GROUPTHINK IN GOVERNMENT

D1232634

GROUPTHINK IN GOVERNMENT

A Study of Small Groups and Policy Failure

Paul 't Hart

The Johns Hopkins University Press
Baltimore

Original hardcover edition published by Swets & Zeitlinger, 1990
Johns Hopkins Paperbacks edition, 1994
03 02 01 00 99 98 97 96 95 94   5 4 3 2 1

The Johns Hopkins University Press
2715 North Charles Street
Baltimore, Maryland 21218-4319

Library of Congress Cataloging-in-Publication Data will be found
at the end of this book.

A catalog record for this book is available from the British Library.

ISBN 0-8018-4890-3 (pbk)

Contents

Preface to the Johns Hopkins Paperbacks Edition

Almost five years have elapsed since the original version of this book was written. During this period, groupthink has not lost its popularity among social scientists. A sizable number of follow-up studies testifies to this fact. Some of these, unfortunately, continue to use the concept of groupthink loosely and indiscriminately as a symbolically powerful pejorative label to stick on any controversial episode of organizational action or public policy-making. It is this kind of gratuitous use and conceptual stretching of what was designed to be a serious and, above all, contingent analytical framework which prompted the writing of this book. In that sense, this book has so far failed to achieve one of its main purposes, namely, to prevent groupthink theory from becoming a kind of analytical garbage can for commentators and analysts in need of a powerful metaphor when they seek to blame policymakers or managers for a variety of ills and evils of governance. The wider circulation made possible by this Johns Hopkins Paperbacks Edition may, I hope, help to turn this ongoing tide.

Yet, there have been numerous serious scholarly efforts to critically review, apply, test, and modify groupthink theory.[1] Although they have taken different paths and sometimes arrived at different conclusions than I have, these authors clearly share my view of groupthink theory as an intriguing, innovative, and policy-relevant contribution to our understanding of the dynamics of high-level decision making and management. At the same time, they all recognize that groupthink analysis entails a number of delicate conceptual, methodological, and theoretical issues and problems that call for carefulness, caution, and creativity in its application.

Some of these issues and problems arise from the much neglected fact that groupthink analysis uses an essentially micro-level, social-psychological approach to the understanding of decision making and more often than not applies this approach to the analysis of meso-level processes of institutional action. High-level corporate or governmental decision making tends to involve actors from different parts of the organization or policy community, whose behavior, as we know from research in political science, public administration, and organizational analysis, is shaped by the broader historical, bureaucratic, and political contexts in which they operate. These contextual factors provide a rich set of constraints and opportunities for decision makers, quite apart from the particular policymaking groups they may happen to be part of. Therefore group processes and thus social-psychological mechanisms can only become the most important forces shaping the behavior of these policymakers if and when particular configurations of these other contextual factors enable them to be. For this reason, the analysis of group decision-making processes in government should always take place within a broader interdisciplinary, mutli-level framework that examines these configurations.

Social and political psychologists cannot afford to ignore the broader institutional forces that govern the perceptions, calculations, and behavior of real-world policymakers.[2] They do so at the risk of arriving at reductionist explanations and identifying all sorts of biases, irrationalities, and information-processing pathologies, whereas seasoned observers of organizational and political behavior, who are more aware of meso-level considerations and constraints and of paradigms of governance that do not accord a central place to its problem-solving and information-processing functions, would find these conclusions to be both overly simplistic and normatively crude.[3] In this book, I have tried to deal with the problem of multi-disciplinary perspectives and levels of decision-making analysis in the context of groupthink theory. I still regard that attempt as worthwhile and as the core contribution this book has to make. I welcome the opportunity of exposing this attempt to the critical evaluation of a wider audience. Also, readers of this edition may want to reassess the Iran-Contra case study in view of the new evidence uncovered since 1989, especially the report of Special Prosecutor Walsh. Insofar as I have been able to study it, nothing in the report contradicts the groupthink explanation developed here, on the contrary, but a more systematic analysis would be called for.

Less central in the present book, but in my current view quite essential to a better understanding and application of groupthink analysis, are several outstanding issues that I would encourage readers to reflect on when reading it. First, is groupthink an exclusively American phenomenon? Most of the documented cases of groupthink concern U.S. foreign policymaking, and Janis speculated that groupthink would occur twice as much in the United States as in European countries. Andeweg, observing these national differences, argues convincingly that they can be traced in part to institutional differences in the organization of government.[4] In his view, the lack of continuity in the U.S. presidential staff makes this administrative system more vulnerable to groupthink than are Western European systems, in which the government can rely on a more permanent, experienced, and more independently operating civil service (which, of course, has other potential drawbacks). In addition, vulnerability to groupthink is presumably determined by the amount of political heterogenity within government. Coalition cabinets such as those in Belgium and Holland, with ministers having different political backgrounds on top of different departmental portfolios, are less likely to exhibit premature and extreme consensus than are one-party governments such as those in the United Kingdom and the United States, not to mention dictatorial regimes. At the same time, in countries with strong political parties and strong government departments, the chances of group-think may be weak at the top of government, but much stronger at lower levels, for example, within cabinet committees, specific departments, or political party factions. This is less likely in the American system, where parties are weak and departments often characterized by internal bureau-political infighting.

Second, how serious a problem is groupthink for good government? Janis has always asserted that there is a strong probabilistic link between the quality of decision processes and the quality of their outcomes. Consequently, groupthink, being a low-quality decision process, should lead to low-quality outcomes; an assertion that found empirical support in a careful reanalysis by Tetlock et al. of Janis's original cases. As a criterion for success, they used the decision makers' own objectives, which is less ambiguous than the criterion of "national interests" used by Herek et al. in a comparable study some years earlier.[5] At the same time, in two new cases mentioned but never fully analyzed by Janis, Tetlock et al. found disastrous outcomes produced by high-quality, "vigilant" decision processes. These results do not contradict the idea of a probabilistic relationship between quality of process and outcome, but they do indicate that this hypothesis has its limits as a basis for predicting, let alone preventing, policy fiascoes. Apparently, there are circumstances in which methodical decision-making procedures are of no avail. Part of the problem in this discussion on groupthink and decision quality comes from the choice of criteria for assessing quality. This choice is ultimately a political one, a fact insufficiently realized by Janis and other micro-level decision theorists, whose view of good policymaking derives from an essentially rationalistic, problem-solving framework. However, if one departs from organizational and political paradigms of decision making, other types of rationality and other standards for measuring decision quality come into view. These focus, for example, on the symbolic rather than the substantive nature of many decision-making procedures and problem-solving activities; the requirement for decision makers to gather and maintain a workable amount of political and bureaucratic support; the need to balance the pros and cons of not a single but a series of interrelated decisions and episodes; the tradeoff between short-term and long-term considerations; and the problem of allocating scarce decision-making resources to the many salient issues competing for attention.[6] Adhering to a limited, functionalist perspective on rationality and decision quality in government and organization, many groupthink theorists run the risk of propagating a one-sided view of the success and failure of policy decisions. Combined with a lack of adequate data on the relative frequency of groupthink phenomena and the availability of several of high-profile cases in which groupthink apparently led to major fiascoes, there is a distinct danger that we make it seem as if groupthink is a bigger threat to good government and good management than it really is.

Finally, if groupthink is the problem, what are the feasible solutions? So far there have been few attempts to review, elaborate, or test the prescriptive hypotheses to prevent groupthink put forward by Janis. In the final chapter of this book, I provided some preliminary thoughts on this matter, but I have since come to realize that we should devote more attention to the policy implications of groupthink analysis.[7] Revisiting Janis's prescriptions, I realize that they are not unproblematic. For one thing, they raise the costs of decision making by prompting policymakers to devote more effort to each decision. When fully implemented, they are certain to overload the capacity of the policymaking system. In addition, they demand the near impossible from group leaders. They are supposed to be powerful enough to control the flow of policy process internally and to have its results accepted externally, yet at the same time they are urged to refrain from exhibiting any substantive or manipulative policy leadership during decision-making sessions with their advisers. Also, more adversarial decision-making procedures, designed to stimulate heterogenity of viewpoints and functional forms of internal conflict within decision-making groups, are in danger of disintegrating into the opposite extreme: stiffling forms of uncompromising bureaucratic politics that will make it more difficult to reach any collective decision at all.[8] The challenge is to find ways of balancing heterogenity and uniformity, effectiveness and efficiency, and consensus and dissensus in and around high-level decision-making groups. Appropriately contextualized and situation-specific policy prescriptions for restructuring decision procedures are probably a more viable way of achieving this balance than any set of sweeping, universalistic principles of high-quality policymaking based on a narrow, White House centered, non-comparative empirical base.

Having continued to work on follow-up research on group decision making, crisis management, policy fiascoes, and other matters related to the subject matter of this book in the years since its first appearance, I am very grateful to the Royal Dutch Academy of Sciences, for a generous five-year research fellowship; to Uriel Rosenthal, for ten years of exemplary mentorship and friendship; to Mark Bovens, for showing that, for us ordinary mortals at least, there is a tradeoff between the quantity and quality of academic research and writing; to Alex George and Ned Lebow, for continued long-distance encouragement and support; to my other colleagues at the Crisis Research Team and the Department of Public Administration of Leiden University, for providing a challenging and congenial professional environment; and above all to Marieke, for her love, wit, cogent criticism, and patience.

Notes

1. Notably, W.W. Park (1990), A review of research on groupthink, *Journal of Behavioral Decision Making*, 3, pp. 229-245; M.B.R. Kroon (1992), *Effects of Accountability on Groupthink and Intergroup Relations*, PhD diss.: University of Utrecht; M.B.R. Kroon, D. van Kreveld, and J.M. Rabbie (1992), Group versus individual decision making: Effects of accountability and gender on groupthink, *Small Group Research*, 23, no. 4, pp. 427-458; P.E. Tetlock, R.S. Peterson, C. McGuire, S. Chang, and P. Feld (1992), Assessing political group dynamics: A test of the groupthink model, *Journal of Personality and*

Social Psychology, 63, no. 3, pp. 403-425; M.E. Turner, A.R. Pratkanis, P. Probasco, C. Leve (1992), Threat, cohesion, and group effectiveness: Testing a social identity maintenance perspective on groupthink, *Journal of Personality and Social Psychology*, 63, no. 5, pp. 781-796; R.J. Aldag, S. Riggs Fuller (1993), Beyond fiasco: A reappraisal of the groupthink phenomenon and a new model of group decision processes, *Psychological Bulletin*, 113, no. 3, pp. 533-552. P.R. Bernthal and C.A. Insko (1993), Cohesiveness without groupthink: The interactive effects of social and task cohesion, *Group and Organization Management*, 18, no. 1, pp. 66-87. Apart from doing empirical work, in some of my own subsequent writings on groupthink I have tried to think through more carefully the prescriptive implications of the theory and research findings. See, for example, M.B.R. Kroon, P. 't Hart, D. van Kreveld (1991), Managing group decision making processes: Individual versus collective accountability and groupthink, *International Journal of Conflict Management*, 2, no. 2, pp. 91-116; P. 't Hart (1991), Irving L. Janis's *Victims of groupthink, Political Psychology*, 12, no. 3, pp. 247-258; P. 't Hart and M.B.R. Kroon (1994), Groupthink in government: Pathologies of small group decision making, in J.L. Garnett (ed.), *Handbook of Administrative Communication*, New York: Marcel Dekker, (forthcoming). See also F. Gaenslen, Decision-making groups, in E. Singer and V. Hudson (eds. 1992), *Political Psychology and Foreign Policy*, Boulder: Westview, pp. 165-194; R.L. Moreland, J.M. Levine, Problem identification by groups, in S. Worchel, W. Wood, J.A. Simpson (eds. 1992), *Group Process and Productivity*, Newbury Park: Sage, pp. 17-47; H.E. Purkitt, Political decision making in small groups: The Cuban missile crisis revisited—one more time, in E. Singer, V. Hudson (eds. 1992), *Political Psychology and Foreign Policy*, Boulder: Westview, pp. 219-244; C.F. Hermann, Avoiding pathologies in foreign policy decision-making groups, in D. Caldwell, T.J. McKeown (eds. 1993), *Diplomacy, Force, and Leadership: Essays in Honour of Alexander A. George*, Boulder: Westview, pp. 179-208.
2. An example of a similar plea with respect to the study of accountability as an independent variable in decision-making analysis can be found in P.E. Tetlock (1992), The impact of accountability on judgment and choice: Toward a social contingency model, *Advances in Experimental Social Psychology*, 25, pp. 331-376. Also, various authors in the special issue on prospect theory of *Political Psychology* (13, no. 2, 1992, ed. by B. Farnham) call for an integration of political and psychological approaches to decision making, but they are quick to sensitize readers to the methodological difficulties of doing so.
3. For astute comments on this point, see R. Jervis (1989), Political psychology—some challenges and opportunities, *Political Psychology*, 10, no. 4, pp. 481-493. See also J.G. Stein (1988), Building politics into psychology: The misperception of threat, *Political Psychology*, 9, no. 3, pp. 245-271.
4. R.B. Andeweg, Balanceren tussen consensus en conflict: Besluitvorming in de nederlandse ministerraad, in P. 't Hart, P. de Jong, and A.F.A. Korsten (eds. 1991), *Groepsdenken in het openbaar bestuur: Cruciale beslissingen in kleine groepen*, Alphen: Samsom, pp. 207-225 (in Dutch).

Acknowledgements

This study is about some of the darker sides of the interaction between public officials in making important decisions that affect many people's lives. In certain circumstances, groups of sensible, smart, even shrewd men and women think and act in a way that can only be described with the term "collective stupidity". Research on groupthink brings up troublesome questions about the performance of policymaking groups in positions of great, even awesome, responsibilities. It attempts to alert us to the need for extreme care in organizing and managing collective decision processes. However, the underlying premise of groupthink research is that there are ways in which to overcome the pitfalls of collective stupidity; the big problem is how to identify these in theory and how to mobilize these in practice.

In writing this book, I have had the good fortune of enjoying the direction and assistance of a number of individuals whose contributions have been absolutely vital to the completion of this project. First of all, I am very grateful to Uriel Rosenthal and Jaap Rabbie who have supervised this research project. Discussions with Uri and Jaap have been my main source of inspiration in completing this study.

In addition, I greatly appreciate the efforts of Sonja Balsem, Vicky Balsem, Mark Bovens, Clark McCauley, Michael Charles, Wim Derksen, Menno van Duin, Alexander George, Dorothé Hammecher, Alexander Kouzmin, Albert Kersten, Karin Kisjes, Marceline Kroon, Richard Ned Lebow, Hanneke van der Linde, Erwin Muller, Joseph Scanlon, Roger Stough, Ger Teitler, and Sandra Timmermans, who have either contributed important comments on previous versions of this text or rendered assistance in the making of this book. I would like to single out especially Jan Hakvoort for constant support and constructive criticism. Secondly, I am, of course, heavily indebted to the late Irving L. Janis. His work on groupthink is among the most exciting and thought-provoking studies in Social Science. It was the first book I read as a student, and it has kept me busy ever since!

In her own special way, Marieke has showed me that there is more to life than research, and will hopefully continue to do so ever after.

Finally, I would like to dedicate this book to my mother and father, who have raised me with love, patience, and intellectual stimulation. I love them very much.

PART I
GROUPTHINK IN GOVERNMENT

1 – Introduction:
groupthink and policy fiascoes

1.1. Backgrounds

Why do governments or public agencies take stances, develop programs or engage in actions that lead to disastrous or, at least, highly undesirable outcomes? Policy fiascoes are of many kinds. They can stem from financial mismanagement of public programs. They can take the shape of planning disasters, i.e., large-scale public ventures such as infrastructural and building projects gone astray. They can be actions by political or administrative authorities that lead to intense public criticism and outrage, severely compromising the legitimacy of the incumbent authorities, the regime, or, indeed, the political system as a whole. They can entail maltreatment of individuals and groups within society. They can result in the use of unnecessary or disproportionate violence by government agencies. And the most chilling policy fiascoes are those that plunge governments into needless, costly, and potentially hopeless international confrontations-including war. To be sure, there may be good reasons for governments to embark on a course of action that entails risks or afflicts harm on third parties. For instance, during a major economic crisis, governments virtually cannot escape the need to cut back on public spending and this, in turn, may strike a severe blow to large groups of citizens. Equally, governments may have compelling reasons for taking part in international confrontations. These examples are not policy fiascoes. A governmental course of action may be called a policy fiasco if it leads to the kind of outcomes that are generally perceived to be highly negative, without a good set of reasons for doing so, and without a proper consideration of the risks involved. Policy fiascoes come in different degrees, according to the type and extent of negative consequences resulting from government action, as well as the degree of responsibility that can be reasonably ascribed to government actors for bringing these about.

The Watergate scandal is a clear-cut example of a political fiasco affecting high-level policy makers. The burglary of the Democratic National Headquarters ordered by over-zealous Nixon campaign strategists was in itself little more than the kind of petty electoral crimes that occur with great regularity. However, the subsequent cover-up attempt by the President and his closest associates was not only ill-guided in the sense that it was doomed to fail from the start, but more importantly, it brought about a political showdown that seriously hurt Nixon's presidency and the general public's faith in the American political system as a whole. Equally, the Argentinean Junta's decision to re-occupy the Falkland Islands and its subsequent intransigence in the face of international mediation attempts led the country into a war it could not win and this, ultimately, brought about the fall of the junta. A less dramatic class of policy fiascoes is exemplified by various 'planning disasters': the Sydney Opera House project, the Concorde project, San Francisco Bay Area Rapid Transportation (BART) system.[1] The common denominator of these projects is that their cost-effectiveness ratio falls far below any reasonable standard: greatly escalated production costs, political controversy, and repeated downward adjustments of the projects' strategic and operational goals and norms. A related category of fiascoes pertains to policy decisions or operations that contribute to or fail to prevent the development of 'real' disasters: NASA's Space Shuttle project, the role of public and private agencies in the development and mismanagement of the reactor crises at Three Mile Island and Chernobyl, the Bhopal petrochemical disaster, and many more examples of 'compulsive', 'wanted' and 'willful' crisis events.[2]

Policy fiascoes can be studied in many different ways, but the most obvious issue concerns their causes: "How could it happen?" In any specific case, however, such a general question is easier to pose than to answer in a satisfactory manner. Most of the examples that have been cited thus far pertain to relatively large-scale projects or operations that involve a host of different actors within and outside government. Furthermore, they stretch out over longer periods, sometimes years. In these rather complex policy settings, it is generally very hard to come up with a solid diagnosis of *the* cause of the fiasco. There are more factors at work than analysts or investigators can grasp or weigh according to their relative potency. To be sure, this limited capacity to explain the course and outcomes of the policy process does not remain limited to fiascoes. It is equally problematic to adequately diagnose the anatomy of policy successes. The complexity of high-level political and administrative decision making and implementation presents a magnificent challenge to the analyst.

The present study seeks to make a contribution by analyzing the causes of policy fiascoes. Given the inherent complexity of the subject, this contribution will be limited to the extent that this study will examine closely just one type of explanation of the development of policy fiascoes. Specifically, the focus of this study will be on *flaws in the operation of small, high-level decision groups at the helm of major projects or policies that become fiascoes.*

A theory of flawed group decision making contributing to the occurrence of policy fiascoes was set forward in a book published in 1972 (with an expanded second edition in 1982). It is called *Victims of Groupthink* and was written by Irving L. Janis. Janis' study can be considered a path-breaking effort to develop a mature small group-level explanation of

4

instances of political decision making. Although its scope is limited in principle – explaining certain specified fiascoes – his work has received wide attention and has alerted many students of political decision making to the potentials of using the unexplored avenues of small-group theory and research.

Here, the aim is to critically reexamine Janis' theory in the context of governmental decision making. In the course of this study, the notion of 'groupthink', which is central to Janis' diagnosis of policy fiascoes, will be explained and cast in a somewhat more comprehensive theoretical framework. To be able to do so, a survey of the literature in two different social-scientific disciplines has been conducted: Social Psychology and Public Administration. The revised model of groupthink that will emerge during the course of this book reflects this interdisciplinary perspective. The result of these theoretical endeavors is illustrated empirically in an elaborate case study of a recent U.S. foreign policy fiasco in the final part of this book.

An important caveat to be taken into account concerns the problem of levels of analysis and explanation. In the present study the focus lies with the formation and operation of small, high-level decision groups within government. It is from the decision processes within these groups that explanations of (the success and failure of) government policy are derived. This involves an analytical leap that is not wholly unproblematic. For this reason, elaborate attention is paid to defining more clearly the conditions under which small-group action has indeed such a decisive impact on government policy as a whole. Secondly, it will become apparent that part of the explanation of the occurrence of groupthink must be sought in the wider intergroup and organizational context in which the groups under study operate. Therefore, while retaining the original focus on small-group action, the level of analysis will be 'lifted up' occasionally to examine how intergroup and (inter)organizational phenomena shape the context and process of group formation and decision making.

1.2. Janis on groupthink

Victims of Groupthink: A Psychological Study of Foreign Policy Decisions and Fiascoes by Irving L. Janis was published for the first time in 1972. Consider the following list:
- The preparedness policies of the US Navy at Pearl Harbour in December 1941.
- The decision to pursue the defeated North Korean army on its home territory by president Eisenhower and his advisors.
- The Bay of Pigs invasion plan by president Kennedy and his advisors.
- The series of decisions to continue and escalate the Vietnam War by president Johnson and his advisors.

These were no 'trivial' matters dealt with by artificial groups in the laboratory. These were real-life decisions, made by some of the most powerful decision makers in the world. They were also evident failures, all of which caused great losses not only to the decision makers themselves, but, more importantly, losses to countless people who happened to be wound up in them.

In an unprecedented way, Janis applied ideas from small group analysis to explanation in these policy fiascoes. He made plausible the hypothesis that each of these events can, to a considerable extent, be attributed to the occurrence of a very specific and obviously detrimental phenomenon within the groups of decision makers involved in their making. He called this phenomenon "Groupthink", cleverly picking this highly suggestive Orwellian mode of expression (cf. "doublethink" in Orwell's novel *1984*). According to Janis, groupthink stands for an excessive form of concurrence-seeking among members of high prestige, tightly-knit policy making groups. It is excessive to the extent that the group members have come to value the group (and their being part of it) higher than anything else. This causes them to strive for a quick and painless unanimity on the issues that the group has to confront. To preserve the clubby atmosphere, group members suppress personal doubts, silence dissenters and follow the group leader's suggestions. They have a strong belief in the inherent morality of the group, combined with a decidedly evil picture of the group's opponents. The results are devastating: a distorted view of reality, excessive optimism producing hasty and reckless policies, and a neglect of ethical issues. The combination of these deficiencies makes these groups particularly vulnerable to initiate and sustain projects that turn out to be policy fiascoes.

The idea of groupthink took social-psychological theorizing about small groups largely by surprise. Few analysts had ever reckoned that cohesive groups may also perform worse rather than better on certain 'problem-solving' tasks. They had spent years developing techniques to mitigate conflicts and promote team spirit. They had never really considered sociological assertions about the dysfunctional effects of tightly-knit worker groups (as evident from Coch and French's study of working groups in a factory who set and imposed upon their members informal 'production norms' independent of management's objectives) or the eu-functions of conflict.[5] The groupthink concept actually turns around some of the traditional ideas about the effects of 'cohesiveness' on group performance. To a great extent, Janis' contribution lies in pursuing a – within his own discipline, at least – counter-intuitive logic. Moreover, he went on applying it to actual cases of public policy making.

From 1972 on, the groupthink phenomenon entered the columns of scholarly magazines in various strands of social science, as well as in popular editorials and newspapers. It became a standard item in textbooks on Social Psychology, Organizational Psychology, Foreign Policy and Political Decision Making, and Management. A revised edition was published in 1982, containing another case study: the attempt to cover up the true story of the Watergate burglaries by president Nixon and some of his advisors.

Yet there is something ironic to be noted in the reactions towards groupthink. While the volume certainly became what Brian Barry has termed an "in-book", surprisingly little research using the groupthink thesis has been undertaken.[4] Was it that Janis' statements were so powerful and conclusive that no further work seemed necessary? That is highly unlikely. Janis himself was quite cautious in his formulations as to the theoretical solidity and explanatory power of groupthink. It seems rather the sort of suspense pervading the book (also because of the cases discussed) that has managed to strike people's imagination. If so, this is at least an indication that Janis was on the right track. Still, in scientific terms, the validity of a concept or a theory entirely depends upon the results of theoretical and empirical scrutiny. This has been considerably lacking in the case of groupthink.

How can one identify groupthink? How does it come about, what are its defining characteristics, what are its effects? The most systematic treatment of these matters in Janis' work can be found in the second edition of his book, which extends and above all systematizes the earlier formulation.[5] In his recent study on "crucial decisions", he has presented the groupthink phenomenon within a much wider decision-analytical context, however, without changing the theory as such.[6]

Definition

Originally, Janis defined groupthink as follows:

> "A mode of thinking that people engage in when they are deeply involved in a cohesive in-group, when the members' strivings for unanimity override their motivation to realistically appraise alternative courses of action." [7]

As Longley and Pruitt have pointed out, this definition is confusing as it incorporates not only the process itself (a certain mode of thinking), but also some of its antecedents (a cohesive in-group; personal involvement in it by individual members), as well as some of its effects (a reduced capacity to realistically appraise alternative courses of action.[8] In his later formulations, Janis has not, as Longley and Pruitt imply, changed his definition. Rather, he has provided an operational formulation of it. By then, the causal connections between antecedents, indicators and effects are made explicit in a flow chart (see figure 1.1.).

Herefrom, it turns out that groupthink stands for concurrence-seeking, that is, excessive concurrence-seeking.

Antecedent conditions

Consider the flow chart. It shows three types of 'causes':
1) High cohesiveness of the decision making group.

Figure 1.1. Janis' theory of groupthink

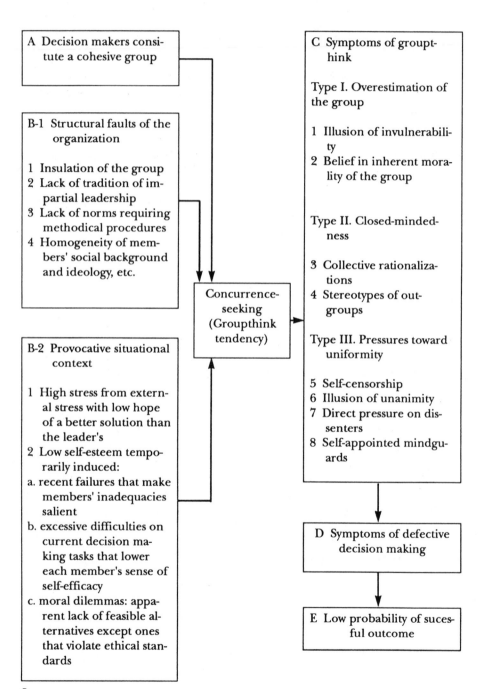

ANTECEDENT CONDITIONS

OBSERVABLE CONSEQUENCES

A Decision makers consi-
   tute a cohesive group

B-1 Structural faults of the
     organization

1 Insulation of the group
2 Lack of tradition of impartial leadership
3 Lack of norms requiring
   methodical procedures
4 Homogeneity of mem-
   bers' social background
   and ideology, etc.

B-2 Provocative situational
     context

1 High stress from external stress with low hope
   of a better solution than
   the leader's
2 Low self-esteem tempo-
   rarily induced:
a. recent failures that make
   members' inadequacies
   salient
b. excessive difficulties on
   current decision ma-
   king tasks that lower
   each member's sense of
   self-efficacy
c. moral dilemmas: appa-
   rent lack of feasible alternatives except ones
   that violate ethical standards

Concurrence-
seeking
(Groupthink
tendency)

C Symptoms of groupt-
   hink

Type I. Overestimation of
the group

1 Illusion of invulnerability
2 Belief in inherent morality of the group

Type II. Closed-minded-
ness

3 Collective rationalizations
4 Stereotypes of out-
   groups

Type III. Pressures toward
uniformity

5 Self-censorship
6 Illusion of unanimity
7 Direct pressure on dissenters
8 Self-appointed mindgu-
   ards

D Symptoms of defective
   decision making

E Low probability of suces-
   ful outcome

2) Specific structural characteristics ('faults') of the organizational context in which the group operates.
3) Stressful internal and external characteristics of the situation.

These are not equally important for the occurrence of groupthink. "The explanatory hypothesis about why groupthink occurs gives preeminence to the provocative situational factors...(box B-2)"[9] And then:

> "(the) explanatory hypothesis implicitly assigns a secondary role to the structural faults of the organization (box B-1)... Those structural features can be regarded as moderating variables involving the presence or absence of organizational constraints that could counteract the concurrence-seeking tendency."[10]

Janis actually implies a picture different from the flow chart, namely the picture in figure 1.2.

Figure 1.2. Groupthink dynamics: a specification[11]

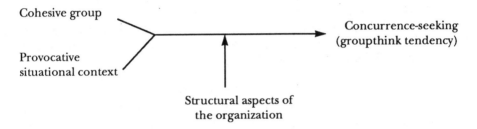

Let us be more specific about the antecedents of groupthink. When is it likely to occur? While the boxes in the flow chart have already answered this question in theoretical terms, it may be useful to consider some examples from actual decision groups that, according to Janis, have displayed groupthink.

1. Group cohesiveness. Take president Truman's group which dealt with the conduct of the Korean war. Janis quotes Glen Paige:

> "...Truman's group of advisors developed a high degree of solidarity. Glen Paige...calls attention to the 'intra-group solidarity' at all the crisis meetings. He concludes that 'one of the most striking aspects...is the high degree of satisfaction and sense of moral rightness shared by the decision makers'...The members of the group continued to display esprit de corps and mutual admiration throughout the many months they worked together. It was a group of men who shared the same basic values and dominant beliefs of the power elite of American society,

particularly about the necessity for containing the expansion of 'world communism' in order to protect the 'free world'."[12]

2. *Structural aspects.* One of the structural aspects mentioned by Janis is a lack of impartial leadership. Consider the following passage on the way president Kennedy presided the meetings of the Cuban invasion planning group during the Bay of Pigs episode:

> "(At) each meeting, instead of opening up the agenda to permit a full airing of the opposing considerations, he allowed the CIA representatives to dominate the entire discussion. The president permitted them to refute immediately each tentative doubt that one of the others might express, instead of asking whether anyone else had the same doubt or wanted to pursue the implications of the new worrisome issue that had been raised."[13]

3. *Provocative situational context.* Groupthink does not easily occur in routine situations involving equivocal decisions. Rather, the chances of groupthink markedly increase when decision makers are under stress, dealing with a crisis situation. In these circumstances, decision makers may perceive threats to their self-esteem because of the tremendous burden of having to decide about impenetrable, morally complex issues. Then, the group may become a key source of consolation. See Janis' remarks on the Watergate cover-up by Nixon and his associates:

> "(during) this stressful period they spent much more time talking about what to do, but their rambling conversations invariably ended up reaffirming and extending the cover-up policy. These long conversations could be characterized as displaying collective uncritical thinking (...). Apparently under conditions of high stress the members had become highly dependent on the group for social support, to maintain their morale as well as to protect them from criminal liability through their affiliation with the presidency."[14]

Characteristics

Janis mentions three types of characteristics of groupthink:
1) Those producing an overestimation of the group (illusion of invulnerability; belief in inherent morality).
2) Those producing closed-mindedness (collective rationalizations; stereotyped images of out-groups).
3) Those producing pressures toward uniformity (self censorship; illusion of unanimity; direct pressures on dissenters; self-appointed mindguards).

From these characteristics, one cannot doubt the negative evaluation of groupthink that pervades Janis' writings on the subject. All characteristics seem malicious: while the pressures toward uniformity can be viewed as indicator of excessive concurrence-seeking as such, the other two types of characteristics (overestimation, closed-mindedness) assure that this concurrence-seeking takes place in the context of 'bad' policies.

Concurrence-seeking as such is a necessary element within each collective decision process (especially when unanimity is called for). At a certain point in the deliberative process, discussions need to be concluded and actions taken. In this respect, there is not so much difference with processes of individual decision making, where decision makers start 'bolstering' their preferred alternatives.[15] However, concurrence-seeking becomes excessive when it takes place too early and in too restrictive a way. This need still not be fatal, if the group would be embarking on, more or less accidentally, a sound alternative. It is the other types of characteristics of groupthink which prevent this from happening: closed-minded, stereotyped, overconfident and morally exempt decision makers are highly unlikely to strike the right, or at least a satisfactory, key.

Effects of groupthink

The effects of such a decisional process are quite clear: bad decisions. Still, on this point Janis maintains a certain caution. His "symptoms of defective decision making" are exclusively couched in procedural terms. In his view, groupthink leads to a serious deterioration in what can be called the quality of deliberation. The seven indicators that he mentions are derived from what he regards as critical tasks for any decision maker to arrive at optimal solutions. They resemble, but are not identical to, the procedures of the normative decision models of rational synopticism and optimizing.

Having gone this far, Janis then hypothesizes that under these conditions, the probability that a successful decision will result from these flawed decision processes, sharply diminishes. In his work on groupthink, as in his other studies on decision making, Janis comes out as a proponent of the idea that the quality of decisions is contingent upon the soundness of the procedures through which they are taken. Simply put: 'good' procedures strongly promote the chances of successful decisional out-comes, while 'bad' procedures almost guarantee failing results. Note that Janis, as virtually all decision theorists do, does not talk about the underlying value problem in decision making which has been the source of long debates in Political Science and Philosophy. A decision is good if it enhances the attainment of the ends of the decision makers; what these ends and values are, and how they ought to be evaluated, is of no concern to the decisional theorist. Analysts of government and politics may find this a crudely functionalist perspective. That cannot be denied. But it does permit the researcher to abandon fundamentalist debates which are likely to go on for a long time and get to work and do empirical research which at least illuminates the context and some of the premises of these debates.

1.3. Other analysts on groupthink

Real world replications

Only very few analysts have produced articles or monographs applying, like Janis, groupthink analysis to government and public policy making. In 1974, the Watergate scandal dominated the American political and scholarly community.[17] Several analysts have tried to interpret this domestic policy fiasco in suggesting that groupthink was operating within the group of president Nixon and his advisors. His account, however, is quite loose and journalistic and does not pretend to be a detailed psychological study. However, Green and Connolly have directly linked groupthink to the Watergate cover-up.[18]

Raven has made a very detailed effort to use groupthink in explaining the Watergate cover-up.[19] He found many conditions and symptoms present, but he also concluded that some very crucial conditions, such as high group cohesiveness were lacking. Nixon's 'big team' and his 'young team' were analyzed using sociometric techniques. It appeared that there were highly competitive and conflict-laden relationships within the Nixon group, which made groupthink quite unlikely. "On the other hand", Raven notes,

> "the Nixon group could still be considered a highly cohesive group in some sense – despite their personal antagonisms, all of them wanted with all their hearts and souls to be in that group and to be central to that group"... (...) dependence upon and admiration for their leader was the glue which held the Nixon group together." [20]

Raven, not entirely satisfied with the groupthink hypothesis as explanation of what happened, also suggested other theoretical perspectives from group dynamics that may be useful in this respect.[21] Wong-McCarthy has presented the results of a detailed content analysis of the White House tape transcripts, which also points to many symptoms of groupthink.[22] In the second edition of his book, Janis also examined the Watergate-affair, and reintroduced the groupthink explanation by focusing on a much smaller in-group: Nixon, Haldeman, Ehrlichman and (until his 'defection') Dean.

Tetlock has made content analyses of speeches by decision makers associated with groupthink and non-groupthink decisions, as they were outlined in Janis' book. Using a technique called integrative complexity coding, he found that,

> "relative to non-groupthink, decision makers were more simplistic in their perceptions of policy issues and made more positive references to the United States and its allies (own group). Inconsistent with Janis' theory, groupthink decision makers did not make significant more negative references to Communist States and their allies (opponents)."[23]

In assessing the contributions of this specific technique, Tetlock stretches its heuristic value: detecting probable cases for groupthink analysis. His method has not been pursued since.

Gero used a questionnaire to further examine the effects of a consensus style of group decision making on expectations of intra-group conflict among group members. She found that there may be a strong inclination toward amiability and agreement in consensus climates, and discussed the potentially adverse effects on decision quality.[24]

Finally, attempts have been made to add more cases to the groupthink catalogue. Following a magazine article by Janis, Smith has attempted to document the suggestion that the groupthink has dominated the Carter decision-making process with respect to the hostage rescue mission to Iran. Heller, in an article in the Guardian, linked groupthink to the conduct of the Falkland Islands War by the Thatcher cabinet. These latter examples cannot always be considered successful.[25] They are all very casual and lacking in psychological proficiency to make them serious contributions. On the contrary, such quick-and-easy characterizations may create an illusion that groupthink is an all-purpose, little-effort label explaining just about any case of policy failure. This is deplorable, as Janis has gone to great lengths in calling for caution in linking groupthink to policy outcomes, as well as in providing a sound framework of all relevant factors to be actually used in groupthink analysis.

A more substantive effort was undertaken by Rosenthal. In a comprehensive analysis of several cases of crisis decision making in the Netherlands (disasters, riots, terrorism), he systematically checked the evidence of groupthink. In some cases, positive indications were found, in others not.[26] Similarly inconclusive or even negative about the role of groupthink were both Etheredge and Polsby in their respective studies of the evolution of the United States Middle American policy and several cases of policy innovation.[27]

Hensley and Griffin have performed a full-fledged groupthink analysis on the case of a protracted conflict about the location of additional sports facilities at the campus of Kent State University. The authors found clear-cut evidence for the presence of groupthink in the University's board of trustees.[28] Similarly, Verbeek used groupthink to explain the British fiasco of the 1956 Suez invasion, thereby extending and substantiating tentative claims to this effect put forward by Janis in his book.[29] Barrett has reexamined the U.S. decision process concerning the escalation of the Vietnam war and has argued that, contrary to Janis' findings, groupthink did not play a role at all.[30]

McCauley used the original case studies by Janis to substantiate his theoretical claim that groupthink comes about not only through 'amiability-induced' internalization of group norms and opinions, but also through mere compliance (public agreement on the part of individual group members not accompanied by private acceptance of the prevailing perspective). McCauley's analysis rightly calls attention to the status and power dimensions of group decision making.[31] Similarly, Whyte has made an attempt at comparing the groupthink construct with related approaches of high-risk group decision making based on framing and prospect theory, and examine the relative merits of these alternative approaches in explaining empirical cases of decisional fiascoes.[32]

Laboratory replications

Some very interesting attempts have been made to investigate whether groupthink (unconventional to many experimental psychologists because of its empirical basis in political decision making), can also be found under laboratory conditions. Moorhead, while initially not doing any authentic research himself, did develop a clear model of what would be needed to adequately test for groupthink in decision making groups.[33]

Flowers conducted an experiment with problem solving groups in which he systematically varied leadership style (closed; open) and group cohesiveness (high; low). He hypothesized that decision processes of the high cohesiveness/closed leadership variant would most likely be characterized by groupthink. We need not go into the details of his design at present, suffice it to say that his operationalization of the cohesiveness variable was quite loose, while other preconditions of groupthink were almost totally neglected in the design. His findings stress the importance of the leadership variable, while no evidence could be obtained with respect to cohesiveness (remember again the McCauley interpretation in terms of groupthink as compliance).[34] A much more sophisticated design was presented by Courtright. He also focused upon group cohesiveness and (non-)directive leadership, but he devised much more credible experimental procedures to attain them. Also, he put forward a convincing measure of the dependent variable, that is, the quality of decision making. His major findings suggest:
a) the feasibility of the groupthink phenomenon as such (in particular types of decision groups);
b) that the absence of disagreement in directive leader/high cohesiveness groups is one of the major factors contributing to the – alleged – low quality of decision making in these groups. As such, Courtright seems to have come across a plausible operational measure of concurrence-seeking.[35]
A comparable design and similar results were later reported by Callaway, Marriot and Esser.[36]

Fodor and Smith also studied the leadership and cohesiveness variables in an experimental group problem-solving design. They, however, did not manipulate the style of leadership by instructions. Rather, they sought out group leaders high, respectively low in n-Power, that is, in power motivation. Strikingly, the low n-Power leaders presided over the groups that produced better decisions that those headed by high n-Power leaders. Like Flowers, Fodor and Smith could also not find significant effects of group cohesiveness. Again like in the Flowers study, this lack of results can largely be attributed to the crude and simplistic experimental manipulation of the cohesiveness variable (similar results were obtained by Leana).[37]

Finally, 't Hart, Kroon and Van Kreveld have developed a decision-simulation design testing the effects of different modes of accountability for decisions among group members, upon the quality of decision making. The decisional context was designed to incorporate many of the theoretical antecedents to groupthink. It was found that decision making groups that do not have to account for their judgments and choices displayed more tendencies toward groupthink-like patterns of group decision making than groups whose members, either collectively or individually did have to render account.[38]

Reviewing the various findings of replication studies, it should be remarked that their number is modest, their quality mixed and their findings only partially conclusive.[39] Case-study replications often lack in analytical rigor, while laboratory replications are plagued by the seeming impossibility of incorporating more than only a very limited number of variables in their designs. Especially, they have failed to study groupthink in a more stressful context.

1.4. Discussing groupthink: a closer examination

It is time to analyze the theoretical structure of groupthink in greater detail. In particular, three issues need to be addressed: the causal mechanisms implied in groupthink theory, groupthink and decision quality, the broader theoretical context of groupthink. These points generally coincide with the issues raised in an elaborate critique of groupthink by Longley and Pruitt, who signal three main deficiencies of groupthink theory: an inadequate definition, certain unclarities about the relationships between variables, and an oversimplified evaluation of groupthink.

With regard to the definitional issue, Longley and Pruitt signal the evolution of Janis' thinking on this point. They stretch the necessity of this adjustment in limiting the definition of the *concept* to an understanding that pertains to only one of the (causal) steps implied by the *theory*. Yet, they remain critical of the causal flow of the theory.

Causal mechanisms in groupthink theory

The crux of Longley and Pruitt's criticisms of groupthink, however, lies with what they consider to be Janis' confusing statements on how the process of groupthink actually works. As Janis defines groupthink as (extreme, or premature) concurrence-seeking, the eight symptoms of groupthink should be manifestations of such a concurrence-seeking tendency. Yet, according to Longley and Pruitt, four of the eight symptoms of groupthink cannot be considered as such: "(the) illusion of invulnerability and the illusion of unanimity appear to be *antecedents* of premature concurrence rather than

15

consequences of a desire for concurrence."[40] And further, "the ... belief in the inherent morality of the group and stereotypes of outgroups .... seem unrelated to concurrence-seeking except that, *like all other issues,* they are topics on which concurrence can be achieved. These processes apparently got into the list because they were found in several of the case studies of inadequate decision making examined by Janis. But is this a proper reason to include them in a *theory* of groupthink? A theory should be a logical progression of ideas, not a grab-bag of phenomena that were correlated with each other in a sample of six cases."[41]

Longley and Pruitt subsequently note that Janis also brings in the self-esteem factor as an underlying cause of groupthink: concurrence-seeking as an attempt by group members faced with perplexing issues to bolster their own views and to maintain self-respect. But, the authors conclude "this explanation serves to add greater confusion to Janis' theory since (1) self-esteem is not mentioned elsewhere in the theory ... and (2) this explanation does not help to clarify the causal link postulated between the concurrence-seeking tendency and the symptoms of groupthink."[42]

These are no light charges. It should be remembered, though, that they were written in 1980, before the revised edition of Janis' book. In his 1982-version, the role of endangered self-esteem is elaborated as one of the key antecedents to groupthink; especially under stressful circumstances, the need for social support may push group members towards painless agreement with others.[43] As such, it is certainly not at variance with the idea of concurrence-seeking as the essence of groupthink. Furthermore, by making it clear that the symptoms of groupthink should also be viewed as serving certain ego-preservation functions for group members, the self-esteem concept does give additional insight in the reasons why concurrence-seeking in groupthink takes the specific form (the eight 'symptoms') that it does.

As to the charge that four of the eight symptoms of groupthink cannot be seen as a product of high cohesiveness and concurrence-seeking, two remarks are made. First, it is true that the direction of the causal linkage between cohesiveness and groupthink is far from perfectly clear. Steiner, for instance, observes that groupthink may just as well be the product of a desire for cohesion as of cohesion itself.[44] So Longley and Pruitt's observation that the illusions of invulnerability and unanimity appear to be antecedents rather than consequences of concurrence, is not refuted by Janis' later statements. Clearly, the subject needs additional research that is able to clarify the direction of causality.

Second, Longley and Pruitt appear to be overly critical in stating that symptoms such as the belief in the inherent morality of the group and stereotypes of outgroups are unrelated to concurrence-seeking. In the literature of international, inter- and intragroup relations evidence does exist that in situations of conflict, stereotypes of members of outgroups prevail among members of a group; the same goes for the evaluation of the moral standards of that outgroup (in fact, it is argued in chapter 7 that the intergroup context plays a vital role in bringing about the conditions for groupthink).[45] The least that can be said is that these two symptoms, at least, are not opposite to concurrence-seeking.

In my view, there are more problems associated with the first symptom of groupthink. Janis presents groupthink emphatically as a defensive mode of coping with decisional stresses. In particular, the group becomes a source of emotional support for its members. Hence, their anxieties are somewhat relieved. But to imply that this promotes an "illusion of invulnerability" seems to be stretching the idea. Here, Janis seems to have fallen prey to his inductive method of theorizing after all. He witnessed clear symptoms of invulnerability illusions in some of his cases (notably Pearl Harbour), and subsequently included them in his conceptual model. Yet, as pointed out, it does not fit in with the underlying logic of groupthink and its alleged context (threat) in the original model. How to reconcile these extremes? The literature provides no clues here. I shall return to this point and suggest a possible solution in this study, when talking about accountability, responsibility and decision making.

Groupthink and decision quality

A key concern underlying this study is with the quality of governmental decision making. Decision makers need to anticipate and circumvent the complexities of decision making in the multi-actor, multi-interest environment that characterizes high-level policy decision settings. Government authorities need to deal with cognitive and value complexities. Few behavioral decision theories deal with these problems.

Groupthink theory is one of these. But, what does it have to say on these matters? How does it deal with the difficulties in outlining a truly comprehensive standard of decision quality? And how thoroughly does it examine the effects of a particular mode of decision making (groupthink) on the quality of the resulting decisions?

Longley and Pruitt note that "a negative evaluation of groupthink pervades all of Janis' writings about the topic".[46] They signal that even in the revised conception of groupthink as concurrence-seeking, the flow chart directly links concurrence-seeking and groupthink characteristics to symptoms of defective decision making. Hence their conclusion. Yet, in his 1982-edition, Janis is not entirely as deterministic about the alleged adverse effects of groupthink as Longley and Pruitt suspect. In the final analysis, according to Janis, groupthink is not a necessary, nor a sufficient condition for policy failure.[47] He does suggest that groupthink increases the likelihood of defective decision processes, which, in turn, increase the likelihood of disastrous policy outcomes. Still it is quite clear that, in Janis' mind, groupthink is a certain road to failure. In fact, in his research strategy, he departed from this premise: he chose cases of (alleged) policy failure first, and then applied groupthink analysis to see whether the decision process was affected by it. If so, groupthink was implied to be one of the causes of failure.

17

As to the link between concurrence-seeking and defective decision making, it is evident from the specification of the eight symptoms of groupthink: from a procedural point of view, they appear to be all bad (see Boxes C. and D. in flowchart). However, to understand the implied link between defective decision processes and decisional failures, one must first take a look at Janis' broader views on the issue of decision quality, as formulated in his study of decision making, written with Leon Mann.[48]

As noted earlier, Janis (and Mann, for that matter), appears to be a true adherent to the 'good-procedures —> good-results' paradigm of decision theory. In his view, decision making quality is contingent upon, if not identical to the quality of the deliberations preceding the actual choice. Good procedures virtually ensure good results (defined as optimal outcomes within the limits of the situation). Therefore, the authors have adopted a model of decision quality that is entirely procedural. It comprises of seven "critical tasks" for high-quality decision making:

  a) canvassing a wide range of available courses of action;
  b) surveying the full range of objectives to be fulfilled and the values implicated by the choice;
  c) careful weighing risks, costs, and benefits of each alternative;
  d) intensive search for new information relevant to further evaluation of each alternative;
  e) assimilating and seriously considering new information or expert judgement, even if it is critical of the initially preferred course of action;
  f) reexamining positive and negative consequences of all known alternatives before final choice;
  g) making detailed provisions for implementation of chosen option, making contingency plans to be used if various known risks were to materialize.

The symptoms of groupthink, the authors hold, are squarely opposed to an adequate fulfillment of these tasks. Hence, defective deliberations about decisions, and hence (logically deduced from the authors' premises), the near-certainty of failing policy outcomes.

This line of reasoning is not entirely unproblematic.

1. Longley and Pruitt contend that the linkage between the symptoms of groupthink (Box C) and defective decision making (Box D) is one-sided. They signal that "symptoms of groupthink as self-censorship, urging dissenters to curtail their remarks, avoiding the influx of outside opinions, and even collective rationalizations are *eventually* necessary in many decision making sequences".[49] In other words, they maintain that these features can also be detected in decision-making processes that would qualify as high quality. Mechanisms for consensus building are necessary to come to a decision at all. If no limits would be put upon the duration, scope and likely outcomes of their deliberations, decision groups would never come around to anything. According to Longley and Pruitt, the crucial factors involved in determining whether the above characteristics of groupthink really obstruct a sound process of deliberation about choice are:

a) their *timing* (if one curtails discussion too early one falls into the trap envisaged by Janis; but if one, for instance, uses these mechanisms to short-circuit repetitive and low-utility discussions, they might actually enhance the quality of deliberation);

b) the *type of decision task* that the group faces (Longley and Pruitt cite Katz and Kahn, who differentiate between dilemma-like issues requiring innovative solutions – which, in turn, demand very elaborate and wide-ranging discussions with a minimum of closure and focusing during the key deliberations on the one hand – and normal problems that are less complex and can be solved more easily – thus, not necessitating all too elaborate discussion).[50]

It follows that the above-mentioned groupthink symptoms will probably hurt the quality of decision making about 'dilemmas', while they may be neutral or even functional in 'regular problem solving.' This calls for a better specified, *contextual* perspective on groupthink. In other words, groupthink is a partial rather than a generalistic theory of group decision making. It is interesting to see that in his recent book, Janis has paid ample attention to specifying the conditions under which his newly-developed 'constraints' model of decision making is applicable.[51] Specifically, he asserts that the problematic nature of distorted decision procedures is most clearly felt when decision makers are faced with important decisions, necessitating consequential choices – as opposed to more simple routine choices. The heuristics, biases, and other cognitive and motivational barriers to strictly rational-synoptic or, in Janis more realistic terms, 'vigilant' decision making, are problematic only when decision makers are faced with difficult problems for which there are no standard solutions. This suggests that, as far as groupthink is concerned, it is not really interesting to perform groupthink analyses of regular problem-solving groups at some lower-level of management or policymaking. Instead, and compatible to Longley and Pruitt's assertion, one should concentrate on high-level decision groups at the pinnacle of the organization or government where the stakes are high, standard solutions are lacking, and 'bad' procedures for deliberation and choice are likely to be self-defeating.

2. As far as this linkage between procedures and failing outcomes is concerned, it could be suggested on theoretical grounds that the linkage between the symptoms of defective decision making as produced by groupthink and the incidence of policy failure is truly one of probability, and not of necessity. In other words, 'bad' procedures need not always produce bad results; decision makers may get lucky. Similarly, well-conceived decisions may result in fiascoes, because of failing implementation, unforeseen adversities, and so on. This is why Dror has recently characterized policymaking as "fuzzy gambling".[52] Janis is obviously aware of this need for qualification. However, in groupthink analysis, the *de facto* line of reasoning has, nevertheless, been that groupthink produces defective decision-making procedures which, in turn, produce policy fiascoes.[53]

It is surmised here that this is too deterministic a general position even when confined only to high-level decision groups making consequential choices. However, it is a perfectly plausible and usable hypothesis to inspire empirical research.

Recently, Herek, Janis, and Huth have presented some empirical evidence suggesting that the implied direct connection between processes and outcomes of decision making is indeed highly relevant. They examined 19 cases of U.S. presidential decision making during international crises, using a selection of high-quality academic studies. Subsequently, they rated the quality of the decision-making process using operational definitions of the seven procedural criteria mentioned above. Then, they had two experts (from opposite ends of the conservative-liberal continuum in their personal views of the cold war – in order to control for ideology effects) make ratings of the outcomes of each of the crises – using two criteria: advancement of U.S. national interests, and reduction of international tensions in the post-crisis period. This design enabled them to investigate their hypothesis that high-quality decision making procedures during crises are associated with better crisis outcomes than are defective decision making procedures.

There proved to be 'sizable' correlations between process and outcome scores. Higher scores on symptoms of defective decision making were related both to more unfavorable immediate outcomes for U.S. vital interests, and to more unfavorable immediate outcomes for international conflict. Correlations do not allow statements about causality. Therefore, several alternative, third-factor and methodological explanations were probed – and discounted. So the authors conclude that:

> "The findings of the present study thus bear out the surmises of those social scientists who have concluded that poor-quality procedures used in arriving at a decision give rise to avoidable errors that increase the likelihood of obtaining an unsatisfactory outcome."[54]

While this piece of research does not explicitly deal with the effects of groupthink on policy outcomes, the gist of its argument is quite pertinent in this respect. The assertions by organizationally and politically oriented analysts appear to be incorrect: decision process does matter in determining policy outcomes; groupthink, therefore, is a real danger to effective decision making.

One might object to this conclusion by criticizing the highly imaginative, yet in many respects debatable research design. Take the operationalization of outcome quality. What are vital U.S. interests in any given crisis? Is it not conventional wisdom that national interests are, at best, an ambiguous measuring-rod for success and failure of policies – for instance, if one takes seriously the organizational politics view of high-level decision making? How relevant a criterion is the short-term reduction of international tensions from a broad, strategic geopolitical perspective? Yet, on the other hand, Janis c.s. rightly assert that their interpretation of process-outcome linkages is, at least, not contradicted or disconfirmed by empirical evidence.

20

Groupthink is but one amongst many constructs in group dynamics. There are other theories in Social Psychology which cover similar grounds. As such, one could view groupthink as being embedded in a whole area of social scientific theorizing about people in groups. Still, Janis' theory has been developed mainly by induction from his case studies, rather than by a rigorous deduction from existing theories of group behavior. This is not to say that Janis did not take into account theoretical work done by others; far from it. Janis' ideas of the functions and dysfunctions of group cohesiveness, reactions to opinion deviance and the role of group leaders in promoting consensus, certainly stem from a thorough reading of the literature. He has personally been actively engaged in research on individual and group behavior under stress.[56] Yet his actual treatment of the literature in the two volumes on groupthink is rather minimal and somewhat selective. Only occasionally is some particular idea or notion illustrated by examples from the field.[57] Indeed, many of the explanatory mechanisms developed in the revised edition were based on Janis' own conflict theory of decision making.

Other analysts discussing groupthink have noted striking similarities between elements of groupthink and other current insights in social science, however, in particular certain elements of social-psychological theories. Raven has elaborated the use of sociometric techniques in groupthink analysis. Also, he has put forward the risky-shift phenomenon as one for further discussion in this respect.[58] In their review article, Longley and Pruitt suggest yet other bodies of theory that could be related to groupthink, while Steiner has provided a more elaborate presentation of "heuristic models of groupthink", linking groupthink to theories of group problem solving, the risky-shift model, and normative models of group decision, emphasizing the role of group leaders and group norms in the quality of information processing by a group.[59] Goleman has put groupthink in line with several other psychological mechanisms of self-deception. In their analysis of entrapped decision makers, Brockner and Rubin suggest that groupthink may be one of its social antecedents.[60]

Further, students of intergroup competition and conflict have provided evidence about the intra-group (cohesiveness) effects of external conflict, which merit more elaborate analysis. Finally, in basic texts on group decision making, groupthink is frequently mentioned as one among several related dynamics of destructive effects of groups on individuals.[61]

All in all, there are sufficient reasons for engaging in a somewhat more thorough discussion of the relationship between groupthink and other theories in Social Psychology and group dynamics. Such a discussion may serve to better clarify the causal mechanisms at work in producing groupthink and in assessing the effects of groupthink. More importantly, in this respect, it may result in a certain amount of simplification of the groupthink phenomenon. In its present form, groupthink appears to be a highly complex construct. If related to current social-psychological theories, groupthink may turn out to be far less intricate. In fact, groupthink might even well turn out to be a specific variant of well-known modes of group behavior. In the next part of this study, the task of discussing groupthink in a broader social-psychological context is undertaken.

1.5. A theory in need of elaboration

Having gone through a rather detailed conceptual and theoretical discussion of the groupthink syndrome, it is time to present the main conclusions. These serve as a starting point for a somewhat broadened examination and – eventually – adaptation of the theory. They are summarized in a number of key points.

A. What Groupthink is: Objectives, Definition, Dynamics

1) Groupthink is a theory originally developed to illuminate and explain certain historical fiascoes in U.S. foreign policy.
2) The basic idea underlying groupthink is that these failures can, at least, in part be attributed to faulty decision-making processes in the small, informal groups of officials that made these decisions.
3) In particular, groupthink theory posits that the decision makers fell victim to the groupthink syndrome, that is, they constituted highly cohesive groups which displayed a forceful tendency toward concurrence. This concurrence-seeking (groupthink) tendency led the group to uncritically decide upon faulty courses of action.
4) Groupthink can, thus, be defined as a strong tendency for quick concurrence-seeking among members of decision groups.
5) There are three crucial antecedents of groupthink: highly cohesive groups, structural aspects of the organization, provocative situational characteristics (notably stressful situations). Specifications are provided in Janis' conceptual model of groupthink.[62]
6) There are eight symptoms (indicators) of groupthink: illusion of invulnerability, belief in inherent morality of the group, collective rationalizations, stereotypes of outgroups, self-censorship, illusion of unanimity, direct pressure on dissenters, self-appointed mindguards.
7) The symptoms of groupthink tend to produce defective decision making characterized by: incomplete survey of alternatives and of objectives, failure to examine risks of preferred choice, failure to reappraise initially rejected alternatives, poor information search, selective bias in processing information, failure to work out contingency plans.
8) Defective decision making qua groupthink almost certainly leads to unsuccessful policy outcomes.

B. Characteristics and Shortcomings of the Theory

9) The *definition* of groupthink as concurrence-seeking has the advantage of not blurring the distinctions between the descriptive function of a definition and the negative connotation attached to the idea of groupthink. Yet in practice, concurrence-seeking is preceded by adjectives such as 'extreme' or 'premature' which nullify this advantage, which make more clear to the reader as to what is the 'essence' of groupthink.

10) The *theory* of groupthink, that is, the causal model of groupthink presented by Janis, is a valid starting point. Yet Janis is not entirely clear about the direction of causality, notably between cohesiveness of the decision group and the concurrence-seeking (groupthink) tendency in group decision making.

11) The model is, in a sense, also incomplete. It does not account for certain significant similarities between groupthink and other social-psychological phenomena. A more thorough assessment of these matters may shed a different light on the 'causes' of groupthink and provide a more solid empirical basis for the model.

12) The strong relationship between decision processes and decision outcomes implied in the groupthink model remains open to critical scrutiny. In particular, attention should be paid to the organizational, administrative and political factors that may mitigate the shape and quality of policy outcomes resulting from groupthink.

C. Theoretical and Research Perspectives

13) The theory of groupthink should be further elaborated, confronting it with current insights from group dynamics and other fields of social science.

14) More specifically, the immediate and underlying contextual and group-dynamic causes (antecedents) of groupthink need to be clarified.

15) Groupthink theory, whether in its original or in some revised version, is in need of more empirical research, along the lines specified by Janis. That is, by using a variety of research methods tackling different aspects of the theory, combined into an integrated research strategy.

1.6. Plan of the study

The present study makes an attempt to use, compare, and combine theory and research from various disciplines, notably Social Psychology and Political Science/Public Administration, to arrive at a more comprehensive understanding of a specific phenomenon, e.g. groupthink. In this sense, then, the study has two interrelated objectives. First of all, an attempt is made to further develop the theory of groupthink, both conceptually and empirically. At the same time, the specific manner of analysis adopted in this study reflects a second objective – call it the 'hidden agenda' – namely, to provide an example of the potentialities and limitations of a truly interdisciplinary approach for studying social phenomena. To achieve this second objective, the book contains separate sections reflecting social-psychological and political-administrative perspectives on the groupthink phenomenon; in addition, these various disciplinary contributions are confronted with one another and combined in various ways throughout the study.

The attempt to present an elaborate and systematic interdisciplinary analysis has several implications. First of all, the book is designed to be of interest to readers from various disciplinary backgrounds. Hence, a social psychologist interested in decision-making analysis will find not only a concise overview of some of the main strands of research in this area in his own discipline, but also a presentation of how political scientists and students of public administration have tended to study processes of group decision making, what their main conclusion are, and how this compares to some of the results of social-psychological studies. The same holds, *mutatis mutandis,* for readers with a political science background. So one function of this study may be to serve as a multi-disciplinary kaleidoscope. The objective looming behind this design is to alert mono-disciplinary students from various backgrounds to the fact that, parallel to their own research traditions, there are others studying the same or comparable phenomena, but using different analytical angles, propositions, and empirical methodologies – and that it is useful, indeed imperative, to incorporate this knowledge into one's own work whenever possible.

Secondly, the book makes an attempt at in-depth theorizing about groupthink. Throughout the study, the steps in the argument are outlined in detail. In this respect, the book may read as a kind of 'voyage of discovery': the reader will experience, as the author did, the surprising parallels, as well as occasional discrepancies, between, say, social-psychological and political-administrative perspectives on the different components of groupthink theory. Reading through parts II and III of the study, he will sense the possibilities, problems, and pitfalls of combining multiple perspectives on groupthink.

In summary, while in this chapter an 'internal' examination of groupthink has been presented, focusing on issues as internal consistency and the validity of causal connections, parts II and III of the book will contain a much broader, 'external' examination. There are several layers in such an external examination. Firstly, there are several insights and theories within Social Psychology that may shed light on the dynamics of groupthink. A broader social-psychological perspective may serve to remedy some of the criticisms raised by, for instance, Longley and Pruitt. If one examines the psychological roots of excessive concurrence-seeking, it may very well be the case that the symptoms of groupthink are more than a 'grab bag' of loosely related ideas, and, indeed, fit the evidence of various strands of theory and research within the field.[63]

Secondly, groupthink has been put forward as a theory of (failing) policies in and around government. Yet, the groupthink concept does not appear to take into account the analytical perspectives on decision-making processes developed in Political Science and Public Administration. In other words, groupthink is a very unpolitical theory on a subject matter which, according to other analysts, gives rise to very specific and very powerful organizational and political dynamics. The second leg of the external examination thus pertains to confronting groupthink with context and process variables from political and administrative theories of decision making. For example, one of the purposes of such an examination is to see how realistic the idea of a concurrence-seeking, close-knit group of high-level executives as the main locus of decision making in key political events is, in view of what we know goes on in the political domain during such episodes. In other words, we can try to establish the range of situations in which groupthink analysis may be realistically applied.

The external examination of groupthink thus has two main elements: a social-psychological orientation and a political-administrative orientation. Bearing in mind the themes put forward in the previous chapters, a number of key topics serve to structure the format of the present discussion. These themes are as follows:
a) the *preconditions* of groupthink, with specific attention for the role of crisis (stressful) circumstances;
b) the *dynamics* of groupthink;
c) the *effects* of groupthink, notably the quality of decision making.

The purpose is, above all, to arrive at greater conceptual clarity and a broader theoretical basis for groupthink. Heuristic hypotheses about the sources and effects of groupthink are developed, resulting eventually in a revised model of groupthink.

Part II will be devoted to a social-psychological examination of groupthink. Firstly, the antecedents and dynamics of groupthink are reexamined, using three social-psychological topics: cohesiveness (a logical starting point given its central place in Janis' original formulation), conformity and compliance, and deindividuation (chapters 2-4).[64] Secondly, the effects of groupthink will be discussed in view of the literature on group polarization (notably the risky shift hypothesis), as well as current theorizing about commitment and entrapment (chapter 5-6). Thirdly, the focus of groupthink analysis will be extended from exclusive attention for intragroup processes toward consideration for the intergroup context of group action (chapter 7).

The analysis of part II works toward a revision of Janis' original conceptual model of groupthink, which explicitly links concurrence-seeking to a number of other familiar group processes. Chapter by chapter, the components of this revised model are elaborated. It will be summarized in full at the end of part II.

It must be noted that the treatment of social-psychological theory and research in part II is not comprehensive. The phenomena discussed at greater length have been selected by referring to the more applied literature on group decision making in organizations. More specifically, the focus is on group phenomena which are commonly associated with 'bad decisions' or group performance failure.[65] Consequently, little attention is paid here to other potentially relevant phenomena such as social facilitation, group impact theory, and modelling.[66]

Part III confronts the social-psychological conceptualization of groupthink with empirical information and analytical perspectives on government policymaking. Groupthink has been advanced as a theory purporting to explain (certain types of) government policy decisions. Since then it has become commonplace to suggest groupthink as one among several factors producing government policy fiascoes. In part III these claims are examined critically. Specifically, the preliminary revised model developed in part II is reexamined with one underlying question: to what extent do the interpersonal and group phenomena that together constitute 'groupthink' occur in and around 'real-life' decision makers and decision groups in government and politics?

First of all, in chapter 9, the underlying assumptions of groupthink theory are critically examined: to what do decisions get made in the deliberate, choice-like manner presumed by groupthink and many other notions of decision making? Evidence from research on organizational decision making suggests that only a small part of a complex organization's output is produced in this manner. Furthermore, the chapter attempts to show that of this category of decisions, again only part is taken by one single group operating in relative isolation and autonomy from other groups within and around the organization. Next, in chapters 10 and 11, the antecedents and dynamics of groupthink as presented in the model at the end of part II are reassessed in a similar manner. Subsequently, a specific political-administrative elaboration of groupthink theory is attempted. In chapter 12, an analysis of the impact of different structures of accountability on group decision making in government leads to the distinction between two generically different modes of groupthink: a pessimistic variant (groupthink type 1: collective avoidance as outlined by Janis), and an optimistic variant (groupthink type 2: collective over-optimism). Part III is concluded in chapter 13, which summarizes the main amendments and changes to the revised model of groupthink that emerge from the political-administrative reexamination of groupthink theory.

Part IV seeks to provide a critical empirical illustration of the ideas developed in the two theoretical overviews. In an introductory section, the revised model of groupthink is operationalized into a set of research questions. These provide an empirical framework for case study of U.S. decision making with regard to the arms-for-hostages deals with Iran under president Reagan (chapter 14).

The main conclusions of the study are drawn in chapter 15. It includes a final assessment of groupthink theory; it suggests leads for future research in this area; it reflects upon the pros and cons of interdisciplinary work in social science; and, finally, it discusses some of the measures that might be taken to prevent groupthink.

Notes

1. Hall (1982).
2. The cases mentioned as well as several others are dealt with at length in: Rosenthal, Charles and 't Hart (eds.1989).
3. Coch and French (1948), Homans (1950), Coser (1956).
4. Barry (1974), speaking about Hirschman's Exit, Voice, and Loyalty.
5. Janis (1982a); see also Janis and Mann (1977); Janis (1982b).
6. See Janis (1989), pp.56-63; 275-283; see also Wheeler and Janis (1980).
7. Janis (1972), p.9.
8. Longley and Pruitt (1980).
9. Janis (1982a), p.259.
10. Janis (1982a), p.301.
11. Arrows 1 and 2 converge to point to the possibility of interaction effects among the antecedent conditions, suggesting that it is the combination of a provocate situational context and the existence of a cohesive group that produces the strongest tendencies towards concurrence-seeking; see Janis (1982a), p.303.
12. Janis (1982a), p.49; see also De Rivera (1968).
13. Janis (1982a), pp.252-253; on these affiliative tendencies under external pressure, see also Schachter (1959), and Rabbie and Wilkens (1971).
14. Janis (1982a), p.42.
15. Soelberg (1967); Janis and Mann (1977).
16. Janis and Mann (1977) and Herek, Janis and Huth (1987) deal at length with the issue of the relationship between procedures of decision making and the quality of decisional outcomes.
17. See Janis (1982a).
18. Green and Connolley (1974).
19. Raven (1974); see also Raven and Rubin (1977).
20. Raven (1974), p.311.
21. Ibid, pp.313-318.
22. Wong-McCarthy (1976).
23. Tetlock (1979), p.1314. Integrative complexity coding is described more fully in Suedfield and Tetlock (1977).
24. Gero (1985).
25. Janis (1980), Smith (1984) and Gabriel (1985) on the Iran rescue mission; Heller (1983).
26. Rosenthal (1984, 1986a).
27. Etheredge (1985), Polsby (1984).
28. Hensley and Griffin (1986).
29. Verbeek (1987).
30. Barrett (1988).
31. McCauley (1989).
32. Whyte (1989); I came across this article during the final editing of the manuscript, so it was not possible to do full justice to Whyte's analysis. See also Esser and Lindoerfer (1989).

33. Moorhead (1982). Later on, Moorhead did try to use his model in actual research, see Moorhead and Montaneri (1986).
34. Flowers (1977), pp.890-892.
35. Courtright (1976, 1978).
36. Callaway, Marriot and Esser (1985).
37. Fodor and Smith (1982), pp. 180-184; Leana (1985).
38. 't Hart, Kroon and Van Kreveld (1989); see chapter 14.
39. In a long footnote in his recent book, Janis (1989) has answered some of his empirically-oriented critics, such as Barrett and Etheredge by reexamining their arguments and providing evidence that their assertions are not damaging to the groupthink interpretation of the cases (Bay of Pigs, Vietnam) at all.
40. Longley and Pruitt (1980), p.79; see also Moorhead (1982).
41. Longley and Pruitt (1980, pp. 79-80).
42. Longley and Pruitt (1980, p.80); see also McCauley (1989).
43. Janis (1982a), pp.250-259.
44. Steiner (1982).
45. Deutsch (1965, 1973), Jervis (1976), White (1984, ed.1986); see further chapter 7.
46. Longley and Pruitt (1980), p.77.
47. Janis (1982a), pp.11, 196-197, 259.
48. Janis and Mann (1977). This study contains an integrated model of individual decision making under stress, as well as a broad range of empirical illustrations of the authors' ideas.
49. Longley and Pruitt (1980), p.77.
50. Katz and Kahn (1978).
51. Janis (1989).
52. Dror (1986).
53. It is used by many decision analysts involved in quality assessment. With regard to group decision making in empirical cases, the work of Hirokawa and colleagues is quite similar to groupthink analysis. See Hirokawa (1987); Hirokawa and Scheerhorn (1986); Hirokawa, Gouran and Martz (1988).
54. Herek, Janis and Huth (1987); the article was reproduced with minor corrections in Janis (1989).
55. See, however, George (1980).
56. See, for instance, Janis (1968, 1971), as well as his work within the American Soldier project - Stouffer et al. (1949).
57. Janis (1982a), pp.3-7, 194, 218-219, 246-250, 257.
58. Raven (1974); see also Raven and Rubin (1977).
59. Longley and Pruitt (1980), pp.86ff.; Steiner (1982) mentions the well-known work on group problem solving by Maier – including Maier and Solem (1952); Hoffman and Maier (1964), and the risky shift literature (see chapter 5).
60. Goleman (1985); Brockner and Rubin (1985).
61. See Swap et al. (1984), as well as Hirokawa et al. (1988).
62. Janis (1982a), pp.242-259.
63. Longley and Pruitt (1980), p.80.
64. Note that an important theorist on deindividuation, Zimbardo, views it as an intrapsychic state brought about by environmental conditions, and thus not specifically as a group phenomenon. Others thake a different view, however, and do stretch the group-dynamic aspects of deindividuation; see Zimbardo (1970), Diener (1980).
65. Most notoriously in Buys (1978), see also Swap (1984), Hirokawa (1987).
66. For overviews, see Shaw (1981), Forsyth (1983), Brown (1986).

PART II – GROUPTHINK:
A SOCIAL PSYCHOLOGICAL INVESTIGATION

2 – The cohesive group: a re-assessment

2.1. Cohesiveness: introduction

The inclusion of group cohesion (cohesiveness) in a discussion of the factors at work in producing groupthink comes as no surprise. Indeed, the cohesiveness of decision making groups is the crucial linchpin in Janis' own depiction of the dynamics of groupthink. In fact, it is the sole group-level factor that he singles out as a substantive, independent cause of groupthink. And it is, of course, the idea that is most impressive in its counter-intuitive power: the realization that, depending upon the content of group norms, harmonious, cooperative, team-like entities may be a liability rather than an asset in producing high-quality decisions. This is not what one would expect. At face value, it seems perfectly sensible that a tightly-knit group where members like each other and cooperate smoothly, is likely to produce better decisions at lower costs than groups where members cooperate less, groups where there is little common ground between members and groups characterized by internal conflicts. The basic thesis of groupthink is, of course, exactly the reverse: the very cohesiveness of the group may become a value in itself for each of the members, and to such an extent that they may be reluctant to say or do anything that might disturb it, such as voicing criticisms against the ideas and opinions of other members or the group's majority. Furthermore, it may even affect (delimit) their capacity to think critically.

This lack of frankness is detrimental to the making of consequential decisions, where discussion and a certain amount of dissent are indispensible in arriving at well-grounded choices. The characteristics of groupthink are, in fact, geared to the preservation of group cohesion and high spirits through the quick attainment and preservation of consensus on the issue the group confronts. Ultimately, this can produce unsound decisions leading to the kind of policy fiascoes analyzed by Janis.

Recently, the nature of the causal linkages between group cohesion and groupthink has been questioned by several theorists. Before entering this discussion, some current insights and issues in cohesion research shall be presented specifically, because I think that much of the discussion about the specific role of cohesion in producing groupthink hinges upon different conceptions and interpretations of cohesiveness itself.

Cohesiveness, viewed by Janis and most other small-group theorists as the extent of 'sticking-togetherness' of members of a group, is one of the crucial factors in group functioning. It is also one of the most intensely researched variables in Social Psychology (in particular in group dynamics). Perhaps partly because of its very pervasiveness, it is also one of the most elusive and multi-faceted aspects of (decision) groups. Firstly, there are several competing notions of cohesiveness. Secondly, there are different techniques of measuring cohesiveness which do not always yield consistent results. Thirdly, cohesiveness affects group behavior in numerous ways. It pervades both group structure and process, and cohesiveness factors may act as either independent, intermediate, or dependent variable. Essentially, many of the unresolved problems in the analysis of group cohesiveness reported twenty years ago by Cartwright, still exist today: how do various sources of attraction combine in a composite measure of cohesiveness, what is the importance of different sources of attraction on group cohesiveness and its subsequent effects upon group behavior, and what is the nature of causal linkages involving group cohesiveness and other aspects of group structure and process.[1]

The main focus in the present discussion will be on cohesiveness as an independent (and occasionally, as an intermediate) variable, more specifically on the effects of cohesiveness upon group performance, notably on group decision making. From there on, a re-examination of the relation between cohesiveness and groupthink comes as a logical final step.

2.2. Cohesiveness: definition

Just after World War Two, cohesiveness research moved swiftly by the systematic efforts of Festinger, Schachter, Back, and their associates. Their empirical approach necessitated a clear-cut definition of group cohesiveness. The following definition was employed: cohesiveness is the resultant of (or: the total field of) all forces acting on members to stay in the group. The keyword was attraction. Using this definition, Festinger et al. investigated patterns of informal social communication, notably pressures to uniformity of perceptions and judgements that may arise in cohesive groups. Expanding the theme, Schachter also examined the effects of group cohesiveness on the treatment of deviants (group members with differing opinions) by the majority.[2]

The attractiveness of the group for its members was said to derive from various sources. People may want to be in a group because they like the other members. The group may be attractive to its members because the group can accomplish things which they alone cannot. The group may also be prestigious in itself: being part of the group is regarded as an honor within the organizational context the members are operating in, enhancing the individual's status and self-esteem. In short, there might be a whole range of reasons why groups are attractive to members. Therefore, there are also many different sources of group cohesiveness. Cartwright lists four general sets of variables determining a person's attraction to a group:

a) his motive base for attraction (personal needs for affiliation, respect, security, and other values that can be mediated by groups);
b) the incentive properties of the group (group goals, style, prestige, etc.);
c) his (subjective) expectancy of the rewards and costs associated with his group membership;
d) his comparison level – his evaluation of the expected outcomes of group membership against his personal standards of what constitute (un)favorable results.[3]

Criticism: Gross and Martin

This diversity of sources of cohesiveness was one of the points of criticism raised against Festinger et al.'s interpretation of cohesiveness-as-attraction. Gross and Martin criticized the operational elaborations based on this definition both on conceptual and empirical grounds. Their main contention was that Festinger et al. – using the measures they did, notably friendship choices and experimental manipulations in terms of ascertaining subjects of the alleged compatibility between themselves and their fellow group members – did not measure what they set out to do. According to Gross and Martin, such operationalizations tapped only one of the large number "forces" which attract members to a group. Also, objections were raised against the idea put forward by Back that cohesiveness was a unitary concept. Back, on the basis of some of his experiments, asserted that the behavioral effects of group cohesiveness were always the same, regardless of the specific source of attraction. In other words, a group that is cohesive because the members like each other, is considered virtually identical to a group whose cohesiveness was derived from interdependence between members. Criticizing Back's research design, Gross and Martin charged that this proposition was untenable.

Gross and Martin, in turn, put forward an alternative notion of cohesiveness that substituted the "additive conception" of Festinger et al. with one that emphasized the relational bonds between and among group members. Although they did not provide a specific formulation, their notion of cohesiveness would be something like "the extent to which the ties between group members remain intact in the face of disruptive conditions".[4] From the polemic that followed, Cartwright and Zander put forward the idea of group cohesiveness as a function of the individual member's *resultant* attraction-to-group.[5]

Other interpretations

It should be pointed out that the notion of group cohesiveness has been treated in very different ways as well. Lott and Lott, for instance, took the perspective of S-R learning theory and defined group cohesiveness as that group property which is inferred from the number and strength of mutual positive attitudes among the members of a group.[6] Their underlying idea was that these positive attitudes are, in essence, dependent upon the receipt of rewards – thus a dominantly voluntaristic, pragmatic perspective. Similar ideas can be found in exchange theory.[7] Later on, the distinctions between pragmatic and relational dimensions of groups were elaborated in the split between task fulfillment and social-emotional (group maintenance) aspects of small group processes. This dichotomy gained prominence in leadership research.

Nowadays, few people seem to bother. Cohesiveness is considered an unproblematic factor which needs no elaborate conceptual or operational discussions. In various organizational and management studies, it is regarded a self-evident concept, lingering between attraction to group, mutual liking and group identification.[8] This compromise outcome may be a realistic understanding, but it does present some problems if one studies group decision making using a theory (groupthink) which hinges upon cohesiveness as the key explanatory factor.

In the absence of a single, fully developed notion of cohesiveness, it seems wise for the purposes of the present study to settle for the Cartwright and Zander notion of cohesiveness as the resultant attraction of a member to a group. However, at the same time, it is important for analytical purposes to try and differentiate whenever possible between the types of cohesiveness factors that pull group members together, f.i. between primarily functional ties (interdependence) and groups characterized primarily by friendship and amiability (affection) – although in reality these two dimensions cannot always be separated (see below).

2.3. Cohesiveness: research

Firstly, various sources of cohesiveness are briefly presented (cohesiveness as a dependent variable). Yet, as mentioned, the primary interest here lies with cohesiveness as an independent or intermediate variable. More specifically, the effects of cohesiveness upon the processes and outcomes of group decision making will be examined.

Sources of cohesiveness

In his review of cohesiveness research, Cartwright cites studies describing various reasons why individuals become attracted to groups, most of which pertain to characteristics of the group itself: the attractiveness of fellow members, (perceived) similarities among members, the goals and activities of the group, its size, its atmosphere, as well as other structural properties (such as the communication structure).[9] These are all quite obvious elements that need little comment: small groups are more tightly-knit than large ones; decentralized groups have greater member satisfaction than centralized networks. Yet, there are a few other sources of cohesiveness, in part also mentioned by Cartwright. These are the following:

Interdependence between members. There appears to be an important distinction between consensual and symbiotic groups. In the former, cohesiveness derives mainly from the perceived similarities in characteristics and opinions of the members (esprit de corps). In symbiotic groups, it is the perceived interdependence between the individual members which provides the bonds. There may be differences between the various members, yet they feel that they need each other to function most effectively: the sum is considered bigger than its parts. In practice, these two sources of attraction may co-exist.

Conflict with out-groups. Interdependence may also be a source of conflict: promoting more contact between various groups in an organization or community may not always succeed in resolving tensions – far from it.[10] The interests of group members can be partly overlapping, partly mutually exclusive. Within-group competition lowers cohesiveness. More important, however, is the widely documented finding that a group that enters into conflict with one or more other groups, will become more tightly-knit – provided they anticipate success from joint action.[11] This thesis of "intergroup conflict = intragroup solidarity" has found its way beyond Social Psychology. An entire school of theory and research in International Relations uses this thesis at the level of nation states – with mixed results, it should be added.[12] The intergroup context of groupthink is discussed in full in chapter 7. Here it suffices to remark that an important source of attraction between members of a group may lie *outside* the group's domain, i.e. in certain environmental conditions.

Rituals and symbolism. Some groups are hard to become part of. Membership may be considered an honor. The prestige of the unit reflects upon its members. The group is, therefore, highly attractive for its members and generally tends to be quite cohesive. Pleasant contacts are almost an end in itself. Examples abound: a secret society, a local women's circle, a gentlemen's club, the governing committee of a scientific association. Often, such prestigious groups have their own particular initiation rituals and symbolism, all geared to enhance esprit de corps among members. It may be a meticulous appointment procedure, it may be a special medal or a tie, it may be regular exclusive inner-circle meetings: all create or reinforce a sense of we-ness among core members.[13]

Leader-centeredness. Captains, foremen, presidents, and chairmen: they are all examples of group leaders. Group leaders can exert a persuasive influence in establishing and maintaining the atmosphere of interpersonal relationships within groups. The field experiments by Lewin, Lippit, and White have shown that the style of leadership ("democratic", "laissez-faire", and "autocratic") shapes the group climate and members' satisfactions with the group.[14] A powerful leader is able to induce a bond between the group's members that chiefly consists of their mutual loyalty to him.[15] Indeed, the common admiration for a charismatic political leader may well be the only tie that binds his otherwise sharply divided advisors together. Some leaders deliberately use this strategy of group leadership. A marked example of this was U.S. president Roosevelt, who deliberately pitted his advisers against one another, and sought to benefit from the conflicting point of view this produced.[16]

External adversity and stresses. Even if a group fails to achieve its ends, its cohesiveness may remain unshocked. It may, indeed, even grow. Lott and Lott signal that when failures are perceived by the group members to be arbitrarily imposed by sources outside the group's control, there is a good chance that attraction to the group increases.[17] This is even more so when group members lack an exit option: they cannot dissociate themselves, so they decide to make the most of it.[18] In crisis circumstances (high stress), group cohesiveness generally increases: task groups may actually become 'primary groups' under the pressure of outside events. This thesis has been extensively documented in field settings. The most striking examples of primary group ties can be found in military groups in combat situations. Loyalty to the small combat unit was what kept many soldiers going during World War Two (in terms of combat effectiveness and resistance to enemy propaganda), both in the German and the U.S. armies. Similar findings were obtained in other theatres of war.[19] In fact, Janis – as co-researcher in the American Soldier Project – obtained most of his initial data and insights on group cohesion under stress in this period. Other field studies can be found in the disaster literature, for instance in Lucas' study of two groups of miners trapped underground for many days following a major accident.[20] A third example concerns Mulder et al.'s research among Dutch associations of shopkeepers threatened by supermarket take-overs.[21]

Sophisticated laboratory research, however, has made it clear that there exists no simple and clear-cut linkage between external stress and increased group cohesiveness. Hamblin hypothesized that group integration actually decreases when members either feel that they can do better by a timely retreat from the group, or perceive that there is no solution to the crisis available at all. In these situations, group members may display more self-oriented behavior and indulge in imposing negative sanctions upon their colleagues.[22] In his research on stress in task groups, Payne emphasized that for groups under stress to become more integrated, it is necessary that the members need to have interpersonal skills.[23] In sum, it appears that there are various intermediate factors which determine when and to what extent groups in crisis situations become more cohesive.

Cohesiveness and group decision making

The effects of cohesiveness upon group process, productivity, and performance are widely documented. The same goes for the effects that cohesive groups can have on the thoughts and actions of their members. The number of studies on cohesiveness and decision making in groups is far more limited, however. Drawing on both sources, some of the findings that are most relevant in the present context are discussed.

Cohesiveness and group atmosphere. Communication between members of cohesive groups is more frequent, more intense, and positive in tone than in non-cohesive groups. This results in more pro-active behavior of individual members and more efforts to coordinate one's actions with those of the others. This, in turn, is one of the factors which enhances members' satisfaction with the group. Cohesive groups tend to be congenial groups.

Cohesiveness and group influence upon its members. Much of the research program on informal social communication by Festinger and his colleagues was devoted to studying group effects on individual members. The investigators, soon to be followed by a vast number of others, found that cohesive groups exert certain pressures toward uniformity upon their members. More generally, as Shaw observed: "(Groups) characterized by friendliness, cooperation, interpersonal attraction, and similar indications of group cohesiveness exert strong influence upon members to behave in accordance with group expectations. Members of cohesive groups are motivated to respond positively to others in the group, and their behavior should reflect this motivation."[24] In cohesive groups, the explicit or implicit norms and standards that underlie the functioning of any collectivity, gain importance. It is held that the more cohesive the group, the more its members tend to abide by its norms of conduct.

There appears to be a compelling logic in this proposition: the more cohesive the group, the greater the members' satisfaction with it and the greater their willingness to remain part of it, hence the greater their incentives to think and act as the group does. Yet, this final step is taken too hastily. Whether a group member feels compelled to go along with the group, depends entirely upon the *content* of the group's norms. Group norms may very well encourage critical discussion and dissent by minorities or individual members. It should be added that this is not very often the case. Usually group norms to tend to stress the importance of consensus and joint action; hence the tendency towards uniformity. Yet, the key point to remember is that cohesiveness increases the power of group norms, and these may or may not favor uniformity (cohesiveness may even foster detrimental conformity, as will be explained in chapter 3).

In practice, the tendency for conformity in cohesive groups is widespread. Research has illustrated this in many laboratory and field settings.[25] The very cohesiveness of the group promotes this: because group members emphatically want to remain in the group as a respected participant, the group enjoys considerable sanctioning power. It has at its disposition a wide range of techniques for changing the opinions and behaviors of a deviant member: from occasional remarks or jokes that alert the deviant to the group norm, to (threats of) rejection and expulsion. The group member who is able to withstand such pressures has to be a formidable individual. Yet, as the literature on deviance and psychological reactance has shown, under certain conditions, deviants may persist and serve as catalysts for group changes.[26]

Cohesiveness and problem-solving abilities. At a very general level, field studies have shown that highly cohesive groups are more effective in accomplishing group goals than low-cohesive groups. Similarly, studies of group problem solving show that cohesive groups perform well.[27] In the literature contrasting individual and group performance, the benefits of group cohesion have been stretched again and again. The advantages of groups are said to lie mainly in the sphere of the quantity and quality of information storage and retrieval. Also, groups are more successful than individuals in generating a wide range of alternatives. At the same time, group decision making has some costs: it takes more time and it requires sometimes difficult give-and-takes between group members. In this context, the value of cohesiveness is stretched as promoting a congenial and task-oriented atmosphere, which allegedly facilitates group discussion.[28]

These are all familiar arguments. And it is precisely this line of thinking that Janis is contending with. His position of course is that at a certain point, high cohesion becomes detrimental to the quality of decision making. However, in the experimental literature on group decision making and task performance, little support for this contention can be found. Janis' case rests more on the above-discussed findings on pressures toward uniformity and on his studies of combat units. At the same time, studies of U.S. foreign policy decision making provide mostly anecdotal support for Janis' ideas. In his detailed analysis of the decision-making process of president Truman and his advisors at the time of the Korean invasion, De Rivera signals that, at times, the high cohesion of Truman's group (despite bitter personal rivalries between key advisors) seemed to cause distortions of the advisement process: the withholding of information that might shatter the consensus of the group. After the publication of Janis' study, many other analysts signalled such distortions of information processing and choice making, also in the sphere of organization and management theory.[29]

A specification: cohesiveness and group decisions within the environment

In organizational and political life, groups hardly ever operate in a vacuum. That is, they are influenced by what goes on outside the group domain. They occupy a certain position within the organizational part of this environment. They get inputs and feedback from it: information, resources, commands, advice, cooperation, opposition. And, in turn, they attempt to cope with their environment: they react to its inputs, send their own outputs to it, and generally try to influence their environment so as to enhance their interests or purposes.

Real-life groups, therefore, ought to be studied in context. The social context can affect every aspect of group functioning to varying extends. Actors and agencies within this context may exert a high degree of control: select the group membership, set the group tasks, actively steer the group process, and determine the criteria of group performance. Or they may be merely a malleable object of manipulation by an all-powerful (small) group. In reality, the relations between groups and their organizational and interorganizational context will vary between these extremes. In any case, real-life groups act and react to certain parts of their environment. This affects the group process in many ways.[30] Just as organization theory at a certain point 'discovered' the environment and started to develop typologies of environments and contingency models of organizational effectiveness, so has small group analysis in management theory begun to recognize the importance of context variables.[31]

One way in which group process and environmental factors interact relates to group cohesiveness and its effects upon group performance. Top management may either stimulate or frustrate its advisory groups through its policies of allocating tasks and providing resources and support. This affects the internal processes of these groups. For instance, advisory and planning groups do not like to see their work being ignored by strategic decision makers. If this happens, these groups may lose their attractiveness for their members. Cohesiveness diminishes, and the speed and quality of their work decrease.

That is but one scenario. A very interesting variant occurs when a group is in a state of conflict with the organization as a whole. The group wants or does things that run counter to the wishes of organizational leadership or the official norms and goals of the organization. This occurs during strikes and mutinies, or in cases of collective excesses and desertions by military units. At the societal level, one may regard the conflict between extremist groups and the prevailing social and political order from this perspective. In these circumstances, group cohesiveness actually disfavors group performance (if judged by the official standards). One way to put an end to this is, of course, for organizational and political authorities to try and disrupt the cohesiveness of the deviant group by promoting internal disagreement or defections. For the group members, these situations entail a conflict of loyalties. They have to chose between solidarity with the group and respecting the wider demands of the organization or society in general. If the group in question is a sort of 'full-time', primary group (such as an army unit in combat), it can be extremely hard to break group cohesiveness in favor of compliance with 'official' rules and desires.[32]

Conclusion

Cohesiveness is a pervasive factor in any group process – by its presence or absence, and in both 'positive' and 'negative' ways. This brief review of cohesiveness research has revealed that the picture with regard to both the sources and effects of cohesiveness is quite diverse. No easy generalizations are available. There is a large diversity of sources of cohesiveness, and it is not known precisely how these various origins affect the impact of cohesiveness upon the group process. We know that, in any case, highly cohesive groups are congenial groups; that highly cohesive groups can, in principle, exert considerable influence upon their members through the operation of group norms and standards, up to the power to go against the values and expectations of their wider (organizational) environment. And finally, it has been concluded that the effects of cohesiveness upon (the quality of) group decision making are contingent upon a number of intermediate factors, including the type of decisional issue at hand, and the content of the group norms.

2.4. Cohesiveness and groupthink: analysis

The time has come to try and relate cohesiveness again to groupthink. That is not as simple as it may seem. Even Janis himself is ambiguous on this point. In their review article, Longley and Pruitt signal at least four linkages between cohesiveness and groupthink in the work of Janis. Steiner turns things around and suggests that, "...it was the *desire for cohesion* rather than cohesion itself that promoted groupthink..."[33] (my emphasis, PtH). In this view, groupthink does not necessarily occur only in highly cohesive groups. Striving for cohesion rather than its maintenance becomes the crucial causal factor, thus, apparently, broadening the scope of the groupthink thesis. The two points of view expressed above can be restated in the form of two hypotheses:
a) the occurrence of groupthink is contingent upon the decision group being highly cohesive (cohesiveness as a necessary condition for groupthink as suggested by Janis);
b) the occurrence of groupthink is a by-product of a desire for cohesiveness in decision groups. Groups that are not cohesive, but who are actively striving to become more cohesive, may exhibit the same kind of extreme concurrence-seeking as cohesive groups who attempt to maintain their close-knitness (revised hypothesis suggested by Steiner).

Is this a soundly based correction? This is hard to determine from Janis' work alone, as it lacks more formal measurement of the crucial variables.

The first thing to note is that the hypotheses are not mutually exclusive. In fact, they are complimentary. But, if considered together, they depict a vital theoretical issue in groupthink analysis, namely the question whether Janis was right to consider high group cohesiveness a *necessary* condition for the occurrence of groupthink (Janis made it quite clear that it is not a *sufficient* condition for groupthink).[34] If the second hypothesis is valid, the range of groups susceptible to groupthink phenomena is increased to certain types of non-cohesive groups. Such a finding may prove to be of significant importance in assessing the potentialities of groupthink in

40

political decision making. On the other hand, the issue may spring from the failure to differentiate between different sources and types of cohesiveness, such as cohesiveness based on functional interdependence and cohesiveness based on interpersonal attraction (see below).

Conceptual and causal factors. The variability of interpretations of the relation between cohesiveness and groupthink is in part a function of the elusiveness of the concept of cohesiveness. Janis offers no clear-cut definition of cohesiveness. In fact, only in his analysis of the Watergate case does he elaborate at length upon the question whether the group under consideration was indeed highly cohesive (which – it should be remembered – is the key antecedent condition in his model). His attention in that particular case was triggered by Raven's article which essentially dismissed the possibility of full-fledged groupthink occurring in the Watergate case, because Nixon's group was ridden by conflict and competition. Janis, however, carefully reassessed Raven's assertion and showed that a plausible case can be made that during the critical early months of the cover-up there was a cohesive in-group consisting of Nixon, Haldeman, Ehrlichman and Dean.[35] Unfortunately, in other cases, Janis stops short of such an analysis, thus leaving room for various interpretations.

This does not mean that one can readily accept Steiner's hypothesis. Cohesiveness research has shown that in cohesive groups, strong pressures for can occur. However, nowhere has the even more elusive concept of 'desire for cohesiveness' been put forward as a meaningful variable. And there are indeed some doubts. In attributing the same powerful effects to groups desiring to be cohesive (and thus, allegedly, not being it at the point in time under study – which in itself is strange if one views cohesiveness as attraction-to-group: if all group members feel so positively about the group, it is cohesive according to many established definitions), Steiner puts a high premium upon the effects of anticipatory socialization and upon the effects of group norms-to-be. It would seem from cohesiveness research that the very power of group norms and standards derives from their being (a) well-known to all members, (b) backed by a repertoire of shared signals and sanctions derived from the members' strong desire to remain a respected group member. It seems that such conditions can exist in a meaningful and substantive way only in ongoing groups that have been cohesive for some time.

Groupthink and sources of cohesiveness. An alternative interpretation of the Steiner hypothesis may be attempted on the basis of our overview of various *sources* of cohesiveness. What Steiner calls a desire for cohesion might very well be merely a reference to a different type" of cohesiveness than Janis had in mind while formulating the groupthink thesis. If one examines Janis' cases, very different sources of cohesiveness have operated. While in the Nixon group common loyalty to the leader was a major factor, the conflict with outgroups and the gravity of the situation seems to have been pivotally in the Vietnam and Korean episodes, respectively. Ritualism and prestige play a role in all of the groups, but appear most markedly in admiral Kimmel's group at Pearl Harbour with its emphasis upon decorum and off-duty social contacts. It is an open question how strong the effects of different sources of cohesiveness are. However, it can be argued that a group whose sole cement lies in common admiration for the leader rests upon a more volatile footing than a group whose cohesiveness derives from symbiosis-interdependence between the members. There might be a continuum of cohesiveness, based on (combinations of) different sources of cohesiveness. If this is the case, the two hypotheses about the relation between cohesiveness and groupthink are complementary instead of mutually exclusive.

Cohesiveness and groupthink: towards an alternative view. Recently, an alternative interpretation of the relation between groupthink and cohesiveness has been offered by McCauley. It does not concern the issue of the importance of cohesiveness as antecedent factor per se, but instead suggests a reassessment of the process dynamics that occur in cohesive groups. McCauley wonders whether groupthink is a matter of group members actually internalizing the group's perspectives and policy alternatives (internalized consensus), or whether it can also pertain to group members going along with the group despite the fact that they privately doubt the wisdom of the group's course of action (compliance).[36] He argues both exist, and illustrates this by reexamining Janis' own case studies. Especially the Bay of Pigs and Vietnam cases appear to be examples of compliance rather than internalized consensus: throughout the decision-making process, there were serious 'doubters' who continued to harbour private concerns about the prevailing policies, but who did not want to keep raising them in the group. Janis calls this the suppression of doubts, or potentially the silencing of dissenters through mindguards. Yet McCauley rightly notes that the fact that the dissidents did not speak up does not mean they privately accepted the group majority's (or leader's) opinion – far from it. Rather, their behavior may have been due to their need for securing the group's approval. Similarly, he discusses the situational and structural conditions conducive to groupthink presented by Janis, and shows that these same conditions conduce to compliance (without private acceptance) as well; the relationship between compliance and groupthink shall be taken up at length in the next chapter.

Here it is important to take note of McCauley's reassessment of the diversity of sources and effects of high cohesiveness. First of all, he indicates that "high cohesion can come from extrinsic rewards and punishments mediated by the group and from prestige of group membership, as well as from the attractiveness of group members (....) Acceptance by other group members can increase cohesiveness, presumably by increasing the attractiveness of other group members to the one accepted, but this is only one of the possible sources of cohesiveness." [37]Similarly, he discusses the situational and structural conditions conducive to groupthink presented by Janis, and shows that these same conditions conduce to compliance (without private acceptance) as well.

Then, he criticizes the way in which Janis singles out cohesiveness based on feelings of we-ness and a clubby atmosphere, as being the most powerful (and necessary) antecedent to groupthink:

"With the perspective of the discussion above (e.g. about different sources of cohesiveness – PtH), we can interpret this as a suggestion that internalization of group influence is greater when cohesion is based on attractiveness of group members or prestige of membership than when based on task-related rewards. This suggestion has some precedent (....) even if it is not generally accepted (....) But it is also possible that internalization is greater when cohesion is based on attractiveness of members or prestige of membership in addition to task-related rewards. This alternative amounts to saying simply that groupthink is greater when cohesion is greater, recognizing that there are multiple and additive sources of cohesion rather than assuming special power for some of these sources."[38]

Once again, one encounters suggestions that Janis may have moved too swiftly in formulating the original groupthink hypothesis. He appears to have discounted too quickly the evidence from experimental studies of the sources and effects of group cohesiveness. On the other hand, the discussion so far has not provided any solid evidence suggesting that high cohesiveness – whatever its specific effects on different modes of group concurrence-seeking and consensus formation – is *not* a necessary antecedent to groupthink. It will take going beyond the cohesiveness literature to illustrate that there are *generically different paths to groupthink*. This task is taken up in the next two chapters.

Another key component of Janis' analysis concerns the role of threat-induced psychological stress – stemming from external (crisis-like situations) and internal (low self-esteem) sources. To what extent do these factors indeed give rise to high group cohesiveness? And to what extent will this stress-induced cohesiveness produce excessive concurrence-seeking? These questions pertain to the situational component of groupthink theory. By singling out these situational conditions, Janis de facto implies that groupthink is a contingent, situation-bound theory, rather than a general phenomenon that may occur at any time in any decisional group.

Research by Hamblin cited earlier suggests that the stress->cohesiveness linkage is mediated by group members' appraisal of the situation and their estimation of the effectiveness and chances for success of group action (as opposed to alternative coping patterns) in dealing with the threat. Similar evidence was obtained by Rabbie et al.: only (anticipated) success in competitive interaction with other groups *increased* the cohesiveness of a group under pressure; when members felt they would not prevail at the end, cohesiveness under threat *decreased*.[39]

These results indicate that perhaps the most intense form of group cohesiveness occurs in those groups that, under threat, continue to function as a unit, with sufficient esprit de corps. It is up to further research to establish more precisely the conditions under which this is likely to be the case.

The second question that emerges concerns the quality of group performance under conditions of high threat. Here, one of the key issues to be resolved is embedded in the following question: if group cohesiveness increases under stress because individuals view the group as a sort of hiding place and source of social-emotional support, and thus serves to decrease the stresses and tensions upon the individual members, how is it possible that such groups fall prey to the very symptoms of collective cognitive closure that are normally associated with high or increasing stress? Because this is what Janis, in his assessment of the situational dynamics of groupthink seems to imply: there is a threat; faced with it, the group becomes more closely-knit; this relieves some of its members' anxieties; one would then expect them to be able to operate better; and yet the group falls prey to groupthink. Is this a contradiction or merely a paradox? It is only a paradox if one accepts the underlying motivational theory. The decrease of individual stress is achieved through the seeking of group unity and solidarity, yet this is done at the price of adequate reality-testing. The focus on the group acts as a motivationally-based perceptual barrier: group members are no longer adequately sensitized to the problems they are facing.[40] It is up to leaders and influential group members to find ways in which to avoid the trade-off between stress reduction through group integration and the need to maintain the group's critical facilities in coping with its environment.

Notes

1. Cartwright (1968), pp. 105-107; see also Golembiewski (1962); Verba (1962); Golembiewski et al.(1969); Hare (ed.1976).
2. This early work in group cohesiveness studies can be found in, by now, classical articles and books, such as Festinger (1950); Festinger, Schachter, and Back (1950); Festinger and Thibaut (1951); Back (1951); Schachter (1951); Asch (1951).
3. Cartwright (1968), p.96; see also Thibaut and Kelly (1959).
4. See Gross and Martin (1952), p. 554, as well as the sharp reaction by Schachter and Gross and Martin's reply in the same issue.
5. Cartwright and Zander (1968), pp. 77-78; see also Golembiewski et al. (1969) p.71.
6. Lott and Lott (1961); Lott and Lott (1965).
7. For instance, Homans' (1950) analysis of the human group, as well as the more formal analysis by Thibaut and Kelley (1959). Compare this with March and Simon's (1958) analysis of why people join organizations.
8. For instance, Gladstein (1984); Miesing and Preble (1985).
9. Cartwright (1968), pp.95-103.
10. Hewstone and Brown (eds 1986).
11. Deutsch (1949); Sherif and Sherif (1953); Blake and Mouton (1961); Meyers (1962); Smith (1972); Deutsch (1973); Rabbie (1982).
12. See Rummel (1963); Tanter (1966); Wilkenfeld (ed. 1973). Galtung (1968)

provides a lengthy discussion on the isomorphism between small groups and international systems.

13. See Parillo, Stimson and Stimson (1985).
14. Lewin, Lippit and White (1939).
15. This was already pointed out by Freud in his essay on group psychology, Freud (1927).
16. On Roosevelt's leadership style, see Barber (1972); George (1980); Morgan (1985).
17. Lott and Lott (1965); see also Mulder and Stemerding (1963).
18. Schachter (1959).
19. Grinker and Spiegel (1945); Shils and Janowitz (1948); Stouffer (ed. 1949); George (1968); Chodoff (1983).
20. Lucas (1970). For an overview of small-group level findings of disaster research, see Drabek (1986).
21. Mulder and Stemerding (1963); also Mulder et al.(1971).
22. Hamblin (1958); Hamblin (1960).
23. Payne (1981).
24. Shaw (1981), p.218.
25. Asch (1952); Kiesler (1969); Hare (ed.1976); McGrath (1984).
26. The problem of deviance and pressures to conform was addressed for the first time in full by Schachter (1951). Subsequently, a whole range of studies elaborated on the subject. See the overviews by Diener (1980) and Dickenberger and Gniech (1982); See also Moscovici's analysis of social change, presented in chapter 3.
27. Shaw and Shaw (1962); Maier (1970).
28. See, for instance, Miesing and Preble (1985).
29. For example, George (1974), Smart and Vertinsky (1977) Tjosvold (1984); Gero (1985); Hirokawa and Scheerhorn (1986); Hirokawa et al. (1988).
30. See Hackman and Morris (1975); Gladstein (1984); for a specific discussion of the effects of context on group process with respect to political groups, see Verba (1978).
31. Gladstein (1984); in part III of this study, this line of reasoning is pursued more fully.
32. Janis (1945); Janis (1949); Coser (1956); Shils and Janowitz (1948); Chodoff (1983).
33. Steiner (1982), p.519.
34. See Janis (1982a), pp.245-256.
35. Raven (1974); Janis (1982a), pp.211-216.
36. McCauley (1989), employing the familiar distinction between compliance, identification and internalization put forward by Kelman. See Kelman and Hamilton (1989), see also chapter 3.
37. McCauley (1989).
38. McCauley (1989).
39. Rabbie et al.(1974).
40. The purest form of this argument in Janis' work can be found in his 1963-article, reprinted in Cartwright and Zander (eds 1968).

3 – Conformity, compliance, and groupthink: a new perspective

3.1. Conformity and compliance: introduction

Decision making by consensus nearly always requires some participants in the decision making process to adjust their views, or at least to abide by what appears to be the group's (or the majority's) judgment. In groupthink, group members are willing to do so rather quickly and to a large extent. In fact, 'true' victims of groupthink will only very rarely find themselves in disagreement with the group because the very dynamics of groupthink lead to the development of *shared* perceptions and opinions among group members. In that case, adjustment of private views is unnecessary.

But in many decision situations, especially when they concern highly ambiguous and volatile policy problems, such perfect and clear-cut a-priori consensus will not exist. Consensus will have to emerge. Different assessments have to be brought into line – be it often very quickly (due to real or perceived time pressure). Some group members, in other words, will have to bend their judgments. Groupthink is a process in which this occurs very quickly through strong tendencies for concurrence-seeking. Why were the members in the high-ranking and powerful policymaking groups examined by Janis who originally differed from the group's majority judgement, prepared to 'give in' so quickly and painlessly? Why did most potential 'dissenters' silence themselves or allowed others to do it?

Considering the groupthink phenomenon from the perspective of the individual group member, one is dealing with processes of social influence, in particular (implicit or explicit) conformity and compliance. Concurrence-seeking implies that potential dissidents conform to what appear to be the group's perceptions and judgments. Now the topics of conformity and compliance stand for a large body of knowledge in the social-psychological literature. In it, different causes and effects of conformity are identified. Studying research on conformity and deviance, one quickly recognizes that the conformity of victims of groupthink needs a wider explanation than merely in terms of "concurrence-seeking in highly cohesive groups". To be sure, highly cohesive groups are able to put strong pressures toward uniformity upon their members. This has been discussed in the previous chapter. But it is held here that this is not the only way in which group members are influenced toward uncritical acceptance of the apparent group consensus. In this chapter in particular a distinction is made between influence upon group members stemming from relations with their peers (pressures to uniformity in cohesive groups as discussed in the previous chapter) and influence stemming from hierarchical differentiations within groups (most notably conformity and compliance in leader-member relations).

In order to probe deeper into these differentiations, a change of focus is needed. Let us not view groupthink from the perspective of the group as a whole, but take a 'bottom-up' view instead: studying groupthink from the perspective of an individual member. Why did Janis' group members go along with the group? To be sure, concurrence-seeking as a form of group pressure -direct and/or subtle – is one explanation. But could it not also be that some of the group members merely complied as a form of obedience to the group leader or to certain high status members? Did they not act in the group in a manner that they were more or less 'instructed' to? These questions draw attention to the structural differentiation between the members of decision groups. As in almost any collectivity, in the policy-making groups studied by Janis, some members were 'more equal than others.' There were leaders (for instance Truman, Johnson, Kennedy, Kimmel, Nixon), senior members (for instance McNamara, Acheson, Haldeman) and juniors or relative 'outsiders' (for instance Schlesinger, Dean, Ball). With differing positions came different roles, different rules of conduct, and most of all, differences in 'weight' – power and authority within (and outside) the group.

In this chapter, an attempt is made to explore some of the implications of a bottom-up perspective on groupthink. The discussion will be focused upon conformity and compliance in the small-group context. This is a very broad topic. It involves, amongst others, group pressures on individuals, reactions to deviance and relations between majorities and minorities, obedience to authority, and the role of leaders and leadership. These are all substantive areas of theory and research in their own right. So they cannot be dealt with here but in a highly selective manner, focusing on the role of conformity and compliance in groupthink.

3.2. Conformity and compliance: definitions

To keep a clear view of such a broad and complex field, it is inevitable to make some terminological distinctions at the outset. Conformity is used as an over-all concept. It is taken to be a cognitive, attitudinal, or behavioral change on the part of a group member as a result of real or perceived pressures put upon him. [1]

There are several analytical dimensions of conformity, however, which have to be taken into account.
– The *extent* of change; does it involve personal cognitive or motivational adjustments or is it merely a superficial 'giving in' to external pressure?

Kelman and Hamilton distinguish between processes of compliance (conformity as obedience to commands and rules); identification (conformity based on need to preserve valued relationships with influencing agents); and internalization (conformity as an intrinsically rewarding process of behavioral change: influence is accepted because it is congruent with the actor's value system).[2] In the context of groupthink, internalization is the key factor at work in the cohesiveness interpretation: a basic value consensus among members of highly cohesive groups. In this chapter, the conformity processes that require more explicit steering by majority members or group leaders are the central focus of attention: identification and, in particular, compliance.

- The *object* of influence; conformity may pertain to changing one's view of reality, but it may also pertain to an individual's attitudes or choice behavior (perceptual change due to informational influence, versus attitudinal or behavioral change due to normative influence).

- The *source* of influence; conformity pressures may stem from the group as a whole, transmitted in a group context (see chapter 2), or from single group members, most notably high-status members such as the group leader.

- Related to the source of influence is the *direction* of the influence process. If conformity arises from collegial or (peer-)group pressure, it can be thought of as a product of horizontal influence. If it arises as a result of specific status differences within the group, we call it hierarchical (or vertical) influence. Conformity as a consequence of hierarchical influence usually amounts to compliance as defined by Kelman and Hamilton.

The framework presented above allows for some clear-cut understandings:
- the bottom-up perspective on influence processes in decision groups is best represented through taking conformity as the generic term for socially-induced individual change;
- conformity arises out of pressure upon the individual group member (real or perceived); it can pertain to both perceptual/cognitive and motivational/behavioral states;
- apart from conformity pressures as a result of peer influence, conformity may result from the explicit use of (in)formal power, hierarchy and authority -in that case, conformity takes the form of compliance (conformity based on commands from authoritative sources – notably group leaders).

An important factor in hierarchical influence processes are high-status group members and group leaders. Leadership functions in a group include the guarding of the group's goals and purposes, the enforcement of norms, the maintenance of group atmosphere, and the management of the group decision process. Theoretically, then, group leaders are those members who at one point or another in the group decision making process perform these functions. But reality is more complicated. This is because leadership also has formal and psychological dimensions. Group leaders may have been appointed, regardless of their specific abilities or prestige within the group. Consequently, discrepancies may exist between official and de facto (informal) leaders: the two categories may coexist – and come into conflict – within one and the same group. The psychological dimensions of leadership and leaders within groups are equally important. In terms of power and status differences between group members, wide varieties of leadership patterns exist. Some leaders are simply 'first among equals', with little psychological distance between themselves and the rest of the group, whereas other leaders may be highly charismatic, all-powerful, dictatorial – with obvious consequences for member attitudes.

Talking about leaders and the effects of leadership in small (decision) groups, one should keep an open eye to the diversity and fluidity of leadership patterns that may exist. It is, in other words, too simple to just look at the highest ranking official within a group and simply assume that this must be the leader. Rather, in any empirical discussion, one should: firstly, identify the leader(s) in various stages of the group process; secondly, assess their leadership style and its consequences for group maintenance and task performance; thirdly, carefully analyze the power and influence processes within the group without presuming simple, 'downward only' directives and influence attempts.' Only then can one start to analyze in detail the hierarchical influence processes and their conformity effects within the group under study.

3.3. Conformity and compliance: research

Under this heading, three related strands of research relevant to conformity are examined. These describe two variants of 'horizontal' and one general class of 'vertical' sources of conformity. They are studies of:
a) the impact of group norms and role expectations;
b) majority and minority influence in groups;
c) obedience to leaders or high-status members.

Group norms, member roles, and conformity

Almost any group develops components of a specific structure and culture specific to itself. This goes for families or peer groups such as sports teams and street gangs, but also for task groups such as workers' teams, military units, management teams, and other decision-making groups. Group members get a sense of their positions (and status) in the group, and develop a somewhat predictable pattern of relationships, i.e., the group structure. Group norms – the formal or informal 'rules of conduct' that specify what behaviors are acceptable for the various members – are a key element of the group structure. For the individual member, the norms of the group are a primary guideline in his thoughts and actions. If a group member wants to become or remain well-appreciated by his fellows, he must conform closely to the norms of the group. If he fails to do so, he risks negative sanctions from the others, even up to expulsion from the group.

Extensive research has gone into finding out how group norms develop and change, how they affect group task performance and to what extent they bind group members.[4] Sheriff's classic experiments on the autokinetic effect have illustrated how norms develop in a situation of almost total ambiguity, and how they serve as a convergence point for the judgments of individual members. Research on the development of norms has persisted ever since. It has shown that norms serve to create order and predictability in group interaction: they serve a protective function by reducing uncertainty. They also help a group to function in a larger social context. Similar findings stressing the impact of group norms were reported in studies of political groups.[5] A few pointed examples of the conformity-producing functions of group norms are the following:

1) Coch and French studied the effect of group norms regarding work unit production in a factory. They found that new workers in the unit met with intense social disapproval from the rest of the group if they produced well above the groups' output norms. In order not to become outcasts, they subsequently adjusted their output downward. Similar pressure to conform with performance standards developed by groups (note: mostly irrespective of larger organizational goals or expectations) have been observed in many other settings since.[6]

2) In threatening circumstances, groups may become highly cohesive. Studies of military combat units show that increased cohesiveness and the threat to survival also lead to a strong increase in the 'strictness' of group norms. Whereas in everyday settings the degree to which group norms are truly accepted by each and every group member varies, in combat situations norms become pivotal in maintaining the integrity and the morale of the group and in promoting the (perceived) chances of survival. It is deemed necessary that everyone acts in concert, and that members can rely upon one another. Therefore, the range of permissible deviations from the norms of the group is greatly diminished.[7] A key mediating factor, however, is the content of the group norms. Some groups, even under threat, may develop norms that favor nurturant and supportive treatment of 'deviants'.[8]

3) Roles of group members vary: there may be decision makers and advisors, specialists and generalists, managers and departmental heads, and so on. Role differentiation often brings along status differentiation. Differences in status and prestige, in turn, lead to different requirements to conform to group norms. Yet analysts disagree as to how these requirements actually differ. Some say that leaders are the top conformers. Actually, they regard it as a necessary condition to achieve high status and maintain leadership. Others maintain the reverse: high status members have already proven themselves in the past and have built up what Hollander calls an "idiosyncracy credit".[9] This allows them more leeway for (temporary) deviations from the norms of the group. More recently, attempts have been made to specify under what conditions 'leaders' have

(or less) room to maneuver away from group norms.[10]

4) An interesting conformity problem occurs when a group member is part of a group whose norms come into conflict with wider organizational or societal norms. It is the classic dilemma for members of 'deviant groups' (gangsters, juvenile delinquents, dissidents, derailed military units): which set of norms will be adhered to? Whichever is chosen, negative sanctions can follow. As it turns out from research, in many cases the hold of the immediate peer-group is stronger than that of the wider organization or society. The peer-group is close and important to the member's everyday life. He may identify strongly with the group's norms or with its leader(s). The group will, moreover, tend to be highly cohesive, given the perceived conflict with outgroups, increasing its importance for the self-esteem of its members. And it has at its disposition direct and impressive sanctions (positive, but often quite brutal negative sanctions as well). Compared to the conformity-inducing power of the in-group, the counteractive potential of the formal organization (in combat, the official command structure can be far away), or society (for instance the law-and-order apparatus) is considered remote. A comparable conformity dilemma is posed by membership of policy decision groups that are in the process of going astray (producing failing policies; initiating morally unsound or criminal actions) is crucial in understanding the action of potential dissident members in some of Janis' cases of groupthink (Vietnam, Watergate, Bay of Pigs, Appeasement). Chapter 7 provides a more elaborate discussion of the in-group/out-group differentiation that may occur in these circumstances, and its effect upon the intragroup decision processes.

Peer pressures, majority and minority influence, and conformity

Group members attempt to influence the judgments and actions of their fellows not only with regard to group norms, although the boundaries are difficult to draw. But in research on conformity pressures, several other factors have been identified. For instance, in the area of perception, Asch's experiments have shown that purely informational pressures can be put upon a group member by his peers. Asch showed that even in a situation that was practically devoid of any ambiguity (assessing from three markedly different alternatives the correct length of a line on cardboard), thirty percent of the subjects followed the obviously incorrect answer given by members of his group (who were all, of course, confederates of the experimenter). Since then, Asch's paradigm has been replicated in many cultural and occupational settings. Results have varied, but it appears that his basic findings (under certain conditions individuals may distort their private judgements when confronted with a different, but incorrect, group assessment) stand out.[11] The possibilities and limitations of peer pressure on individual group members are examined more closely by way of a few marked examples.

Examples of peer pressure. In their research program on informal social communication, Festinger and his colleagues developed an interest in pressures to uniformity in small groups. They performed both field and laboratory studies to test their theory, which posited that pressures to uniformity arise from two sources: (a) social reality – group members want to obtain support for judgments that are not anchored in physical reality; (b) group locomotion – group members seek consensus to attain group goals. When opinion discrepancies exist among group members, uniformity pressures produce communication directed toward reducing the discrepancies. From these basic theoretical statements, Festinger deduced numerous hypotheses about the magnitude of pressure put upon individual members and the likelihood of opinion change.[12]

As discussed in the previous chapter, group cohesiveness is one of the factors increasing pressures to uniformity in situations of opinion divergence. But it is by no means the only factor. Apart from interpersonal and group-level dynamics, there are also intrapersonal factors at play: seeking conformity to assess the correctness of one's own opinion and thus by satisfying the drive for a favorable self-appraisal (self-esteem).[13]

More or less as a spinoff from the Festinger research, several other factors influencing the strength and effectiveness of conformity tendencies have been identified. In a review of situational and experimental variables related to conformity, Kiesler summed up seven main factors:

- task difficulty and stimulus ambiguity: the greater the difficulty/ambiguity, the greater the conformity;
- group size and unanimity: a unanimous group of at least three people triggers maximum conformity; the marginal utility of more persons is small – at the same time, even one person can effectively apply conformity pressures upon another in dyadic situations, even without communication; moreover, if a group is not unanimous, its conformity-inducing potential virtually vanishes;
- the discrepancy between the opinions within the group: Kiesler suggests that there might be a U-curve, where both very low and very high degrees of discrepancy produce the strongest conformity pressures;
- the (perceived) competence of the dissenting subject vis-a-vis the group: the less competent the dissenter is at the task relative to the group, the greater the chances that he will conform;
- the relative status of the dissenter: high-status members are more steadfast than low-status members;
- the previous success or failure of the group: groups with a history of success are able to obtain greater conformity than groups that have previously failed; there may be elements of imitation and 'modelling' involved here;
- public commitment: members who have to speak up in public are more inclined to conform with the group, than if their point of view would remain private -at the same time, if a person publicly has committed himself to a certain position, his resistance to conformity pressures grows (the notion of commitment and resistance to change is a crucial element

Figure 3.1. Functionalist and genetic models of conformity and social influence in groups[16]

FUNCTIONALIST	GENETIC
1 Social influence in a group is unequally distributed and is exerted in a unilateral manner.	1 Every group member, irrespective of his rank, is a potential source and receiver of influence.
2 The function of social influence is to maintain and reinforce social control.	2 Social change is as much an objective of influence as social control.
3 Dependence relations determine the direction and the amount of social influence exerted in a group.	3 Influence processes are directly related to the production and resolution of conflicts.
4 States of uncertainty and the need to reduce uncertainty determine the forms taken by the influence processes.	4 When an individual or subgroup influences a group, the main determinant of success is behavioral style (of the influence source).
5 The consensus aimed at by influence exchange is based on the norm of objectivity (i.e. the belief that there is only one correct answer).	5 The course of the influence process is determined by objectivity norms, preference norms (the self-enhancement function of consensus) and originality norms (desire for nov elty).
6 All influence processes are seen from the vantage point of conformity, and conformity alone is believed to underlie the essential features of these processes.	6 Conformity is but one form of social influence, aimed to reduce conflict through the elimination of deviance. Other modalities are normalization (avoiding conflict) and innovation (change through minority influence).

of both Festinger's and Janis and Mann's theories of decision making; the wider implications of commitment are discussed in chapter 6).[14]

A bottom-up perspective on peer pressure. The study of peer pressure has taken more and more a true 'bottom-up' perspective by focusing on the role of deviants, group rejection of deviants and the effects of minorities on group judgements and performance. Deviance research was greatly stimulated by Schachter's experiments, showing that pressure to communicate and to conform are directed towards a deviant. A persistent deviant will meet with disapproval and, ultimately, rejection. Since then, cumulative research and theory have expanded on these initial findings. The most far-reaching developments were initiated by Moscovici and his colleagues. They questioned the underlying functional assumptions of conformity research.[15] The old and the new lines of thinking are contrasted by juxtaposing their main propositions (see figure 3.1.)[16]

Based on his genetic model, Moscovici has emphasized the potential power of minorities in groups, specified conditions for minority influence, and stressed the innovative potential of dissenting minorities in decision groups. Active minorities can be the key to innovative solutions. They can promote learning. In doing so, they may enhance decision quality. This takes the focus of conformity analysis far away from the detrimental conformity effects mentioned earlier: non-conformity is possible, and can be useful. In a way, Moscovici has adopted a functionalist perspective as well, but his focus is change, not control.[17] Much work on 'deviance' has been performed by Levine. His model of reactions to opinion deviance – while grounded in the old, functionalist 'paradigm' – seems to incorporate most of the empirical claims and factors put forward by 'genetic' analysts.[18]

Obedience, leadership, and conformity

The discussion of this chapter on conformity and compliance was begun by pointing to the 'vertical' dimension of influence processes in groups. Nowhere becomes this element more clear than in studies of obedience to authority. In many situations people, individually and in groups, appear prepared to do what they are told to do by authority figures (leaders), even if this amounts to performing cruelties on other people. Milgram's classic obedience experiments have made this painfully clear. In the base-line condition, sixty-three percent of naive subjects playing the role of learner in an alleged experiment on memory and learning, continued giving increasingly severe, painful, and dangerous electric shocks to a 'student' failing to give correct answers to a memory test (also held to be a naive subject in the experiment – in reality a paid actor faking dramatic reactions to the 'shocks' given by the real research subject, the learner). They did this because they were requested to participate by a figure of authority, the experimenter (the authority in the case was 'scientific').[19]

Though controversial because of its methods involving deception and the amount of stress put upon the subjects, the significance of Milgram's findings was hardly contested.[20] In military history, numerous examples of cruelty-under-orders can be found. Significantly, Milgram's work has been called the Eichmann-experiment (the experiment coincided with Eichmann's trial). Later on, stories of American atrocities in Vietnam, notably the My Lai massacre, brought the message home in the U.S.; especially because lt. Calley and other participants at My Lai claimed they had been executing 'superior orders'.[21]

Milgram ran numerous variations on his basic paradigm in order to tap factors which would make for variations in the level of obedience. Accordingly, he moved the site of the experiments to an obscure office building, had the victim give feedback on his bad heart condition, brought the learner and the victim in one and the same room. Yet in all these conditions, substantive levels of obedience were obtained. Only in one condition did he manage to get a very large percentage of subjects to defy the experimenter. Most significantly to the present study, this happened when there were three learners instead of one, with two of them quitting early in the procedure. Milgram called this the "liberating effects of group pressure": peers-induced social support and conformity pressures overcame the authority-induced obedience impulse. Based on this analysis, Milgram and others vested some hope in peer rebellions against malicious organizational commands.[22]

Administrative obedience? Milgram's experiments, like Asch's, have been replicated many times in many different cultures and occupational settings. Despite some variations, the main obedience effect was always present. One of the most sophisticated and interesting replications is provided by Meeus and Raaymakers. They set out to develop a procedure in which: (a) there was no ambiguity in the credibility of the test procedure; (b) there would be a minimum of 'demand characteristics' in the experimental situation; (c) the type of destructive action required would be less extreme and more comparable to the everyday practice of organizational and administrative performance.

They summarized their research procedure as follows:

> "(The) experimental design involves an X-Y-Z structure similar to Milgram's: X is the experimenter, a research worker at the university, Y is the subject and Z is a person applying for a job. The applicant (a trained accomplice) has been invited to the laboratory to take a test. The test is crucial in the selection procedure. If the applicant passes the test, he gets the job. If not, he will remain unemployed. The subjects are instructed to disturb the applicant while he is doing the test. They are to make negative remarks (to be indicated as 'stress remarks') about his test achievements and denigrating remarks about his personality. The subjects are told that this procedure is not part of an evaluation of the applicant's suitability; the ability to work under stress is not an essential feature of the job. The procedure must be followed solely to assist in the experimenter's research project, which focuses on the relationship between psychological stress and test achievement. The subjects are to make the remarks despite the applicant's objections. The applicant's objections become increasingly strenuous as the procedure continues. Due to the stress remarks, the applicant suffers considerable psychological strain, so that his test achievements are unsatisfactory and he consequently fails to get the job. The subjects are thus faced with a moral dilemma. Must scientific research be allowed to prevail upon someone's chances of a job or a career? Should they cooperate to this purpose?"[23]

Much to their surprise, they obtained no less than 91 percent obedient subjects in their base-line experiment. Despite the more favorable conditions for disobedience, the lowered threshold of having to perform less extreme actions apparently gained the upper hand. Meeus and

Raaymakers' paradigm of 'administrative obedience' raises probably even more disturbing questions to students of public administration and political decision making than Milgram's did. The shuffling of papers and the following of bureaucratic procedures appear to provide an effective context for an official to neglect or play down the adverse or destructive consequences of his actions.

How to relate these findings to the problems of group decision making and the role of conformity in producing groupthink? While the analysis itself must await the next section, the next cluster of research findings provides a preliminary lead.

Groups under stress: search for strong leaders. In a research program on power and influence in groups, Mulder and his co-workers also investigated small groups under stress and their patterns of leadership. They conducted a field experiment involving groups of Dutch shopkeepers allegedly threatened by the impending arrival of supermarket chain stores in their town or neighborhood. It was found that in the high threat condition (high probability of supermarket arrival, presumed 20-30 percent sales losses), the groups displayed not only a tendency for high cohesiveness, but also a need for strong leadership. So cohesiveness of groups under stress is likely to become leader-centered. This finding is supported by evidence from other studies: in situations of threat, people in groups seek for clear and strong leaders.[24] Apparently, strong if not authoritarian leadership is actively (if partly unconsciously) sought and thought to be functional in reducing stress and/or coping with threat.

What are the wider consequences of leader-centered cohesiveness? The key point is that the tendency to seek strong leaders may also lead to an increased willingness to abide by their judgments and commands. It is hypothesized, then, that there is a tendency for obedience to strong leaders among members of 'embattled groups'.[25]

The tendency to obey the group leader in these conditions springs from several motives:
- the need for guidance and security under stress (cf. also Bion's "dependency groups" seeking omnipotent leaders to relieve anxiety);[26]
- the perceived need for loyalty to the leader in difficult circumstances, as well as the identification with the leader and his cause;
- the desire to minimize personal responsibility for decisions and actions during critical episode (obedience to orders and demands brings with it a perception of shifting responsibility for adverse consequences of the obedient subject's actions towards the commanding figure).[27]

If this line of reasoning is valid, a strong case for the relevance of an compliance perspective on a number of cases of groupthink could be made: concurrence-seeking under the impact of hierarchical influence processes. Take, for instance, the case of the Watergate cover-up. Janis has argued effectively that the in-group around Nixon was held together – despite pervasive factional rivalries and constant feelings of insecurity – by the common admiration for the leader as well as the dependency of the advisors upon their leader. This latter tendency became more marked when the investigation directly threatened the positions of Mitchell, Dean, Haldeman, and Ehrlichman, up to criminal liability. Nixon, as their employer and President of the United States, had the formal means to protect his advisors. So they continued to serve him loyally against overwhelming odds – up to a breaking point.[28]

The group as 'liberator'? A final word about disobedience in the small group context is in order. As mentioned before, Milgram and subsequent researchers using his paradigm were impressed by the effects of peer rebellion in neutralizing blind obedience. Similarly, Moscovici took up evidence originating in Asch's findings to develop his theories about resistance to conformity and minority influence. Apparently, both horizontal and vertical conformity pressures can be resisted by the individual – but he needs others to take the lead or to go along.

This is all well-taken. But it is surprising to this author that Milgram c.s. totally failed to explore the other side of the coin: the power of the group in maintaining and perpetuating destructive obedience. Horizontal (peers-induced) pressures to uniformity can also work to reinforce vertically-induced blind obedience. If they do, one can safely hypothesize that, once the group has set a pattern of compliance, the chances of disobedience (both autonomously or due to third-party intervention) are very slim indeed. What, for instance, would happen if Milgram's two confederates would willingly comply all the way, serving as a model to the naive subject?[2-9] Would an additional confederate arriving half-way through the procedure expressing his dismay be able to get the naive subject to discontinue? There is ample reason to doubt this. By that time, group pressures and needs for justification of his past actions are likely to keep him in line, despite being provided with an example of defiance. The mutual reinforcement of horizontal and vertical conformity is to be taken seriously. It should be worthwhile to reexamine Janis' cases to this end (compare the revisionist reinterpretation of the Executive Committee during the Cuban Missile Crisis which stresses the willingness of the group to abide by the President's imposition of debatable premises guiding the earliest discussions about the American response to the missile construction in Cuba).[30]

3.4. Conformity, compliance, and groupthink: analysis

The discussion of conformity in relation to groupthink takes three steps. First, the face-value plausibility of considering patterns of hierarchical conformity pressures and leadership factors in groupthink analysis is stretched. Secondly, based upon the above thematic discussion of conformity research, a specific interpretation of the role of conformity in groupthink is presented. Thirdly, Janis' own thoughts on conformity and leadership factors with regard to groupthink are discussed.

At the outset, it is pointed out that in this section, emphasis is put on the issues of within-group stratification, hierarchical (vertical) pressures to conformity and the role of compliance in concurrence-seeking. This is done as an addition, not as a substitution of Janis' original interpretation, which focused solely on the link between cohesiveness and horizontal forms of social influence. Even the summary review of conformity research presented above should make it abundantly clear that these sort of influence patterns are of great importance in studying group decision making. It is argued, however, that there is more to it than that. Structural differentiation and power differences between group members make for generically different influence.[31] As such, high cohesiveness is not a necessary condition for premature concurrence-seeking (groupthink).

It is argued that similar tendencies may arise from compliance, notably *anticipatory* compliance ('giving in' before manifest pressure is exerted). Processes of anticipatory compliance can be just as subtle as cohesiveness-induced extreme concurrence-seeking; its effects upon the quality of group decision making may be just as harmful.

Leads in the literature

Dimensions of power, hierarchy, and leadership in groupthink have not been entirely neglected in the groupthink literature. Apart from their treatment in the second edition of Janis' book, several other analysts have provided some leads. First of all, Flowers manipulated the leadership style variable in the groups he studied in his laboratory test of groupthink. He hypothesized that:

> "cohesiveness and leadership style should interact so that groupthink in the decision process is most likely to occur under conditions of high group cohesiveness and closed leadership".[32]

Oddly enough, he found that a 'closed' (directive, manipulative) leadership style was much more important in bringing about symptoms of groupthink than group cohesiveness. Though part of these findings may be due to the specific operationalizations in his experiment, Flowers' findings do reveal the possibility that – as argued above – groupthink may occur in both cohesive and non-cohesive groups. To be more specific, consider Flowers' conclusion that "the degree of power of the leader may be an important variable to include in a revision of Janis' hypothesis".[33]

Secondly, in another laboratory test of groupthink, Courtright discussed the role of leadership factors. Due to methodological considerations of operationalization, Courtright manipulated leadership through the experimenter's role-playing. In doing so, he acknowledged that:

"Janis' description of groupthink suggests that members accept the influence of the leader because they 'identify' with the values and goals of the group and its leader. In this study, however, the results of the attempted influence more closely resemble compliance – i.e. performing the desired behavior without the presence of the corresponding attitude or value."[34]

Still, he found traces of an interaction effect between high cohesiveness and a directive leadership style. So the closed, option-limiting style of leadership again proved to be a relevant factor in reducing overt disagreement and fostering quick and 'painless' decision making.

Thirdly, Fodor and Smith obtained results quite similar to those of Flowers. In their study, the effects of cohesiveness and group leaders high or low in power motivation on group decision making processes were examined. They found that leaders high in a power "foster an atmosphere that is detrimental to group decision making", using an operationalization of group decision making quality modelled after Janis' symptoms of groupthink).[35] Like Flowers, they found no significant effect of cohesiveness, which led them to question the validity of Janis' theory. Yet, the authors quite correctly surmised that a main reason for the failure of their study to corroborate Janis' hypothesis on cohesiveness and groupthink, might have been that their (simple) operationalization of cohesiveness was far removed from the real-world 'cohesiveness' that Janis implied.

Fourthly, McCauley has called attention to the role of internalized compliance in producing groupthink. As discussed earlier, he confined his analysis largely to 'horizontal compliance', e.g. stemming from perceived or anticipated peer influence attempts. He interpreted compliance within the broader framework of cohesiveness rather than emphasizing vertical compliance and leadership factors. Yet this seems to be more a matter of definition (broad or limited notions of cohesiveness vis-a-vis compliance), than a substantive theoretical problem.

A specific interpretation

How can the leads above be transformed into systematical inferences about the relationship between processes of conformity and obedience and the concurrence-seeking tendency of groupthink? The analysis so far allows for a specific hypothesis. It is a contingent hypothesis: it focuses on group decision making under stress.[36] It reads very simply: in situations of high external stress, members of a decision group have an increased tendency to quick agreement with the leader's preferred course of action (whether he is physically present or not seems to be a point of interest that would require further research); this tendency may be so strong that it leads to premature concurrence-seeking.

What is the underlying logic of this hypothesis? Take the existence of high external stresses on the decision group as given. Then, two main effects follow:

- the decision group tends to become highly cohesive (as described by Janis and others);
- there is a perceived need for strong leadership among the group members;[37]

These first-order effects, in turn, have specific behavioral consequences:
a) there will be a group leader (either appointed, formal leaders or de-facto, situational leaders) who takes the lead in assessing the situation and proposing a course of action;
b) the members of the group may have personal doubts or misgivings about the leader's alternative, but they feel a need not to oppose the leader at such a critical moment;[38]
c) potential dissenters are subjected to subtle or overt forms of group pressure (which has increased power due to the group's high cohesiveness) not to voice or maintain deviant positions;
d) if necessary, the leader uses his authority – reinforced by the face-to-face character of the interaction in the decision group – to ensure compliance with what, by now, has become the group position.[39]

This may seem a rather 'narrow', highly specific scenario. To a certain extent, this is correct. The interpretation of compliance-induced group-think offered here is certainly not meant to depict some new general pattern of group decision making under stress. Far from it. It requires the availability of a strong and commonly accepted group leader. It requires a closed leadership style as described by Flowers and others. It may even require a pre-existing climate of toughness, or at least of compliance. Certainly, these conditions will not apply to each and every group of government officials faced with, say, a crisis situation.

However, in real-life policy settings, these conditions at times do apply and produce the sort of leader-centered, anticipatory concurrence-seeking suggested here (see chapter 11). It appears that certain types of organizational 'climates' may be more conducive to self-evident compliance to authorities than others.[40] More generally, the organization's task or position within the policy network can influence members' attitudes towards loyalty and obedience.[41] Apart from this rather specific interpretation, research on conformity, peer pressures and leadership suggests that other factors than cohesiveness may bring about groupthink-like patterns of concurrence-seeking, self-censorship, mindguarding and stereotyping.

Janis' view (and a rejoinder)

How would Janis respond to such a line of reasoning? First of all, it should be noted that in some of Janis' cases, quite clear examples of compliance-based, leader-centered concurrence-seeking can be found. Even after the fatal attack which lay bare their failure, the members of admiral Kimmel's group at Pearl Harbour continued to express their great admiration for him and pledged their loyalty.[42] Similar patterns can be found in the Korea case and the Bay of Pigs case. And although Nixon's aides were surely much more than merely 'yes-men' in the interaction with the president, Raven does remark that "they were all bound to the group through loyalty, acceptance, and identification with their leader, Richard M. Nixon. They had been carefully selected for their loyalty (....) Their dependence on Nixon was of the very highest (....) So long as Richard Nixon was successful and powerful, and they demonstrated proper loyalty and proper tactics, they could be assured of an important role in one of the most powerful offices in the world."[43]

Janis has also devoted some attention to conformity behavior in group decision making. Yet his treatment is very limited in scope. He only discussed conformity arising out of fear of recrimination, and used it to illustrate the perils of decision making in non-cohesive groups. According to Janis, deliberate conformity out of fear of recrimination crisis in conflict-ridden on 'pecking-order' type of groups low in cohesiveness.[44] He hypothesized that the lower the cohesiveness, the stronger the tendency for deliberate conformity, and the greater the chances of errors in decision making. In a graphic illustration, Janis presented this as the exact mirror image of groupthink (see figure 3.2.).

Figure 3.2. Conformity and groupthink according to Janis (Janis, 1982a, p. 299)

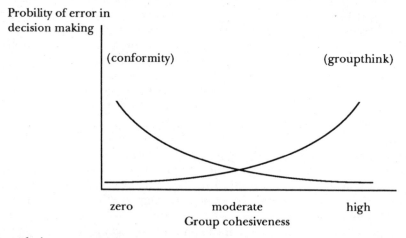

The analysis presented in this chapter, suggests that this is indeed a valid, but merely one amongst other patterns of conformity. For one thing, fear of recrimination is not the only source of conformity. Many more distinctions are important: leader-centered or peers-centered conformity, normative or informational bases for conformity, positive or negative sanctions under-lying conformity, compliance versus internalization, and others.

The structural differentiation between group members and, with it, the hierarchical component can pervade the deliberations of real-world decision groups in ways that are more subtle than Janis' deliberate conformity – indeed in ways that closely resemble the subtle processes of concurrence-seeking at work in groupthink. This makes for generically different patterns of groupthink (and, importantly, requiring different preventive and remedial strategies). The specific hypothesis regarding stress-induced, leader-centered (anticipatory) compliance outlines one such pattern. Moreover, the analysis of this chapter suggests that there are ways in which horizontal and vertical patterns of conformity can reinforce one another so as to almost totally 'grasp' the individual group member.

Notes

1. Kiesler (1969).
2. Kelman and Hamilton (1989), pp.103-112.
3. Some basic sources on leadership include Fiedler (1967); Vroom and Yetton (1973); Stogdill (1974); Kellerman (1978); Hollander (1978); Blondel (1987).
4. Sherif (1936).
5. Fenno (1959); Verba (1962); Fenno (1962); Barber (1965).
6. Coch and French (1948); Homans (1950); Berkowitz (1954).
7. Shils and Janowitz (1948); Chodoff (1983); Gal (1985).
8. Stock et al. (1958); Dentler and Erikson (1959).
9. Proponents of the former view are, for example, Homans (1950); Berg and Bass (eds 1961); as opposed to Hollander (1978).
10. Wahrman (1977); Hamilton (1978); Shaw (1981), pp.280-289; Latané (1981).
11. Asch (1951); Asch (1952); Kelley and Shapiro (1954), Crutchfield (1955); Asch (1956); Milgram (1961); Ross, Bierbrauer, and Hoffman (1976).
12. Festinger (1950); Festinger et al. (1950); Festinger and Thibaut (1951); Festinger et al. (1952); Gerard (1953).
13. Israel (1956).
14. See Kiesler (1969) for specific references for each of the factors mentioned here; see also McGrath (1984) for a similar overview.
15. The main source to be consulted is Moscovici (1976). See also the overview of ten years of research in Moscovici (1985).
16. Derived from Moscovici (1985).
17. See Coser (1956) on the productive and dynamic functions of social conflict.
18. See the overview in Levine (1980).
19. Milgram (1974) provides an overview of the experiments.
20. For a comprehensive discussion, see Meeus and Raaijmakers (1984).
21. For a comprehensive discussion of the My Lai-case, see Kelman and Hamilton (1989).
22. Milgram (1964); Milgram (1965).
23. Meeus and Raaijmakers (1986), p.313. In their joint 1984-dissertation (in Dutch), the authors provide a comprehensive and sophisticated methodological discussion of Milgram and the replication experiments conducted throughout the world.
24. Mulder and Stemerding (1963); Bettelheim (1943); French (1944), p. 299; Shils and Janowitz (1948); Janis (1958), pp. 91 ff.; Ellemers (1956), pp. 51-62;

see also Lanzetta (1955); Hamblin (1960).

25. Note: this is not to imply that relations between leaders and members cannot become strained under stress, see, for instance, Krantz (1985).

26. Bion (1961); Rabbie and Wilkens (1971).

27. Milgram (1974); Kelman and Hamilton (1989).

28. Janis (1982a), pp.211-216; also Raven (1974).

29. On the dynamics of behavioral modellig in a social context, see Bandura (1977).

30. Lebow (1981), p.300; McCauley (1989).

31. See French and Raven's (1959) analysis of the different bases of social power; see also Kelman and Hamilton (1989), chapter 3.

32. Flowers (1977), p.890.

33. Ibid, p.895.

34. Courtright (1978), p.232. To explain this phenomenon, it is useful to consider Kelman and Hamilton's distinction between different types of conformity; compliance as rule-based, identification as role-based, and internalization as value-based conformity.

35. Fodor and Smith (1982), p. 183.

36. In chapter 7 it will be shown that the hypothesis outlined here is especially plausible in situations of intense intergroup conflict.

37. Note that Rabbie and Bekkers (1978) have also explored the reverse situation: the tendency for group leaders whose position within the group is insecure to favor more competitive group stances toward outgroups (f.il in negotiations), provided the group thinks it can "win" the confrontation.

38. See Janis (1982a), pp.250-254, for a balanced view on this point.

39. Helm and Morelli (1979), pp.335-338.

40. Etzioni (1977) used compliance as the central concept in his typology of organizations.

41. Woolsey-Biggart and Hamilton (1984) discuss the relationship between roles, positions and perceived requirements of loyalty and conformity with political leaders' whishes or programs.

42. Janis (1982a), pp.77-80, see McCauley (1989).

43. Janis (1982a), pp.210-211; Raven (1974), pp.310-311.

44. Janis (1982a), pp.299-300.

4 – Deindividuation:
reduction of restraints in a group context

4.1. Deindividuation: introduction

The concept of deindividuation has been put forward by Festinger and his associates. It was subsequently elaborated by many social psychologists in and outside of the laboratory. Amongst others, deindividuation has been proposed as an explanation of disinhibited, extreme and apparently irrational behavior by collectivities, be it crowds or small groups. This includes such divergent phenomena as lynch mobs, soccer vandalism, bystander passivity during emergencies as well as a range of socially unacceptable behaviors at the micro level. [1]

According to Zimbardo, deindividuation is an intrapsychic state characterized by an absence of self-awareness, and disinhibited behavioral propensities. Regular mechanisms of social control based on guilt, fear or shame lose importance.[2] A more sociological interpretation of deindividuation has been offered by Turner and Killian, who see deindividuation arise when individuals that are part of a crowd, group or social category develop a new set of emergent norms, which in turn enable them to engage in behaviors otherwise precluded by their conformity to regular social norms.[3]

In certain circumstances, therefore, people get so tightly involved in or 'consumed' by the collectivity they belong to that they – temporarily – lose their distinct self-awareness and self-identity. It is the group rather than they themselves which provides the reference point for their activities – substituting individual goals, norms, and standards of behavior for those perceived to be the ones of the group.

Deindividuation-like states of mind among group members are provoked by certain situational characteristics confronting a group. When viewed as a group-level phenomenon, the loss of the capacity for self-perception and self-regulation among individual members is so strong that the de-individuated person does not even become self-aware when he is facing choices or performing behaviors that normally would evoke such self-perception and self-regulation.[4] De-individuating situational factors (to be elaborated shortly) provide positive impulses for acting in unconventional and restrained manners and, at the same time, lessen the perceived impact of possible sanctions against such behavior. These types of behavioral patterns and consequences make deindividuation in many ways quite similar to groupthink.

The origins of deindividuation as a concept can be traced to early crowd theorists, such as Le Bon, Sighere, and Mc Dougall.[5] In their works, the notion of a 'group mind' featured prominently. Also, personality theorists such as Fromm, Horney, Jung, and Maslow have touched upon the question under what conditions individuals are inclined to yield to the homogeneity of a de-individuating environment their sense of individuality and distinctness.

4.2. Deindividuation: definition

Like the concepts of cohesiveness and conformity discussed above, deindividuation is conceived of in different ways by the various authors that have studied it. In the first article using the term, Festinger et al. define it as "a state of affairs in a group in which individuals are not seen or paid attention to as individuals. The members do not feel that they stand out as individuals."[6] Subsequently, they hypothesized that certain behavioral consequences would follow from deindividuation, in particular a reduction of inner restraints.

Zimbardo broadened this notion substantially. He defined deindividuation as "a complex, hypothesized process in which a series of antecedent social conditions lead to changes in perception of self and others, and, thereby, to a lowered threshold of normally restrained behavior".[7] In this definition, there are three interrelated elements: a *process* of changing perceptions, a resulting *internal state* of the person (the feeling of being 'de-individuated'), and the resulting *behavior.* The antecedent factors are not included in the definition, although Zimbardo identified several plausible antecedents of deindividuation, notably anonymity and large group size. The internal state of being de-individuated is specified. It consists of: (a) feeling of indistinguishability from one's environment, (b) lowered self-awareness and self-evaluation, and (c) decreased concern about the evaluation of other people.

Although most researchers have been in agreement with the thrust of Zimbardo's thinking, several criticisms have been made. Zimbardo has not been entirely clear as to whether deindividuation is necessarily a group-level phenomenon, or whether it might also be caused solely by an individual's perception of himself and his environment.[8] For instance, in Turner and Killian's sociological interpretation, it is crucial that there is an identifiable group as the basic source of emergent norms triggering deindividuation.

Perhaps the most useful operational notion is provided by Diener: "A de-individuated person is prevented by situational factors present in a group from becoming self-aware. De-individuated persons are blocked from awareness of themselves as separate individuals and from monitoring their own behavior."[9]

66

A final conceptual-theoretical point of division in deindividuation research concerns the underlying dynamics of deindividuation. One perspective sees deindividuation mainly as a process of reducing behavioral restraints which comes as rather spontaneous and often quite pleasurable to the individual. A second view presumes that everyone strives for a unique identity of his own. Consequently, a state of deindividuation arouses negative affect, and a renewed search for identity. In this second view, the very perception of deindividuation sets off attempts to reduce it. Dipboye has compared these two different assessments of the effects of deindividuation on, for instance, aggressive behavior, self-presentation, conformity, and risk-taking in decision making.[10]

In the present analysis, the notion of deindividuation as presented by Diener is adhered to, mostly because of its analytical soundness. With regard to the distinction outlined by Dipboye, the view of deindividuation as a reduction of restraints is by far the most widely accepted and used in deindividuation research. So the present study will coincide with it, acknowledging, however, that further clarification of the distinctive features of deindividuation along the lines proposed by Dipboye is needed.[11]

4.3. Deindividuation: research

A well-known example of deindividuation research is the Stanford Prison experiment by Zimbardo. He enrolled eighteen normal students to participate in a two-week full-time experiment concerning prison life. By lottery nine students were assigned as guards and nine as inmates. The nine inmates were eventually arrested without any warning by the local police, which had agreed to cooperate with the experiment. The 'suspects' were given the standard treatment for severe criminals: handcuffs, fingerprints, a naked briefing in front of their cells (rebuilt in the cellar of Stanford's Psychology laboratory). The inmates were put with three men in one cell. The prisoners were wearing prison clothing, the guards wore a uniform and sunglasses; they worked in eight hour shifts. In addition, they held the keys to the cells and were in total control over the fate of the prisoners: the guards determined smoking and toilet rules, visiting hours, and the like. They were instructed, however, not to use any physical violence against the prisoners.

The reality of the simulation proved to be considerable. Within only a few days, both the guards and the prisoners were totally absorbed in their respective roles. The guards were strict and occasionally inflicted cruel punishments: midnight inspections of the cells, cutting off prisoner privileges at will, forcing prisoners to do a large number of push-ups. As time went on, the guards became tougher. The prisoners had likewise internalized their role: they addressed each other by number, they were demoralized and apathetic, they neglected their personal sanitation. They grew to hate the guards, but nevertheless obeyed their stringent orders.

After several days, some prisoners displayed serious psychosomatic symptoms: periods of intense crying, depressions, hysteria. Zimbardo felt obliged to discontinue the experiment after six days. He was surprised by the speed and intensity of the subjects' accommodation to the extreme situation and the internalization of their roles. He explained the process using the idea of deindividuation: individuals 'submerged' in the two clearly defined, uniform role patterns supported by all kinds of physical devices fostering individual anonymity. For the guards, the situation became a legitimation for unrestricted cruelty, for the prisoners hiding in the collectivity provided a means for survival in a hostile environment.

Anonymity

Zimbardo has suggested that real or perceived anonymity of group members is the principle cause of deindividuation. Such anonymity may derive from the sheer size and density of the group or collectivity (e.g. crowds), indistinguishability of clothing, and the consistent categorization of members in group interaction.[12] The effects of anonymity are not only reduced self-awareness and disinhibition but also a perceived diffusion of responsibility on the part of group members for the behavior of the group and for their own behavior as part of it. This responsibility diffusion, in turn, leads to more aggressive behavior towards outsiders, competing groups, and victims.[13]

On the other end of the spectrum stands the Turner and Killian perspective, which holds that not anonymity but mutual identifiability of group members is crucially important for the development of emergent norms:

> "If crowd behavior results from the absence of social control or the release of repressed tendencies, then anonymity would indeed be of primary importance in accounting for the elimination of controls that ordinarily keep impulses in check. If, however, crowd behavior is subject to social control under an emergent norm, it is important that the individual in the crowd have an identity so that the control of the crowd can be effective. Thus evidence should be sought to test the hypothesis that the control of the crowd is greatest among persons who are known to one another rather than among anonymous persons."[14]

Still, the evidence about the link between anonymity and deindividuation is mixed, to say the least. Diener cites a whole range of studies that found exactly opposite effects of anonymity: more restrained behavior, heightened self-awareness. He concludes his review with five hypotheses that take the form of contingency statements: the effects of anonymity of deindividuation tendencies appears to be mitigated by intermediate factors, such as the type of behavior at stake, the role of internal standards, the type of anonymity (from other group members, from outside observers; induced by clothing or otherwise).[15]

To put it differently, anonymity is certainly not a necessary condition for deindividuation. It can be hypothesized that for deindividuation to emerge most strongly, anonymity to outsiders should go hand in hand with identifiability of the group members amongst each other.[16]

The type of groups that are central to this study regularly are all but anonymous. They are at least partly composed of highly visible public figures, who are identified as separate individuals by their environment. Yet, one should keep a balanced view in this respect. Many public policy decision groups lack the presence of high-profile members. Medium-level policy planning groups in the bureaucracy are perfectly anonymous to the general public, if not to the higher echelons of policy making. Often chief executives cultivate a group of loyal but faceless assistants: 'the president's men'. Although anonymity as such is – on balance – not a major factor in the type of policy-making groups examined in this study, the alleged effects of anonymity can be and are brought about by other factors, as will be indicated below.

Group cohesiveness

Cohesiveness reenters the picture. A recurrent theme in deindividuation research is the idea that there is an intimate linkage between a feeling of group unity (a high rating of the group as such; positive affect towards group members) and the occurrence of deindividuation. It is hardly coincidence that deindividuation research has been inspired by crowd theorists who spoke of the 'group mind': a collectivity thinking and acting as one.[17] Being in a highly cohesive group tends to cause people to take the group as their main point of reference rather than their individual perceptions, opinions and interests.

Here one detects a rather strong similarity between deindividuation and groupthink: in both cases group cohesiveness appears to be an underlying factor. Yet, as has been pointed out earlier, deindividuation as such also appears to be one of the possible dynamics underlying groupthink. This suggests a causal linkage between cohesiveness, deindividuation and groupthink; it is depicted in figure 4.1.

Figure 4.1. Deindividuation and groupthink (I)

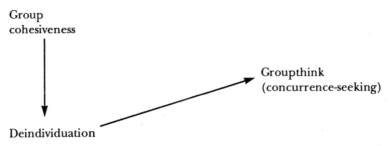

One note of caution should be stressed. Janis' analysis of cohesiveness and groupthink departs from the assumption that the concurrence-seeking that occurs in highly cohesive groups results in very subtle as well as more overt pressures to unanimity. And group members respond to these pressures: they conform. In deindividuation research, however, it is found that de-indivuated persons, for instance, in highly cohesive groups, tend to display less conformity.[18] The socially disapproved behavior of de-individuated groups apparently results from other factors than conformity or compliance with deviant group norms. On the other hand, emergent norm theory does suggest that conformity to norms, be it newly-developed group norms, is crucial. This is a matter that awaits further clarification.

External demands

The parallels between deindividuation and groupthink do not stop here. There are several studies that indicate that certain types of external demands or pressures are also a cause of deindividuation. For instance, Cannavale and his colleagues suggested "that when the effect of 'danger' on group behavior through time is considered, there are several circular causal processes underlying the correlation between deindividuation and the reduction of restraint."[19] Diener proposed that external events that require group response may serve to install in members an outward focus of attention. Secondly, he has suggested that intense group action – which may or may not be due to external demands – uses up individual members' processing capacities, thus contributing to reduced self-awareness.[20]

Again, cohesiveness is a factor at play. Both Diener and Cannavale et al. rephrased the proposition that external threats serve to increase group cohesion and the members' sense of unity which, in turn, is a principal cause of deindividuation. The first half of this proposition is, by now, familiar terrain (see chapter 2). The second half of the proposition has been elaborated above. It is depicted in full in figure 4.2.

Figure 4.2. Deindividuation and groupthink (II)

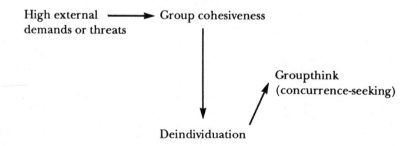

What actually happens when a person or a group of people is becoming de-individuated? In the introductory passages to this section, several characteristics have already been mentioned. Most basic is the loss of self-perception and self-regulation among group members. According to the comprehensive model of deindividuation by Diener, the process of deindividuation displays itself to the person in the following forms (both affective and cognitive reactions):
- difficulty in monitoring one's own behavior and in perceiving the products of one's actions;
- difficulty in retrieving personal and social standards of behavior and in comparing one's own behavior to these standards (cf. diffusion of responsibility);
- as a consequence, no tendency to engage in or self-correction;
- constrained time perspective, lack of foresight;
- consequently, a lack of concern about future punishment that might restrain behavior;
- more reactive to immediate cues, emotions and motivations.[21]

These behavioral symptoms, in turn, tend to produce certain types of consequences of group action. The consequences have been elaborately researched and discussed in the literature. They include: aggressive action, violation of norms seemingly dictated by the situation, conformity to group judgments and actions, increased risk-taking.

The similarity of the consequences of deindividuation to the effects of groupthink are quite clear. Yet, while groupthink is explicitly designed to explain decision-making activities by groups, this has not been the case with deindividuation. It would be of great interest to investigate deindividuation more explicitly in the context of decision making and try to establish more its effects systematically upon the course and outcomes of decision processes.

4.4. Deindividuation and groupthink: analysis

Reviewing the discussion of this paragraph, one cannot help but notice the striking similarities between groupthink and deindividuation. The connections between the two are manifold.[22] First, one cannot overlook the many face-value similarities that exist between the behavior of de-individuated persons and victims of groupthink. They are both group phenomena. In both instances, individual group members relinquish their critical facilities in favor of an emerging group consensus or group behavior. In the process, situational factors, group norms, and group atmosphere combine to bring about a powerful, if largely unexpected and unnoticed behavioral impetus. In terms of behavior, both are suggested as explanations for failure: aggressive policies, neglect of moral aspects, and high risk-taking. In this respect, the 'how-could-I-have-done-this reaction' of individual

71

members after the event is characteristic for both mechanisms.

From a more theoretical point of view, the linkages of both groupthink and deindividuation to group cohesiveness, group goals, anonymity of group members, and conformity need to be further explored. In terms of situational antecedents, cohesiveness and external pressure stand out. In terms of behavioral effects, there is increased recklessness (aggression, risk-taking), a tendency to neglect the consequences of group actions, and a collapsed time perspective. By now, there is sufficient evidence to make plausible the idea that given the similar antecedents and effects of both concepts, there might also be a link in terms of processes: the concurrence-seeking tendency of groupthink can be seen as a manifestation of deindividuation. Deindividuation posits the development of a group mind, groupthink occurs during its maintenance and preservation. This specific linkage has not yet been researched in the literature, although there are some hints in this direction.[25]

At this point, the discussion on deindividuation and groupthink is concluded with a very general hypothesis: groupthink is enhanced by a state of deindividuation among group members. In other words, deindividuation is one of the group-level mechanisms bringing about groupthink, conceived of as premature and excessive concurrence-seeking.

Notes

1. Festinger, Pepitone, and Newcomb (1952); Ziller (1964); Klapp (1969); Zimbardo (1970); Turner and Killian (1972); Diener (1976); Diener (1977); Dipboye (1977); Diener (1980); Prentice-Dunn and Rogers (1983).
2. Zimbardo (1970).
3. Turner and Killian (1972).
4. Diener (1980), p.22.
5. An excellent review of early crowd theory is provided by Van Ginneken (1989).
6. Festinger, Pepitone, and Newcomb (1952), p.382.
7. Zimbardo (1970), p.251.
8. Cf. Singer, Brush, and Lublin (1965).
9. Diener (1980), p.210.
10. Dipboye (1977).
11. Ibid, pp.1069-1972.
12. See Festinger et al. (1952); Zimbardo (1970).
13. Dion (1979).
14. Turner and Killian (1972), p.25, quoted in Rabbie and Visser (1984), p.104.
15. Diener (1980), pp.221-223.
16. Rabbie and Visser (1984), pp.120-123 suggest this.
17. McDougall (1927).
18. Cannavale et al. (1970); Dipboye (1977), pp.1062-1068.
19. Cannavale et al. (1970), p.145.
20. Diener (1980), p.227.
21. Diener (1980).
22. Swap (1984), p.74.
23. Swap (1984); Hirokawa and Scheerhorn (1986).

5 – Effects of groupthink (I) : risk-taking and recklessness

5.1. Risk-taking: introduction

Recklessness might be a suitable characterization of the outcomes of the decision process by the groups in Janis' groupthink case studies. The decisions arrived at were irresponsible and proved to be ineffective, with dramatic consequences. Another way to look at this is to say that groupthink decisions are excessively risky. That is, groupthink invariably arises in situations where there is a considerable risk of aversive consequences; and the defective decision process (the groupthink syndrome) results in the group setting out on a course of action which tends to cause the risks of failure to materialize.

While this may be too simple a picture, it does alert one to the correspondences that may exist between groupthink and the well-known phenomenon of risk-taking in individuals and groups. Ever since its 'discovery' in 1961, a dazzling number of social psychologists have engaged in research on the so-called 'risky shift': group decision processes were said to lead to the choice of a more risky course of action in dilemma situations involving different probabilities, than if the problem had been decided upon by individuals.[1] Over 300 studies have examined the risky shift and its later-discovered corollary, the cautious shift. These phenomena have shown both the strengths and weaknesses of modern social-psychological theory and research. They have induced intense discussions and debates among researchers with regard to the question of how to explain these mani-festations of the general phenomenon of group polarization, also called the extremization of individual members' attitudes (the 'choice shift'). At the same time, they have laid bare the limitations of 'normal' science: it took more than ten years before people started questioning the risky-shift paradigm as developed and investigated on the basic of a rather ambiguous methodology (the *Choice Dilemma Questionnaire*). Throughout this period, investigators sought to illustrate, disqualify, and explain the choice-shift, while the timely use of a more fundamental conceptual and theoretical reflection might have led them to ask whether they were actually pursuing the right question.[2] For what is risk? What are the differences between the researcher's and his subjects' assessment of what constitutes a risky course of action in a given problem situation? And why this focus upon the outcomes of a group decision without granting a similarly important place in the research paradigm to the cognitive and social *processes* that are producing it? Reviews of the choice shift and group polarization literature are nearly always cast in a negative tone. More recently, there have been somewhat interesting new explorations.[3]

Several authors discuss the possibility of relating the risky shift to the dynamics of groupthink.[4] And as hinted at above, there is at least some face-value correspondence between the two phenomena, embedded in the idea of a decision group being more than merely the sum of its members, but above all in the notion of groups taking extreme positions in risky situations. Yet, there are many questions to be resolved before we can really tell how the two phenomena fit together.

One of these problems lies in the very meaning of risk. How is it perceived by those who decide? What psychological processes and mechanisms of information processing and choice making are triggered once a perception of (high) risk has occurred? What is the effect of overlapping versus differing definitions of risk by members of one decision group? How do the antecedents and symptoms of groupthink relate to risk-taking?

Some of these questions shall be discussed in this section. The starting point is the working hypothesis that a groupthink decision process enhances excessive risk-taking (which is a 'type' of decisional outcome). The discussion will go beyond the choice shift literature. Both in cognitive psychology (decision theory) and in the sociological and administrative literature on technological risk and disaster management, interesting conceptual and theoretical leads can be found.

5.2. Risk-taking and choice shifts: definition and research

The risky shift paradigm

One of the reasons for the popularity of choice shift research has, undoubtedly, been the counter-intuitive findings of early researchers such as Stoner and Kogan, Wallach, and Bem that groups tended to be more risky and bold than individuals, and not – as was commonly held – more cautious and conservative. Nevertheless, another powerful source of attraction was the relatively simple and cheap research design of risky shift experiments. The basic procedure is as follows. The researcher administers a set of standardized questions involving real-life choice dilemmas to an individual. For every dilemma, the individual is given a certain proposed course of action. Now the subject has to decide the lowest probability of this option materializing that he is willing to accept in choosing it. For example, there is the situation of a local businessman invited to try and pursue a political career in the next congressional election. Now the question is, when would you advise this man to go ahead: when his chances are four out of ten, or higher, or lower? The probability chosen indicates the score on each dilemma: from one to ten. The lower the probability chosen, the more risk one is willing to run. Once the individuals' questionnaires have been completed, the subjects are to form small groups and re-discuss each of the dilemmas to reach a group decision. The choice shift can be found by comparing the mean score (per question or in sum) of the individuals in a certain group A with the group's scores. A risky shift occurs when the group's score is lower than the individuals' mean score. Afterwards, a post-test (again using individuals) may be held.

About 80 percent of all choice shift research has used this experimental design, which was developed by Kogan and Wallach.[5] Later research has employed, amongst others, specific choice dilemmas in the field of intergroup negotiation and international politics, and (attitude) questions which do not necessarily involve risk, but merely mutually exclusive or more or less 'extreme' options or judgments.[6]

Key findings

Stoner's results were confirmed again and again, not only in the United States with college students, but also in many different countries, cultures, and social and occupational settings.[7] At the same time – using a different set of choice dilemmas – it was found that groups may also shift towards a *less* risky (more cautious) position. Hence, the phenomenon became a two-sided one: the choice shift. Thirdly, Moscovici and his colleagues found that a group opinion shift was not limited to problems involving risk. Using attitude questions, they found evidence of a more general phenomenon of group 'extremization' or group polarization: group judgements tend to be more extreme (again: in either direction in a given 'dilemma' situation: for or against the U.S. and its foreign policy, and so on) than individual judgments.[8]

Explaining choice shifts

The quick and pervasive developments and changes in research findings (from risky to choice shift; from dealing with risk to group polarization in general), startled investigators who had zealously put forward numerous explanations for the early findings, pertaining only to the risky shift. In just a few years time, explanations had to account for three theoretical patterns of group decision making instead of one. Many traditional risky shift explanations could not account for the newly-found tendencies and faded into the background. Yet to date, a number of different explanations remain, which despite evidence of considerable overlap – are still generally depicted as competitive. They are briefly summarized here:

1) Diffusion of responsibility. In the context of a group, individuals feel no

longer solely responsible for the outcomes of decisions. They are, therefore, more inclined to pursue a risky strategy. This tendency may be reinforced by the existence or development of emotional bonds between group members which serve as a source of emotional support for risky endeavors (this thesis cannot account for cautious shifts and has lost prominence because of that).

2) Leadership and persuasion. The basic thought is that in a group discussion, those favoring the riskiest options also tend to be the most forceful and dominant group members. These informal group leaders, in turn, persuade others to follow their example. This explanation can be reinterpreted in a 'cautious leaders' variant.

3) Familiarization. It has been suggested that as individuals become more familiar with a problem, they will take greater risks. Other forms of choice shift cannot be explained with this hypothesis, which in effect asserts that the risky shift is in fact not really a group-level effect at all.

4) Group majority influence. Not only a dominant leader can shape the outcome of group decisions. Cartwright has illustrated the validity of majority models: if groups operate upon consensus, the group decision equals or approaches majority opinion; if no consensus can be obtained, majority rule is often applied. In this way, group polarization may result without actual opinion change on the part of its members: decision making as a process of negotiation.[9]

5) Emergent norms. Group discussions can be highly unstructured. This may cause members to develop a need for help in pinpointing a certain direction. In due course, direction may be provided by a certain alternative that gains support among the group members. This alternative will be used as a norm for making choices. It can enhance either risk or caution.

6) Risk (or caution) as value. There are many variants of 'value hypotheses'. In 1965, Brown put forward the risk-as-value hypothesis, stating that in the U.S., risk-taking was a socially desirable trait. In group discussions, members would therefore want to be perceived to be, at least as risky as their fellow members, in effect modifying their initial opinions to this effect (via social comparison mechanisms). Similarly, a caution-as-value corollary has been put forward. A related idea is that of risk(caution)-as-ability: a belief in group members that risk-takers c.q. cautious decision makers are generally more able and efficient; this belief would lead group members to conform to this image. Pruitt has suggested a specific variant of this hypothesis, the release hypothesis, stating that group members experience value conflict in making their choice: there is the heroic ideal of riskiness versus golden rules of caution.[10] The conflict is resolved by taking the most risky group member as a model and shifting in his direction: social constraints are released through modelling. Image maintenance plays a role in itself in producing choice shifts when individual members' individual choices are made known to the group. In that case, mechanisms of commitment come into play: group members want to appear steadfast and

will not be inclined to modify their position towards the middle.

7) Involvement. In their work on group polarization as a more general phenomenon which subsumes risky and cautious shifts, Moscovici, Doise and their associates have suggested that risk in itself is irrelevant in explaining choice shifts. Choice shifts are a function of more common psychological processes. Specifically, Moscovici and Zavalloni proposed that in the course of the group's discussion, group members become cognitively and emotionally involved in the issue or decision at hand, they gravitate to polarization. In short: group discussion leads to involvement, involvement leads to polarization.[11]

8) Persuasive arguments. A separate class of hypotheses emphasizes the role of argumentation in group discussions: options that represent the dominant values of group members will also be the ones most discussed. Members get more information about them as deliberations go on. At a certain point, they are provided with so many 'relevant arguments' that group decisions tend to shift forwards these dominant alternatives.[12]

9) Profit maximization. The interdependence structure between groups in an intergroup bargaining situation determines the strategic choices of the group members. Choices for cooperative or competitive strategies vary with interests: the greater the perceived dependence on in-group members, the greater the in-group favoritism while the greater the perceived interdependence with out-group members, the greater the out-group favoritism.[13]

Discussion of choice shift explanations

It is impossible to provide a balanced assessment of all these theoretical explanations here. Yet, there are some pertinent general observations from comprehensive reviews of the literature, which deserve to be mentioned. Firstly, the empirical evidence regarding the various hypotheses is mixed. There is no single hypothesis which adequately explains the whole gamut of data on choice shifts and group polarization which, by now, been obtained. Yet, there are marked differences in the empirical adequacy of various hypotheses. For instance, the confident leader explanation of choice shifts has received very little empirical support. The same goes for explanations solely aimed at explaining shifts towards more risk, such as the diffusion of responsibility thesis. These hypotheses are said to lack generality, because they cannot account for shifts in other directions. One could counter this charge by noting that there is no reason why it should be necessary that both types of shift are caused by the same sort of mechanisms. It is not per definition impossible that *different* dynamics underlie shifts towards risk and caution.

This leads to a related point. Generally, the hypotheses are depicted as mutually exclusive, whereas much of the empirical evidence supports two or more theoretical explanations. It is time to develop integrative models of choice shifts, taking into account complementary mechanisms affecting the course and outcomes of group decisions. A theoretical advance in this direction also presupposes a more precise and valid operationalization of key concepts, such as 'risk' and 'caution'. This would involve a conceptual analysis of key terms in, for instance, the decision-theoretical literature.[14]

A final problem concerns the perennial question of external validity of choice shift findings and explanations. While there may be striking examples of face value correspondence between choice shifts as established in social- psychological research and instances of real-life group decision making, very little work on the subject has been performed outside the laboratory. That is, although the phenomenon itself has been observed to take place in a wide variety of settings, the explanatory research has been typically conducted in experimental environments, mostly with non-permanent groups of college students as research populations and the Choice Dilemma Questionnaire as the measuring instrument. It was not until Moscovici and Zavalloni's work that the focus of research:

a) was broadened from risk-related situations to group polarization of judgments and actions in general, and

b) became more oriented towards general mechanisms of the group process than towards ad-hoc explanations of certain specific outcomes (e.g. risky shifts).

A major task ahead is to broaden and deepen this line of work, including a major effort to investigate the process of group polarization and choice shifts more extensively in naturalistic settings.[15]

5.3. Risk taking and recklessness: a broader view

At this point, it is useful to expand the view a little. Talking about risk-taking in naturalistic settings, one encounters dimensions and problems associated with the concept of risk not taken up in the choice shift literature. In fact, as a political scientist by training, I was stunned to see the far-reaching inferences about foreign policy and 'nuclear' decision making that some of the authors just mentioned were drawing from their risky-shift research based on the Choice Dilemma Questionnaire. As if the relatively trivial and structurally simple problem situations of the Questionnaire could in any way be compared to the complex ('wicked') problems and policy environments faced by real-life high-level political and administrative decision makers.[16] To be sure, Minix's adapted questionnaire is a first step in this direction.[17] But the problem is more fundamental. I would argue that it is inappropriate to jump to conclusions about risk-taking and decision quality without a thorough examination of the specific meanings and roles of the concepts of risk and recklessness in politics and administration.

When doing so, it becomes evident that risk-taking is a very relative concept. Often, the actions of certain organizations or governments are dismissed as foolishly risky. But most of the time such evaluations come about with the benefit of hindsight. Barbara Tuchman's book *The March of*

Folly is a case in point. Amongst others, she describes U.S. policy making with regard to Vietnam as a clear example of almost willful foolishness. Yet, as Wagenaar has shown, such a harsh judgement is inappropriate, for the decision makers at the time lacked the clear-cut view of all the stakes and the actors at play that we have in retrospect: it is wisdom with the benefit of hindsight to call failures like Vietnam examples of compulsive recklessness and foolishness.[18] On the other hand, one would also want to avoid the logical conclusion of Wagenaar's position, which would render any evaluation of policy making useless. In many cases, decision makers can know who or what they are dealing with and which are the risks and benefits of various options.[19]

The key point is that risk and risk-taking are relative concepts. While one actor A may perceive himself as risk-avoiding, someone else may think A is a high risk-taker. This may happen because they have different understandings about what constitutes risk.

This relates to one of the main issues in the social-scientific literature on risk-taking, risk assessment, and risk management. This literature ranges from studies of decision making on technological hazards to treatises about the cultural dimensions of risk in society.[20] Let us signal some key points, which will induce caution when speaking about ill-fated and reckless policies springing forth from faulty decision making processes such as groupthink.

1) Policy problems involving risk are difficult problems. For example, Fischoff et al. signal five generic difficulties in deciding about risk-related ventures:
- there is uncertainty about the definition of the problem, as various actors may perceive a certain situation, for instance the prospective construction of a nuclear power plant, in a number of different ways, depending on their specific backgrounds, values, and interests);
- it is difficult to get all the necessary facts needed for a proper consideration of the alternatives;
- it is difficult to ascertain what types of values should prevail in assessing the merits of each alternative;
- the human element in many high-tech environments adds to the already existing uncertainties: unpredictable and unmanageable human errors may trigger a major disaster – and can one take chances in this respect;
- from these four points it follows that it is difficult to assess the quality of decisions reached in such an environment.[21]

2) Risk, in other words, is a concept open to contestation. In a policy context, formal decision-theoretical notions of risk do not hold, nor does a purely technical approach to decision making about risky ventures. Risk-related decisions occur in a multi-actor setting. This inevitably entails social conflict.[22] Such conflict goes back to the very meaning attributed to various dimensions of risk. Talking about risks always involves selection. Many people are deeply worried about air pollution and about the threat of nuclear war, but not about the danger of an economic world recession. We

select the trade-offs we face. We also select the time perspective we apply to risk-related problems. How do we weigh short-versus long-term risk and benefits? Often by simply ruling out some considerations. This is partly a function of psychological factors, but it may also reflect a deeply-ingrained cultural bias. Recognizing this may lead to surprising outcomes. As Douglas and Wildavsky point out:

> "In the traditional view, bureaucracy is extremely cautious and risk averse. Our way of analyzing its perceptual processes suggests the opposite. It is never deliberately risk seeking, but its blind sports make it take risks because it cannot see them."[23]

3) This testifies to the need to pay attention to the intricate relationship between the (multiplicity of) subjective and objective dimensions of risk. Simple dichotomies do not apply. One needs to examine individual differences in perception, the effects of different roles and interests of actors in a decision situation, and the broader organizational, political, and cultural environment of decision making. The same goes for the time perspective. Take, for instance, the dilemma facing policy makers during terrorist hostage-takings: from the short-term perspective of ending the current crisis without loss of life a conciliatory attitude towards the terrorists is called for, but this entails serious long-term risks of inviting repetition of terrorist challenges, and vice versa. In the choice shift literature, quick assertions are made with regard to risk (or caution) as a value in itself. It is suggested here that there is much more to that than generally acknowledged. This makes it hard to talk about success and failure of risky decisions. Risk may be unrecognized by decision makers. Risks may be deemed irrelevant by a biased choice of criteria. And risks may be acknowledged and well-taken, but consciously out-weighed by other factors. Given all this, it is impossible to equate high or low risk-taking with high or low quality of decision making without further qualifications.

5.4. Risk-taking and groupthink: analysis

Minix has applied choice-shift analysis in the context of political decision making.[24] He set out to examine crisis decision making in foreign policy. The key question was whether decision groups, confronted with various feasible scenarios of international crisis events, would reach different (e.g. more or less risky decisions) than individuals. To enhance external relevance, Minix's subjects included military officers, the closest he could come to running the experiment with officials who actually make these decisions in real-life situations. In his theoretical discussion, Minix discussed at length the crisis literature in order to illustrate the validity of a small group approach to the analysis of crisis decision making. He stressed that maintaining decision quality under stress was a vital problem in crisis decision making. Further, he elaborated upon groupthink as a syndrome that was not only likely to appear in crisis decision making by small groups, but also detrimental to the quality of decision making. Excessive recklessness was regarded as a pivotal factor in this respect.

In the analysis of his results – which showed a rather differentiated pattern of risk propensities in his three populations – Minix hinted at elements from the antecedents and symptoms of groupthink being operative in the dynamics of choice shifts. These included, first and foremost, the operation of group norms and standards, but also phenomena such as collective psychological rigidity, defective information processing (for instance, excessive reliance upon historical analogies), and the steering role of group leaders.[25] Yet, nowhere did he come around to explicate the implied link between the well-known manifestations of decision making under stress by individuals and groups on the one hand, and his own findings and explanations regarding the choice shifts on the other. Similarly, he refrained from discussing the nature of the relationship between risk-taking and the quality of decision making.

These omissions can partly be understood from the fact that Minix's subjects did decide about crisis scenarios, but without actually being placed under stress themselves. So whatever levels of risk-taking were reached in the experiments, they would certainly not be due to manifestations of individual or collective psychological stress. Yet one would wish that Minix had managed to incorporate this final element in his design (for instance, by including the experiment as a form of examination within the regular curricula of his student subjects) because it would have enabled him to actually connect the two lines of research presented in his theoretical introduction. Now his analysis primarily focuses upon assessing the relative power of the familiar choice shift explanations. The other elements are acknowledged, but cannot be taken to a solid conclusion.

Despite these shortcomings, Minix has clearly shown that there may be connections between groupthink and risk-taking in crisis situations. In that respect, his work can be viewed as lending support to earlier assertions by De Rivera, who examined the risk-taking process in the Korean Decision – an episode which Janis later explained as a groupthink decision.[26]

Groupthink and recklessness revisited

It is time to reassert the working hypothesis of this paragraph: groupthink enhances excessive risk-taking. In other words, (some, probably not all) instances of highly risky decisions taken by groups can be explained by the dynamics of groupthink. The corollary to this hypothesis is more important to the present study, however. It reads as follows: if groupthink is shown to dominate a decision process over a problem involving risk, it is likely that excessive risks will be taken.

There are several ways to render plausibility to these propositions. Firstly, Minix's findings with regard to the high-risk-taking groups in his study can be discussed and more explicitly related to groupthink. Secondly, the other way can be followed by reassessing the antecedents and symptoms of groupthink on the basis of what has been said here about the dynamics of risk-taking and the subjective meaning of risk.

Minix's risk-takers. Minix's analysis of the data from his crisis-oriented choice shift simulation provides some interesting leads with regard to groupthink. He obtained very clear choice shifts: group decisions amplified the direction of the mean choices of the individual members. But there were both cautious and risky shifts. Which groups tended to shift towards caution? Which groups tended to shift towards risk? Minix found that groups composed of Fort Knox officers tended to shift towards risk (72 percent of these groups) and tended to do so quite manifestly (+1.31 on a scale of ten). A much smaller risky shift took place in (55 percent of) groups composed of ROTC cadets. Groups of college students, on the other hand, tended to shift not toward risk, but toward caution (57 percent of the student groups, with a mean shift of -0.43).

To explain these patterns Minix examined several of the explanatory hypotheses, dividing them into group process and group attributes hypotheses. Using the transcripts of the group meetings as process data, he inferred qualitative support for the hypothesis that risky shift groups placed great reliance upon historical analogies in their choice process, tended to focus on one option from the very outset of their discussion, and were more or less dragged into the direction of the most extreme member who tended to assume informal leadership. All of these process patterns bear similarities to groupthink.[27] With regard to group attribute variables – based on test score results – Minix found strong support for the hypothesis that decision groups whose members have a high political belief score, i.e. are more conservative, will shift to risk more than groups composed of individuals with low scores do not. Secondly, given the clear differences between choice behavior of his three sub-samples, Minix also managed to gain strong support for his hypothesis that the magnitude and direction of the choice-shift is primarily dependent upon the content of group norms and standards. With the officers, the military norms of 'toughness' led them to adopt strong (and increasingly escalatory and risky) postures. Cadets – still in the socialization process – tended to gravitate towards such stances as well, but (as yet) less pronouncedly so. As to the students, their political science training may have caused them to operate on a different set of assumptions and principles.[28]

In his conclusion, Minix suggests that attribute and process characteristics interact in bringing about choice shifts. Prior beliefs of members set the basic direction; the homogeneity and norms of the group reinforce these tendencies; the group process is structured to amplify the initial choices. So norms and values *do* play a role in choice shifts, but these are not values regarding the intrinsic desirability of risk or caution. Rather it is notions regarding views of the world and role performance within the group that seem to determine the course of the decision-making process.

Groupthink processes and the dynamics of risk-taking. This brief excursion into the literature on societal and technological risk has made it clear that the subjective component of risk is pivotal for decision making. If a group of decision makers fails to perceive dangers and uncertainties in the problems it is facing, then one cannot really speak of 'decision making under risk'. And that is where groupthink comes in. Because it can be argued that the groupthink process does exactly that: through information – distortion and dominant – image formation victims of groupthink neglect the trade-offs and dilemmas they are facing and create their own illusions of certainty. This, in turn, leads them to be over-optimistic about the outcomes of their decisions. And so they are driven to recklessness: undertaking highly risky ventures without a proper assessment. The crucial danger of such a decision strategy is, of course, that if members of a decision group perceive their situation as non-risky, it might very well prove fatal to them, because there may be factors in their environment which assure that the group's over-optimistic strategies will backfire.

This, in effect, amounts to a paradox: because the risk dimension of their actions becomes largely irrelevant to decision groups caught up in the groupthink syndrome, they will tend to take decisions that are excessively risky. In certain circumstances, this will lead to dramatic failure when the risk inherent in the situation materializes (yet note that failure is not inevitable: excessive risk-taking may bring great profits, but that would be a matter of 'luck' or 'coincidence').

Why do groupthink groups neglect the risk dimension? The fact that they do so should be quite clear from some of the symptoms of groupthink. The overestimation of the group through the illusion of invulnerability and the belief in the inherent morality of the group sets the stage for overoptimism. It is reinforced by closed-mindedness (rationalizations and stereotypes), while cautionary forces within the group are prevented from gaining leverage by the operation of uniformity pressures.

Reconsidering the psychological processes underlying groupthink, there are some remarkable resemblances. For instance, the characteristics and consequences of de-individuation contain forces which provoke a negligence of risks. For de-individuated groups, the future as such loses relevance. They become less concerned about the longer-term consequences of their actions; they are insensitive to the thought that they are taking any 'risks' at all.

While this may seem an extreme form of risk negligence, there are striking correspondences between this psychological syndrome and the complacent groups of admiral Kimmel and president Nixon examined by Janis. In both the Pearl Harbour and Watergate cases, there were marked tendencies for the groups to fail to realize the future consequences and risks of what they were advocating. Alternatively, highly-stressed groups such as Truman's Korean group and Johnson's Vietnam Tuesday Luncheon group seemed to suffer from a collapsed time-perspective, a cognitive pattern that is frequently found as a (defensive) response to overload and stress. With only the very short-term consequences of decisions deemed relevant, the concept of risk faded into the background. Hence, reckless action resulted, such as the decision to cross the 39th parallel in Korea.

Groupthink and risk-taking: conclusions

The conclusions of this inquiry into the linkage between groupthink and risk-taking are somewhat ironic. There is definitely a strong relation between groupthink and highly risky (and subsequently failing) courses of action. But this relation emerges only from a post-hoc, analytical point of view. Decision makers and groups in the groupthink mode fail to see this linkage themselves -and that is exactly one of the main reasons why it exists. Would decision makers caught in the groupthink syndrome be more aware of the risk-dimensions of their actions, they would probably stop and think. But as it is, the brief reexamination of the antecedents and symptoms of groupthink shows that there are various ways in which groupthink leads to recklessness:
– Groupthink is said to breed overconfidence, so the very idea that risks are involved may fade into the background. Often, this happens in a very subtle way, for instance by ritualized talk about possible 'cons' of certain decisions, such as in Johnson's Tuesday Luncheon Group. But risk negligence by the group also occurs in a very a-priori and definite manner: Pearl Harbour was deemed invulnerable by admiral Kimmel and his group, and there was no way to challenge this belief.
– Groupthink facilitates disregard of risks that are thought to affect outgroups only. Stereotyped images of 'outsiders' and 'enemies' legitimize the exporting of risks in these directions. What is wrong with Union Carbide exploiting a badly managed petro-chemical factory in a densely populated area in the middle of India? India is a far-away country, used to all kinds of hazards anyhow? While this may be an exaggerated representation of the line of reasoning involved in the Bhopal case, these sorts of culturally of geographically biased concerns over risk occur all the time.[30] Groupthink reinforces them. Chamberlain's Inner Circle had no difficulties sacrificing Checheslovakia to Hitler as it meant short-term safety for Britain.[31] Everything else was of secondary importance.
– Groupthink, especially under conditions of crisis, promotes a collapsed time perspective. This causes the decision makers to neglect an entire class of risks, namely those springing from the indirect, longer-term consequences of decision. By playing it safe in the short run, decision makers in a complex problem situation may invite disaster in the longer run. Groupthink obscures this fact.

In sum, groupthink tends to push policy decision groups toward ill-conceived risk-taking. This can take many different forms, ranging from hyper-activism in unrealistic and dangerous projects toward continued inaction in the face of serious dangers. However, not every reckless decision group is necessarily affected by groupthink; group extremization can have many different causes.[32] It is up to future research to provide us with a more refined understanding of the linkages between the two types of phenomena. In this study, the focus is limited to studying the impact of groupthink on risk-taking, and not vice versa.

Notes

1. Stoner (1961).
2. See Cartwright (1973) for a critical assessment.
3. Compare, for instance Cartwright (1971); Burnstein and Vinokur (1977); Meertens (1980), pp.17-25, and Moscovici (1985), pp.396-403.
4. Raven (1974); Myers and Lamm (1976); Meertens (1980); Steiner (1982); Minix (1982); Swap (1984); Hogg and Abrams (1988).
5. Kogan and Wallach (1964).
6. For studies on negotiation, see Rabbie and Visser (1984); Rabbie, Schot and Visser (1989); for studies of international politics see Semmel and Minix (1982); Minix (1982) for non-risk item studies see Moscovici and Zavalloni (1969); Myers and Bishop (1971).
7. See the overviews of findings in, amongst others, the special issue of the Journal of Personality and Social Psychology (20, 1971); Myers and Lamm (1976); Lamm and Myers (1978); Meertens (1980).
8. Moscovici and Zavalloni (1969); Doise (1969).
9. Cartwright (1971).
10. Pruitt (1971a).
11. Moscovici and Zavalloni (1969).
12. Burnstein and Vinokur (1977).
13. Rabbie, Schot and Visser (1989).
14. MacCrimmon and Taylor (1976).
15. Campbell and Stanley (1966); Moscovici and Doise (1974).
16. For a critical assessment of the prevalent methodology of choice shift research, see Van der Vlist (1976).
17. See Minix (1982).
18. Fischoff et al (1981); Kahneman, Slovic and Tverksy (eds 1982); Wagenaar (1987).
19. Compare, for instance some studies of crisis management in Israel: Stein and Tanter (1980), and Maoz (1981), who provide a decision-theoretical assessment of risk-taking and choice by the Israeli cabinet in the face of threat and uncertainty.
20. Lagadec (1982); Perrow (1984), and Douglas and Wildavsky (1982), respectively.
21. Fischoff et al. (1981).
22. Griffiths (ed.1981); Nelkin (ed.1985).
23. Douglas and Wildavsky (1982), p.100.
24. Minix (1982).
25. Minix (1982); the selection of subjects - students, naval cadets, and navy officers-reflects Minix' emphasis on the importance of normative orientations as an explanatory factor; see also Tetlock (1979).

26. De Rivera (1968).
27. Minix (1982), pp.127-143, in particular pp.143-144; see also Janis (1982), p.300.
28. Minix (1982), pp.146-148.
29. This idea is explored further in chapter 12, where a distinction is made between groupthink type 1 (collective avoidance) and groupthink type 2 (collective overoptimism). Both variants may lead to excessive risk-taking, but the underlying patterns of reasoning are likely to differ.
30. Shrivastava (1987); Shrivastava (1989).
31. A sketchy analysis of the appeasement episode can be found in Janis (1982a).
32. Note that, amongst others, Hogg and Abrams (1988), pp.112-113, 183, view groupthink as one manifestation of the more general phenomenon of group members' adherence to group norms favoring extremitized or polarized courses of action. See also Wetherell's (1987) discussion of group polarization from the perspective of social identity theory.

6 – Effects of groupthink (II) : commitment and entrapment

6.1. Commitment and entrapment: introduction

Sometimes, people are the victims of their past actions. Having once set a particular course of action, they may find it very difficult to divert from it. Resistance to changes can be quite intense indeed. Also, it is widespread. Many people have difficulties in reversing choices they have made earlier on. One of the reasons for this is that change can be interpreted as admitting that past choices were wrong. The need to justify one's past behavior may, in this respect, enhance its perpetuation.

The problem with this pattern of commitment is that it can be so strong that people even continue to refuse making changes in the face of repeated and unambiguous information that their present course of action does not bring the results they had in mind. Then, commitment – in itself necessary to get things done at all – becomes counterproductive. Staying on course while the ship is heading for collision is, in almost any case, a bad decision. The same goes for continuing to invest in a project that keeps losing money without any prospect for a turnabout, and for continuing a war that is of little importance, or that cannot be won. Yet, these things happen. They represent a special sort of decisional failure: a series of interconnected bad decisions, with unwanted, ineffective or damaging outcomes. They have been identified in many variants and they have been given many names: the dangers of sunk cost, social traps, "too much invested to quit", escalating commitment, "knee-deep in the big muddy", entrapment in a course of action.[1] It happens in interpersonal relationships as well as in business and politics. How long do you keep waiting for a bus that is long overdue? Why don't you tell your partner that the affair is over? Why did Iran and Irak keep on fighting a stalemated war for more than seven years? Why did the United States continue pouring people and equipment into the Vietnamese war? Why did the Concorde project go ahead despite dubious results? What will happen with the Chunnel project in the face of the escalated costs of building the tunnel underneath the English Channel? All of these cases are candidates for an analysis of commitment and entrapment in decision making. They pertain to 'trapped administrators': decision makers that lack the capacity to make timely changes, to abandon earlier plans, to terminate important projects and relationships.[2] How do these decisional pathologies come about? What are the relationships between groupthink and entrapment?

6.2. Commitment and entrapment: definition

The phenomenon of commitment to a course of action is, actually, a broad heading which encompasses a number of specific variants, commitment being a traditional and well-researched topic in various branches of Social Psychology.[3] In this study, it is the possible escalating effects of commitment that are of interest. Defined in very general terms, escalating situations are "predicaments where costs are suffered in a course of action, where there is an opportunity to withdraw or persist, and where the consequences of persistance and withdrawal are uncertain".[4] A more specific interpretation of decision making in escalation situations is given by Brockner and Rubin in their analysis of entrapment. Entrapment is conceived of as "a decision-making process whereby individuals escalate their commitment to a previously chosen, though failing, course of action in order to justify or 'make good on prior investments'."[5] More specifically, these authors identify a number of situational and behavioral traits that characterize entrapment. The *situational* component of entrapments pertains to the following: a prior investment in the pursuit of the goal has been made; a choice exists between getting (or staying) into or getting out of the situation; decision making takes place under conditions of uncertainty; a repeated series of investment decisions is required to achieve the objective. The *behavioral* (response) component has three characteristics: with each decision to continue, the conflict over future steps increases (both 'avoid' and 'attract' factors increase in significance); entrapped decision makers, eventually, shift from a rational-economic to a non-rational 'psycho-logic' involvement in the situation; entrapment behavior tends to be self-perpetuating, each additional 'investment' increasing the degree of commitment.

Staw and Ross hold a somewhat different view of the role of (non)-rationality in entrapment situations. Rather than switching from a rational to a psycho-logical assessment of the situation, entrapped decision makers adopt a form of retrospective as opposed to prospective rationality. They focus upon events which will correct or reduce the magnitude of previous errors rather than seeking out strategies to increase future outcomes. This line of reasoning suggests that self-justification is a crucial factor in producing escalation decisions.[6] As will be discussed shortly, there are several other possible causes and dynamics. Still, it seems wise to be cautious in denouncing entrapment as a non-rational process: it may simply be a case of shifting types of rationality.

6.3. Commitment and entrapment: research

Escalation and entrapment phenomena have been the subject of three different lines of research. As summarized by Staw and Ross:

"One group of studies by Teger (....) used an experimental game to simulate an escalation context. An unusual auction was held (....) – one where the highest bidder wins a dollar prize but the loser also has to pay the amount of his bid, thereby placing participants in the position of having to continue bidding in order to avoid a certain loss. A second series of studies has been conducted by Brockner, Rubin, and their associates (....) These researchers used various laboratory games to simulate (....) contexts where subjects are likely to expend resources working toward a receding or elusive goal. A third series of studies consisted of role-playing experiments conducted by Staw, Ross, and Fox. In most of these experiments, students were asked to play a role of an administrator in charge of allocating resources to a money-losing project, with the option of withdrawing or increasing their commitment of funds to the original course of action."[7]

Research has gone through three distinct stages. At first, the occurrence, pervasiveness, and stability of the entrapment phenomenon needed to be established. This was accomplished by the early publications in the field.[8] Subsequently, the search for causes and explanations began. This has resulted in a wide range of articles manipulating the basic research paradigm in order to trace what variables enhance or diminish the tendency to persist in a failing course of action. The variables considered were manifold, for instance: personal responsibility for decisions, timing of negative feedback, value of rewards, cost awareness and goal proximity, temporary versus structural causes of setbacks, the specific decision structure (active versus passive escalation decisions), biased or 'framed' presentation of information, job insecurity and external resistance to policy decisions, and individual versus group decision making.[9]

The third step has been to develop somewhat more integrated models and theories of entrapment. This final step has proven to be quite difficult. As Staw and Ross rightly note "the field has been functioning more with a methodological than with a conceptual paradigm. Although some research procedures have become popular or even commonplace in recent years, there has been less agreement on the relevance of various theories for explaining escalation behavior."[10] Yet, there have been some major attempts to provide general models of the entrapment process, as well as efforts to link entrapment phenomena to established theories in cognitive and social psychology.[11]

A model of the escalation process

In order to provide a summary picture of the various elements of the escalation processes at work in entrapment, two figures are presented. The first, adapted from Staw and Ross provides a very general picture of the decisional situation, whereas the second figure, adapted from Fox and Staw, illustrates the basic steps in the decision maker's process of reasoning in an entrapment (escalation) situation (see figure 6.1.).

It follows from the diagrams that the basic dynamic is one of decision makers confronted with bad news about the effects of their past decisions, who engage in a process of deliberation. They assess why the setback occurred (exogenous or endogenous setbacks, temporal or structural setbacks). They acknowledge its importance, and they consider whether it is worth it to go on. Now, the key to the entrapment process is that the forces of justification tend to override and influence other elements of the assessment. Cognitive dissonance theories suggest that people tend to strive for consistency between actions and judgments (perceptions). In that case, the main impetus is to go on with what one is doing, for instance, because reversal would amount to admitting previous failures, or because organizational and political interests seem to demand so. Consequently, people play down the severity of the setback, attribute it to unique causes beyond their control, and come to believe that one more effort will be sufficient to achieve the objective.

Theoretical exploration

Yet, the cognitive dissonance explanation of entrapment is but one type amongst many others developed in recent work. A very useful attempt to categorize different findings of the literature has recently been made by Staw and Ross. They posit four distinct types of determinants of what they call behavior in escalation situations. These are: variables pertaining to the problem situation at hand (project variables), psychological factors, social factors, and structural factors.[12]

Project variables. Project variables refer to characteristics that affect the financial gains or losses of persistance versus withdrawal (private sector), or the utility of abandoning versus stepping up efforts to achieve certain – non-financial – policy objectives (public sector). Take the example of the construction of the nuclear fission plant at Kalkar, West-Germany. This project was the result of a concerted effort by the governments of West-Germany, the Netherlands, and Great Britain to enhance their capacity for highly sophisticated civilian applications of nuclear technology. Enormous sums were invested, yet the construction took much longer than expected. This was partly due to technical problems, but also because of several juridical complications concerning claims raised by protesting

Figure 6.1. Dynamics of entrapment

A. *General process (from: Staw and Ross, 1987, p. 43)*

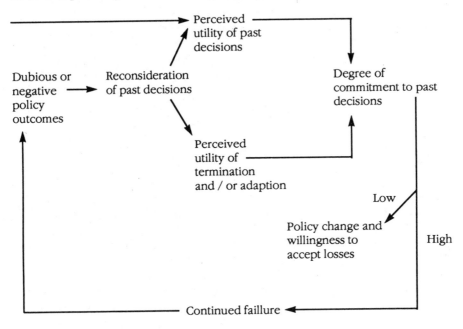

B. *Specification (from: Fox and Staw, 1979, p. 452)*

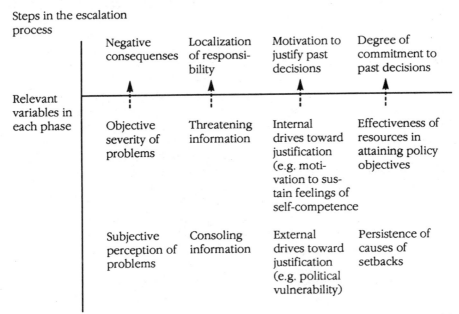

Steps in the escalation process	Negative consequenses	Localization of responsibility	Motivation to justify past decisions	Degree of commitment to past decisions
Relevant variables in each phase	Objective severity of problems	Threatening information	Internal drives toward justification (e.g. motivation to sustain feelings of self-competence	Effectiveness of resources in attaining policy objectives
	Subjective perception of problems	Consoling information	External drives toward justification (e.g. political vulnerability)	Persistence of causes of setbacks

environmentalists. In all these years, money was poured into the project without any benefits coming in return before completion of the installation. No policy maker would have supported the project if all this had been known in advance, yet all governments maintained their commitments. Like in other cases of entrapment, the project was structured in ways to maximize commitment despite negative feedback. Each setback was perceived as temporary and correctable with some additional expenditures. Secondly, the goal of the project was considered large, yet it was known to be a long-term venture. It was a definite investment situation: the Kalkar factory would cost quite a sum to build, but once production would have started, the gains were held to be considerable. So, there was an easy pattern for justifying incremental extra expenditures. Thirdly, the salvage value of prior investments was close to zero: the factory was more than the sum of its parts. Unfinished parts could not easily be put to use elsewhere. It was 'all or none'.

Psychological variables. Psychological processes at work in entrapment go beyond 'mere' cognitive dissonance effects. In an earlier article, Staw and Ross examined the role of six familiar psychological phenomena in producing (excessive) commitment to a course of action. These included motivational dynamics such as reinforcement effects and expectancy effects, but also more cognitively oriented phenomena – apart from self-justification as put forward in dissonance theories – such as reactance effects, learned helplessness effects, and invulnerability (over-optimism) effects.[13] Using a simulation design involving decisions about major infrastructural investments in a Third World country, they found that the resulting patterns of commitments were best explained by reactance theory originally developed by Brehm. This approach suggests that an individual is much more attentive to causal information and more focused on attaining future benefits after a failure as opposed to a success experience. When the decision maker then attributes the setback to an exogenous as opposed to an endogenous cause, he will be most eager in trying to set things straight with an additional efforts, since the cause of failure is less likely to recur.

In their 1987-article, however, Staw and Ross put more emphasis on reinforcement effects. They suggest that a history of past successes or early benefits in the current project serve to reinforce the decision maker's confidence in the chosen course of action. He will be more likely to pay no attention to or discount negative information. Similarly, the self-justification effects at work in entrapment are elaborated and related to tendencies for ego defensiveness in 'trapped administrators'. Other psychological mechanisms suggested are self-inference (where individuals examine their own behavior in terms of its 'social desirability' and infer personal preferences and values from their prior actions), and dynamics of distorted or inadequate information processing.[14]

Social variables. Like many decisions, escalation decisions are seldom taken by one individual in a social vacuum. In organizational and public policy contexts, decision makers operate in various social settings and environments. Decisions are often made in groups. Decisions affect other actors in the environment. Decision makers are judged by their peers and superiors on the basis of their performance record. Decision makers regularly find themselves in competition with others. These and other social factors affect the course and outcomes of decision making.

In escalation situations, social, organizational, and political factors may promote a desire for face-saving and external justification in decision makers. Put under external pressures (job insecurities, resistance against policies, organizational conflict), decision makers tend to feel a strong need to 'stand firm' and not to admit past mistakes or reverse course.[15] They may engage in 'impression management', manipulation of signals sent to others so as to manage others' interpretations of recent setbacks.[16] In competitive situations, such as the Dollar Auction, strong motivations to avoid losses and defeat the opponent can develop, and will then encourage to persistence.[17]

The organizational environment also furnishes decision makers with external norms and values. Commitment against all odds may be in line with the dominant corporate or political culture which respects heroism. Some evidence of this phenomenon was found: in a survey on judgments about entrapment situations, respondents highly rated the competence of consistent and ultimately successful administrators in a comparative case scenario, while they were considerably less enthusiastic about either inconsistent/successful ones or consistent/unsuccessful ones.[18]

Structural variables. Structural factors enhancing entrapment pertain to structural characteristics of an organization and its interaction patterns. In Staw and Ross' reading, these include:
1) economic and technical side-bets (the tools installed or hired for implementing a project may themselves generate a drive for its continuation);
2) political support for the project at crucial points in the organization – no matter its economic or political rewards;
3) administrative inertia (willingness to change or reverse course is often not enough, administrative interia heightens the costs of initiating change), and
4) certain long-standing programs may become so institutionalized in the norms, values, and culture of the organization or policy network that altering or abolishing them is literally 'unthinkable'.

6.4. Commitment, entrapment, and groupthink: analysis

Relating entrapment to groupthink involves several steps. First, it needs to be shown that entrapment occurs not only in individual but also in group decision making. Second, similarities (and differences) between groupthink and entrapment must be outlined. Then, it becomes possible to specify our view of the relationship between the two phenomena.

Strikingly little work has been done on escalation and entrapment in decision units other than individuals. However, the few studies of group entrapment that are available, seem to confirm that groups are just as susceptible to becoming prisoners of past decisions and actions as individual decision makers are. Actually, bearing in mind the risky-shift hypothesis, one might suspect that groups may even be *more* tempted to become entrapped. That does not seem to be the case, at least not necessarily so.

Evidence on group-level entrapment came from Bazerman et al.[19] They designed a role-playing 2 x 2 design testing for individuals/groups and high/low responsibility conditions. In the high-responsibility conditions, groups, like individuals, became more entrapped. Yet they could not find any specific effect of the group variable.

Teger has found that there are certain intermediate factors which determine whether groups become more or less entrapped than individuals. Using his Dollar Auction paradigm, he found that (two-person) groups of females became significantly more than individual females but also more than groups of males. Female groups, in other words, experienced a risky shift, whereas male groups experienced a cautious shift. Teger attempted to explain this remarkable finding by a specific interpretation of the diffusion of responsibility notion. Brockner and Rubin present this argument:

> "...males are socialized to behave more competitive or aggressively than females: that is why males became more entrapped in the individual condition. However, in the presence of group members, individuals feel less responsible for acting in a manner consistent with socialized rules. As Teger puts it, groups as opposed to individuals give the subject social support for defying the norms which they see as operating in this situation. Thus, males in groups are free to deviate from the macho, tough guy image, whereas female teams are released from their socialized inhibitions against aggressive behavior."[20]

Teger's line of reasoning deviates rather sharply from the diffusion of responsibility explanations in the risky shift literature, where it is the responsibility for the outcome of the decision that is diffused rather than the drive to act in accordance with societal norms and expectations. The former type of 'diffusion' would seem to lead to more entrapment rather than less, and Teger does not make it clear why he neglects this alternative (yet, in reality very common) interpretation of the role of diffusion of responsibility.

Brockner and Rubin

In their book-length review of entrapment research, Brockner and Rubin speculated about possible relationships between groupthink and entrapment. Taking the example of U.S. decision making in the Vietnam War as a case example, they pointed out some remarkable similarities between "the processes underlying entrapment and the groupthink tendencies that produced the fiasco".[21] They cite various quotations from Janis' analysis to make their point. Take the statement by Bill Moyers, one of the key members of Johnson's *Tuesday Luncheon* in-group of advisors:

> "With but rare exceptions we always seemed to be calculating the short term consequences of each alternative at every step of the policy making process, but not the long term consequences. And with each succeeding short-range consequence, we became more deeply a prisoner of the process."

This comes very close to the entrapment perspective. Yet entrapment is also adherence despite negative feedback, which was widely available during the Vietnam episode. Opposition to escalation in Vietnam came from numerous sources, including the U.N., as well as from individuals and agencies within the American government. Yet, Johnson's group persevered, closely following the commitment pattern of the trapped administrator outlined by Fox and Staw, where decision makers who adopt a policy in spite of initial resistance to it, will be strongly motivated to justify the appropriateness of the plan, even when it produces undesirable short run results. As White House historian James Thompson put it:

> "the men in Johnson's inner circle convinced themselves that the Vietnam War was of crucial significance for America's future – a conviction that grew directly out of their own explanations and justifications (...) Instead of reevaluating the policy in response to clear-cut setbacks, their energetic proselytizing led them to engage in 'rhetorical escalation' that matched the military escalation."[22]

Janis also noted the significant role of the group's commitment to the Vietnam policy. With the basic beliefs unaltered, the advent of setbacks required rationalizations and the invention of new arguments to continue on the same course. That is where groupthink comes in: the very cohesiveness of the group reinforced and perpetuated the prevalence of strong beliefs of moral righteousness, as well as group norms emphasizing solidarity instead of open-minded discussion and reexamination of past actions.

Entrapment becomes a 'type' of groupthink: highly cohesive groups making bad decisions through the self-justification processes underlying entrapment. Brockner and Rubin are quick to add that there are many other cases involving groupthink and entrapment where the pattern might be different. A remarkably similar fusion between groupthink and entrapment is found in Hensley and Griffin's case study of defective decision making by the Kent State University Board of Trustees concerning the location of a new gymnasium on the university campus. Despite vehement criticisms from all echelons within and around the institution, the Board persevered, causing major unrest at the campus and a wave of negative publicity.[23] And there are many more candidates for a combined groupthink entrapment analysis, such as the Nixon group at the time of Watergate, and British and French appeasement to Hitler Germany in 1936-1939.

Entrapment and groupthink: a hypothesis

It is time to come to a more systematic assessment of the linkages between entrapment and groupthink. In this study, a rather specific option is taken, based on the following assumptions:

a) entrapment occurs in situations involving a series of sequential, interrelated decisions;

b) entrapment is conceived of as a concept which, in itself, describes the structure and outcome of a set of decisions rather than the choice process; a situation of entrapment exists when decision makers have persevered in a certain course of action despite repeated signals that its current results are negative. (Note that this somewhat limited conception of entrapment differs from the definition by Brockner and Rubin presented earlier, see also c).

c) entrapment is not to be equated with a specific type of decision process; rather, there are various dynamics and processes of decision making that may lead to entrapment (based on and interacting with the four classes of causal variables cited by Staw and Ross).

With these notions as a starting point, the linkage between groupthink and entrapment becomes clear. It is hypothesized that groupthink is one of the modes of decision making that produce entrapment. In turn, entrapment is viewed as one of the possible outcomes of a groupthink decision process. In other words, entrapment is a specific pattern of 'defective decision making' resulting from groupthink.[24]

A few comments are in order to illustrate the plausibility (there is as yet no empirical evidence available) of this linkage. These comments further elaborate some analytical similarities between both concepts.

– Both concepts are associated with defective decision making and policy failure: groupthink describes how failure may arise, entrapment describes a specific pattern of failure. The two concepts fit nicely, yet it should be reminded that groupthink may result in other types of failure and that at this point, entrapment is still very much an individual-level phenomenon, whose group ramifications need to be researched more thoroughly.

– The antecedent conditions of groupthink bear some striking similarities to elements in the determinants of escalation behavior and entrapment. Janis singles out three classes of antecedents: group cohesiveness, structural faults of the organization, and stress on decision makers. Elements of the latter two come very close to some of the social and structural variables put forward by Staw and Ross. For instance, both analyses emphasize the role of organizational and group norms as barriers to cautiousness and systematic information processing, instead favoring boldness (in Staw and Ross' view, boldness and heroism are authentic values; in Janis' view, the norms of the group may encourage toughness of the decision makers).[25] Another example concerns the role of external pressures and competition. In entrapment situations, these factors strengthen the tendency to keep firm and reinforce earlier-made choices with self- and external justification and impression management. In groupthink, competition with out-groups manifests itself in the devaluation and 'dehumanization' of competitors, strengthening the insulation of the decision group and encouraging stereotypic thinking.[26] Thirdly, low self-esteem as a stress factor in groupthink is comparable to the self-justification and ego-defensiveness at work in bringing about entrapment.[27]

Finally, it should be noted that the psychological function fulfilled by the symptoms of groupthink is basically a protective one: through concurrence-seeking, the group members seek to maintain their emotional equanimity in the face of the stresses of making vital decisions. In Janis' view groupthink is a form of defensive avoidance. The same logic lies underneath entrapment: decision makers persist against all odds because a change or reversal is considered too painful (self-esteem!), or too costly in terms of power status and reputation.

Notes

1. In the order of phenomena, see Wolf and Conlon (1984); Platt (1973); Teger (1980); Staw (1981); Staw (1976); Brockner and Rubin (1985).
2. This term comes from Fox and Staw (1979).
3. Kiesler (1969); Janis and Mann (1977).
4. Staw and Ross (1987), p.40.
5. Brockner and Rubin (1985), p.3.
6. Staw and Ross (1978), p.44.
7. Staw and Ross (1987), p.41; see also Brockner and Rubin (1985), chapter 3.
8. See Platt (1973); Rubin and Brockner (1975); Staw (1976); Teger (1980).
9. In the order of factors mentioned in the text, see Staw (1976); Staw and Fox (1977); Rubin and Brockner (1975); Staw and Ross (1978) and Levi (1982); Brockner et al. (1979) and Rubin et al. (1980); Arkes and Hackett (1984) and Brockner et al. (1984); Fox and Staw (1979); and finally Bazerman et al. (1984) and Varca and Levy (1984).
10. Staw and Ross (1987), p.42.
11. See Staw and Ross (1978); Fox and Staw (1979); Brockner and Rubin (1985); Staw and Ross (1987).
12. Staw and Ross (1987).
13. An elaboration of each of these hypotheses and their original sources can be found in Staw and Ross (1978).
14. Staw and Ross (1987).
15. Fox and Staw (1979); Brockner et al. (1981); Levi (1982).
16. Caldwell and O'Reilly (1982); O'Reilly (1983).

7 – Beyond the group process: the intergroup context

7.1. Introduction

One of the key questions underlying this study concerns the issue of the conditions under which groupthink is likely to occur. In other words, which kinds of problem situations or, more broadly, external contingencies provide a decisional setting well-suited to the development of groupthink?

In his own work, Janis has paid comparatively little attention to the problem of identifying in workable detail the circumstances that favor groupthink, as well as to the explanatory potential these context —> process linkages may have regarding the groupthink phenomenon as a whole. In the representation of his theory, Janis has pointed out several 'antecedent conditions' of groupthink. These pertain to: (a) the existence of a sole, cohesive, decisional group; (b) structural faults of the organization; (c) a provocative situational context, notably high stress from external threats, and (temporarily) low self-esteem.

Only the notion of threat comes close to an identification of the way in which the external problem context influences the group formation and decision process. The notion of structural defects brings in the role of the organizational context of group decision making (to be discussed more fully in part III of this study). However, Janis does not elaborate upon the issue, and leaves the reader with the general notion that groupthink is a stress-related phenomenon. This, in turn, seems to imply that the entire variety of stress-inducing factors identified in the literature may bear upon the tendency of a policymaking group to fall prey to groupthink tendencies.

This shortcoming must, in part, be explained by self-imposed limitations on the part of Janis and other groupthink analysts. Traditionally, discussions about groupthink have been almost exclusively couched in terms of intragroup processes. This is understandable to the extent that the very idea of high cohesiveness as potentially 'bad' already constituted a major break with the mainstream literature on group performance – and thus required much attention in its own right. Nevertheless, by taking for granted the contextual ramifications of groupthink in the highly generalistic manner outlined above, groupthink analysts have missed a chance to enhance the precision of the theory.

To illustrate this within the context of social-psychological theory and research, it is useful to explore in this chapter the role of *intergroup* dynamics, and in particular the effects upon group decision-making processes of a group's relationships with other groups in its direct environment. In doing so, a number of specific and testable hypotheses regarding 'situational' contingencies favoring groupthink, are formulated. These hypotheses should be considered a first step toward more detailed answers to the question of when groupthink is likely to occur and when it is not.

7.2. Intergroup behavior: a social-psychological perspective

It is not altogether surprising that Janis and other groupthink analysts have paid little, if any, attention to intergroup dimensions. This only reflects the relative neglect of that field of study within Social Psychology as a whole.[1] Explanations for this persistent blind spot have included the fact that during the late forties till the early sixties, intergroup relations were not a dominant social concern in the United States, and therefore not incorporated into mainstream research programs. Part of it has also been explained by the methodological individualism prevalent in American social science, inducing an individualistic bias in group studies, focusing on the individual member and his relations with other group members and the group as a whole.

Despite this relative marginality, a noteworthy theoretical and empirical literature has been building up since the late sixties, which has a lot to offer for students of group decision making. In examining this literature here, some caveats are in order. First, the focus here is on the *intragroup impact* of different varieties of relations that exist between this group and other groups (e.g. its social environment). Therefore, no attention is paid to other-level ways of studying intergroup relations. Furthermore, given the topic of this study, the primary interest will lie with intergroup relations involving at least one *small* group rather than societal categories at large.[2] Finally, this brief discussion of intergroup studies does not aspire in any way to be comprehensive. Only themes and perspectives deemed salient from the perspective of groupthink are presented.

Intergroup behavior: two key theories

Like many other areas in Social Psychology, intergroup studies have long been characterized by a dispersion of ad-hoc mini theories and hypotheses seeking to explain results of laboratory research. Gradually, however, there have developed several distinct, more general ways of interpreting relations between groups. Among these theoretical perspectives, two have been most influential: realistic conflict (or functionalist) theory inspired by the work of Sherif and Blake and Mouton; and social identity theory, developed by Tajfel and expanded by Turner and associates.[3]

Realistic Conflict. Realistic conflict theory finds its roots in the pioneering experiments on intergroup competition and cooperation, conducted by Sherif and associates. They conducted several field experiments in boys' summer camps. They were able to create intergroup divisions between groups of boys attending the camps, and have these escalate into intense forms of intergroup conflict by engaging the groups in a variety of games and other modes of competitive interaction. Intergroup hostility, once it existed, proved to be very difficult to break through. Merely promoting more contact between members of opposing groups proved ineffective. Having group leaders appeal for a relaxation of tensions was insufficient, too: they only risked losing their prominent position by taking a compromising stance. The only measure that worked, according to Sherif, was to manipulate the goal structure of the groups. Only when the experimenter introduced a so-called superordinate goal – such as the need for the two groups to collaborate in crossing a river or in coping with other types of campers' adversities – did the groups proceed to overcome barriers of hostility and, eventually, reintegrate.

Based upon these studies, Sherif and other researchers postulated that intergroup relations are determined to a large extent by the perceived structure of interests governing the intergroup situation. Cooperation is likely to result when groups have compatible goals and interests, whereas conflict is produced when goals and interests diverge. And intergroup conflict can be resolved by introducing superordinate goals, i.e., goals that have "...a compelling appeal for members of each group, but that neither group can achieve without participation of the other".[4]

An important finding of these early intergroup experiments was that the presence of a negatively valued and 'threatening' outgroup increased intragroup solidarity in each of the groups. Also, there was a marked tendency for group members to hold biased perceptions favoring their own in-group, consistently overestimating in-group products and achievements vis-a-vis the out-group. This in-group bias also pertained to notions of fairness and justice: for instance, when their own group was caught out by a surprise attack or unexpected move, the in-group members accused the other group of deception and cowardice, while the other group 'got what they deserved' when they were attacked without warning by the in-group.

Realistic conflict theory was subsequently expanded in both basic and applied settings. With regard to applied research, Blake and Mouton's research into the dynamics of intergroup relations in industry confirmed most of the basic propositions of intergroup theory.[5] Stimulated by these results other researchers have sought to apply insights derived from the theory to a wide range of situations, ranging from racial prejudice and segregation to the escalation and reduction of international conflict.[6]

In basic research, in series of experiments conducted by Rabbie and his associates support has been found for the interests-based perspective on intergroup relations developed by realistic conflict theory – although not without qualifications. In an experiment designed to identify the minimal factors necessary for group formation and in-group/out-group differentiation, Rabbie and Horwitz found that simply classifying into two distinct groups yielded no difference between the evaluations of ingroups and outgroups.[7] However, flipping a coin to decide which of the two groups would receive a gift produced a significant bias in favor of the in-group and its members. Intergroup bias was created by the fact that group members expected better outcomes from encounters with in-group members than with outgroup members. This occurred despite the fact that the original means of classification between the two groups were trivial.[8] Later, Rabbie found that the degree of bias expressed was less when the awarded bonus was smaller.[9] To obtain the bias effect, it was not necessary that group members actually interacted with each other. Even the expectation of ingroup interaction enhanced in-group bias.[10]

Many other factors affecting in-group/out-group differentiation and, likewise, cooperation and competition have been identified in various laboratory experiments. However, the key point to be made here is that these results in general have been interpreted by realistic conflict researchers to indicate that considerations of perceived rewards and costs associated with group membership are crucial to understand the dynamics of groups and intergroup relations. In other words, the interdependence of members and groups is a crucial mediator of groups as goal-seeking entities.[11]

More recently, research in this tradition has made extensive use of the Prisoners Dilemma Game to further investigate the conditions of co-operative and competitive behavior. By manipulating the pay-off matrix in the game, researchers are able to investigate the effects of different interdependence structures on the behavior of participants in the game (individuals or, as in the most recent research of Rabbie and associates, small groups).[12] Best known in this respect is the tit-for-tat rule of co-operative behavior, the best-performing maxim in a comparative test based on an infinite series of PD games.[13]

Social Identity. Tajfel et al. further elaborated the minimal group research conducted by Rabbie and discovered that factors other than instrumental considerations (e.g. interest representation) were at play in intergroup interaction.[14] To begin with, one should discriminate between purely instrumental competition (and cooperation) between groups, and more purely 'social' forms of competitive interaction. In fact, what emerges from the minimal group studies is that social categorization – the classification of individuals into two distinct groups – is sufficient to generate intergroup competition. Social identity theory argues that following group designations made by the experimenter on the basis of some trivial criterion (for instance, favoring a Klee or a Kandinsky picture), the individuals concerned are categorizing themselves in terms of these social categories. Having done this, the individuals' basic need to achieve a positive identity (self-esteem) becomes linked to their membership of the group, i.e. personal identity becomes socially defined. This affects their perceptions of the in-group, thus providing the basic impetus for the in-group bias. At the same time, positive social identity can only be meaningfully established by a process of social comparison with other groups, hence providing the impetus for out-group depreciation.

Although social identity theory introduces a key motivational assumption (individuals seek to enhance their self-esteem by striving for a positive identity, which is socially defined in terms of their group memberships), it otherwise argues mostly along strictly cognitive lines: social categorization is viewed as a cognitive process of differentiating objects and people according to some basic perceptual criterion.[15] In more recent accounts of the theory it is argued that the purely cognitive interpretation of the roots of intergroup differentiation, as propagated mostly by Turner, is not tenable. It is only through the operation of social identification mechanisms that this cognitive differentiation is 'transplanted' to other dimensions as well: from differentiation to appreciation and depreciation of in-groups and out-groups.

Elaborating the fundamental assumptions of social identity, the theory seeks to identify the basic strategies that people use when they experience an inadequate social identity through their present in-group/out-group identifications and comparisons:
- individual mobility, i.e. exiting from one's own group, trying to assimilate into a higher status group;
- social creativity, i.e. change the basis of the original comparison by either using different criteria or comparing with different types of outgroups more likely to result in positive comparisons;
- social competition, i.e. seeking direct confrontation with the other groups in order to achieve positive self-esteem (i.e. there is presumably a tight coupling between the well-being of one's group and personal self-esteem); this last strategy is presented as a key explanatory factor for many instances of open ethnic or racial conflict.

These propositions have been extensively researched in recent years, generally showing results which indicate the usefulness of this conceptualization. Subsequently, these and other components of social identity theory have been used to enlighten historic instances of intergroup conflict, such as in industrial relations, ethnic tensions in South Africa or in Northern Ireland. In this extension, social identity theory indeed accommodates some of the criticisms raised against realistic conflict theory, especially those pertaining to the need to study open as well as closed groups, and the need to study relations between groups with differential power.[16] It should be noted that in its implications for managing intergroup conflict, social identity theory is rather pessimistic. As Caddick notes, "(....) it provided no grounds for expecting intergroup cooperation or adjustment to a mutually more satisfying intergroup relationship as the consequence of social identity motivations" (my emphasis, PtH).[17] While in realistic conflict theory, conflict resolution can be engineered through mediation and manipulating the interdependence structure, the basic notions of comparison and competition within social identity theory render these strategies less useful. It appears that only the elimination of the cognitive and social bases of intergroup differentiation (e.g. fundamental reintegration) provides for long-term resolution of conflict.[18]

Toward integration? It should be noted that some of the differences between the two approaches in explaining group formation and intergroup behavior may be overcome. Indeed, in the concluding chapter of a volume which contained pieces by representatives of both theories, Tajfel has suggested that the two perspectives may be complementary rather than mutually exclusive:

> "There exists therefore strongly suggestive evidence that intergroup comparisons reflect a pattern in which both instrumentality and social identity must be taken into account."[19]

Elaborating on this point and comparing Turner's and Horwitz and Rabbie's contrasting chapters in the book, Tajfel comments:

> "There is one important point in common in the discussions of group formation (....) of this book. They agree that it is neither simple 'similarities', nor various forms of 'cohesion' (such as mutual liking of individuals who then become members of an ingroup), nor personal interactions, which can provide the first basis from which the formation of groups can be understood. The fundamental and *sine qua non* condition for the group process to be set into motion is to be found, according to Horwitz and Rabbie, in the group members' perception of their interdependence of fate (....) In contrast, for Turner (....), this basic condition for group formation needs to be sought in social identity conceived as 'the cognitive mechanism which makes group behavior possible' (....) Yet it is very possible that (....) each of them concentrates on a different stage of the same process which is then treated as if this one stage amounted to the total sequence."[20]

Tajfel then proceeds to suggest that while Rabbie and Horwitz may indeed be right in their assertion that interdependence of fate is the crucial factor in the earliest stages of group formation, they subsequently ignore the social identification mechanisms which serves to strengthen group formation once set in motion.[21] Similarly, Turner overlooks what Tajfel calls the pre-history of group formation as pointed out by Rabbie and Horwitz. As yet, however, these real or spurious differences of interpreting group formation and intergroup behavior have not been satisfactorily resolved; empirical evidence concerning each of the positions is building up gradually but seems somewhat biased by the different research paradigms associated with these different theoretical positions. Recently, Rabbie et al. have attempted to provide a more comprehensive test of the validity of the two basic perspectives in a series of laboratory experiments involving choice shifts.[22] At the same time, some more elaborate attempts have recently been

104

undertaken to integrate the contending perspectives in a much broader psychological framework explaining interactive behavior.[23]

For the purpose of this chapter, it is not necessary to further discuss these different interpretations. Suffice it to note that the intergroup literature as a whole provides an agenda for studying intra-group processes which is often overlooked by analysts of group decision making. In the rest of this chapter, this literature shall be used to illuminate some of the basic tenets of the preliminary revised model of groupthink that has been emerging from chapters two to six. In particular, the focus shall be on how different modes of intergroup relations may affect the group process in ways conducive to the development of groupthink.

7.3. The intergroup context of groupthink: an exploration

It is perhaps most clear to start this exploration with the most general proposition that emerges from it: from the intergroup literature it appears that groupthink in groups that are part of an intergroup situation is most likely to occur when the intergroup relationship is characterized by intensive competition up to the point of intergroup aggression. In other words, intensive intergroup competition gives rise to group processes that have been identified earlier in this study as the basic components of groupthink, in particular high group cohesiveness and anticipatory compliance in the face of strong leadership. Also, certain intragroup consequences of intergroup conflict relate most directly to the symptoms of groupthink, such as a belief in the inherent morality of the group and stereotypes of out-groups.

· It should be reminded at the outset, that in some cases, it is hard to establish the direction of causality. In other words, intragroup conditions may in turn affect intergroup behavior. For example, Rabbie et al. showed the group's perception of its bargaining strength affects its predisposition to engage in more far-reaching competitive behavior.[24] Hence, intragroup factors may influence intergroup behavior just as much as the other way around; in fact, earlier findings of this sort have inspired a lot of research and debate in international relations about the correlates of aggressive behavior of states.[25]

To introduce the reader to the core of intergroup research, it is helpful to examine figure 7.1. Based on the work of Schein, it provides a concise overview of the consequences of intergroup competition on both the nature of the relations between the competing groups, as well as the conditions within each of the groups, as they have become apparent in several decades of·intergroup research. Also, he indicates the differential effects of 'winning' and 'losing' in such a situation. In the rest of this chapter, key elements of this figure are discussed in greater detail.

Figure 7.1. Consequences of intergroup competition (based on: Schein, 1979)

A. *Within* each competing group

1 Increased cohesion, internal differences are overcome, loyalty to group increases
2 Group climate becomes more focused on task accomplishment; concern for members' psychological needs lessens
3 More autocratic leadership styles and group willingness to tolerate this
4 Group becomes more highly structured and organized
5 Great emphasis on presenting 'solid front' to outsiders

C. Effects on *winning* group

1 Cohesion retained or increased
2 Release of tensions and switch to more complacent and playful mood
3 More emphasis on intragroup cooperation and concern for members' needs; low concern for work and task accomplishment
4 Reinforced stereotypes of itself and of outgroups; little motivation for reevaluating perceptions and operations; learning incentives

B. *Between* competing groups

1 Each group sees the other group as enemy rather than as neutral object
2 Distorted perceptions: negative views of outgroup, overestimation of own group; negative stereotypes
3 Hostility toward other group increases while interaction and communication with other group decreases; hence stereotypes are easily maintained
4 When forced into interaction, group members listen more closely to the group's own representatives, while other group's agents are listened to only to find faults

D. Effects on *losing* group

1 When outcome leaves room for interpretations, group will tend to deny or distort the reality of losing
2 If loss is psychologically accepted, strong urge to look for external scapegoats; when unavailable, internal conflicts come to the fore
3 Group climate more work-oriented, desperate to achieve success
4 Low intragroup cooperation, low concern for members' needs; high concern to recoup losses
5 Shattered stereotypes require reevaluation; greater incentives to learn and reorganize

106

In an overview article reflecting on the relationships between intergroup conflict and intragroup cohesiveness, Dion distinguished two main lines of inquiry.[26] First of all, he mentioned the early work of Sherif, Deutsch, and Blake and Mouton examining the intragroup effects of intergroup competition per se. As noted above, this research yielded two main findings.

a) intergroup conflict tends to promote intragroup cohesiveness in each of the groups involved;

b) intergroup conflict leads to outgroup depreciation.

The behavioral consequences of intergroup conflict were manifest. In-group cohesiveness was evidenced from subjects reporting greater attraction to members of their own groups, by 'selective altruism' in locating rewards towards in-group rather than out-group members, and by an over-evaluation of the in-group products. Out-group biases were reflected in a range of behaviors from 'ethnocentrism' of perceptions of in- and out-group members all the way to open hostility in intergroup encounters. Based on these observations, it was concluded that crucial factor involved in evoking these behavioral patters was the perceived incompatibility of goals.

Subsequent research, the second component of Dion's presentation, sought to establish the differences between the intragroup consequences of intergroup competition and intergroup cooperation. In other words, the factor of 'perceived incompatibility of goals' was made variable, and linked to other sets of variables. Early research in this vein found that there were significant differences between competitive and cooperative groups in, amongst others, the quality of task performance in training situations (better in competitive settings), and the development of a more pronounced hierarchical structure in competitive groups.[27]

Also, competitive groups were found to be more cohesive. However, there has been some discrepant evidence with regard to this latter point. On a number of occasions, Rabbie and his associates have found no significant differences between the cohesiveness of competitive, coaching, or cooperating groups.[28] This lack of evidence may be due to a critical mediating factor, namely, the *perceived likelihood of success* resulting from group action in the intergroup situation. For instance, it was found that competitive groups with a strong bargaining position were more cohesive than those with a cooperative orientation.[29] Similarly, in-group attraction increases strongly when the extent of group success increases.[30]

Worchel and others found another interesting factor mediating in-group/out-group evaluations in intergroup encounters. They found evidence for the idea that the *anticipation of further group interaction* and the *publicness of group evaluations* influences group members' perceptions of the in-group and its products: when further competition is anticipated, publicly shared evaluations of group products serve the instrumental function of sustaining members' motivations for future interaction. In other words, in evaluating their in-group, members anticipate the likelihood of future interaction. The study by Worchel et al. points to the necessity of taking into account a broader time perspective in assessing the intragroup effects of intergroup cooperation and competition. It also suggests that group members' evaluations of their in-group can very well be derive from instrumental considerations.[31]

This instrumental hypothesis runs parallel to evidence from the cohesiveness studies presented in chapter two, which emphasize the affective, social, support-seeking functions of group identification under threat. This hypothesis can easily be transplanted to situations of threat deriving from intergroup conflict (see proposition 2 below – note that this ego-defensive, self-esteem related function of group solidarity in intergroup conflict can also be understood from the perspective of social identity theory).[32]

Cohesion in context: propositions

Reviewing the evidence so far, it is possible to formulate a number of hypotheses relevant to groupthink:

Proposition 1. The larger the intensity of intergroup conflict, the higher the cohesiveness of each of the competing groups, provided group members perceive their own group to be successful in gaining leverage over out-groups.

Proposition 2. The larger the intensity of intergroup conflict, the higher the cohesiveness of the competing groups, provided group members share a sense of collective threat, and perceive the group as the most appropriate manner of mitigating or countering these threats posed by outgroups.

The two propositions offer alternative explanations for the increased in-group cohesiveness that tends to accompany heightened intergroup conflict, yet they make the same basic point with regard to the preconditions of groupthink: along the continuum ranging from intergroup integration via intergroup cooperation all the way to intergroup hostilities, situations of intense intergroup conflict are the most likely candidates for groupthink analysis. This argument can be enhanced using other evidence.

Intergroup conflict, group leadership and compliance

In chapter three, it has already been pointed out that there is a tendency for small groups under threat to assume a more differentiated, even authoritarian, leadership structure: group members seek for strong leaders as a means of countering the threat (and absolving themselves from some of the responsibility of accomplishing this). It was further argued that the tendency to accept directive leadership may, in fact, lead to processes of anticipatory compliance: group members going along in advance with what they perceive to be the options and demands of group leaders.

Again, this hypothesis is applicable to the more specific context of intergroup competition and hostility. Research has shown that leadership positions and relations between leaders and members can exert a pervasive influence on a group's attitudes vis-a-vis other groups in its environment. This is not a one-sided process, however. The course and outcomes of intergroup relations in turn affect the leadership structure of the groups involved.

For example, in an experiment by Rabbie and Wilkens, it was found that intergroup competition leads to a more centralized leadership structure. Also, competitive groups had a more clearly pronounced hierarchical structure as a whole: intergroup conflict apparently breeds an intragroup 'pecking order.' There is some evidence that an authoritarian leadership style (in the Lewinian sense) seems more 'suited' to intergroup conflict.[34] In studies of competitive bargaining it emerges that the extremity of a group's bargaining position is related to the stability of the position of the group leader or main bargainer: threatened leaders tend to opt for more aggressive bargaining stances.[35] In sum, the following proposition seems warranted:

Proposition 3. The higher the intensity of intergroup conflict, the stronger tendency on the part of group members to accept strong leadership, and the more hierarchically structured the group becomes, provided group members perceive the leader to be effective in defining and defending the group's interests vis-a-vis opponents.

Intergroup conflict and symptoms of groupthink

The intergroup literature is scattered with indications that intergroup conflict seems to give rise to behavioral tendencies among groups and their members that directly resemble some of the symptoms of groupthink.

Illusion of invulnerability. In several but not all studies of intergroup conflict, the tendency of in-group members to over-evaluate the group product provides a hint for this phenomenon.[36] Indeed, the conflict-induced (more generally: threat-induced) tendency to become more attracted to their in-groups is often accompanied by ideas like "if we just stick together, nobody can touch us." This can be observed in the behavior of youth gangs, combat units, and soccer hooligans alike.[37]

Belief in the inherent morality of the group. The sense of collective self-righteousness in parties involved in intergroup conflicts is particularly well understood from the perspective of social identity (although the phenomenon can also be explained in functional terms). Groups strive to

109

achieve positive social identity. When they find themselves in conflict with other groups, a key imperative for the group is to maintain a positive moral self-image: "We are the good guys, not them." It has been found that this tendency is most marked when intragroup interaction between the members is possible. The collective deliberations serve to bring about polarization tendencies, and through mutual reinforcement (also called 'enhancement' in the group polarization literature) the group becomes more self-righteous. As a consequence, there is a lowered threshold for engaging in aggressive behavior towards outgroups.[38]

Collective rationalizations. As intergroup conflict increases, intragroup cohesiveness is heightened. This not only strengthens the operation of group norms, it also pervades the perceptual-cognitive domain of group members. Group members' views of the world become more and more socially determined through the operation of categorization and identi-fication mechanisms. This provides a convenient basis for collective rationalizations, as any more 'objective' yardstick for assessing the situation and the adequacy and acceptability of the group's actions in the course of the conflict, is increasingly lacking. The group members define and evaluate the world and their own actions against outgroups in terms of their own biased perspective. This diminishes the chances for reflection and constructive self-criticism.

Stereotyping. This is one of the best-documented features of intergroup behavior. From Sherif till the present wave of studies of intergroup conflict in different paradigms, this has been a topic for research and discussion. While Sherif and others have concluded that the negative stereotyping of out-groups was a corollary of intergroup competition and conflict, more recent studies have shown that the mere classification of subjects into distinct groups where members experienced some form of 'common fate' was sufficient for tendencies to devalue and disfavor members of other groups to emerge. Intergroup conflict merely amplifies these tendencies, up to the point of 'depersonalizing' out-group members and viewing them solely as representatives of the depreciated out-group, and 'dehumanizing' them as targets that can be harmed mercilessly (see also chapters 3 and 11).

Examples of these far-reaching tendencies for group-based stereotyping abound. The most dramatic examples are associated with ethnic and political violence, such as Northern Ireland, the Arab-Israeli conflict, the Iran-Iraqi war, but most of all the atrocities of the Nazi era. Many applied studies of intergroup relations have elaborated on the problem of how to break through escalatory spirals of prejudice and stereotyping in intergroup conflicts.[39] Here, too, the group proves to be more than the sum of its members. For instance, groups express more indignation and more subsequent aggression when confronted with deceptive or confrontative behavior on the part of other parties in the conflict. This goes especially for groups harboring a relational motivational orientation: they are 'hurt' by the opponents' behavior, and are inclined to take strong punishing measures.[40]

110

A final similarity pertains to behavior in intergroup conflict situations and the behavioral outcomes of groupthink. More specifically, it should be pointed out that both risk-taking and entrapment are oft-encountered features of intergroup conflict. For instance, intergroup social comparisons provide a plausible explanation for some of the typically social-competitive dimensions of risk taking and entrapment: increasing the in-group's commitment to a particular project or decision in order to 'outdo' other groups, and hence increase individual and in-group self-esteem.

7.4. Groupthink and intergroup relations: conclusions

It is interesting to notice that where the groupthink literature has neglected the intergroup dimensions of this phenomenon, the same has happened the other way around. I have come across only one study in the field which discusses at some length the groupthink phenomenon, be it within the framework of an intragroup application of social identity theory.[41]

The view developed in this chapter has been laid down in some preliminary propositions, limited in scope in that they regard the group's relations with other groups in its environment as a 'contextual' factor, hence in essence external to the group. This contrasts with some of the intergroup literature where it is argued that the very formation and maintenance of a particular group needs always to be seen in the broader intergroup context. Nevertheless, a preliminary attempt has been made here to identify the kinds of intergroup settings conducing to groupthink among groups involved in intergroup encounters. As the propositions formulated above illustrate, situations of (intense) intergroup conflict, be it socially or instrumentally defined, are the most likely candidates for groupthink analysis. It has been shown that many of the basic process dynamics as well as some of the major symptoms of groupthink are among the foremost intragroup consequences of intergroup competition and hostility, with perceived chances of winning and losing as crucial mediating factors. 'Winning' may easily lead to self-satisfied complacence, while 'losing' may lead to external blaming and redoubled and rigid efforts to yet gain the upper hand (see figure 7.1.; see also chapter 12 where a distinction is made between optimism-driven and pessimism-driven types of groupthink).

Illustrating the face-value plausibility of this line of thinking, one could go back to the case studies by Janis and other analysts: in each and every case, there was a vitally important conflict going on between the key group under study, and competing groups in its environment. Many of the ill-fated decisions taken were designed to defeat opponents, outsmart competitors, mislead rivals, or, reversely, to defend against aggressors: the Kennedy group versus Castro's Cuba, Kimmel's group versus the Japanese military, Chamberlain's inner circle versus Hitler's Germany, and the Johnson group versus communist expansionists in South-East Asia. Interestingly enough, and elaborated in chapter 10, some of these intergroup tensions involved groups within one and the same government, which, theoretically, is to operate as an integrated whole. In the case of Watergate, for instance, the Nixon group considered itself in conflict not only with the Democratic party, but also with Congress, parts of the Judiciary, and various agencies within the administration (FBI, CIA, State Department). Similarly, in the face of growing opposition to the Vietnam war, Johnson and his group became embroiled in bitter domestic debates over its policies – up to the point of paranoia about 'the enemy within.'

The intergroup perspective on groupthink is potentially fruitful. The propositions outlined here provide a first attempt to further specify the contextual contingencies of groupthink. However, a number of problems remain to be resolved. Amongst these, the problem of establishing the direction of causality stands out: does intergroup conflict cause an increase of intragroup cohesiveness, or might it be that highly cohesive groups are more tempted to engage in competitive intergroup interaction? Both assumptions may be correct – as indicated by some of the research presented above. The challenge is to identify more systematically the factors that mitigate these interrelationships.

Notes

1. This goes especially for the United States, as pointed out by a number of leading European social psychologists, such as Moscovici, Tajfel, Doise, Rabbie and Billig. For overviews of this discussion, see Billig (1976); Austin and Worchel (eds 1979); Turner and Giles (eds 1981), pp.7-16, Tajfel (1982); Taylor and Moghaddan (1987).
2. This point refers to the fact that in some theories of intergroup behavior, the notion of group is broadened considerably to include any social category of people that perceive themselves to be distinct from others on one or more characteristics. This holds true especially for social identity theory, as developed by Tajfel and colleagues, see: Turner and Giles (eds 1981); Tajfel (1982); Turner (1987); Brown (1987); Hogg and Abrams (1988).
3. In their recent overview of theories of intergroup behavior covering both social psychological and sociological perspectives, Taylor and Moghaddan (1987) mention four other theories; equity theory, elite theory, relative deprivation theory, and a five-stage model of intergroup relations.
4. Sherif (1966) p.89.
5. Blake and Mouton (1962).
6. For the former, see Aronson et al. (1978); Aronson (1984). For the latter, see Galtung (1968); Deutsch (1973), and also parts of White (1984).
7. Recent replicatory research with greater numbers of subjects does give some classification effects, see Rabbie and Horwitz (1988), and Rabbie, Schot, and Visser (1989).
8. Rabbie and Horwitz (1969).
9. Rabbie (1972).
10. Rabbie and Wilkens (1971); Rabbie and De Brey (1971).
11. Thibaut and Kelly (1959); Kelley and Thibaut (1969); Kelley (1979); Horwitz and Rabbie (1982).

12. Early intergroup experiments in the PD- tradition have been reported by Wilson and Kayatani (1968) and Wilson and Wong (1968), as well as Stephenson and Brotherton (1975). For an extensive treatment, see Lodewijkx (1989).
13. Axelrod (1984).
14. This presentation of social identity theory has made use of the following accounts: Tajfel and Turner (1979); Turner and Giles (eds 1981); Tajfel (ed. 1982); Tajfel (1982); Taylor and Moghaddan (1987); Hogg and Abrams (1988).
15. Turner (1981); notice Tajfel's concealed criticism of this extreme cognitivist position, in Tajfel (ed 1982), chapter 16.
16. Opend and closed groups are differentiated on the basis of the extent of permeability of group boundaries: the degree of liberty with which can join or exit from the reference group. On the study of groups with differential power, see Doise (1978); Caddick (1982); Ng (1982); Ng (1984).
17. Caddick (1982), p.149.
18. See Austin and Worchel (eds 1979); Hewstone and Brown (eds 1986).
19. Tajfel (ed.1982), p.499.
20. Tajfel (1982), pp.501-502.
21. Rabbie and this co-workers do not agree with this assessment as they do include measures of social cohesion etc. in their designs, see Rabbie and Horwitz (1988); Rabbie, Schot and Visser (1989).
22. Rabbie, Schot and Visser (1989); see also Rabbie and Horwitz (1988) for pointed statements about the course of the debate between themselves and the social identity theorists, the empirical basis of the various claims, and the prospects for future research.
23. Rabbie and this associates have made attempts to do so in developing the so-called Behavior Interaction Model, see Rabbie and Lodewijkx (1987); Lodewijkx (1989); Rabbie et al. (1989).
24. Rabbie and Visser (1974); Rabbie et al. (1974).
25. See Rummel (1963); Tanter (1966); Wilkenfeld (1968), Wilkenfeld (ed. 1973).
26. Dion (1979).
27. Meyers (1962); Fiedler et al. (1967).
28. Rabbie and Wilkens (1971); Rabbie and de Brey (1971); Rabbie et al. (1974).
29. Rabbie et al. (1974).
30. Kahn and Reyn (1972).
31. Worchel et al. (1975).
32. To reiterate, some of the literature cited in chapter two included Lanzetta (1955); Hamblin (1958); Janis (1968), and Mulder and Stemerding (1963). An intragroup elaboration of social identity theory is provided by Hogg and Abrams (1988), pp. 93-115.
33. Rabbie and Wilkens (1971).
34. Rabbie and Van Oostrum (1977).
35. Rabbie and Bekkers (1978).
36. This occurs especially in ambiguous situations, where there is no self-evident standard of comparison, and where subjects know they can earn a reward for the group product. See Hinkle and Schopfer (1979).
37. See Whyte (1943); Stouffer (ed. 1949), and Van der Brug (1986) respectively.
38. Rabbie and Lodewijkx (1986), Rabbie and Lodewijkx (1987); Lodewijkx (1989).
39. See Billig (1978); Tajfel (1982); Hewstone and Brown (eds 1986).

8 – Toward a revised model of groupthink

8.1. Social-psychological perspectives on groupthink

This chapter concludes the social-psychological analysis of groupthink. In chapters two to seven, a broad range of theory and research on group processes has been covered. At times, rather complicated reasoning was necessary to elaborate specific ideas and linkages. It seems useful, therefore, to provide first an overall summary of the key arguments made in these chapters, before presenting preliminary conclusions.

In the social-psychological investigation of groupthink, both ends of the conceptual model of groupthink originally put forward by Janis have been examined. On the 'input' side, the concepts of cohesiveness, conformity and compliance, and deindividuation have been explored as possible antecedent and process factors. On the 'output' side, the effects of group-think on risk-taking and entrapment phenomena was probed. Both dimensions are summarized in the appropriate order.

8.2. Inputs and processes

Cohesiveness

In Janis' model, high cohesiveness was the original group-level antecedent factor promoting groupthink tendencies in decision making groups. In the groupthink literature, this view has been challenged in a number of ways. Longley and Pruitt argued that Janis has been unclear about the specific manner in which high cohesiveness leads to groupthink. Steiner hypothesized that it was desire for cohesion rather than cohesion itself which caused groupthink. And both Flowers and Courtright presented experimental evidence suggesting that cohesiveness is not a necessary for groupthink.

In order to explore the merits of these alternative approaches, the cohesiveness literature was consulted. The most striking characteristic of cohesiveness soon turned out to be its diversity. First of all, various competing definitions of the term were found. Secondly, a number of different bases (sources) of cohesiveness were identified: interdependence between the group members, conflict with outgroups, rituals and symbolism, leader-centeredness, and (certain instances of) external adversity and stress. Thirdly, there were multiple effects of cohesiveness on group decision making: positive group atmosphere, increased potential for the group to influence its members' thoughts and actions, contingent effects on group problem-solving abilities, and effects pertaining to the group's relationships with its (organizational) environment.

This excursion through the cohesiveness literature was then used in reassessing the relationship between cohesiveness and groupthink. One of the main findings was that the various assertions of Janis, Steiner, and others are not at all mutually exclusive. The perceived differences between these arguments can, in part, be attributed to the fact that these authors use different conceptions of cohesiveness – in particular, they implicitly refer to different sources of cohesiveness. Also, the analysis indicated the potential role of the stress factor (in combination with group members' perceptions of the group's chances of overcoming problems effectively) in shaping group cohesiveness and its effects on group decision making. Further, the content of the group norms was found to be vitally important in determining the implications of the pressures to uniformity of thought and action acting upon members of cohesive groups. In sum, it appears that there are mediating factors which determine: a) whether a decisional group will become or remain highly cohesive when confronted with different problem situations, and b) the specific impact of cohesiveness on the group decision process.

Conformity and compliance

Taking groupthink analysis beyond a reassessment of the cohesiveness factor, a bottom-up perspective on groupthink proved very useful. What does it entail? It requires taking the point of view of the individual group member participating in a group decision-making process. Then, a new set of questions emerges. The key issue becomes: why does a member of a decision group go along with the apparent group consensus, even when he disagrees and (or) sees that the group is heading for failure? Posing the question in these terms means focusing on conformity and compliance of group members. Hence, an attempt was made to establish the interrelationships between conformity research (in its broadest sense) and the groupthink literature.

The concept of conformity focuses attention not only on peers-induced pressures to uniformity ('horizontal' pressures – as in cohesiveness research), but also on vertical pressures flowing from the – formal and informal – hierarchical differentiation within groups. Some group members are more equal than others. Their viewpoint weighs heavier. Also, these influential members or group leaders may possess all kinds of possible sanctions to induce other members to go along with their preferred course of action. It is suggested, therefore, that the 'concurrence-seeking' of the groupthink phenomenon may – under certain conditions – stem very well from compliance and obedience of members to leaders or authoritative majorities. This boils down to a generically different pattern of groupthink than outlined in Janis' original thesis.

Support for this basic thought was found in the conformity literature. Various ways of bringing about individual conformity were identified: the impact of group norms and member roles, direct peer pressures and the impact of majorities and minorities on group decision making, and the role of leaders and authority figures. Taken together and put in a small-group context, these three variants of conformity were shown to be potentially complementary and mutually reinforcing.

Next, these findings were confronted with the groupthink literature. Power, influence and conformity factors have been given some attention by Flowers, Courtright, Fodor and Smith, and McCauley. They all found evidence of a leadership effect in bringing about groupthink: a closed, authoritarian leadership style seemed to provoke leader-centered con-currence-seeking detrimental to high quality decision making. The interesting thing was that most researchers found the effects of leadership style on group decision making to be much stronger than cohesiveness effects. Or: vertical patterns of compliance appeared to be more powerful in bringing about groupthink than horizontal patterns of conformity. These findings provide support for the contentions that: (a) conformity and compliance play an important role in bringing about groupthink; (b) cohesiveness may not be a necessary antecedent to groupthink; (c) consequently, tracing the causal mechanisms of groupthink may involve identifying different paths, which may but need not overlap.

In a further elaboration of the linkage between conformity and groupthink, the role of external stress was elaborated. The group literature provides support for the thesis that under stress, group members tend to develop a need for strong leadership. Along comes an increased tendency to obey these leaders. This makes for a contingent view of conformity-based groupthink: it is more likely to occur in groups operating under stressful conditions than in groups not under pressure.

Deindividuation

A third body of literature shedding light on the causal dynamics of groupthink focused on the phenomenon of deindividuation. The reason to focus on deindividuation was simply that there exists a great face-value correspondence between deindividuation and groupthink: both are group-level phenomena, and both are generally, correctly or not, associated with ill-founded, irrational, and ineffective behavior. Probing into the deindi-viduation literature, much more correspondence was found.

The value in combining deindividuation and groupthink primarily lies in the fact that in (experimental) Social Psychology – unlike groupthink and despite its seemingly elusive character – deindividuation is a relatively well-researched concept. So it became possible to discuss the antecedents, 'symptoms' and consequences of deindividuation in view of what we know about groupthink. Three antecedent factors were considered: anonymity, cohesiveness, and external demands or pressures. The latter two showed a marked resemblance to some of the antecedents of groupthink. The same goes for some of the documented effects of deindividuation, such as the violation of commonly accepted norms, little concern about the future, and recklessness.

Based on this analysis of the structural similarity between groupthink and deindividuation, a specific interpretation of the linkage between the two phenomena was offered. It was hypothesized that groupthink is one type of manifestation of deindividuation, specifically to be found in small-group settings. Other, more widely known manifestations pertain to crowd behavior (lynch mobs, audience phenomena, vandalism).

8.3. Outcomes

Risk-taking and recklessness

Groupthink decisions often entail rather extreme positions on a certain issue. This is very similar to the well-known phenomenon of group polarization. The logic of groupthink – a group-level process that shapes and reshapes individual members' judgements – resembles the basic ratio of choice shift research: groups are more than the sum of their members. Janis contends that groupthink generally leads to bad decisions. One of the dimensions of low decision quality he identified, was excessive risk-taking. Numerous social psychologists have since hinted at the possible relationship between groupthink and risk-taking.

Firstly, the concept of risky shift was introduced, and the development of this area of research since 1961 was briefly described. The development from risky shift, via conservative shift, to group polarization shows a gradual broadening of the interest in group-induced dynamics of choice behavior. Different explanations of choice shifts were presented, and it was concluded that – despite ongoing polemics between adherents to various explanatory hypotheses – not one but numerous explanations of choice shift behavior fit the evidence. Indeed, the different hypotheses possibly are complementary.

Secondly, the concept of risk itself was critically examined using sociological and anthropological studies. This was done because this author was unsatisfied with the easy generalizations using evidence from experimental choice shift research to explaining and predicting risk-related political decision making. It was shown that in real-life situations, risk is often hard to recognize. And if it is at all recognized by participants in the decision-making process, its shape and importance will often be judged differently by different authors. Formal, decision-theoretical notions of risk do not apply. The relationship between subjective and objective dimensions of risk is very complicated. This makes it hard to equate high or low risk-taking with high or low quality of decision making.

These insights provided a basis for reassessing the relation between groupthink and risk-taking. Support for the original contention that groupthink leads to risky or reckless choices was found, for instance by examining the work of Minix who conducted risk-taking experiments in the context of crisis decision making. Yet the explanation for this link between groupthink and risk-taking that was put forward, differs considerably from current notions. It is contended that groups caught in the groupthink syndrome make more risky decisions because the entire 'risk dimension' of their actions becomes irrelevant to them. They have little concern about the impact of their decisions, they have a collapsed time perspective (cf. deindividuation), they are over-confident. In short, groupthink leads to risk-negligence, bringing about (objectively) risky choices; these choices may work out well, but often they do not. In the latter case, the picture painted by Janis indeed emerges: groupthink —> risk-taking —> policy failure.

Commitment and entrapment

In many cases, public policy making involves a set of interrelated choices rather than one single moment of decision (in crisis circumstances this may be somewhat different). One pattern of decisional failure is entrapment: becoming entangled in a negative spiral of faulty decisions that turn out badly. The entrapment phenomenon has emerged from research on commitment to past decisions and it has received ample support in experimental research. Policy fiascoes such as United States' involvement in the Vietnam conflict have been explained in terms of entrapment.

As a well-circumscribed instance of decisional failure, entrapment seemed highly appropriate to be investigated in relation to groupthink. In particular, it should be of interest to see whether groupthink could be one of the causes for entrapment. To establish this, a survey through the entrapment literature was conducted. Brockner and Rubin's speculations on the interrelations between entrapment and groupthink were taken as a starting point. The variables underlying entrapment were systematically scanned (project variables, psychological variables, social variables, structural variables). It was found that although entrapment is usually conceived of as an individual-level process, the psychological and social dimensions of entrapment come very close to the state of mind and the group dimensions of groupthink. Therefore, it was hypothesized that in multi-decision situations, when the decision-making process is characterized by groupthink, entrapment in the chosen (and failing) course of action is likely to occur.

8.4. Groupthink in context: intergroup perspectives

Moving beyond the conventional boundaries of group decision-making studies proved to be very useful in getting a better understanding of the contextual factors setting the stage for a group's deliberation and choice activities. Both the 'cohesiveness-based' and 'compliance-based' dynamics of groupthink are illuminated by exploring the nature of a group's relationships with other groups in its environment. After a sketch of two of the main lines of thinking in intergroup research – realistic conflict theory and social identity theory – the focus of the chapter was on the intragroup effects of intergroup conflict.

On the basis of evidence from a number of studies focusing on the relationship between intergroup conflict and intragroup cohesiveness, it was hypothesized that, under certain conditions, intense intergroup conflicts provide the kind of context for a decision group to become highly cohesive and congenial. These specific conditions are as follows: (a) faced with the threats posed by the stances or actions of outgroups, group members must perceive collective action within their respective groups to be the most adequate line of defense, and/or (b) the group has already proved to be successful in countering outgroup-related threats.

As regards the effects of the intergroup context upon leadership and compliance dynamics within groups, evidence from this research confirms the basic line of thought developed in chapter five. In situations of intergroup conflict, groups tend to become more hierarchically structured, increasing the potential for strong leaders to expect loyal behavior from members of the group.

Finally, reviewing evidence from the effects of intergroup conflict, it was found that many of the symptoms of groupthink occur in groups engaged in competitive or conflict-ridden interaction. In particular, the tendency to stereotype and depreciate members of outgroups combined with a strong in-group bias (belief in the inherent morality of one's own group, occasionally combined with a belief in the effectiveness or invulnerability of the group) set the stage for ill-conceived group decisions that do not do justice to the inherent complexity of the intergroup situation.

8.5. General conclusions

1) The groupthink phenomenon has been 'discovered' (put forward) only relatively recently (1972). As we have seen in chapter one, it is also an inherently complex phenomenon, involving a multitude of actors, factors and processes. Therefore, it is not surprising that the dynamics and effects of groupthink are not yet fully understood. To be more specific, the model of groupthink put forward by Janis should be viewed as a preliminary model.

2) Taking a broad social-psychological perspective, it appears however, that

the basic idea of groupthink is well-entrenched in the literature. The analysis of chapters two to seven shows that it is possible to use groupthink as a focal point for combining various theoretical and research traditions within social psychology. This not only does justice to the complexity of the concept, it has the added advantage that it ties together strands of research which were previously largely unrelated. As such, this analysis serves a more fundamental heuristic function.

3) It appears from this examination that groupthink can indeed be more fully understood by taking a broader view of its antecedents and consequences. Having attempted this, a number of interesting conclusions emerge:
- high cohesiveness is not a necessary condition for groupthink to occur; high concurrence seeking may also derive from very different sources, such as tendencies for group members to comply with the demands or points of view of leaders and other authority figures; this would make for a leader-centered variant of extreme concurrence seeking;
- once it occurs, high cohesiveness does bring about very powerful tendencies towards uniformity of thought and decision within groups; as Janis suggests, these need not always take the form of direct pressure upon individual members; more subtle and intractable patterns of concurrence seeking exist;
- the specific effects of cohesiveness on group decision making may be mitigated through other phenomena occurring in cohesive groups (deindividuation is a case in point);
- again and again, the (external) stress factor came up as a significant contingency element in triggering groupthink-related processes; it appears that groupthink is very much a partial, contingent theory of decision making;
- any analysis of groupthink should take into account the intergroup context of the specific group under study, because it is there that may lie the antecedent roots of the groupthink syndrome.

Taken together, these conclusions suggest that it is necessary to develop a multi-path understanding of groupthink, in order to be able to grasp more fully the range of its antecedents and consequences. This is attempted in a very provisional manner in the section below.

8.6. Remodelling groupthink

On the basis of these reviews, an attempt is now made to provide a revised model of the groupthink phenomenon. It will be a split analysis: an input model describing paths towards groupthink, and an output model describing the decision-making effects of groupthink. They are depicted in figure 8.1. and 8.2.

Figure 8.1.

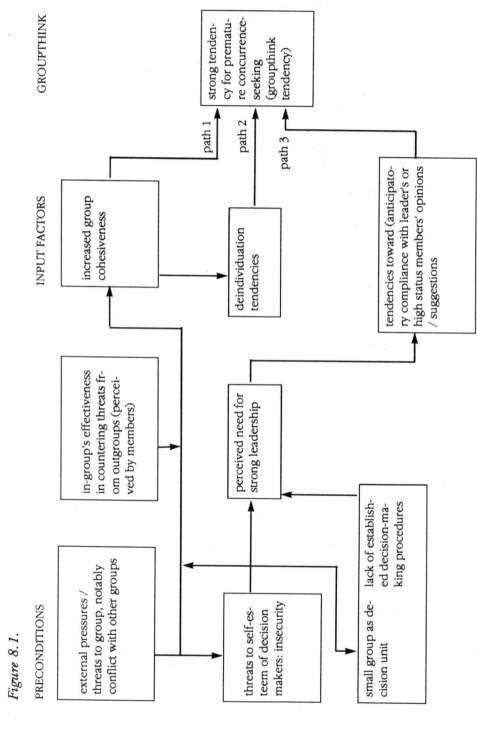

This model of groupthink rests on the assumption that groupthink can arise in a number of different ways; hence there are several identifiable pathways to groupthink. These pathways are not mutually exclusive. On the contrary, they may reinforce each other. Yet, they are all substantive pathways: each one is in itself a sufficient 'cause' of groupthink.

Before explaining the three pathways, it should be stretched that there are two general situational/structural preconditions; these conditions must be present for groupthink tendencies to arise. These are:

– there must be a group as the key decisional body (i.e., the decisions made should involve group discussion and collective deliberations);

– the group must be relatively informal or unstructured (i.e., there must be no well-circumscribed and adhered-to sets of procedural guidelines guiding the decision process).

In addition, there are grounds for arguing that there must be a certain amount of stress among the group members, either because of direct external threats or pressures (e.g. crisis conditions), or because of 'internal' sources of discomfort, anxiety and uncertainty which threaten self-esteem. Note, however, that the idea of groupthink as a phenomenon which exclusively arises under conditions of external demands or threat-induced stress cannot resolve the problem that at least one of the symptoms of groupthink identified by Janis, the illusion of invulnerability, does not seem to fit into such a defensive collective mindset.

Exploring in greater detail the nature of the relationships between situational conditions and the group process, one class of situations in particular stands out as conducing to groupthink, that is, situations of intense intergroup competition and conflict – provided group members perceive their own group as an adequate and successful forum of countering the threats posed to them by the intergroup situation (threats arising from intergroup conflicts may also be resolved by group members by resignation or defection from their original in-groups). This particular class of situations is therefore embedded as one specific, though not the only, category of situational antecedents of groupthink processes, impacting upon at least two of the three alternative pathways to groupthink.

Path 1. The first path is almost identical to the original groupthink hypothesis put forward by Janis: high cohesiveness as a direct and sufficient cause of groupthink. This formulation invites specification. This involves the above-mentioned contingency view of groupthink as a stress-triggered phenomenon: the cohesiveness that causes the groupthink tendency cannot be found in just any group; it is hypothesized that it is a product of external ('objective' – arising from intergroup conflict or other types of stressors such as impending disasters) or internal ('subjective') stress among group members. Let it be repeated that it is acknowledged that high stress only leads to increased cohesiveness if group members perceive the group as a viable protective mechanism; if not, cohesiveness under stress decreases).

Path 2. This path describes a specific route to groupthink in which the combination of external pressure and cohesiveness produce deindividuation phenomena in the group, which in turn foster groupthink. The difference with the first path may be quite thin, yet – as chapter six has shown – it is meaningful at least in theoretical terms. The distinction between the two may be found by analyzing the various different sources of cohesiveness in greater detail. It is hypothesized that in groups where the basic source of cohesiveness lies in the prestige and rituals of the group, as well as the mutual liking of its members, deindividuation is more likely to occur and serve as a kind of intermediary stage towards groupthink. Whereas in groups who are bound together by the interdependence of the members, with esprit de corps as an additional (not a primary) factor, there is a greater chance of more direct and probably somewhat less profound groupthink tendencies to occur.

Path 3. The third path towards groupthink is decidedly different from the other two. It starts with another effect of stress on groups, namely the tendency to search for strong leaders within the group; this is all the more likely if there are no tightly fixed decision-making procedures, or when the formal group leader does not display sufficient leadership in the given situation. Based on the analysis of chapter five, it is now hypothesized that the stress-induced tendency to search for strong leaders will lead to (excessive) drives towards conformity and compliance in individual group members; these drives are reinforced by the pressures to uniformity towards the perceived group judgement that occur in cohesive groups in general. With the individual members predisposed to resign their private judgements quickly, a specific form of premature concurrence-seeking (groupthink) arises. In the third path, high cohesiveness in the sense of amiability, is not a necessary precondition for groupthink.

Reality is always more complex than the most refined model. It is likely that in real-life cases of group decision making, different patterns of groupthink will occur at the same time. I should just state that this model allows for such an intermingling. The three paths are – I repeat – not presumed to be mutually exclusive, but, conversely, held to be interacting and reinforcing.

Output model explained

Very little now needs to be said about our systematization of the effects of groupthink. We have started from the assumption that it may be possible that the premature closure following from groupthink-ridden concurrence seeking may focus on a solution of the decision situation that is not a priori bad or ineffective. This closely follows Janis' reasoning on this point, as he too maintains that groupthink is not a sufficient cause for policy failure.

Figure 8.2. Decision-making effects of groupthink

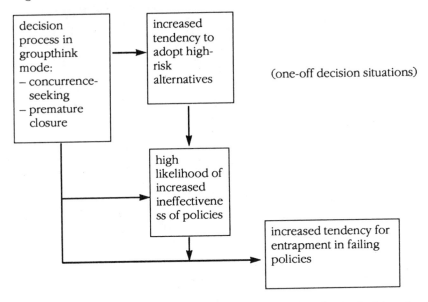

However, the specific dynamics of groupthink seem to ensure that this sort of happy coincidence occurs quite rarely. Groupthink makes for a distorted and biased process of search and deliberation. More often than not, decision makers caught in the groupthink syndrome will go for an ineffective course of action. Hence the common equation of groupthink with decisional failure. In chapters 5 and 6, it has been shown that groupthink also leads to more risky decisions; as a consequence, it can be hypothesized that in policy situations that require a series of decisions, a groupthink mode of collective decision making is bound to result in entrapment.

It is necessary to keep a balanced view of the success/failure issue in groupthink analysis. More generally, the model of groupthink currently proposed here should be put through further theoretical scrutiny before being used in empirical analysis. It is a model based on purely social-psychological elaborations of the groupthink concept. However, groupthink was originally put forward as a theory of high-level policy making. High-level policy decisions do not arise in a vacuum. They take place in organizational and interorganizational settings. If they are political decisions, they also arise in the specific setting of governmental decision making. These factors ought to be taken into consideration if a workable under-standing of the dynamics of groupthink is to be developed. This will be attempted in part III, which contains an organizational-political analysis of complex decision making, focusing on the role of small groups. The primary aim of these efforts will be to test the validity of the model developed here from another literature. Sometimes one has to break things down a bit again before something really useful can be constructed. This is what is designed to happen in parts 3 and 4 of this study.

PART III – A POLITICAL ADMINISTRATIVE EXAMINATION

9 – Groupthink in government decision making: challenging assumptions

9.1. Introduction

Good theory specifies the conditions under which it applies. Good theories have clearly defined boundaries and domains of validity. If these are lacking, risks of over-generalization and misapplication loom large. It has been argued earlier that groupthink theory is in danger of becoming an all-purpose label stuck on flawed policies. The original conditions and caveats provided by its author tend to be disregarded.

In this chapter it is shown that in the context of government decision making, groupthink can, at best, be only a partial theory, i.e., relevant to only a limited category of decision-making events. In the following chapters, an attempt is made to try and specify settings and processes where groupthink analysis may be pertinent. One way to accomplish this is by eliminating classes of situations and settings in which groupthink – given its set of preconditions and antecedents – is sure *not* to occur.

In this study, 'government decision making' is taken to be processes and outcomes of political-administrative decision making within, between, and with regard to, public-sector agencies. It may be true, as Bozeman holds, that "all organizations are public".[1] But still government and its institutions continue to play a crucial role in steering society, operating within the political process, and embedded in a specific structure of rules, obligations, and responsibilities.

A de-bunking approach

The object of the analysis in the rest of this chapter is very much to question what could be called 'psychologists' matter-of-courses'. Many psychologists are quick to talk about decision making in terms of one or more persons facing a problem and choosing a course of action to resolve or diminish this problem. Similarly, students of small-group decision making are quick to generalize their hypotheses and findings to real-life settings, including government. Both of these tendencies can also be witnessed in the discussions about groupthink. By drawing on theoretical and empirical notions from other disciplines – i.G. Political Science and Public Administration – as well as by presenting some original case examples, an attempt is made to illustrate that things are more complex than that. For instance, government decision-making processes resemble the traditional picture of choice-making underlying the groupthink thesis only to a limited extent. Large domains of government action can be more usefully analyzed by employing other perspectives, such as cybernetic organizational-process models emphasizing bureaucratic routines and flows of activity, as well as garbage-can perspectives proposing an altogether different temporal and interpretive order of decision-related activities such as information gathering and processing.[2] Hence, where do the kinds of explicit choice processes implied in groupthink and other conventional theories of decision making take place? While it is difficult to give any specific demarcation, it is often suggested that the decision perspective is most useful in analyzing the processing of non-routine problems requiring involvement from top-level decision makers in the organization or policy setting. A problem is likely to perceived to be non-routine in a number of situations:

– it is *big,* in the sense that it has not only current but also future implications for the performance of a (sub)unit or the organization or policy setting as a whole;
– it is *unconventional,* in the sense that it is felt that it cannot be dealt with by applying the standard repertoire of organizational responses or available 'solutions' and 'choices';
– it is *divisive,* in the sense that it has engendered or is likely to engender serious differences of opinion and conflicts within and between various parts of the policymaking machinery;
– it is *political,* in the sense that the problem has important repercussions for the external relations and strategic position of the organization or some of its key decision makers.[3]

In retrospect, one of the drawbacks of the fact that political decision-making theory has been mainly developed in the foreign-policy field becomes manifest. Because foreign policy, especially at the top layers of politics and diplomacy, is almost by definition non-routine. Models of decision making that were originally developed principally in view of explaining foreign policymaking have later been generalized to other areas of government action, without paying attention to the specifics of the policy context. This may have led to an overemphasis on the making of decisions as conscious and clearly definable choices. The same goes for groupthink theory: developed in a foreign-policy context, yet quickly expanded to explain decision making in other fields of government activity. This is not always appropriate. Instead, it is necessary to specify more clearly the contingent nature of the decision-making perspective embedded in groupthink theory.

Another implication of adopting a political-administrative perspective concerns the evaluative dimension of groupthink. While it is not possible at this stage to fully explore the epistemological and normative implications of the model of decision quality employed in groupthink theory, the analysis does suggest that the negative evaluation that pervades current formulations of groupthink is in part due to somewhat simplistic ideas about rationality and decision making. To illustrate this, it is useful to consider the garbage-can theory of organizational choice.[4] One of its key aims has been to provide analysts with a different kind of (heuristic) logic for understanding how and why organizations and governments act. Garbage-can logic enlightens seemingly chaotic, wasteful and irrational processes. In doing so, it more or less 'rationalizes' the existence of organizational slack, of procrastination, and organizational inaction.

This has important evaluative implications. Taking garbage-can logic seriously leads one to question the usefulness or validity of continuing to employ traditional rationalistic notions of decision making as normative standards by which the actual performance of organizations and state agencies are judged. Taking up the argument in the context of groupthink, a similar question arises. Janis employs a traditional process-outcome model of decision quality. A high-quality decision is identified by examining its genesis: the process of seeking and processing information, as well as the making of choices, need to be as comprehensive and unbiased as possible. If not, decision quality is poor – and less likely to produce favorable outcomes.

However, decision-making processes may have an altogether different meaning for their participants and other organizational members. Traditional models of decision making do not take into account the symbolic dimensions of decision-related activities.[5] This lack of understanding for alternative rationalities involved in organizational decision processes tends to provoke a rather negative evaluation of decision making in field settings. If one would employ a normative model taking into account the symbolic and ritualistic dimensions inherent in organizational choice, seemingly purposeless behaviors would be judged more favorably.

Similarly, groupthink and other conventional theories of decision making pay little attention to the fact that the definition of a successful decision outcome is subject to these dynamic processes of interpretation and sense-making. The simplistic notion of stable and undisputable policy goals provides for a clear, yet unrealistic standard of measuring 'decision effectiveness' – discounting other ideas about effectiveness shared by the participants in the decisions examined. For instance, although the building of the Sydney Opera House was considered by most observers to be a typical fiasco, some of the actors on the scene may have held a different view, whereby the enormous cost escalation of the project did not weigh up to its manifest and latent functions (ranging from providing an appropriate venue for cultural activities, to serving as an instrument to eliminate political opponents).[6]

9.2. Government action: groups in context

Key question – Central to groupthink is the making of decisions in small, informal groups. To what extent does government decision making take place in small groups?

Key proposition – There is a large number of governmental settings in which small groups operate, ranging from cabinets and cabinet committees to planning and work groups at lower levels of the government hierarchy. Yet there are relatively few occasions where the decision-making process takes place within a single, small group.

In the previous section, it was shown that in organizational and governmental settings, decision making processes more often than not differ markedly from the comparatively simple choice model which is presupposed by groupthink theory. Now the focus lies with the question of who makes decisions. Groupthink theory presupposes a small group as the decisional forum. It is contended here that this happens only in a limited number of cases. Most government decisions are taken by decisional units other than small groups. Recent work on comparative government has witnessed the development of typologies of governmental decision-making structures, which serve to show the breadth and variety of decision-making structures operating within modern government. By way of example, two of these typologies are presented.

Blondel. Blondel discerns two basic dimensions in the structure of governments: unity versus division, and hierarchical versus collective decision making.[7] A united government is said to exist when decisions emerge from one center, that is one man, a few men, or a group. If this center is indeed composed of one or no more than three men, and if the center is the dominant force in developing initiatives and guiding the policy process, the government is not only united but also hierarchical. At the opposite end, in collective governments, decision making authority is – ideally – shared by the members of the government, lacking one leader with preponderant influence. Finally, a government is called divided if there is not one but more – mostly two – centers of decision making, as is the case in many Communist states.

Blondel is quick to acknowledge that the governmental structures in his typology are more or less ideal-typical constructs which do not always accurately represent the complexity, diversity and fluidity in patterns of government. Moreover, his typology obviously only pertains to decision making at the top national level.

What factors explain the prominence and development of particular structures in a political system? Whilst again acknowledging that many cultural, historic, ideological and socio-economic factors influence this process, Blondel singles out three specifically institutional characteristics: the personal strength of a political leader, which plays a key role in propelling governmental arrangements along the hierarchical-collective dimension; the weight and character of political groups (parties, churches, armed forces), which has to be taken into account in forming governmental arrangements; and the role and importance of the bureaucracy, to the effect that a big and powerful bureaucratic apparatus tends to breed problems of coordination and divided arrangements at the governmental level. In the country-by-country survey of Rose and Suleiman, similar factors have been put forward to account for cross-national differences in structures of policymaking.[8]

Elsewhere in his study, Blondel elaborates and evaluates various arrangements. Firstly, he notes that there are very few political systems today functioning on a pure, leader-centered hierarchical basis. The leader inevitably runs into serious problems of oversight and control given the increasing diversity and complexity of public decision making. On the political level, only very strong personalities can claim the supreme and unchallenged position implied in the hierarchical model. Usually, such systems last only as long as the incumbent leader; with leader rotation generally comes a change in the decision-making structure as the new leader cannot immediately claim a similar dominance as his predecessor. In this respect, the gradual 'atomization' of the U.S. system of government is discussed. Formally, the President is able to install a leader-directed hierarchical system, given his power of appointment, the spoils system and other constitutional provisions. But in practice, the strong growth of the executive branch has effectively turned the system into a divided and pluralistic configuration. There is a rather weak and divided cabinet, strong congressional influence in policymaking, a large bureaucracy, and a strongly growing 'counter bureaucracy' in the Executive Office of the President. In such a system, the President acts as a broker more than a decision maker.[9]

Mackie and Hogwood. In the collaborative volume *Unlocking the Cabinet*, an attempt is made to further analyze the structure of decision making in political systems with cabinet government.[10] In eight European national overviews, different modes and problems of governmental decision making are explored, concentrating on the role of cabinet committees. In the editorial chapters, however, an attempt is made to provide a more comprehensive typology of decisional arenas at the central level of government. In all, Mackie and Hogwood identify seven types of decisional fora:
a) unilateral decisions by one minister of a department or his designates;
b) 'internalized' decision coordination by a single minister heading more than one department (e.g. superministers);
c) bilateral decisions between pairs of ministers;
d) multilateral decisions involving a number of ministers outside a formal committee;
e) cabinet committee decisions;
f) cabinet decisions;
g) party decisions.

The authors note that there are probably still other, more informal modes of interaction and decision making at the center of government. In elaborating their typology, they emphasize that empirically, it is hard to develop a clear-cut model of cabinet-level decision structures or to pin down the relative frequency and importance of various arenas. In this respect, they make a number of significant observations:

> "(....) the idea of a hierarchical pyramid of individual ministers topped by cabinet committees, topped by the cabinet, topped by the prime minister, with implied delegation downwards and upwards referral of all strategic or important decisions is not convincing. In many countries, authority for political decision-making affecting single departments resides in the individual minister and not in the collective responsibility of the cabinet (....)
> However, even in countries with the doctrine of ministerial responsibility, we find individual ministers exercising a wide power of decision making about their departments, with the minister exercising much discretion about which issue should be referred to colleagues (....) A number of decisions will be taken in full cabinet, but these will not necessarily include all the most important ones (....)
> The model of cabinet structure which best describes most cabinet systems is one of interrelated but fragmented decision arenas derived from membership of a cabinet which gives the system a focus but which itself takes only a small proportion of decisions (....) Cabinet committees or their informal equivalents perform a crucial role in making these systems workable (....)
> The decision arenas we have outlined are not self-contained and isolated from each other: they consist of the same political actors in different combinations. Hence they are interrelated; however, they are fragmented because they consist of different sets of these actors rather than a fully integrated and coordinated system, with clearly defined criteria for delegation from the full cabinet."[11]

Implications: the limited role of small groups

Considering the two typologies and their elaborations from the perspective of this study, some preliminary inferences are drawn about the role of small groups in governmental decision making.

a) From a historical-developmental point of view, the tide has, generally though non-monotonic, been against small-group decision making at the center of government. Modern governments, even if they adhere to a liberal, non-interventionist political philosophy, tend to be big and diversified. The growth of modern governments is largely due to other factors than ideology or purposeful design. Bigness in overall size is reflected in the number of departments and cabinet posts, causing a net increase in group

134

size at the cabinet level. Countertrends such as the notion of 'super-ministers' have only seldom taken hold. In organizational terms, modern governments have displayed strong centrifugal tendencies.

b) Along with growth, increasing fragmentation of decision-making authority and activities has eroded traditional notions of small-group government (be it leader-centered or collective). The Mackie/Hogwood typology testifies to this fact. Even while concentrating at the cabinet type of decision structure, they identified eight different arenas for decision making. Their typology gives rise to the idea that while there might indeed very well be a relatively small core of key decision makers in and around a cabinet, they do not form a stable group. Instead, they encounter each other again and again in different fora depending upon the subject at hand. All decision makers hold a large number of memberships in subgroups and coordinating committees dealing with specific policy issues, with only limited overlap. Attempts to provide for a stable, small group of ministers coordinating key fields of government activity have not been successful.[13]

On the other hand, the rise of matrix organizations and other forms of adhocracy has provided for new ways and channels of small-group prominence.[14] For example, it has become quite common to install special ad hoc committees composed of specialists and political or administrative 'heavy-weights' to plan and oversee big projects, such as organizational or tax reforms, integral retrenchment proposals, major industrial and technology-development policies, and large-scale infrastructural investment projects. These groups work together for a considerable period of time, often quite intensely and comparatively isolated from outside turbulence and interventions.

Another avenue of small-group activity lies not within the government, but at its fringes, in parliament. Parliamentary committees, permanent or ad hoc, resemble in many respects the small group idea. It is suggested in the literature that such committees develop their own formal and informal rules and norms. Their members are to a certain extent bound by these conventions. They can only be effective if they observe the rules of the game. Further, in some committees, a marked sense of esprit de corps develops over the years, as membership – in particular chairmanship – remains rather stable. New members are regarded as freshmen and are put through a variety of initiation rituals.

c) Each of these 'partial' fora can, of course, be considered a small group in its own right, prone to group-dynamic phenomena. Cabinet committees, for instance, generally persist over time during a cabinet's tenure and have a relatively limited membership. Yet there are mitigating factors. For instance, because most authorities will hold numerous memberships, partly encountering the same colleagues in different fora, tendencies to link issues and to develop quid pro quos over a number of issues dealt with in different groups develop. So some issues in a certain cabinet committee may be decided upon considerations that lie largely outside either the issue at hand or the particular decision group dealing with it.

135

9.3. Small groups in complex settings

In this chapter, an attempt was made to indicate that the small-group perspective on governmental decision making has a limited rather than universal relevance. We have not only indicated that there are many other types of decision structures operating within government, but also that these other, bigger settings and not the small group are perhaps a more appropriate angle for analyzing the making of government policy. To political scientists and public administration analysts, this is hardly a startling conclusion.

Modern governments are big. They are complex. Governing involves highly diverse and complex modes of interaction. Most substantive policy issues involve a wide range of actors, not only outside but also within government. Decision making, or rather 'the processing of policy issues' is fragmented. To be sure, there are many, many small groups, formal, semi-formal and formal, scattered throughout government.[15] But it is quite rare that a small group is the key decisional forum in making policies. More often, decision making involves different groups, sometimes separate, occasionally interlocking. This diminishes the applicability of groupthink analysis.

In attempts to use the groupthink explanation, it seems appropriate to delimit the focus to non-routine problem situations dealt with by the top of the organizational/governmental hierarchy. This includes cases of long-range policy planning, project management, highly politicized issues, and different types of crisis management. As to the kinds of groups to be studied in particular, the following stand out: cabinets and cabinet committees, high-level advisory committees, organizational or departmental management teams, parliamentary committees and subcommittees, and policy planning groups.

Having identified situations in which the decision-making process is indeed dominated by a single, more or less stable group, the next step in an applied governmental groupthink analysis is to investigate whether the operation of this group can be explained by either or some of the different process dynamics (paths to groupthink) outlined in the preliminary revised model of groupthink. Therefore, it is now time to analyze in a more generic sense the validity or plausibility of these alternative paths within the context of government decision making.

Notes

1. Bozeman (1987).
2. Allison (1971); Steinbruner (1974); March and Olsen (1986); Hickson et al. (1986); Heller et al. (1988); Nutt (1988).
3. Radford (1977); Dror (1986); Krieger (1986); Nutt (1988).
4. March (1988).
5. Feldman and March (1981).

6. Kouzmin (1979); Hall (1982).
7. Blondel (1982), pp.57-59.
8. Rose and Suleiman (eds 1983).
9. Blondel (1982), pp.80-84; lively illustrations of this same proposition can be found in Smith's (1988) account of the Washington 'power game'.
10. Mackie and Hogwood (eds 1985); see also Baylis (1989) for a recent comparative discussion of cabinet structures.
11. Ibid, pp.31-33.
12. Blondel (1982), pp.175-203.
13. Dror (1986).
14. Mintzberg (1984).
15. See Snyder (1958); Matthews (1959); Francis (1962); Barber (1965); Dodd (1962); Stassen (1972); Golenbienski (ed. 1978); Baylis (1989).

10 – Government decision making:
between cohesion and conflict

10.1. Introduction

Key question – Groupthink theory posits high group cohesiveness and esprit de corps among members as a key factor in triggering groupthink processes. How often does it happen that governmental decision groups are highly cohesive?

Key proposition – Government decision making is characterized by a complex relation between conflict and consensus. Decision groups, however, do not very often display the kind of amiability between members that is posited in groupthink theory. Ironically, one of the primary promoters of such types of cohesiveness may be the existence of conflict within the wider policy community.

In this chapter, an attempt is made to examine to what extent the cohesiveness and deindividuation pathways to groupthink can be found in governmental settings. There are various reasons to be cautious in applying notions of cohesiveness to groups operating in the context of politics and government. From the review of this chapter, it will become clear that group cohesion does play a part in government settings, but mostly very differently than expected by original groupthink theory. In effect, to understand the dynamics of the formation and cohesion (versus dissolution and divisiveness) of governmental groups, it is vital to examine the broader intergroup and organizational context in which they operate. This results in new propositions on cohesiveness and groupthink. With regard to deindividuation, the reality of government decision making allows for very little common ground with the theoretically promising pathway of deindividuation-driven groupthink: in high-level group settings, the antecedent factors of deindividuation are largely absent.

10.2. Conflict and cohesiveness in government

In Janis' model of groupthink, high group cohesiveness is the crucial process antecedent to groupthink. It is a necessary condition for group-think to occur. In the preliminary revised model presented in chapter 8, cohesiveness underlies only two out of three plausible pathways to groupthink. Even so, the concept of cohesiveness remains a key part of groupthink theory. In this section, group cohesiveness is reconsidered from a political and administrative perspective. If ever such a perspective provides for a radically different outlook on the dynamics of group decisions as compared to the social-psychological perspective, it is here.

Conflict rather than cohesiveness would be the appropriate starting point in analyzing the dynamics of governmental decision groups. And if there does indeed exist a certain amount of cohesiveness in such groups, it is more likely to be the kind of functional, interdependence-triggered cohesion rather than the kind of amiability and esprit de corps suggested by Janis. To be sure, such groups do exist. But it is argued here that they are the exception rather than the rule; their existence is contingent upon the occurrence of certain additional factors.

Yet, the picture is more complicated. Because, as known from the literature on intergroup relations, conflict between different parties or factions in a decisional process may in itself become a source of cohesion within the groups concerned. Apparently, in certain situations, 'external' conflict may breed intragroup cohesion (see chapter 7). This seems to be a viable assertion for studying political groups and the dynamics of, for instance, political and administrative coalitions.

In this chapter, the first question is how to substantiate the initial claims about the non-cohesiveness of political and administrative groups. Three pervasive political and administrative factors shall be discussed, that counteract the development of tightly-knit decision groups in government: instability, political heterogeneity, and bureaucratic politics. Once this basic argument is presented, the paradoxal relationship between conflict and cohesion in government is discussed in view of groupthink theory.

Non-cohesiveness: unstable groups

One reason why governmental groups rarely display a high amount of cohesiveness is because they simply lack the time to develop a significant degree of rapport. Politics is a cyclical process. Elections and other events provide for a constant reshuffling of those who govern. In this vein, Heclo has termed the central government of the United States "a government of strangers."[1] While, obviously, there are considerable national differences in the duration and regularity of political cycles as well as in the specific systems of political and administrative recruitments, Heclo's phrase applies to many centers of government. As Heclo notes:

"Much more important than the experience or inexperience of political appointees as individuals is their transience as a group. Cabinet secretaries may bring with them a cadre of personal acquaintances to fill some of their subordinate political positions, but in general public executives will be strangers with only a fleeting chance to learn how to work together (....) One of the most persistent themes in comments from political executives of all recent administrations is the absence of teamwork characterizing the layers of appointees. This absence of unifying ties is foreordained, given the fractionalized, changing, and job-specific sets of forces that make up the selection process. But it is not only methods of selection that put mutually reinforcing loyalties at a premium. Rapid turnover intensifies all the other problems of political teamwork."[2]

In the United States, the phenomenon of executive rotation extends beyond the levels of chief political executives. The spoils system in which many senior administrative appointments in the Washington bureaucracy are attached to the incumbent political power holders magnifies the rotation effects upon the stability of planning and decision groups and the continuity of policy making in general. In countries with a civil-service tradition, things are different. But even within political systems with a large permanent bureaucracy, instability and rotation are important attributes. But here, they may have alternative causes:
- economy drives and retrenchment policies affecting the government bureaucracy;
- continuous efforts at administrative reform resulting in a steady reorganization of departments and directorates, as well as reshuffling of tasks and responsibilities;
- new management techniques stressing the merits of all-round administrators, causing steady rotation and replacements to gather experience in a variety of positions;
- increased vertical mobility of civil servants within the bureaucratic apparatus.

To put the matter sharply: the net effect of these trends is that the chance that a certain policy planning or decision group – be it at the cabinet level or within or between departments – has the stability of leadership and membership which appear to be necessary requisites for achieving some degree of cohesion, is relatively small. The chances for achieving group stability are perhaps largest within one department or policy unit, within long-standing government coalitions, or in policy circuits dominated by either career bureaucrats or long-seated political appointees.

Non-cohesiveness: politics and the group process

There are other factors preventing government decision groups from becoming highly cohesive. It is by now almost a cliche to state that policymaking is a political process, in that it involves the interplay of numerous groups and interests, conflict, negotiation, and compromises. Let us examine how this affects the operation of political councils, such as cabinets.

Whatever the specific structure of the political system, a national-level cabinet is highly unlikely to become a cohesive in-group. Cabinets tend to be fragmented and divided rather than harmonious. Cabinet government may have originally been inspired by ideas about achieving consensus at the highest level of government as a mode of effective coordination and control, the incidence of diversity, descensus, and conflict are among the most pressing current problems of cabinet government in many countries.[3] Indeed, forming and maintaining workable coalitions in the governance process lies at the heart of politics and political analysis. This renders maintaining an adequate balance between conflict and consensus is a key challenge.

Size. There are many reasons for this. First, most cabinets are simply too large to become an effective working group.[4] Remedies against the crippling effects of size and diversity, such as inner-cabinets and 'superministers', have not taken hold. Second, interpersonal compatibility and team-building are generally not amongst the key considerations in cabinet recruitment, which tends to be dominated by political consi-derations of various kinds. As a consequence, the sources of disagreement and personal conflict between members are often 'incorporated' into the design of cabinets.

Further, cabinet ministers can seldom escape serious role conflicts. Besides being 'part of the team', they are, at the same time, heads of departments. They are expected to represent the perspectives and interests of their departmental constituencies. At the same time, the cabinet as a whole is the primary forum for integrating sectoral policies. Its task is to coordinate the highly compartmentalized perspectives and efforts of the ministries. It has to weigh budgetary constraints likely to be put forward by Treasury or Budget departments against the policy claims of the spending departments, and so on. The role conflict experienced by cabinet ministers becomes clear now. On the one hand, if they identify themselves too strongly with their department, they will be quickly accused of 'going native' by the Chief Executive and his staff, or by their fellow cabinet members: in the end, exclusive partisan advocacy on the part of cabinet members is counterproductive. On the other hand, a cabinet minister who bends too easily or frequently for the demands of his cabinet colleagues will quickly get the reputation of being a 'weak' minister. This will not only further impair his effectiveness within the cabinet, it will also make him lose the esteem of the senior civil servants at his own department; this will diminish his ability to 'get things done' and manage his own department.

Departmental fragmentation. Departmental fragmentation and its impact upon the coordinative abilities of the cabinet has been a major source of scholarly and political debate in many European countries. In the Netherlands alone, some five major ad-hoc advisory bodies have studied the topic over a twenty-year time span, without much effect.[5] Similar problems exist in West Germany, where the multitude of departmental perspectives has found recognition and formalization at the cabinet level by the 'Ressort Prinzip' embedded in the Constitution.[6] Similar observations pertain to Norway. [7]

Political fragmentation. But perhaps the most important factor lies in the fact that cabinets are always products of representation and accommodation between a large number of their constituent forces' interests. The predominant considerations in the composition of cabinets are political: accommodating the various wings and shades of the ruling party (in single-party democratic governments and one-party regimes), building a viable coalition between various political factions; appropriate representation of societal groups (e.g. the military, the clergy or the leading religious groups, business interests, regional and/or ethnic groups, especially in new or unstable political regimes). From this point of view, cabinet members are representatives of their political power bases rather than autonomous actors chosen for their abilities at governing. This limits their freedom to take positions in the cabinet.[8] Moreover, if there are great conflicts of interest between the various constituent bases, this will be reflected in a lack of unity in the cabinet.

In this respect, Andeweg's asserts that most cabinets seem to be more in danger of excessive heterogeneity than threatened by the adverse effects of excessive homogeneity (such as groupthink).[9] In his terminology, this is the product of both departmental and political (i.e. representational) sources of heterogeneity. Again it appears that the analyst should take non-cohesiveness of cabinets as a starting point and look for specific factors promoting consensus and cohesion, rather than the other way around.

Non-cohesiveness: bureaucratic politics

A final dimension of non-cohesiveness in governmental groups discussed here focuses in particular upon the government bureaucracy. In the last thirty years or so, empirical observations of policymaking within government, as well as research into the political roles and functions of civil servants have shattered the long prevailing image of government bureaucracy as a 'machinery', or a unitary organization.[10] The separation between politics and administration put forward by many early administrative scholars has contributed to the prominence of an ideology of administration in which civil servants and government departments or bureaus were depicted as the loyal and neutral preparators and implementors of policy decisions. 'Administration' was all about neutral competence; 'politics' was the domain of wheeling and dealing, conflict and strife.[11]

Research has turned this conventional image upside down, and has provided a more 'realistic', though not undisputed, depiction of the workings of government: the 'paradigm' of bureaucratic politics. Two

143

empirical premises about politics and government form the basis of this conceptual model:

a) 'The' government does not exist. The government actually stands for a large and particularly complex conglomerate of organizations, sections, departments, officials, and layers of administration. .

b) 'The neutral, consensual administration' is a fiction. Different parts of the administration as well as different actors within these parts, have different tasks, outlooks and interests, which need not necessarily coincide smoothly. On the contrary, there appear to be perennial clashes between the opinions and interests of various bureaucratic actors. Positions shape the stands one takes; and the stands one takes as well as the game one plays will determine one's future standing. Conflict is the main setting of bureaucratic interaction, power is the currency.

Example: State vs. NSA. To illustrate the pervasiveness and impact of bureaucratic politics on the policy process, consider the following observations by Henry Kissinger in his time as Presidential assistant for National Security Affairs:

> "The Foreign Service is a splendid instrument, highly trained and able. When I was Secretary of State I grew to admire it as an institution, to respect its members, and to develop a close friendship with many of them. But it requires strong leadership to impose coherence on the parochial concerns of the various bureaus which are most conscious of the daily pressures; this is especially true if the policy to be pursued is unpopular or at variance with long-held predilections. That sense of direction must be supplied by the Seventh Floor – the office of the Secretary of State and his immediate entourage. Unfortunately – to the credit of neither of us – my relations with Rogers [William P. Rogers, Secretary of State under Nixon from 1969-1973, PtH] had deteriorated to the point that they exacerbated our policy differences and endangered coherent policy. He was likely to oppose any recommendation of mine simply as an assertion of prerogative; I tried to bypass him as much as possible (....) Rogers was convinced that our course [in this case, with regard to the India-Pakistan crisis of 1971, PtH] was mistaken and that Nixon took it only because of my baneful influence. I believed that Rogers had no grasp of the geopolitical stakes. The result was a bureaucratic stalemate in which White House and State Department representatives dealt with each other as competing sovereign entities, not members of the same team, and the President sought to have his way by an indirection that compounded the internal stresses of our government."[12]

Recollections similar to these can be found in virtually all memoirs and biographies of top policymakers and civil servants, without regard of their specific positions and countries of origin. In some political systems, bureaucratic strife appears to be a built-in phenomenon:

144

"The basic themes of American governmental institutions are distrust and disaggregation. Together, they fuel suspicion. Presidents often come to divide the world into 'us' and 'them'. 'They' typically cannot be relied upon. 'They' will be seen as torpid, bureaucratically self-interested, and often uncommitted or skeptical of presidential initiatives. Above all, 'they' will be seen as an uncontrollable source of hemorrhaging to the press (....) Unmediated by any tradition of, or basis for, a cabinet team, distance defines 'us' and 'them'."[13]

Only in America? The American system is by no means unique. For instance, Cassese provides an account of departmental battles as a perennial feature of the Italian national government.[14] And there are, by now, many other accounts of bureaucratic politics in a variety of countries and settings.[15] Neither is it really a 'new' perspective on government and bureaucracy, as political economists have since long provided positive theories of strategic behavior by bureaucrats as self-interested utility maximizers.[16] Yet, for one reason or another, the basic ideas transmitted by this school of thought were slow to be absorbed by analysts of government decision making (save perhaps for analysts of U.S. foreign and defense policies).[17]

Like other countries the American system is not unified in the sense that bureaucratic politics is found everywhere in as dominant a role as described by Kissinger and Rockman; there are many instances of smoother and more tightly coordinated inter-institutional and inter-departmental relationships in other sectors of policy as well as in state and local levels of administration. Finally, bureaucratic politics need not always be as malignant as suggested in the quotations above. Indeed, there have recently been scholars recommending using the bureau-political perspective as a more realistic guideline for managing the governance process than the conflict-free organizational-reform blueprints so long 'en vogue' among students of public administration.[18]

Modelling bureaupolitics. The model of bureaucratic politics stipulates that considerations of intra-organizational and interorganizational rivalry and conflict play a key if not a dominant role in determining the course and outcomes of policy processes.[19]

How to characterize bureaucratic politics? When does it occur? It should be kept in mind that the 'model' is actually little more than a culmination of research data from very different areas of government policymaking, which have only recently been started to be put in a more coherent framework. It pertains to the factual operation of actors and institutions within government (yet this does not imply that its underlying causes are necessarily intra-governmental, as the patterns of conflicting interests between different sections or departments often reflect similar lines of conflict between departmental clienteles and societal interest groups linked up with the bureaucracy). Further, it is noted that bureaucratic politics not only occurs between institutions or layers of government (central-regional-local clashes), but also within these entities. A bureau-political analysis therefore presupposes a detailed breakdown of the policy process to identify who really are the 'actors.' Decision processes which at first sight seem limited to one and the same institution can be just as well ridden by conflict and strategic interaction between bureaus – witness the making of departmental budgets.

Bureaucratic politics takes place in settings characterized by a number of components:
1) there are many actors in the decisional arena;
2) the actors have diverging interests;
3) no actor has preponderant influence;
4) decisions are made by way of compromises;
5) there exists a gap between the making and the implementation of decisions.[20]

Degrees of administrative conflict. The degree to which bureaucratic politics pervades a policy decision-making process is variable. If characteristics (1), (2) and (3) reach high values, the 'resultant' formation of compromises will be extremely difficult (4), and there will be a wide gap between decision making and implementation (5). Such an extreme and mostly dysfunctional state of affairs has been labelled 'bureau-poli*tism*'.[21] At the other end of the continuum, variables (1) to (3) may assume low values, indicating a less complex and politicized decision arena, making for more smooth and substantive policy formation (see figure 10.1). Hence it is impossible to arrive at general statements about the effects of bureaucratic politics on the quality of policymaking. Contrary to the traditional perspective on administration, the new model allows for the possibility that a certain amount of fragmentation and competition within the bureaucracy may enhance rather than disturb decision quality (by now a long-established idea in the sociology of organizations, which somehow never did get fully through to students of public administration which have long kept on seeking to 'design out' every bit of overlap, redundancy and conflict encountered).[22] This is not to say that bureaupolitics never poses serious problems. Indeed, it does. It may even be a key factor in current problems of big government.[23] But this is because bureaupolitics in many political systems is now tilting towards the right hand of the continuum depicted in figure 10.1.

Why bureaupolitics? In the empirical literature on bureaucratic politics, several antecedent factors are mentioned, that influence the development and specific form of bureaucratic politics in different parts of the administrative system. Yet a systematic and comparative analysis of these factors is still lacking. At this point, one can merely mention the most often cited background variables:

– the structure of the political and administrative system, which determines in particular the number of actors which will claim an input to any given policy process (legal prerogatives, formal designations of

146

Figure 10.1. Degrees of bureaucratic politics

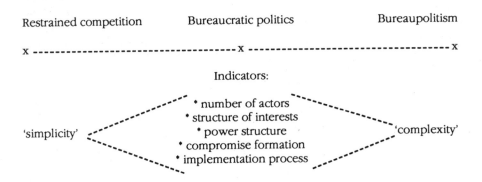

tasks, authority and responsibility relationships between different organizations and administrative or hierarchical levels, recruitment and rotation of political and administrative elites);

– the relationships between government agencies and their political environment (the impact of political parties, pressure groups and clientele organizations on the organization's policies, networks, neo-corporatist arrangements, clientelism);

– political and administrative culture (for instance consociational, accommodative versus majoritarian, win-lose styles of policymaking; norms and values concerning appropriate administrative conduct; socialization of administrative elites);

– the internal organization of government agencies (internal power structure, span of control from top to bottom within the hierarchy, specific organizational culture, relationships and influence patterns between career and political appointees);

– external conditions (budgetary situation, opportunity- versus crisis-triggered decision processes).[24]

Implications for groupthink analysis

The bureaupolitics perspective draws attention to the strategic dimensions of relations within and between government organizations. Applying the bureaupolitics perspective to small-group interaction alerts the analyst to the pervasiveness of interest-driven behavior and multiple lines of conflict which exist within the executive branch. In this view, interdepartmental committees and policy planning groups become sites of conflict and bargaining between competitors, which can be usefully understood by gaming analogies: players, goals, rules, tactics, and sanctions. In such arenas, consensus is the lowest common denominator enforced upon a reluctant set of heterogenous actors under pressure to come up with something, rather than a hearty agreement between people who share a perspective on the problems and prospects of government policy.

In a bureau-political group setting, therefore, the most likely pathology is not a premature consensus among a cohesive set of representatives from various agencies. Rather, it is the inability to achieve any consensus at all, the fact that achieving consensus takes an inordinate amount of time and effort, or the fact that the consensus achieved is only vaguely related or not up to the requirements of the problem situation.[25] Not the most likely but a most serious pathology occurs when bureaucratic politics and conflict amounts to segmentation and non-contact. According to Coser, this is even worse than a high degree of open conflict, because it indicates that conflict has become institutionalized and rigid, with no hope of mitigation or productive side-effects stemming from it.[26]

In terms of small-group theory, a bureau-political perspective would seem to require studying bargaining rather than consensus formation, and modelling zero-sum rather than cooperative game situations. Groupthink seems far away.

10.3. From bureaucratic conflict to group cohesiveness

That, however, is a premature conclusion. Until now, the role of consensus and cohesiveness in government has been played down. Emphasizing the significance of conflict and strategic action, it appears that the final step in pointing out the limits of the applicability of the groupthink hypothesis has been taken. Yet, this is only part of the picture. Not all government decision groups are ridden by conflict. Even while taking interest-driven behavior, politics and intra-government conflict as basic postulates, it is necessary to take note of situations and techniques that serve to mitigate conflict or even provide a basis for cohesion and congeniality. Two classes of factors are discussed: those pertaining to top-level (i.e. cabinet) decision making, and devices mitigating bureaucratic politics (paragraph 10.4).

Mitigating cabinet centrifugality

The potential for conflict within cabinets has long occupied scholars and practitioners in trying to find ways to avoid ending up with a crippled decision-making process at the heart of government. Over the years, a number of structural and behavioral devices have served to mitigate cabinet disagreement. These are used to different extends in different political systems. The first two mechanisms pertain to strategies that, occasionally, prevent matters from being brought to the full group while the other three mentioned here refer to techniques and conditions that facilitate the making of group decisions.

a) Anticipation. Prudent cabinet members or staffers will make sure that if they have a subject on their hands which is likely to engender disagreement, they will consult with some of their counterparts to find out their feelings about the topic, and, if possible, accommodate their critique by adjusting their own positions or proposals before the matter is discussed in the cabinet. Olsen has argued that this mode of conflict mitigation is most likely to be used in comparatively small and fairly transparent political systems, where the number of actors is limited and interests and positions are fairly clear in advance.[27]

b) *Committee work*. Most students of cabinets agree that in many countries cabinet committees and study groups have replaced the full cabinet sessions as the major fora where the direction of cabinet policies is developed. What happens in essence, is that subgroups within the cabinet are formed to deal with major parts of government policy requiring intensive inter-departmental coordination: social-economic policy, administrative reform, European affairs, planning and environmental affairs. The membership of these committees often does not remain limited to members of the cabinet. Usually, assistant secretaries, underscretaries (or their equivalents) and senior civil servants attend committee meetings. There are both permanent and ad hoc committees (the latter often deal with tricky political subjects). Cabinet committees need not have formal decision-making power. Usually, they are to 'prepare' an issue or paper for full cabinet discussion. In practice, however, if agreement is reached in a cabinet committee it is not very likely that the subject will arouse much controversy in full session. If it does, there is always the escape clause to send it back to the committee for further preparation.

The growth of cabinet committees (and other modes of inter-departmental coordination below the cabinet level) has changed the nature of cabinet meetings. On a wide range of subjects, cabinets act more as a rubber stamp than as a decision-making unit. From the perspective of conflict mitigation however, one could wonder whether these developments have really changed something. Is it not simply a displacement of conflict to the committees? For instance, Andeweg has indicated that in a coalition system such as the Netherlands, all the problems of political representation and departmental heterogeneity are transferred to the committee level.[28] There is constant haggling over the composition of cabinet committees; everywhere political and departmental forces have to be balanced. As long as there are diametrically opposed interests involved in the policymaking process, the elimination of a number of fringe actors by splitting policy problems up in committee structures is in itself not likely to result in fostering consensus and cohesion. At the same time, the committee system may contribute to the formation of informal leadership groups within the cabinet, who are able to command support from other members. Then, it is but a small step to the formation of 'inner cabinets', which have frequently gained prominence during wartime situations. As Andeweg notes, there may be strong opposition to the development of such elite groups of cabinet members in systems with a doctrine of 'ministerial equality'.[29]

149

c) *Non-intervention.* Conflict is avoided by the explicit agreement or tacit consent that members of the cabinet will not interfere with matters that fall entirely outside the range of one's own portfolio. For example, a minister of Agriculture is unlikely to start discussing a Police reform bill to be submitted by his colleagues at Interior or Justice. This serves to limit the number of discussants on a large number of topics that come up at cabinet meetings, and hence reduces the likelihood of problems, obstacles and delays in obtaining consensus. Without any rule of this kind, the possibilities for cabinet decision making would be severely reduced. Yet there are important classes of topics for which the rule does not hold: politically sensitive topics which may or may not split up the cabinet; big policy decisions which involve a number of cabinet members anyhow, such as social-economic policies; the annual budget; several classes of foreign policy decisions, such as major bilateral or multilateral treaties; major crisis events. When these types of problems are on the agenda, the strict division of labor and compartmentalization of decision making fade, and the potential for descensus and conflict is increased.

d) *Secrecy.* One way to play down the centrifugal effects of political and departmental heterogeneity in the cabinet is to promote cabinet secrecy. Especially in Great Britain, secrecy has been one of the key pillars of cabinet government. The underlying idea is very simply that cabinet members will be more free not only to say what they think but also to adjust their publicly held views and make deals, if the details of cabinet deliberations will remain secret. This is thought to lessen the pressures from political and departmental constituencies acting upon them to adopt and maintain specific parochial points of view.[30] Similarly, secrecy has been identified as an essential requirement for top-level prudence and accommodation in consociational democracies.[31] Without secrecy it would not be possible to pacify the sharp societal cleavages represented in the political arena; promoting open government in divided societies would be tantamount to having no government at all. Secrecy facilitates the attainment of consensus; but it may do so at the price of no longer adequate probing the assumptions underlying the policies and practices concerned.

e) *Threat-induced cohesion.* A final factor in mitigating cabinet conflicts can best be described as situational. There are situations in which the cabinet or the government as a whole is threatened, either by external events or by tensions within the polity. Examples of internal threats to governments abound: pervasive societal cleavages in 'divided societies', escalated social conflicts and strife (pitting cultural, religious, ethnic, or economic groups against each other on a number of issues), clashes between executive and legislative powers (as in confrontations between one or more ministers and sizeable sections of parliament, which threaten to escalate in ministerial or cabinet crisis).[32] Other internal threats may derive from the activities of social movements demanding social and political changes, hostile outbursts, terrorist activities, revolution attempts, coup d'états, and the like.[33] Threats arising from without the political system range from man-made and natural disasters to international, war-prone crises.[34] Confronted with extreme or otherwise threatening circumstances, cabinets may pull together and become more cohesive in dealing with a common threat. Indeed, the very idea of consociationalism is based upon elite prudence, ad-hoc coalitions, and intensive attempts at consensus-building as means to prevent a political system from being de-stabilized or crippled by societal and political pressures.

However, it is doubtful whether these threat-induced cohesiveness impulses really exist to the extent that has been claimed in the bodies of literature just cited. It appears that the threat —>cohesiveness linkage is contingent upon other factors, such as the pre-crisis atmosphere within the group or wider political system, the size, scope and clarity of problems faced and tasks to be fulfilled, as well as upon the individual calculations of the actors involved. Some players may see more benefits in dissociating from their colleagues instead of riding things out together; they may, in effect, go for an increase in tensions rather than trying to mitigate them as effectively as possible.

10.4. Intergroup conflict within government: breeding groupthink

Several factors and techniques that reduce fragmentation and conflict in government decision making have been discussed. Although generally cabinets may be plagued by centrifugal forces, and bureaucratic politics may pervade the executive branch, this does not preclude the existence of various 'pockets' of cohesive small-group interaction – which can be, in fact, nurtured by this very predominance of fragmentation and competition.

Indeed, there is an other side to the conflict apparent in bureaucratic politics. In a sense, conflict breeds cohesion. Bureaus and agencies may be embroiled in territorial disputes and intense policy disagreement. Yet in the multi-actor setting that government inevitably is, this generally means that coalitions between like-minded are formed. These may be ad hoc and temporary, or more structural. But some of these coalitions generated by the existence of bureaucratic strife can become quite cohesive and con-genial. It is the bureaucratic variant of social psychology's thesis about intergroup conflict which fosters intra-group cohesiveness (see chapter 7). What happens is that once a coalition is formed through bargaining or cooptation, the coalition partners will try to manipulate the context of decision making in such a manner as to get their way. One technique is to narrow the circle of participants in the decision process, by taking the decisions at moments and locations where the main opponents are unavailable.

A remarkable example concerns the decision to attempt a rescue mission to liberate American hostages in Iran. The final decision was made in an NSC meeting at the time that the key opponent to the plan, secretary of State Vance, was known to be out of town; his deputy was led to believe that Vance was aware what was going on and was no longer opposed the idea.[35] Consider also the implications of the observation by Hilsman about Kennedy's style of decision making:

"Kennedy said: And now we have the 'inner club'. He meant that we had together the people who had known all along what we would do about the problem, and who had been pulling and hauling, debating and discussing for no other purpose than to keep the government together, to get all the others to come around."[36]

A more formal system of limiting the number of bureaucratic actors involved in policy making was followed by President Nixon in his design of the foreign policy machinery during his term. He wanted to make foreign policy from the White House, by keeping a tight control over the information flow and the decision process. This was achieved by institutionalizing a formal system of decision procedures and clearances, allegedly to make sure all the views were represented before an issue came up for decision; but at the same time, he wanted to cut out the State Department and the Foreign Service as much as possible by giving wide responsibilities to the NSC advisor and staff, while appointing a 'weak' secretary of State and attempting to diminish the policy roles of other distrusted agencies such as the CIA, while exactly the opposite was attempted during the early reign of President Reagan.[37] A related technique is making use of informal policy circuits and back channels. This was a favorite method of Henry Kissinger in his perennial battles with William Rogers and the State Department.

Secrecy again plays a vital role in these ways of circumventing the bureaucratic struggles. Indeed it is part of these struggles. It ties together parties that have found each other on one or more key issues. It excludes others in the executive branch from knowing what goes on, let alone participating in the decisions.

It is too simple to conclude that the existence of bureaucratic and political rivalries and conflicts of interests totally precludes group cohesiveness to develop. In fact, the issue is partly one of perspective: while *at the overall level of government,* the picture may be one of disintegration and descensus, at the *level of each of the participating factions,* there may be high cohesion and esprit de corps, fueled by the very conflicts with other parties. If one of these contending factions is able to build a strong position of power, it may come to dominate the decision process, thus making for potential cases of groupthink.

This can be illustrated in various ways. Reviewing the various tactics used in conflict-ridden cabinets and bureaucratic settings, one observes a number of processes and mechanisms that can be associated with groupthink tendencies.

Self deception. The politics of accommodation so often practiced in mitigating cabinet disagreement may succeed at the price of neglecting the substance of policy. Moreover, practicing techniques of anticipated reaction and sounding out can easily amount to self-censorship: not voicing concerns which may upset future partners within the cabinet or its leadership in order to facilitate reaching agreements. The motivation to build a workable coalition at the top of a divided political and departmental setting can be so strong as to override the need for open policy discussions.

Eliminating opponents. Manufacturing consensus by reducing the number of actors in the decision process (either by forming cabinet committees, inner circles, or by circumventing opponents by informal policy circuits and the use of backchannels) has the potential of being the victim of its own success. It may totally eliminate important points of view, discussions and critical scrutiny from the decisional forum. The motivation to outsmart political and bureaucratic opponents can easily override concerns about the substantive merits of the policy under consideration.

Leader dominance. Assertive leadership within the cabinet or executive branch may serve to lend coherence to the policy process. But there is a substantive risk of it being pushed too far. The unifying stance adopted by a leader then becomes a tight-jacket from which there is no escape. The leader's power in framing the definition of the group's activities and policy options may limit the group's flexibility in problem-solving (see chapter 11). More fundamentally, in these 'strategically composed' groups, leaders are not likely to be motivated to act as neutral directors of the policy discussions. They want to get things done, and take an entrepreneurial stance rather than acting as guardian of the decision process. They will explicitly advocate their preferred courses of action, and will probably manage the discussion as to maximize support. Doubters or dissenters will have a hard time making their case before the group.

Moral complacency. In conflict-ridden bureaucratic environments, the 'us and them thinking' which develops among the various factions can assume the same dehumanizing proportions as in cases where us and them pertain to, say, opponents in the international system. If bureau-political battles become really hard-hitting (bureau-politism), moral considerations will fade into the background. Then, anything goes in outmanoeuvring opponents. Policy substance or the societal costs incurred by adopting a strategically useful policy, are of less importance than the balance of rewards and punishments within the policy arena.

Pathologies of secrecy. Informal policy circuits and back channels can only be successful if they operate in secrecy. Yet secrecy has the potential of becoming an end in itself. First of all, if rigidly maintained it logically leads to the insulation of the decision-making group. Afraid to let any outsiders in on what they are doing, they lack the benefits of expert or outsiders' advice. Secondly, in line with March's comments about the symbolic dimensions of decision making, consider the psychological impact upon individual members of being part of a small group acting out a secret policy initiative. This will almost certainly enhance self-esteem and feelings of esprit de corps towards the others in the exclusive circle. Hence the group in itself becomes a value, and the preservation of secrecy is held essential for the success of the group. This stimulates a strong motivation to prevent indiscretion or leaks. It will also discourage members from risking their membership by arguing against the gist of the group's course of action. If they experience a role conflict between their private views and individual obligations on the one hand, and the requirements of remaining member of an exclusive elite, the odds are that they will have the latter prevail (they may have been led to expect implicit or explicit career rewards for doing so; take for instance the case of John Dean and the Watergate cover up, where he had long suppressed doubts about the wisdom of the course adopted by Nixon and his lieutenants because of the bureaucratic and psychological rewards connected with it; it was not until he understood that in the long run, Nixon c.s. would likely to be on the losing side of the conflict that he decided to cut his losses and go public).[58]

Generating entrapment. The pitfalls of building cohesion in a divided environment can also come to the fore in the post-decisional stages. Developing consensus and building compromises can be a very time and energy-consuming process. It may take months, even years. It may require substantive concessions from all of parties concerned. If this has been the case, the motivation to preserve and uphold this costly decision is likely to be very strong. In other words, the very difficulty of reaching a decision provides a source of commitment to it once it has been taken. This opens up a great potential for entrapment, for instance when it turns out that other relevant actors or constituencies are not satisfied with the outcomes, or, more seriously, when it becomes evident during implementation that the decision is unworkable. The prospect of having to start all over again will induce the decision makers to do their utmost to maintain the decision.

Implications: reassessing conflict and consensus

It would be very interesting to reassess Janis' case studies from this political perspective of intra-system centripetality, conflict mitigation within top-level policy arenas, and coalition-building in a politicized strategic environment. This perspective alerts the observer to the fact that in each of Janis' cases, the composition of the decision group as well as the decision process were molded not only by the internalized stresses of the external problem situation (e.g. war threats, communist advances, nuclear missiles in the backyard), but to a considerable extent also by the existence of administrative and political pressures and conflicts. This was especially manifest in the Watergate case, where Janis with great precision draws the lines of Nixon's inner circle on this basis, thereby adding the necessary political feel to Raven's early exercise through the groupthink explanation. Especially revealing in this respect are the tape transcripts where Nixon and his lieutenants denounce and radicalize some of their bureaucratic opponents (which, formally, all belonged to the Nixon 'team').

Conflict mitigation techniques going astray can be observed in the Bay of Pigs episode, where President Kennedy and his confidants and appointees showed too big a deference for the CIA officials who had been left on their posts under the new administration. For the sake of bipartisanism and the motivation not to undercut CIA proposals at the first possible moment, the CIA representatives were allowed to dominate the joint sessions preparing the invasion.

On the theoretical level, this analysis raises the interesting question about the role of intergroup (interorganizational) conflict in promoting excessive group consensus. This leads one back to Social Psychology, and the topic of intergroup relations and their impact on intragroup conditions. More specifically, the propositions put forward in chapter 7 seem to provide a valuable alternative (or: additional) frame of reference for explaining the incidence of groupthink in governmental settings. Furthermore, more than Janis' original line of reasoning which pays little attention to intergroup dynamics, it appears to be in concert with the contextual perspective of political-administrative examinations of governmental small group decision making.

From decision making to decision management

The pitfalls of conflict mitigation described above suggest that meta decision making – in other words the management of the decision-making process – rather than the actual making of individual decisions is the key challenge to high-level political and administrative authorities. Some techniques of decision management have been discussed. It has been indicated how by avoiding one class of decisional pathologies (the crippling effects of fragmentation and conflict), decision makers may unwittingly plant the seeds of others (i.e. groupthink). Finding the right balance between consensus and disagreement, between cohesion and dispersion is a crucial task for practitioners and students of decision making alike.[99]

10.5. Deindividuation in governmental settings

Key question – In the revised model of groupthink, a second process dynamic providing a path towards groupthink is deindividuation. To what extent will governmental groups display this feature?

Key proposition – There are great difficulties in assessing deindividuation in governmental settings. On balance, it seems unlikely that a state of dein-

155

dividuation will occur in high-level governmental decision groups other than in highly specific circumstances.

One cannot but be very brief about the occurrence of deindividuation in political-administrative settings. Here, the problems of attempting to combine and integrate concepts and findings from different social-scientific disciplines become manifest. In Social Psychology, deindividuation is a well-established and relatively well-researched topic. This has been due to a curious blend of controlled experiments in the laboratory and more impressionistic accounts from the collective behavior field. But in Political Science and Public Administration, the concept is not only virtually unknown; it is also extremely difficult to handle. How to operationalize it in the context of high-level policymaking groups? At this stage, conventional research simply lacks the methodology or versatility to come up with satisfactory answers.

To be sure, there are field settings which seem suitable contexts for deindividuation phenomena. For instance, in the repressive and military parts of the state apparatus, there is a large reservoir of the type of highly-cohesive, uniformity-inducing, depersonalizing groups acting under external pressures which most closely fit the deindividuation profile. Like Zimbardo's prison guards, police and military are uniformed (compare the appearance of modern anti-riot police, complete with helmets, gas masks – indeed the unrecognizability of individual officers has been a constant source of criticism and claims from protesting groups who claimed this had a disinhibiting effect upon police officers during disturbances, leading to excessively violent behavior). Like the prison wardens also, tight discipline and uniformity of conduct are part of occupational socialization and culture. Finally, in view of the obvious need for groups of soldiers and policemen to perform as one under stress, active attempts are made to build cohesive groups with a strong team spirit. But these groups are not likely to be in the position of making key strategic decisions. Rather, they tend to fit the profile of work groups. Unless decision-making authority is strongly decentralized (or has completely disintegrated under the pressure of extraordinary events), such groups will be involved only in operational domains implementing decisions made higher up the hierarchy. This is not to deny the importance of such groups and the potentially disastrous impact deindividuation may have on the quality of their performance; this is acknowledged. It is just to point out that the administrative settings which, at face value, seem to be the most conducive to deindividuation-like groupthink phenomena, are generally below the policy-making level.

Tentative example: the Nixon White House. Rising up the hierarchy, one might again wonder whether the conditions that, as far as is known from research findings in Social Psychology, give rise to deindividuation, exist at all in the nerve centers of government. To observers familiar with the Nixon era, the concept of deindividuation might seem appealing. Many contemporary accounts of the organization and operation of the Nixon White House mention the quest for uniformity, loyalty to the President, strong depreciation of real or perceived political opponents, and almost mechanistic rules and styles of operation among Nixon aides (cf. emergent norms). Before the Watergate scandal burst open, Chief of Staff Haldeman and domestic advisor Ehrlichman were generally low-profile officials. Nevertheless, their rather rigid and discipline-oriented management style not only earned them a reputation as 'Germans' (or more maliciously 'Nazis'), it also reinforced the idea of a military, drilling climate in the White House machinery.[40] In this system, aides had to be 'faceless'; their anonymity to the outside world went hand in hand with a strong emphasis on loyalty (internal social control). In such an environment, people would perhaps have started to think of the whole (the Nixon administration and its well-being) as something much bigger and worthy than its parts (individual staff members). On the other hand, the above-cited papers of Henry Kissinger tend to strongly emphasize the pervasiveness of ego-conflicts and bureaucratic strife within the administration.

In his case study of the Watergate cover-up, Janis acknowledged this picture, but argues at the same time that in a very select inner circle within the White House staff, considerations of personal ambition and rivalry were in part transcended by devotion to the Common Cause: the defense of the President against hostile criticism and political defeat. Staffers anonymous to the general public were deeply involved in a variety of sensitive operations to this end (e.g. Charles Colson, Howard Hunt, Gordon Liddy and the so-called 'plumbers'). There is some ground for speculating that, at times during these operations, these officials approached the group-minded state of deindividuation. But one must hasten to add that there is little in the way of empirical corroboration of such an interpretation.

Implications for groupthink analysis

In summary, at present there is very little to say about deindividuation in governmental settings. It is impossible to proceed in the same manner as in the sections dealing with decision making, small groups and cohesiveness, and pursue a strategy of elimination and enumeration of situations and decisional fora (un)suitable for further analysis. Where does this leave deindividuation (and the second path to groupthink in our revised model) in an applicationoriented conceptual model of groupthink in government? There are no substantive reasons to include it, nor are there sufficient grounds to eliminate it. The occurrence of deindividuation is contingent upon high group cohesiveness, as well as external anonymity and lack of accountability. In the previous sections, it has been shown that from these perspectives, cohesiveness is a comparatively rare phenomenon in real-life administrative settings. If this line of reasoning is valid, therefore, a preliminary conclusion can be drawn that 'path 2' in the revised model will probably cover a very limited number of groupthink situations. On the basis of the supportive evidence from social-psychological research, it seems nevertheless wise to keep it in, awaiting more sophisticated investigation.

Notes

1. Heclo (1977).
2. Ibid, p.104.
3. Rose and Suleimann (eds 1983), European Journal of Political Research, special theme issue (1988).
4. Blondel (1982), pp.140-173.
5. Andeweg (1988).
6. Mayntz (1983), pp.153-163.
7. Olsen (1983), pp.235-239.
8. Campbell (1983), pp.61-63.
9. Andeweg (1988), p.129; it should be noted however, that homogeneity and heterogeneity are not total equivalents of cohesiveness and non-cohesiveness as they refer mostly to the structural composition of a cabinet (political affiliations, departmental clusters) which may but need not be reflected in the cabinet's performance as a collective decision making body (clique formation, group disintegration).
10. Policy-process orientations of the politics of government can be found in Schilling (1962) Allison (1971), model III; Halperin (1974); Rosati (1981); Jenkins and Gray (1985); role-related orientations are provided by Aberbach et al. (1981); Suleiman (ed. 1984); Campbell (1983b).
11. See, for instance, Page (1985).
12. Kissinger (1979), p.887.
13. Rockman (1981), p. 916; see also Smith (1988).
14. Cassese (1983), pp.192-201.
15. For instance, Dogan (ed. 1975), Suleiman (1975) and Feigenbaum (1985) for France; Jenkins and Gray (1985) for Great Britain; Campbell and Szablowski (1979) for Canada; Rosenthal (1984) and Rosenthal (1988) for the Netherlands; see also the comparative volumes by Aberbach et al. (1981), Campbell (1983b), Suleiman (ed. 1984).
16. Tullock (1965), Downs (1967), Niskanen (1971).
17. For early applications, see Hilsman (1959), Huntington (1961); Schilling (1962).
18. Rosenthal (1988).
19. Chong-do-Hah and Lundquist (1975); Rosenthal (1988).
20. This formulation was first presented by Rosenthal (1988), based on, in particular, Rosati (1981).
21. Rosenthal (1988).
22. See Landau (1969) and Lerner (1986).
23. Fesler (1983).
24. See Halperin (1974); Suleiman (1975); Nossal (1979); Richardson and Jordan (1979); George (1980); Diamant (1981); Jenkins and Gray (1985); Campbell and Peters (eds 1988).
25. The 'policy window' may be closed by the time the bureaucratic consensus is achieved, see Kingdon (1984); Diamant (1981); Jenkins and Gray (1985); Campbell and Peters (eds 1988).
26. Coser (1956).
27. Olsen (1983), p.248.
28. Andeweg (1985), pp.142-144.
29. Andeweg (1985), pp. 142-144.
30. Mackintosh (1968).

158

31. Lijphart (1968), (1977).
32. See, in particular, Nordlinger (1972).
33. Linz and Stepan (eds 1978); Russel (1982); Zimmerman (1983).
34. Barton (1969); Quarantelli (ed.1978); Rosenthal, Charles and 't Hart (eds 1989).
35. Smith (1984).
36. Hilsman (1967), p.6.
37. George (1980) and Pika (1988); see also Smith (1988).
38. On symbolism in decision making, see several chapters in March (1988), on Watergate, see Janis (1982a), Dean (1982).
39. See Neustadt (2nd ed. 1979); Dror (1968); Dror (1986); Allison (1971), p. 71; George (1972); George (1980); Johnson (1974); Pika (1988); this issue is taken up again in the final chapter.
40. See Haldeman (1978), p.55.

11 – Hierarchy and compliance revisited

11.1. Introduction

Key question – In the preliminary revised model of groupthink, an alternative path towards groupthink was identified. It stressed the impact of hierarchical and contextual factors triggering processes of anticipatory compliance among group members, which lead to concurrence-seeking. How and to what extent do these factors play a role in governmental decision groups?

Key proposition – (a) The compliance perspective on groupthink is a plausible and appropriate framework for analyzing the dynamics of governmental decision groups; (b) anticipatory compliance leading to groupthink tendencies is a realistic threat to the quality of decision making in certain high-level government decision groups.

In chapter 3, it was argued on theoretical grounds that cohesiveness is not a necessary condition for groupthink tendencies to occur in decision groups. More specifically, it was shown that premature concurrence-seeking in groups may also stem from conformity and compliance tendencies among group members. This proposition turned the focus of inquiry towards the 'vertical dimensions' of groups, i.e., the impact of hierarchy and status differences between group members. The position and style of group leaders and group norms regarding the interaction between leaders and followers play an important role in determining the quality of group discussion. In several experiments, it was shown that closed leadership styles are quite important in bringing about groupthink tendencies (indeed, more important than group cohesiveness per se). The compliance perspective allows for a 'bottom-up' analysis of groupthink: the group decision process as viewed from the perspective of an average group member. Support for the perspective of (anticipatory) compliance comes, amongst others, from the work of McCauley, who reanalyzed Janis' case studies and found compliance tendencies playing an important role in the Bay of Pigs and Vietnam decision processes. [1]

Following this line of thought, an alternative path to groupthink was incorporated in the preliminary revised model resulting from the social-psychological investigation of part II. Now it is time to reassess and evaluate this alternative mode from a political-administrative point of view. This chapter explores the impact of hierarchy and status differentiation between actors in high-level governmental decision-making groups. In particular, it deals with the question under which conditions and to what extent these factors trigger detrimental compliance and concurrence-seeking within these groups. This topic touches on fundamental issues in the analysis of politics, government and bureaucracy.[2] It encompasses an enormous literature, that cannot be discussed in full here. Therefore, the argument can at best only identify suggestive leads, without aspiring to give a comprehensive treatment.

11.2. Hierarchy and compliance in government organization

In Political Science and Public Administration, few topics have received the kind of sustained and widespread, even passionate, attention as the problem of authority and compliance. It is spread throughout the literature. It can be found in classical philosophical treatises about the nature of politics and government (Plato, Machiavelli, Hobbes, Locke). It emerges in discussions on the stability and change of political elites, regimes, and systems. It is a central component of well-known theories of organization and bureaucracy.[3] And it is an important component of the analysis of public administration and public policy processes. In this study, the primary focus is on the impact of hierarchy and compliance on the decision-making process within government; it is not about compliance of citizens vis-a-vis government actors or demands.

Hierarchical differentiation and meticulous compliance with commands from higher level officials have traditionally been the hallmark of theories of bureaucracy. They were said to enhance the effectiveness, fairness, and predictability of organizational action. Moreover, the strict division of labor combined with a pyramid-like hierarchical structure, were to allow for clear lines of authority and responsibility.

Revisionist theories of bureaucracy have rejected or, at least, modified these ideas, both on normative and empirical grounds. They criticized the rigidity of this ideal-typical bureaucratic structure, and the stifling, even alienating effect it would have on organization members.[4] They challenged its effectiveness by pointing out the problems of coordinating and integrating the behavior of different officials working in different sections on different parts of a policy problem. But most of all, they showed that in reality organizations hardly ever operate according to the strict classical premises. Rather, there exists a continuum of organization structures. The extent to which organizations are compliance-oriented depends upon various factors, such as task structure, tradition, and leadership practices. Military organizations most closely resemble the traditional picture, while more service-oriented bureaucracies have generally developed more horizontal, differentiated patterns of operation.

Within this general context, one should also view the interaction between superiors and subordinates near the top of large government organizations, as well as the interaction between political authorities and high-level bureaucrats and advisors. Most observers agree that the traditional hierarchical model does not adequately describe the power and influence structures and processes that exist at the peak of the government hierarchy. Although in theory, civil servants are subordinate to political office holders, in practice, more complex relationships exist. Bureaucrats possess certain means of exerting influence that overcome their formal position as subordinate advisors: technical and management expertise, delegated or mandated decision authority, mobilization of support in and outside their own organizations (playing the political game).[5] In fact, much of the literature on political-administrative relations is directed to the question of how to assert and maintain sufficient political control over bureaucratic advisors and activities rather than the question of how to break through traditional boundaries of hierarchy.[6]

11.3. Hierarchy, compliance, and high-level decision groups

How does the hierarchical and vertically differentiated context of government and administration affect the policy decision process? In particular, how does it affect the operation of decision groups at the peak of the government hierarchy? These questions introduce to a topic that, compared to the massive literature on authority, power, and compliance at a general level, remains as yet relatively unexplored: the compliance dimensions of interactions between high-level officials in political-administrative settings.[7] To be sure, it is an inherently difficult topic, because to analyze it requires a clear insight into the inner working of these groups (not only in terms of formal and informal structure, but also in terms of the group process), as well as into the motivations and strategies pursued by the different members. There are, nevertheless, some studies available which deal with these issues. Based upon the examination of this literature, I present a number of propositions that reflect the basic argument, with proposition 5 extending it to its logical conclusion.

Proposition 1. In high-level decision groups as compared to other forms of inter-rank interaction within organizations, less emphasis is put on formal positions of authority, and more on the de facto distribution of status and power among the group members.

Proposition 2. In high-level decision groups as compared to other forms of inter-rank interaction within organizations, less use is made of explicit orders and commands; decisions are arrived at to a large extent on the basis of anticipation and consensus seeking, as well as the use of personal influence on the part of key-actors.

Proposition 3. Identification with the basic aims of the organization and the group is a more important means of steering high-level decision groups than control by monitoring and sanctioning on the part of chief executives.

Proposition 4. Despite the less explicitly 'vertical' aspects of high-level decision groups, status and power differences between the group members are critically important in understanding the group process. Therefore, chief executives presiding the group's discussions are in principle able to exert a large amount of control upon the course and outcomes of the decision process.

Proposition 5. In high-level decision groups, directive leadership styles combined with group or organizational norms of compliance may produce groupthink tendencies. This need not involve overt pressures for conformity; instead the group members are prone to excessive anticipatory compliance with the chief executive's assumptions, perspectives, and preferred alternatives.

Compliance and control among political-administrative elites

Status, power, leadership, and compliance – in short the 'vertical' dimension – are clearly manifest in the day-to-day operation of government, even at the highest levels. What makes things more complicated at the top of the hierarchy is the subtle and often hidden nature of power and compliance factors (see also the quote by Thompson at the outset of this chapter). Nevertheless, they are there. This can be illustrated in various ways. Three examples are provided.

War crimes. Perhaps the most compelling way is in examining instances where power and compliance factors have gone astray. This, indeed, is the basic objective of Kelman and Hamilton's recent study *Crimes of Obedience.*[8] While the empirical material of the authors largely focuses on military settings (e.g. the My Lai massacre and its aftermath in the United States), they also provide indications of 'political' crimes of obedience on the part of high-level decision groups. Take, for instance, the Watergate affair. Memoirs of former aides and co-conspirators of the Nixon group suggest that at least part of their unquestioning and enduring involvement in undoubtedly illegal practices must be explained by their relationship with their seniors in and around Nixon's in-group.[9]

Bureaucratic authority. Another illustration of the relevance of a power perspective on government decision-making processes is provided by Woolsey Biggart and Hamilton.[10] They examined the different types of authority exerted by officials with different roles in a government organization: personal staff of a political chief executive, administrative appointees, and regular executive officers. They found that the scope and limitations of the officials' influence in the policy-making process were clearly determined by the pattern of institutionalized expectations associated with their specific roles. Ironically, therefore, the greatest influence in one's position could be wielded by stringently conforming to the intersubjectively determined role requirements of that position. For instance, in the spoils system of the State of California's administrative structure,

> "Staff aides are supposed to suppress their ideas and interests in favor of the ideas and interests of the person they serve. Their whole purpose is to advance the political and personal well-being of the governor. (....) A member of Brown's staff was (....) chastised for conducting a youth job program from the Governor's Office. While it is appropriate for aides to develop ideas that advance the governor's interests, it is seen as inappropriate for aides to manage bureaucratic functions. The staff member's acts were interpreted as self-promotion, 'grandstanding'. However, these same acts would have been appropriate for a cabinet officer."[11]

Note that this need to conform to role requirements presupposed by the organizational context does not limit itself to lower-level subordinates. On the contrary, Woolsey-Biggart and Hamilton extend their argument to all levels in the hierarchy, including leaders (thereby implicitly providing some support for the well-known psychological notion of the group leader as the most-conforming member, under the strongest obligation to abide with the group norms he is held to represent)[12]:

> "This obligation to act within the bounds of a role does not decrease as one assumes higher positions of authority; a role may grant more discretion in how it is enacted, but there are normative constraints to even the highest level positions. The cabinet officers we described had, in some instances, tens of thousands of subordinates and billion-dollar budgets, but they, no less than a clerk, were constrained to perform their roles in such a way as to demonstrate obeisance to norms. Even chief executives must exercise power within the norms of authority."[13]

Anticipating orders. A final illustration of the salience of a compliance perspective on government decision making comes from the work of Dunsire.[14] While developing his own theory of control, Dunsire provides important clues about the way in which authority and compliance affect decision making, which is also embedded in our propositions, namely by anticipation.[15] Like Woolsey-Biggart and Hamilton, he points to the crucial role of social norms (including symbols, and signs shared throughout the organization) governing authority relationships. In doing so, he draws attention to the importance of acting on socially constructed expectations. This, in turn, suggests that in many bureaucratic settings other than army-type of organizations, overt commands or orders are issued comparatively rarely. Understanding the nature of authority and compliance in organizations, therefore, requires looking for more than simply the overt commands and formal guidelines:

"The good higher civil servant (....) makes it his business to 'get to know the mind of the Minister' on a considerable range of questions, and then is able to extrapolate, as it were, to other questions. He can come very close to recommending what he knows the minister will want to see as the recommendation (....)
The boss does not have to issue instructions if his staff know what his instructions would be if he issued them. Thus he can be 'in command' even if he is not there, and is not aware of the facts of a case. His subordinates, by 'learning his mind', will judge what decisions he would make and then act as if he had made those decisions."[16]

Note that Kelman and Hamilton make the identical point:

"(....) an individual may be acting with a great deal of initiative and single-minded zeal, pursuing sundry personal and ideological agenda in the process, and yet be operating fully under the umbrella of superior orders. Even elaborate and innovative initiatives, and even initiatives that are not specifically known to the superior, may be viewed by the subordinates – sincerely and often realistically – as implicitly authorized: as following broad guidelines for implementation of the superior's policy and reflecting what the superior wanted (or would have wanted) them to do."[17]

Like Kelman and Hamilton do in their study, the case study of the Iran-Contra affair in part IV of this book will provide ample illustration of the important role of the unsaid, and of the implicit presumptions governing authority relationships in government decision-making groups. It is time to examine more closely the phenomena of authority and compliance in government.

Toward theory

Kelman and Hamilton set out to explain how and why, time and again, government officials participate in these kinds of illegal and damaging operations, that often involve the inflicting of harm on other people. In their view, the most basic dynamic is one of authorization (a command to engage in a certain damaging action), routinization (the demand is couched in a routine-like structure and context of bureaucratic action), and dehumanization (the targets to be harmed are officially depicted and perceived as not worthy of restraint or caution – because they are 'enemies', 'villains', 'bums', or whatever – compare this with the in-group/out-group dynamics described in chapter 7).

Probing deeper, Kelman and Hamilton go on to develop a general theory of authority, and use it to attempt to explain who and under what conditions are likely to comply with controversial, immoral, or illegal commands by superiors in the government hierarchy.

Following many political theorists on the subject, they assert that for an (implicit or explicit) authoritative order to be effected, it is necessary that subordinates perceive it as rightful (legitimate). Authority is intimately connected with legitimacy. Legitimacy minimizes the need for coercive measures to back up each and every demand issued. In this sense, from the perspective of the leader, legitimacy is the most economically efficient basis for issuing orders, as

> "(....) the influencing agent does not need to convince the person that adopting the induced behavior is preferable for him, given the available alternatives, but merely that it is required of him (....) Authorities activate commitments or obligations that are inherent in the definition of the citizen's role (....), spelling out the requirements of that role under the existing circumstances. The person's focus is not on what he wants to do, given available alternatives, but on what he sees as required of him."[18]

The authors distinguish between three different processes of social influence that affect relationships between superiors and subordinates in a government hierarchy: compliance, identification and internalization. As is shown in figure 11.1, the three processes differ not only in their antecedents but also in terms of their behavioral impact.

Figure 11.1. Compliance, identification and internalization (Kelman and Hamilton, 1989, p. 111)

Antecedents	COMPLIANCE	IDENTIFICATION	INTERNALIZATION
1 Basis for the importance of the induction	Concern with social effects of behavior	Concern with social anchorage of behavior	Concern with value congruence of behavior
2 Source of power of the influencing agent	Means control	Attractiveness	Credibility
3 Manner of achieving pre-potency of the induced response	Limitation of choice behavior	Delineation of role requirements	Reorganization of means-ends framework

Consequents			
1 Conditions of performance of induced response	Surveillance by influencing agent	Salience of relationship to agent	Relevance of values to issue
2 Conditions of change and extinction fo induced response	Changed perception of conditions for social rewards	Changed perception of conditions for satisfying self-defining relationship	Changed perceptions of conditions for value maximization
3 Type of behavior system in which induced response in embedded	External demands of a specific setting	Expectations defining a specific role	Person's value system

The next step in Kelman and Hamilton's analysis is to link these three influence processes to general properties of the socio-political system that serve as different bases for establishing legitimacy and achieving the desired behavior on the part of subordinates – rules, roles and values:

> "(....) one can postulate a hierarchy of rules, roles, and values that can probably be stated most clearly in the negative. Insofar as a person's socialization has not proceeded beyond the acceptance of rules, we can describe him as integrated by way of compliance. Insofar as his acceptance has not proceeded beyond the acceptance of a role, without linking it to the promotion of larger values, we can describe his means of integration as identification. And insofar as his socialization has led to the acceptance and incorporation of societal values in a personal value system, we can speak of integration by way of internalization."[19]

It is postulated that different categories of public officials (as different types of people in general do) typically use primarily one of these three orientations to evaluate the quality of their performance. In this respect, the authors provide evidence that these different orientations are also correlated to individual tendencies to evaluate who is responsible for certain crimes of obedience.

In particular, rule-oriented and role-oriented individuals are more likely to deny an individual subordinate's responsibility for harmful decisions and actions that he was involved in, while value-oriented individuals tend to assert such individual responsibility (DR and AR patterns). According to Kelman and Hamilton, AR-type (value-oriented) individuals are more likely to regard the *consequences* of the behavior in question. In contrast DR-type (rule- and role-oriented) individuals tend to focus on the official's *obligations* to act in accordance with the implicit or explicit commands of legitimate authorities. In other words, rule- and role-oriented individuals are more prone to damaging compliance, while value-oriented individuals are better equipped to overcome barriers that might lead them to question the official course of action, and even to disobedience (e.g. whistle-blowers).[20]

The key question now becomes: what kinds of individuals belong to the DR and AR types? What about high-level 'subordinates' in policy decision groups? For the time being, the answer to these question is restricted. Kelman and Hamilton's research focused on population-survey data of people's attributions of responsibility in the My Lai case, and, consequently, singled out mostly traditional demographic factors (age, education, religion, social status). They did not have data pertaining to government officials themselves, who are directly confronted with compliance dilemmas.

Compliance in a bureaucracy elaborated

This does not mean that the question has to remain open altogether. Returning to Dunsire's work as representative of many writers on compliance and control in bureaucracies, some speculation is warranted.

First of all, using the bureaucracy literature as his frame of reference, Dunsire has developed a typology of superior-subordinate relationships, outlining three idealtypes remarkably similar to Kelman and Hamilton's trichotomy of influence patterns: duress (cf. K and H's compliance); exchange (in certain respects similar to K and H's identification), and identification (cf. K and H's internalization). Dunsire subsequently tried to find out how these different patterns of achieving compliance apply in bureaucratic settings.

Focusing on his analysis of high-level officials (in Dunsire's terminology: policy advisor types and problem solver types), he remarked that at these levels of abstraction and discretion in the policy-making process, the more formal control mechanisms employed by the 'duress' mode are not available to control the substance of decision. The same goes to a large extent for exchange-mode compliance mechanisms. In fact, the author supposes that much of the behavior of high-level officials has to be 'self-regulating':

"It appears that we have reached the limits of a superior's capacity to control the activities of subordinates by the method of setting norms or thresholds, monitoring discrepancies and applying correction. (Consequently,) subordinates must be induced to share the labor, to do their own norm setting, monitor their own activities, apply their own correction. They must be made (at least partly) self-regulating."[22]

Answering the question above about the type of compliance mechanisms that are likely to be encountered at the top of the government hierarchy, Dunsire logically asserted that, at these levels of government interaction, identification (in K and H's terms "internalization") is the most likely pattern of superior's attempts to achieve compliance. This, for instance, holds true for the ways in which most U.S. presidents attempt to select and manage their appointees and, in particular, their personal staff: loyalty to not only the president personally, but also basic agreement with his ideology and policy programs.

Identification has both cognitive and affective aspects. It is achieved through socialization processes, emphasizing not only the substantive purposes of policy, but also procedural norms governing elite-level interactions, including norms of esprit de corps, collegiality, even elitism (note the similarity between these procedural norms and the institutionalized role expectations identified by Woolsey-Biggart and Hamilton in their research).

The rules of the game at the top. On the basis of this discussion, a number of conclusions may be drawn regarding the propositions 1 to 4 formulated at the outset of this chapter.

1) The salience of power and compliance in interactions between officials in high-level government decision-making groups is clearly manifest, even though compliance factors are much more hidden and subtle than

envisaged by classical theories of organization and bureaucracy.

2) Power and compliance relationships near the top of government do have the kind of subtle properties alluded to in propositions 1 and 2. They are subtle, because technically subordinate officials in fact possess a variety of means to exert influence vis-a-vis their formal superiors (if and when they do so is a question that has long occupied analysts of government and bureaucracy).

3) Meanwhile, the repetitive nature of inter-rank contacts in high-level decision groups tends to promote processes of mutual anticipation, thereby obfuscating the need for explicit command relationships suggested in the formal structure. It follows that proposition 3 has indeed plausibility in interpreting the nature of high-level compliance and control processes.

4) Theoretically, there seems to be a remarkable degree of interdisciplinary overlap between strands of research that have co-existed independently of one another: Kelman and Hamilton's social-psychological framework on compliance, and Dunsire's work, which is derived exclusively from Organization Theory and Public Administration.

Compliance in policymaking: the leadership factor

It follows that it is effective for leaders of high-level policymaking groups to offer procedural and substantive guidance that serves to foster and strengthen identification and esprit de corps among their immediate associates. If they fail to do so, they are likely in the long run to be less able to steer the policymaking process. Very few top leaders can continue for a longer period to manage policy activities on the basis of pragmatic exchange relationships or mere coercion alone. Jozef Stalin was probably an extreme exception that confirms this rule (although even Stalin had charismatic, identification-inducing traits in his interpersonal style). Even so, the price was high, both in human costs as well as in policy effectiveness – the self-destructive dynamics of the system were especially marked during the late thirties when Stalin had most of the country's military leadership killed or locked up, seriously affecting the military power of the Red Army.

Despite the fact that, generally, the government leader's room to maneuver vis-a-vis his immediate entourage has its limits, leaders near the top of a bureaucracy may nevertheless exert considerable influence in the course of deliberation and decision making of anyone group meeting they are involved in. That is, if they play the game in accordance with the proper rules and expectations of interaction, as defined by roles, organizational culture, and group norms. An organizational or political leader may, in the first place, be influential in determining the agenda for discussion, and thus in defining the focus and the boundaries of the decision process. Some topics and alternatives are ruled 'in', while others are rules 'out'. Secondly, to a certain extent, some leaders are able to determine the composition of the group by encouraging some officials to participate while not inviting others. These two points of leader influence are illustrated for government

170

decision making by De Rivera in his discussion of President Truman and his group during the Korean crisis of 1950:

> "Towards the end of the meeting, the Undersecretary of State (....) said, 'I'd like to talk about the political aspects of the situation.' Reportedly, the President snapped back, 'We're not going to talk about politics. I'll handle the political affairs.' (....) The Undersecretary of State did not speak again during the meeting and does not appear to have been present at subsequent meetings of the group."[23]

De Rivera is quick to recognize the benefits, but also the risks, of this constraining role of the leader:

> "It must be observed that while the President's authority hindered communication, it pulled his advisors together. A weak leadership might have permitted the development of disputes with resultant disunity and lack of action (....) since a strong leader is bound to exert a normative force that inhibits the expression and development of ideas contrary to his own, he must go out of his way to encourage his group to act freely."[24]

Thirdly, leaders may actively steer the decision process itself by the manner in which they conduct the discussion, and the specific decisional role that is allotted to the group in that respect. Different personalities have different styles, and different situations require different stances:

> "Often, meetings are conducted in quite a different way from the (....) crisis situation where President Truman essentially directed a discussion with the aim of helping *himself* to make a decision. Neustadt's description of one of President Eisenhower's regular cabinet meetings, shows the President *guiding* a discussion with the aim of having the group make a decision or reach a consensus."[25]

There are many other examples that document the potential impact of group leaders on the course and outcomes of group decisions, even in the allegedly 'horizontal' and collegial atmosphere of high-level policy decision groups (this will, of course, partly vary with the formal position of organizational or government leaders: the potential impact of a U.S. president is generally larger than that of a continental European prime minister, personality factors not considered; the same goes for a department head versus the chairman of an interdepartmental committee).

McCauley's reassessment of the ExCom decision process during the Cuban missile crisis is a case in point. Like Lebow, he shows that while president Kennedy may have adopted an open and non-directive leadership style during the agonizing days of deliberation, his actions during the initial stages after the news of the missile bases became known, were very different. His initial definition of the situation was rigid, and ruled out alternative ways of thinking about the situation, thereby strongly delimiting the premises of the work of the ExCom: a forceful response was considered compulsive and there was no room for more relaxed assessments of the situation as the one advanced by Secretary of Defense McNamara who suggested that it did not make much difference for the United States to be hurt by missiles coming from Cuba or from Moscow.[26]

Hollander has commented upon this ability of leaders to stretch their influence in steering group discussion by observing that, even in quasi-egalitarian situations where subordinates possess a variety of means to counteract the leader, legitimate leaders tend to be granted a so-called 'idiosyncracy credit': the benefit of the doubt, extra leeway to present his views as the basis for further action.[27]

The study of the impact of government leaders on their immediate entourage is bound to suffer from the lack of solid evidence available to contemporaneous observers. Only in accidental cases is the public provided with a well-documented picture what goes on behind the scenes of government. This lack of data makes it possible for inaccurate assessments of a certain leader's role and influence to develop and persist unchecked for quite some time. This seems to have been the case with president Eisenhower, who, as it appears new studies using fresh evidence now disclosed, has long been seriously underestimated.[28]

It will be interesting to see whether a similar re-appraisal will eventually befall on the president who has so often been compared with Eisenhower, Ronald Reagan. As the case study of the secret U.S. arms deliveries to Iran in part IV will indicate, the 'Eisenhower image' of Reagan may be an oversimplification and underestimation: for certain issues high on his personal political agenda, Reagan could be quite adamant, and quite able to achieve compliance from subordinates.

Specification: advising the rulers

A final and more elaborate illustration of the importance of (anticipatory) compliance factors is provided by considering the practice of advice-giving and the interaction between government leaders and their advisors in small-group settings.

Speaking Truth to Power: this title of Wildavsky's book on policy analysis neatly reflects the dilemma of policy advisors, whether they be government employees or external specialists (although for those within government, the dilemma is probably somewhat more marked than for those outside). It suggests that advice-giving is a delicate business.

From the perspective of compliance, the adviser's dilemma arises when he or she holds an opinion known to be different from political (or hierarchical) superiors, the advises: should one state one's point of view as frankly as possible, hoping to change the current course of action, yet risking to be negatively evaluated by these 'significant others'; or should one modify

172

one's stance in anticipation of criticism and/or formal and informal sanctions on the part of advises?

The dilemma can be restated more analytically in terms of a number of trade-off choices that the adviser confronts in a situation of policy disagreements between himself and one or more office-holders.

First of all, there is the choice between short-term and long-term considerations: in the short run, the adviser may win the battle over the contended issue by a variety of methods (mobilizing administrative support, going public, making package deals, sabotaging implementation of alternative proposals), but this may prove to be a Pyrrhic victory, in the sense that it will block his future effectiveness as an adviser.

Related to this is the adviser's balance of personal interests: by becoming an advocate for an impopular option, the adviser may – see above – suffer substantial career damage – that is, when his advocacy undermines his personal relationship with the adviser or his broader organizational and political power position. In other words, there is the choice between an interests-based or an issue-based preference structure. From the perspective of not only his personal interests but also those of his own bureaucratic constituency (in general, most bureaucratic advisers represent large organizations or segments in their interaction with peers and political office-holders), it may be wise for the dissenting adviser to modify his position. This has to be traded off against the importance that the adviser and his power base attach to the specific issue at hand.

Furthermore, the dilemma may also involve ethical trade-offs, in particular when the adviser perceives that the office-holders and other actors in the decision-making process are pursuing a controversial or even devious course of action. This problem arose for some of President Johnson and Nixon advisers concerning the use of secret bombing campaigns in Cambodia and Laos, the use of napalm, and the all-out terror-bombing of North-Vietnamese civilian targets.[29] In these situations, the adviser is faced with the choice between the ends-means perspective underlying the official course of action, and his own set of moral or professional norms: will he 'superimpose' his private norms and beliefs upon those provided by his political superiors or his organizational environment?

This advisor's dilemma arises time and again during major policy decision episodes. The best-known examples of this dilemma can be found in national security and defense policies. Take examples such as the Tonkin Gulf incident (North-Vietnamese attacks on American ships and personnel), the Taiwan crisis (Communist-Chinese pressures on the Nationalist-Chinese stronghold of Formosa), strategic issues during the Korean War, the Cuban Missile Crisis, or the Iranian Rescue Mission. In each case both civilian and military advisers had to recommend courses of action which might entail choices between peace and war, and which, consequently, could have a massive impact on the position of – in this case – the United States in general, but the President and his administration in particular. These, in turn, might reflect upon the advisers and their own agencies.

Similar dilemmas of advice-giving can be found with regard to different advisers in different fields of policymaking: natural scientists and engineers in debates on nuclear energy, medical scientists and political advisors during the Swine Flu scare during the Ford presidency, environmentalist scientists concerning conservation of natural resources.[30]

The way in which leaders organize and mange their flows of information and advice is essential for the quality of government decisions and actions.[31] Stated in terms of the analytical perspective presented here, several issues emerge:
– the *selection* of advisors: who participates, and who does not?
– the determination of the *agenda:* what is under discussion and what not?
– the *definition of the issue:* what is the range of debate and alternatives considered for any issue on the agenda?
– the *rules of interaction:* how does the group operate? What is expected of various actors in the group? How does the group reach decisions?
– the *compliance factor:* what is the formal and informal distribution of influence between the leader and different advisors within the group? What balance is found between compliance tendencies and the need for a broad and sharp discussion of the issues?

For the advisor, a key problem is to find a balance between his *obligations* to the leader and the institutionally governed expectations pending on his advisory role on the one hand, and the *assessment of the consequences of alternative options* that he is supposed to contribute to (note that this formulation gropes back to Woolsey-Biggart and Hamilton's and Kelman and Hamilton's categories).

It appears from the literature that more often than not, the participants in advisory groups resolve these questions in a manner that distorts the quality of the resulting decisions that emerge from the advisory process. Both De Rivera and George – who are among the few authors that have investigated the small group dynamics of advice-giving in governmental decision making – point to the potential *distortions* of the advisory process.

De Rivera mentions four kinds of disturbing influences impinging upon the quality of advice-giving:

a) A biased selection of inner-circle advisors. This produces a group that, collectively, tends to go along with whatever the chief executive believes in. Part of this bias can be explained by the political nature of advisory appointments, but probably even more by the fact that advice-giving fulfills important secondary functions next to spelling out and analyzing a great number of options for decision. More often than not, advisors serve as providers of emotional support to executives, assisting them to maintain their psychological balance and composure in the face of disruptive pressures and the stresses of complex decisions. This kind of emotional support is unlikely to be provided by known sceptics and critics of the administration's or the chief executive's policies. The same goes for people temperamentally unsuited to the leader's needs. Therefore, leaders in selecting

174

their advisors, are likely to turn to 'trusted, liked sources'.[32] The importance attached by chief executives of these psychological functions as opposed to the substantive functions of advice-giving, is likely to increase during periods of high stress.

Some political leaders seem especially bent on obtaining emotional support rather than substantive counsel from their advisors. Woodrow Wilson is a case in point – witness his peculiar ties with Colonel House, who lost his effectiveness from the very moment he started to steer a more independent and critical course.[33] Richard Nixon seemed to surround himself with both kinds of advisors: the policy advisors like Kissinger, and chums like Bebe Rebozo for relaxation and getting away from it all. The same goes for Eisenhower's famous 'gang', that complemented trusted political associates as John Foster Dulles and Sherman Adams.[34] The problem with these 'combined' modes of advisors is that it is hard to say who were most influential. It might very well be that Rebozo, even unwittingly, had a major effect on President Nixon's thinking about certain policy issues, more than most cabinet secretaries who were kept at a great distance in the Nixon administration.

b) A tendency among advisors to present a good image to others, in order to maximize their effectiveness. Advisors may be more concerned about living up to these desired images as competent bureau managers, sharp analysts, skillful diplomats, or liberal thinkers, than to provide sound advice related to the problems at hand, and the needs of the chief executive.

c) Advice can be distorted by the role conflict experienced by many high-level advisors: many 'advisors' in high-level government groups are actually at the same time leaders or representatives of bureaucratic or external agencies or units. De Rivera has argued that in many instances, advisors' thinking and actions may be dominated by considerations relating to their institutional constituencies. This may often be at odds with the more generalistic, coordinating perspective of the chief executive that calls upon their opinions. The role conflict thus experienced by the advisors may not always be resolved in favor of the needs of the adviser.

The problem of advisors 'going native' can be exemplified most clearly by the attitudes of high-level military advisors to the political leadership. Certainly in the United States, but also in many other countries, military leaders' advice about certain issues of national defense or war fighting tends to be strongly influenced by their specific position within the armed forces: air-, sea- or land-based. To put it bluntly, military leaders are prone to think in terms of their own respective force's interests first, and only then consider the broader perspectives on the issue. The potentially detrimental effects of this biased advice-giving are partly upset by the fact that these biases are to a certain extent predictable: they are hardly expected to do otherwise. Secondly, the various biased perspectives can be pitted against each other, and, taken together, provide a fairly rich assessment of the situation and the options at hand.[35]

d) Advice can be contaminated by the personal power needs of the advisors. Ultimately, this may induce them to try and persuade, manipulate or even mislead the chief executive into positions that are personally advantageous to the advisor, and do not necessarily make for sound policy.

To some observers, this pathology of advice-giving eventually befell the duo Nixon-Kissinger in certain areas of American foreign policy. Kissinger's personal aggrandizement overcame his desire to serve the president, who, in his second term, was quickly degenerating into lame duck status anyhow, due to the Watergate scandal.[36]

George has taken the argument somewhat further and identifies nine types of 'malfunctions' of the advisory process. Considering these, it is remarkable how many of them can be directly understood keeping in mind the compliance dilemmas for policy advisors outlined above. George mentions the following distorted situations:

1) When the decision maker and his advisers agree too readily on the nature of the problem facing them and on a response to it.
2) When advisers and policy advocates take different positions and debate them before the executive, but their disagreements do not cover the full range of relevant hypotheses and alternative options.
3) When there is no advocate for an unpopular policy option.
4) When advisers to the executive thrash out their disagreements over policy without the executive's knowledge with a unanimous recommendation (pre-arranging inter-bureaucratic compromises that defy political-level control).
5) When advisers agree privately among themselves that the executive ought to face up to a difficult decision but no one is willing to alert him to the need to do so.
6) When the executive, faced with an important problem to decide, is dependent upon a single channel of information.
7) When the key assumptions and premises of a plan which the executive is asked to adopt have been evaluated only by advocates of that option.
8) When the executive asks advisers for their opinions on a preferred course of action but does not request a qualified group to examine more carefully the negative judgment offered by one or more advisers.
9) When the executive is impressed by the consensus among his advisers on behalf of a particular option but fails to ascertain how firm the consensus is, how it was achieved, and whether it is justified.[37]

It appears that distortions 1, 3, 5, 7, and 9 can (but need not) stem from advisers' anticipatory compliance with the chief executive's real or perceived policy stances. Note that the motivation for this compliance may vary, as pointed out by the examples provided by De Rivera, and theoretically underpinned by Kelman and Hamilton's as well as Dunsire's, typology of compliance situations. Advisors, too, may be rule-based, role-based, or value-based persons. Dunsire has made it plausible that at senior levels, value-based individuals are most likely to be encountered. Other than

176

Kelman and Hamilton who seem to think that a value orientation provides a good chance for non-compliance with disastrous or illegal policy proposals from the leader, Dunsire implies that value-oriented individuals, too, can be highly compliant. This merely requires techniques of achieving compliance that are designed to be effective with this category of persons, such as invoking esprit de corps, and generating their basic support for the overall direction of policy at its most general level. Commitments thus initiated are hard to break when an advisor finds himself in disagreement with his (political) superiors over a certain issue.

11.4. Implications for groupthink analysis

These final observations tie together the different strands of the argument, as outlined in proposition 5 stated above and repeated here:

> In high-level decision groups, closed leadership styles combined with group or organizational norms of compliance may produce groupthink tendencies. This need not involve overt pressures for conformity; instead the group members are prone to excessive anticipatory compliance with the chief executive's assumptions, perspectives, and preferred alternatives.

It has, by now, sufficiently been shown that this is a realistic scenario for flawed decision making in government advisory or decision-making groups. The key question for groupthink analysts now becomes under what conditions, how, and to what extent these processes of anticipatory compliance come about and are maintained. While any definite answers to this question can, as yet, not be given due to lack of empirical research, the discussion above does suggest a few facilitating conditions:

1) A chief executive whose status as group leader is firmly accepted by the group members: the more strongly the personal bond between leader and group members, the greater the likelihood of quick compliance with his real or perceived demands.
2) Rules of interaction within the group in which it is accepted unquestioningly that the chief executive sets the agenda and defines the scope of discussion for the predominant policy issues.
3) External conditions such as conflicts over policy that appear to necessitate determined action, enhancing the perceived need for strong leadership from the chief executive.
4) A basic consensus about the general gist of the policy to be pursued among the advisors/group members, as opposed to a situation dominated by bureau-political factionalism and strife.

At the outset of this discussion, Kelman and Hamilton's analysis of 'crimes of obedience' was presented. Might groupthink play a part in the policy process that leads to crimes of obedience? It is surmised here that, given a certain set of conditions, it may very well be. Apart from the conditions that may lead a decision group to fall prey to the second, compliance-based pathway to groupthink identified in the preliminary revised model of groupthink in part II, two additional conditions appear relevant in inducing such governmental groups to engage in or authorize decisions or actions that are extremely harmful to other actors in their environment:

5) The group is confronted with external opposition, criticizing the group's course of action, and, in particular, the effectiveness or the legitimacy of the chief executive's group leader.
6) The group operates in a situation of perceived win-lose conflicts with other groups inside or outside the government (an extension of point 3).

These two additional conditions are derived from the earlier discussion of the social-psychological literature on intergroup competition and conflict, which have also found a certain measure of support in real-life settings.[38]

The Watergate conspiracy and cover-up constitutes one of the best-documented examples of such a compliance-based, extremely harmful mode of groupthink. Both McCauley and Kelman and Hamilton have documented this at length, and it does not need to be repeated here. Are there other examples? Historical examples that spring to mind but that have not yet been fully researched from this perspective are the decision to start the extermination of the Jews arrived at by Hitler and his advisers during the Wannsee conference, Eden's domination of the British cabinet during the Suez crisis of 1956 (matching Chamberlain's powerful hold during much of the appeasement period in 1937-1939), and Egypt's decision to go for war with Israel in 1973.[39]

A more systematically documented instance of compliance-based groupthink concerns the fateful decision episode during a series of teleconferences which amounted in a recommendation to launch the Space Shuttle Challenger in January 1986, despite novel and potentially dangerous weather conditions (low temperatures). Potential dissenters to the unprecedented and inherently risky decision were quick to comply with superiors' signs of displacements at their assessment. This was especially marked when concerned Morton Thiokol engineers were overruled by their company's management, which, in turn, did not want to disturb its important clients at NASA who indicated a strong determination to proceed with launched – pressured as they were by the agency's political and funding-related need to keep up the NASA image and proceed with a tightly planned flight schedule involving commercial transport. This cumulative chain of (anticipatory) compliance produced an ill-fated choice to ignore the initial recommendation not to launch.[40]

In part IV of this study, a preliminary start is made to further test the usefulness of the compliance perspective on groupthink. However, it remains for more systematic experimental research to assess the relative salience of the different pathways (cohesion-based, compliance-based) to groupthink.

178

Notes

1. McCauley (1989).
2. Blau and Scott (1962), Thompson (1961), Downs (1967), Etzioni (1977).
3. Simon et al. (1950), Dunsire (1978).
4. Merton (1957), Crozier (1964).
5. Rourke (1969), Heclo (1977), Jenkins and Gray (1985), Suleiman (ed. 1984).
6. Dunsire (1978), Etzioni-Halévy (1982), Gruber (1987).
7. See Crozier (1964).
8. Kelman and Hamilton (1989).
9. Haldeman (1978), Dean (1982).
10. Woolsey-Biggart and Hamilton (1984), see also Hambrick (1981).
11. Woolsey-Biggart and Hamilton (1984), pp.544-545.
12. Compare Homans (1950) with Hollander (1978) on this point.
13. Woolsey-Biggart and Hamilton (1984), p.548.
14. Dunsire (1978), who fits into a long tradition of authors on problems of control and coordination in bureaucratic settings. See Etzioni (1977), Perrow (1979), Gruber (1987), Bovens (1990).
15. See also Friedrich's famous rule of anticipated reactions, Friedrich (1963), as well as Olsen (1983).
16. Dunsire (1978), p.29.
17. Kelman and Hamilton (1989), p.50.
18. Kelman and Hamilton (1989), pp.90-91.
19. Kelman and Hamilton (1989), p.114.
20. On whistle-blowing, see Glazer (1983); Bovens (1987b).
21. Dunsire (1978), pp.133-137.
22. Dunsire (1978), p.131.
23. De Rivera (1968), p.222.
24. Ibid, p.223.
25. Ibid, p.225.
26. McCauley (1989), see also Lebow (1981).
27. Hollander (1978).
28. See Ambrose (1985); Greenstein (1982).
29. Gelb and Betts (1979).
30. See Ford (1986), Neustadt and May (1986), Preimack and Von Hippel (1974), respectively for each of these instances.
31. See the compelling argument made by George (1980), as well as by Janis in the final chapter of Janis (1989).
32. Milburn (1972).
33. George and George (1956).
34. For Nixon, see Nixon (1978); Haldeman (1978); Mazlish (1972); for Eisenhower, see Ambrose (1985).
35. On the dynamics of military advice-giving, see Betts (1977).
36. Hersch (1986).
37. For a fuller discussion, see George (1980), pp.121-136.
38. See chapter 7, in particular also Rabbie and Visser (1976).
39. See Janis (1982a); Jervis, Lebow and Gross Stein (1985).
40. Hirokawa et al. (1988), Charles (1989), and also Kelman and Hamilton (1989).

12 – Two modes of groupthink: optimism, pessimism, and the impact of accountability

12.1. Introduction

Decisions by the kind of high-level policy-planning groups that are most salient to groupthink analysis, are highly consequential for many people and organizations outside the membership of the group. For instance, many non-routine decisions by government agencies affect individual clients, client groups, other government agencies, and, occasionally, foreign organizations and governments. They may even affect the entire population of the country, as in major tax reforms.

For that reason, government decision making is embedded in structures of public accountability: provisions that serve to substantiate the responsibility of key political and bureaucratic actors for the quality of their decisions, and their impact upon different segments of society. There are many forms that these accountability provisions can take: juridical liability, political control by representative bodies, hierarchical oversight by bureaucratic superiors, and informal accountability through the media and public opinion. Many of these provisions also constrain the decision makers of large corporations, be it in different ways, e.g. by a different set of societal rules and expectations.

Through the existence of accountability provisions, major policy decisions become consequential not only for the recipients, but also for the actors involved in taking them. The 'bigger', the less routine a decision, the greater its potential impact upon the position and reputation of the decision makers. Ultimately, decision makers are judged by their environment in terms of success and failure. The criteria that are used may differ (goal effectiveness, moral and political acceptability, juridical soundness), as well as the fora before which decision makers can be called to render account (ranging from a board of directors in a firm to parliamentary committees, and the courts).

The existence of accountability provisions makes visible the idea that, in general, most corporate or governmental decision makers and decision groups do not operate autonomously in a social vacuum, but instead can be called upon to justify, defend, and face sanctions with regard to their past, present, and future decisions.[1]

It seems interesting to examine the effects of different structures of accountability in different types of problem situations on the processes and outcomes of group decision making. It is to be remembered, however, that in reality, accountability structures constitute but one of the organizational-environmental constraints operating upon decisional groups, competing for prominence with considerations of cost-effectiveness, organizational traditions and norms, political strategy, and power. In practice, these other factors may very well interact with or overcome accountability-related considerations in influencing the behavioral dispositions of decision makers.

In this chapter, it will be argued that, from a contextual point of view emphasizing the impact of accountability structures upon the reasoning and calculation of organizational actors operating in decision groups, two generically different patterns of groupthink can be discerned:
– type I groupthink: collective avoidance;
– type II groupthink: collective overoptimism.
Before arriving at this conclusion, a brief introduction to the issue of accountability is in order.

12.2. Accountability and group decision making: a conceptual model

How does the fact that most high-level corporate and governmental decision groups operate within a structure of accountability affect the behavior of decision makers that are part of these groups? What follows is an attempt to sketch a simple model that produces with certain hypotheses concerning the impact of accountability structures at a very general, undifferentiated level; these may be specified according to specific institutional contexts. This model rests upon some key assumptions:

1) decision makers generally tend to anticipate the consequences which their stances and actions within the decisional group may have for their individual position within that group and its organizational and/or political environment (group decision makers as individual, self-interested calculators)[2];

2) the behavioral dispositions that flow from structures of accountability that operate upon a decision group are mediated by individual members' perceptions of these structures and their possible implications (perceived accountability impact rather than 'objective' structures).[3] The model is depicted in figure 12.1.

The following propositions (elaborated below) have been inspired by this general model:

Proposition 1. If members of a decision group perceive the issue confronting them as a problem that may result in failure rather than an opportunity for success, they will attempt as much as possible to avoid being associated with the decision process concerning the issue. The stronger the perceived likelihood of a major policy failure, the greater the motivation to avoid being associated with it.

Figure 12.1. Structures of accountability and decision-making behavior

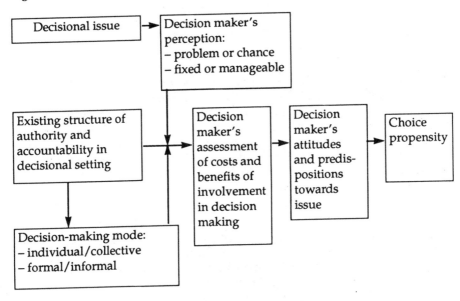

Proposition 1a. There are three main strategies open to individual group members who want to avoid being held personally accountable for an issue they perceive as a potential fiasco, and who are – for one reason or another – convinced that they will not be able to change the outcome of the group's decision process:

a) non-participation in decision making or termination of group membership;

b) hiding within the group in an attempt to spread responsibility as broad as possible and thus minimize adverse personal consequences;

c) engaging in a process of ritualized dissent not aimed at achieving policy change, but primarily to cover one's personal position in the face of future evaluations.

Proposition 2. If members of a decision group perceive the issue confronting them as an opportunity for success rather than as a problem that may result in failure, they will be strongly motivated to cooperate with one another in achieving the expected gains. The stronger the perceived likelihood of a major policy success, the greater the motivation to be associated with the group responsible for achieving it.

12.3. The irony of accountability: propositions elaborated

Based on these propositions, it is illustrated how, given specific definitions of the decisional issue by group members, structures of accountability can

183

promote groupthink tendencies. This, in turn, leads to the two types of groupthink outlined above.

Type 1 groupthink: collective avoidance

Re-examining the three modes of response to pessimistic perceptions of a decisional issue by individual group members, two of these seem particularly conducive to the kind of stress-induced defensive avoidance on the part of decision groups, that was originally outlined by Janis. However, expanding upon Janis' analysis, propositions 1 and 1a provide alternative, complementary indications of when and why this may happen. Other than Janis – who would conceivably argue that accountability provisions are to be viewed simply as one type among other stressors acting upon the group – it is not supposed here that all (or the great majority other than the lone dissenter) members of a decision group involved in a major policy fiasco adhere to the collective (and inadequate) perception of the situation, and strongly supportive of the group's course of action. Rather, their adherence or lack of substantive opposition stems from an individualistic calculation of personal interests: the desire to escape individual responsibility.

Voice?

One of these modes of escaping or minimizing responsibility for impending policy failures is voicing dissent during decisional deliberations. The obvious intention of voicing dissent is to change the outcomes of the group choice. However, and most interesting from the perspective of groupthink, it may serve another function, namely to provide cover for the record. This pattern of 'strategic, ritualized' dissent is exemplified by the role of the city of Amsterdam's Public Works department during the flawed decision making process concerning a new City Hall annex Opera House (the so-called Stopera fiasco, which triggered a budget increase of more than 150 million guilders on an original budget of 300 million guilders). Irritated by earlier attempts by the planners to keep Public Works out of the 'decisional loop', its director and other representatives considered themselves absolved from the responsibility to use their expertise in managing large-scale projects to prevent the fiasco from happening. During the meetings of a municipal committee overseeing the construction project, Public Works did note some points of concern to make clear its reservations about the project – yet it never pressed the issue. Afterwards, Public Works was quick to assert the predictions and its own lack of responsibility for the failures that were made.[4]

In this example, the very structure of accountability for decision making and coordination of construction appeared to carry the roots of failure. Relevant expertise (within Public Works) was not put to adequate use – probably for reasons of protecting or extending bureaucratic turf. As a consequence, competent experts did not feel the obligation to go to great lengths in trying to correct the built-in weaknesses of the project. To do so would mean stirring up political and bureaucratic irritation at City Hall, where the Stopera project was a pet issue. So Public Works officials perceived only one remaining strategy: clearing one's tracks for the future by taking a formalistic approach without really attempting to influence the decision process.

It is surmised that this is a very common strategy. An official or agency involved in something perceived as 'bad news' calculates or assesses what parties and coalitions are involved in the project. If political leverage and commitment to the issue or project are judged to be substantive, there is little hope of being able to block it: the costs of doing so in terms of engendering the disfavor of patrons or other influential actors are likely to be judged as too high. Subsequently, the official or agency will assess the extent of his or its own involvement in the issue: "Will we be blamed when things indeed go wrong?" If the answer to this question appears to be a positive "yes", there is no alternative but to stay involved and make the best of it (damage containment). If the question can be answered in the negative, minimalization of responsibility through strategic formalism and dissociation from the main current of decision making, will be pursued. Registering dissent for the record fits into this framework. It is the administrative mirror image of the 'domestication of dissenters' strategy encountered in groupthink – such as in the case of the making of President Johnson's Vietnam policy.[5]

Hiding

An alternative response to anticipated accountability problems is seeking refuge in the group. In an organizational or political context, not everyone can distance himself from a collective commitment or effort that one is supposed to be involved in. Also, not everybody can realistically expect not to suffer from giving consistent (be it ineffective) criticism of ongoing policies. Many actors simply do not have the formal or hierarchical independence or self-confidence to be able to take such a stance.

This type of response to impending policy failure or embarrassment is probably the most common one: trying to avoid individual responsibility by shifting the burden to a group or collectivity. If anything goes wrong, the blame will be shared, not focused.

Using the group as refuge comes very close to Janis' original formulation of groupthink. But whereas his emphasis is on the personal-psychological functions of shifting responsibility for decision making, it is argued here that formal and informal structures of accountability operate to the same effect. The political and bureaucratic balance of rewards and costs can lead individual actors to resort to an identical, yet generically different, strategy of collective defensive avoidance. Consider the following example.

Towards the end of March 1980, the occupation of the American Embassy in post-revolutionary Tehran had been going on for five months. Secret negotiations to set free of the fifty-five American hostages had produced nothing and were getting more and more deadlocked. The hostage crisis was seriously affecting the Carter presidency. With elections coming up in November, the President's poll ratings were at an all-time low. There was great pressure to 'do something.'[6]

At this time, U.S. authorities had begun to recontemplate the option of a military rescue attempt, which had originally been discounted as too dangerous. By March, this seemed to have changed. Under the supervision of the Joint Chiefs of Staff, preparations had progressed up to the point where it was said that a rescue mission was 'feasible'. As the pressures mounted, the military option gained momentum among Carter and his advisors, notably National Security Advisor Brzezinski. The only major opponent of the rescue plan was Secretary of State Vance. One of the most intriguing features of the decision-making process – which predictably was heavily criticized soon after the failure of the raid (in the Holloway Report reflecting the official investigation) – was that the operational details of the mission were left largely undiscussed. No one questioned the information provided by the military on this point. Yet at least one participant in the key meetings must have had serious doubts about what he heard. The Director of Central Intelligence, Admiral Turner, had been given an internal CIA-evaluation of the rescue plan. It was highly critical of the operation and questioned many of its key assumptions. In particular, it stated that "a loss rate of 60 per cent for the embassy hostages represents the best estimate".[7] There is no evidence that Turner ever mentioned the report and its contents to any of his colleagues or the President.

Why did he not speak up? Turner's silence can only be explained if one takes into account the context of decision making, in particular the enormous public and political pressures which acted upon the President and his advisors at the time: grave damage to the personal and international authority of Carter and the United States in general, impending presidential elections in the face of all-time low poll ratings, and permanent congressional pressures for action. At the end of March, all but Vance were desperate that some action be taken. That even Carter supported a military operation was in itself a dramatic illustration of the effects of the crisis. Carter had come to the presidency advocating the peaceful settlement of international disputes as a basic principle of foreign policy. It had taken him great pains to now acknowledge that force was necessary.

Turner was of course aware of all this. He was also aware of the broad consensus supporting the rescue option: it had to be tried. He just could not bring himself to disturb the momentum which had developed in the group, despite the gloomy figures at his possession. Finally, as a player in the continuing bureaucratic battles at the top of the policy apparatus, Turner was quick to notice the speed and depth of Vance's demise following his continued opposition to the mission. So Turner remained silent and hid in the group.

The Iran example reads like a classic manifestation of mindguarding and suppression of personal doubts as formulated by Janis. This is not denied. Yet it is argued here that they sprang not solely from group-dynamic factors but also from an assessment of the bureaucratic pros and cons on the part of the DCI. He reckoned that his explicit 'opposition':

a) would greatly disturb the growing sense of faith in the mission;
b) would probably not change the outcome of the decision anyhow, because all seemed determined to proceed;
c) if effective after all, would only earn him the scorn of Brzezinski and Carter's staff for blocking the only promise of a quick termination;
d) no matter what the outcome, would probably hurt his relationship with the President who was in no mood to distinguish between the bad message and its messenger.

Under these conditions, it was far more secure not to rock the boat. Turner and the CIA would not be among the chief culprits if the mission would fail, because the CIA was hardly involved in its actual planning. Moreover, the key decisions were made by the group, not by Turner alone. Formally, the rescue decision was the President's. Turner must also have reckoned that it was his duty to support the President through the depths of the crisis, and not criticize him. Giving support by withholding disquieting information was an act of loyalty, an example of team playing – at least in Turner's perception.[8]

Type 2 groupthink: collective overoptimism

The second main way in which accountability structures can adversely effect the quality of group decision making occurs with an entirely different class of decisional issues, and decision makers' perceptions of these issues: golden opportunities, chances-not-to-miss, strategies that cannot fail, and the like. This line of reasoning hinges upon the idea embedded in proposition 1 concerning decision makers' desires to be associated with successes.

Being associated with successful decisions enhances an actor's political or bureaucratic reputation and status. In these cases, it is less important who is responsible for what elements in the policy. The main thing is to have taken part in the project – and have the right people know it (cf. bandwagon effects). Moreover, in many cases, a successful outcome can only be achieved through the cooperation of others. In a political and administrative environment, this usually boils down to obtaining the consent of all the sections and bureaus concerned, either by formal consultation ('obtaining initials on a memo') or by engineering consensus in interunit or interdepartmental committees or joint task forces.

The combination of the perception of the likelihood of obtaining a specific success and the perceived need for collaboration as a prerequisite to effectively implement the necessary policy decisions, leads decision makers to value their membership of the policy planning group or committee in question. In this respect, they perceive the preservation of a congenial, cooperative atmosphere as an important asset in achieving the desired outcomes. Hence some of the basic preconditions for groupthink come into existence. What kinds of policy situations are likely to give rise to such dynamics? The following examples are singled out:

- Policymaking during the so-called 'honeymoon period' of newly-established regimes or governments, which occurs mostly in spoils-system democracies and politically volatile states experiencing regime changes. This is a limited period in which newly-prominent groups of policymakers are given more leeway than usual by domestic political forces to formulate and implement the programs which brought them to power.
- Decision making concerning the planning and preparation of 'big projects' (infrastructural investments, the development of public enterprises, policies).
- Military contingency planning, in particular instances where the military is called upon to perform high-profile missions).[9]

In each of these cases, a spirit of optimism or 'can-doism' prevails, which may easily lead to overconfidence on the part of the decision makers in question. The desire to score a point can easily overcome day-to-day prudence ('we are on to something, and if everyone sticks together, we are going to make it').[10] Here, the structures of responsibility breed not defensiveness and caution but eagerness and high group morale. And as we know since Janis, this can be a two-edged sword. Each of the aforementioned classes of decisional situations is elaborated briefly.

Honeymoons destroyed

The classic example of disastrous overconfidence during a honeymoon period is the Bay of Pigs episode, analyzed by Janis' initial and most convincing case study. The spirit which existed at the time in the new Kennedy administration has been pointedly described by Schlesinger:

> "The currents of vitality radiated out of the White House, flowed through the government and created a sense of vast possibility. The very idea of the new President taking command as tranquilly and naturally as if this whole life had prepared him for it could not but stimulate a flood of buoyant optimism. (....) Intelligence was at least being applied to public affairs. Euphoria reigned; we thought for a moment that the world was plastic and the future unlimited."[11]

This pervasive sense of self-competence and optimism contributed to the lack of critical questioning of the ill-fated and thoroughly misconceived invasion plan, as analyzed by Janis in his book.

Hensley and Griffin's study of the Kent State Controversy illustrates the second type of situation. The University's Board of Governors had developed the idea to build a new Gymnasium. This was a prestigious project, which would enhance the University's facilities and hence its reputation. Moreover, it would be a visible testimony of the Board's administrative and fund-raising abilities. Ventures like these generally become pet projects for their initiators and supporters. So when protests were voiced against the planned location of the Gymnasium, the Board would not give in. This provided a starting point for a drawn-out conflict, resulting in the building of the Gymnasium at the price in an upsurge of negative publicity, and serious conflicts within and between students, faculty staff and administrators. The building was there, but it was a Pyrrhic victory for the Board.[12]

The Kent State case is quite typical for the pitfalls that can beset big-project decision making. Big projects – such as the construction of dams, bridges and roads, the development of airports and urban renewal plans, decisions to produce and market new products – are intrinsically attractive to policy makers who want to accomplish something (this was also true for the city administrators and planners initiating the Stopera project discussed above – not for Public Works, who held a fundamentally different perception of the costs and benefits of the undertaking). Many people, from the planners and R&D people to the construction contractors, have a stake in the project's continuation. At the same time, however, big projects because of their very scale and impact are certain to attract a fair amount of critical comments and opposition: they often require the destruction or removal of other valued things, they cost a lot of money, they abruptly change the environmental or scenic status quo, they affect prerogatives and aspirations of organizations not involved in the plan's development, they employ new, untested technologies, they have large opportunity costs.[13]

In such a complex strategic, tactical and often technocratic environment, balanced decision making is exceedingly difficult. First, there is the expertise gap. Planners and contractors will present their ideas and tabulations using highly detailed and technical facts and figures. They will have reached agreements and formed coalitions or consortiums on that basis long before the formal political decisions are made. Public authorities, especially at the local level, seldom possess the technical sophistication necessary to really challenge the experts' assessments. They are presented with 'accomplished facts'. Finally, there is the blurring of responsibilities. The political decision makers themselves might be among the most intensely-committed advocates of a project. It might have been a key point of action in their political programs or administrative agendas. They are not interested in making a balanced decision: they simply want to see their project move ahead as quickly as possible – whatever the costs.

Elaborated examples over overconfident and otherwise flawed military operations are provided by Gabriel in his analysis of the five big post-Vietnam U.S. military missions: the raid on Sontay prison to free American Prisoners of War, the seizure of the captured U.S.S. Magayez, the Iran rescue mission of 1980, the deployment of Marines in war-torn Beirut, and the invasion of Grenada.[14] Gabriel argues that from a purely military perspective, each of these operations was either a complete failure or showed serious deficiencies. He identifies a number of causes for this. Apart from a set of structural factors (such as the quick rotation of officers leading to loss of operational expertise at command levels, and the lack of institutional memory in the armed forces), Gabriel also refers a failures of coordination and reality-testing in the decision-making process, which are of interest here. In particular, he shows the adverse effects of ad hocery in the planning of missions: every military agency wants a share in a prestigious operation, no matter whether it has something substantial to contribute or not. It is a consequence of the built-in pathology of the peacetime condition of the military: an organization geared to perform in a situation which is not present, in other words an organization temporary out of work, eager to prove its worth. For these reasons, any prospect of the opportunity to conduct a 'real' operation short of all-out war, will be welcomed by a fair number of the organization's membership. Even at the senior levels, the call for a certain mission put forward by the politicians will be perceived as a rare opportunity, never as a problem. All parties are quick to assert that what is asked can be done. Each section of the armed forces will want to take part. This produces bureaucratic infighting, which can be quite intensive. At the same time, the planning effort produces inter-service planning groups where the need to obtain bureaucratic consensus overrides specific operational considerations of the situation. As Gabriel states:

> "(The) propensity to compromise operational standards for bureaucratic considerations leads to major difficulty: group think. Group think may be defined as a condition in which the major assumptions of an operational plan go unexamined by the planners in order to protect the bureaucratic consensus. In the Iranian raid, once the decision was made to use Marine pilots (to satisfy the Marine Corps demands for a role in the mission), that decision was no longer subject to scrutiny or question. This remained so even though in the six months of planning prior to skills required to put the plan into effect. From one point of view, there are great virtues in groupthink and in sustaining the bureaucratic consensus. If things go wrong, the entire planning staff has a vested interest in defending each component. This, in turn, minimizes responsibility, or deflects it altogether, reducing the probability that any individual or component will be penalized for failure to execute the plan successfully."[15]

190

Over-optimism regarding big and prestigious projects exists among policy makers, even in trying times. Whether and to what extent it occurs and pervades the decision-making process depends largely on the skills and abilities of the decision makers, and upon their definition of the situation. If optimism is sufficiently widespread among the members of a decision-making group, it can have serious effects upon decision quality along the lines of groupthink put forward by Janis.

12.4. Accountability and groupthink: some preliminary conclusions

It is possible to go beyond this conclusion and discern some theoretical issues emerging from the discussion. First of all, examples such as the quotation from Gabriel suggest that while groupthink is indeed a recognizable and significant phenomenon in certain administrative settings, its specific dynamics may differ from the mere stress-induced, defensive cohesiveness interpretation. Cohesiveness and sticking together do not occur spontaneously in a political-administrative context: they are there for a reason. By speculating about the effects of structures of accountability and responsibility and the way they affect the calculi of actors in situations of 'opportunities', the analysis suggests that it is necessary to trace some of the specific administrative antecedents and dynamics of group decision making and groupthink in government.

Further, linking the incidence of groupthink to opportunity-triggered decision making constitutes a break with original groupthink analysis, which was typically problem- or crisis-triggered. Janis interpreted groupthink primarily as a defensive mechanism, as a collective response to decisional stress and threats to self-esteem. Here it appears that groupthink can also come to affect decision making by inordinately strengthening the confidence of already optimistic decision makers. It may be, therefore, necessary to distinguish theoretically between 'optimistic' and 'pessimistic' variants of groupthink. To do so can resolve the issue of inconsistencies between the eight characteristics of groupthink. For one thing, such a differentiation between types of groupthink may resolve some of Longley and Pruitt's doubts about the eight definitional characteristics of groupthink.[16]

In particular, the distinction between two types of groupthink made here helps to explain the indeed rather peculiar 'illusion of invulnerability', which seems at odds with the assertion of groupthink as a collective defense mechanism. The illusion of invulnerability may be a key characteristic of the 'optimistic' variant of groupthink, which lead to the Bay of Pigs, and possibly contributed to the genesis of the Watergate cover-up during President Nixon's immensely successful (at least at the time) reelection effort.

To summarize, based on an investigation into the effects of perceptions of accountability on the part of group members upon the processes and outcomes of group decision making, it became possible to identify two different types of groupthink. These are restated here once more.

Groupthink *Type I* closely resembles the logic behind Janis' original formulation: a pattern of collective defensive avoidance in the face of a perceived problem or threat. In particular, threat may stem from a decisional group perceiving a certain issue as a crisis, with little hope of finding an adequate response. In addition, this perception of crisis is influenced by an additional antecedent factor, namely low self-esteem among key group members leading them to seek refuge in the group. Actors on the fringes of the group may react differently, however, and attempt to disassociate themselves from the group decisions – either by physically exiting or by becoming in-house, marginalized dissenters.

Groupthink *Type II* has a radically different generic pattern. It occurs among high-confidence groups working on high-prestige projects, expecting major policy successes and career advancements as a result of their efforts. Specific prototypes of such situations have been outlined above.

There are two key differences between the two types of groupthink:
a) the preconditions: high self-esteem and a sense of competence versus low self-esteem and a lack of confidence in decision-making outcomes; and opportunities versus threats as triggering events.
b) the symptoms (characteristics) of groupthink: Type II has all eight characteristics mentioned by Janis, while in Type II the illusion of invulnerability ought to be eliminated.

It is obvious that this specification of groupthink theory needs further scrutiny. In part IV, the evidence of the Irangate case will be checked for groupthink type II.

Notes

1. Hart (1968); Spiro (1968); Thompson (1980); Beauchamp and Bowie (eds 1983); Jonas (1984).
2. See, for instance Olson (1965); Hirschman (1970); throughout this chapter, Hirschman's trichotomy of exit, voice and loyalty plays an important role.
3. This follows, from amongst others, the Thomas theorem: if men define their situations as real, they are real in their consequences.
4. Due to lack of space, no detailed account can be presented here. Many examples of the kind of attitudes and behaviours suggested here, as displayed by actors in the Stopera case, can be found in the report of the Committee of inquiry into the City Hall/Opera House project, Stopera Report (Amsterdam, 1987, in Dutch).
5. Janis (1982a).
6. An insider's account is Sick (1985). Other sources include Jordan (1982); Salinger (1981); Smith (1984); Christopher (ed. 1985); Gabriel (1985).
7. Salinger (1981), p.238.
8. See Turner's (1985) memoirs for this conception of loyalty.
9. These examples are derived from the groupthink literature. They are inspired by, in particular, the Bay of Pigs and Kent State case studies, as well as the entrapment literature.

10. Janis (1989) discusses some of these phenomena under his 'Wow, grab it!' heuristic.
11. Schlesinger (1965), pp.213-214.
12. Hensley and Griffin (1986).
13. Hirsch (1977); Kouzmin (1979); Hall (1982).
14. Gabriel (1985). Note here that there may have been a discrepancy of perceptions between the political and some of the military actors planning the Iran rescue mission. While for the politicians, it may have been a case of high stress and collective pessimism, some of the military specialists viewed the operation as a welcome opportunity to assert their organization's importance and effectiveness. This explains in part why all major services wanted to be included in the operation: Army, Navy, Air Force, and Marines - although the latter were actually not needed. Hence, in groupthink type I as a plausible hypothesis for explaining strategic political-military decision making, while military operational planning may have given rise to groupthink type II phenomena.
15. Gabriel (1985), pp.20-21.
16. Longley and Pruitt (1980); see also chapter 1.

13 – The groupthink model: an assessment

13.1. Introduction

In this chapter, an attempt is made to summarize the main findings. of the political-administrative examination of groupthink in part III. Following the structure of the argument of part III, the various components of the revised model of groupthink as formulated in chapter 8, are discussed. On the basis of this discussion, specific elaborations and amendments to the model are suggested. To a large extent, these revisions seek to promote a more fine-tuned and qualified use of groupthink analysis in explaining historical cases of government decision making and/or policy fiascoes. They are, to a large extent, delimitations of the applicability of groupthink analysis in real-life organizational and administrative settings. In addition, some of the more speculative elaborations of groupthink analysis, such as the attempt to differentiate between 'optimistic' and 'pessimistic' variants of groupthink, are recapitulated here.

13.2. Reworking the revised model

Assumptions

Groupthink analysis, like many other theories of policy processes, harbors some explicit or implicit assumptions about the nature of decision-making processes in and around government. Specifically, embedded in the group-think explanation of policy fiascoes are two key assumptions: that policies come about in a process of decision making conceived of as making a choice between two or more alternative options in order to solve a particular problem; and secondly, that key decisions underlying these fiascoes are taken by one small, informal group of policymakers and advisors.

On the basis of the analysis of chapter 9, it is concluded here that these two assumptions considerably limit the applicability of the groupthink explanation. The number of policy issues facing government actors and agencies that are processed in the manner suggested by these two assumptions, is rather small.

The current literature on organizational problem solving and decision making clearly points to the fact that many decisions in organizational settings are the outcome of complex interactions widely beyond the simple choice model. The garbage-can model of organizational choice suggests that 'problems', 'decision makers' and 'solutions' are flee-floating streams rather than logically related elements of the decision process. In some cases, the sum of activities undertaken by actors in the decision process results in a situation where no decision is taken at all: non-decision making or non-action. The literature on organizational symbolism suggests that the choice-model serves more as a normatively-valued idea of rational social action than as an accurate description of organizational practices. Finally, empirical research on organizational decision making indicates that there is great variety in the ways in which different issues are processed in various types of organizations; the choice-model is only one category of decision processes that can be found.

Regarding the second assumption, research on the structure of governmental policymaking reveals that, in a variety of ways, decision authority is fragmented, involving two or more 'knots' in the decisional maze rather than a single dominant group. Checks and balances, even in non-democratic states provide for multiple power centers. Secondly, there exists a great variety of decisional fora available in which government decisions can be taken. Few of these conform to the small, informal groups presupposed by groupthink analysis.

This does not imply that groupthink analysis is trivial. It does suggest that one should be careful in applying the groupthink explanation to historical cases of governmental decision making, and that one should take caution not overgeneralize findings from groupthink analysis.

On the basis of this survey, it is argued that groupthink analysts would do well to concentrate on non-routine types of decisional issues when contemplating the use of the groupthink framework:
- large problem scope (present and future ramifications);
- unconventional (standard solutions are perceived to be unapplicable);
- divisive (controversial, inherent potential for conflict);
- political (external and strategic implications for the policymakers and their organizational constituencies).

Non-routine problem situations may be found most markedly toward the higher levels of the organizational/governmental hierarchy. They include instances of project management, long-range policy planning, high-politics controversies, different types of crisis situations. While these kinds of issues are not necessarily settled through deliberate choices made by a single, informal group, they depict the range of settings in which groupthink analysis might be salient.

Among the kinds of groups most salient to groupthink analysis are: cabinets (in particular 'kitchen' or 'inner' cabinets), cabinet committees, high-level advisory committees, organizational or departmental management teams, parliamentary committees and subcommittees, ad-hoc policy planning groups.

It is up to the analyst to establish in any specific case whether the assumptions of groupthink analysis really apply. Only after these questions are answered positively can the analyst start to seriously probe the preconditions and dynamics of groupthink within the context of the case.

Dynamics

In the preliminary revised model of groupthink, three alternative pathways toward groupthink have been identified:

- Cohesiveness, which stresses the stifling impact of highly congenial groups, through subtle processes of social influence; in particular, this high group cohesiveness arises under conditions of external threat as a means of emotional support for the individual group members, and/or in situations of intergroup conflict when group members belief their team can prevail over its competitors or rivals.
- Deindividuation; in certain cohesive groups, the group can become so dominant a force acting upon the individual members that they lose their sense of individuality as become more or less automated 'agents' of the group norms and standards; in certain situations this may lead to a loss of moral restraints and reckless and aggressive behavior similar to the kind of desensitized problem-solving behavior associated with groupthink.
- Anticipatory compliance, which suggests that from the perspective of the individual member, pressures for conformity with the group judgment can arise independent of group cohesiveness; in particular, the hierarchical structure underlying each decision group may induce group members to preemptively comply with real or perceived policy preferences of group leaders or high-status members.

Cohesiveness. These three dynamic pathways to groupthink have been reconsidered from a political-administrative perspective. From this examination it turns out that the original groupthink hypothesis (i.e. the first pathway), appears at first sight to be a relatively rare phenomenon. High-level political-administrative groups are often characterized by fragmentation and divisiveness. High cohesiveness and amiability are easily overshadowed.

Firstly, the high degree of instability of membership composition due to individual job rotation and regime changes (notably in spoils systems or in systems with a tradition of short-tenured executives) may preclude or disturb the development of a truly congenial esprit de corps. Similar effects result from the large size of many political decision bodies or executive groups. This is caused in part by the logic of representation of numerous political and bureaucratic interests involved in any major policy decision. Indeed, as shown by studies of cabinet decision making, political and departmental fragmentation exert a pervasive influence upon the structure and functioning of high-level decision groups, to the effect that these groups seldom develop the kind of high cohesiveness suggested by the first pathway.

The apparently most pervasive threat to group cohesiveness in political-administrative decision making is posed by the development and persistence of intra-bureaucratic divisions and rivalries, better known under the label of bureaucratic politics. In a growing empirical literature on this topic it is explained in detail how many endemic factors in the governmental structure and process contribute to bureaucratic rivalries, stalemates and guerilla wars between different agencies within government. It appears that administrative reality is far removed from the harmony and consensus view embedded in groupthink path 1.

However, a more subtle analysis is required here. There are two ways in which the existence of intra-governmental conflict unwittingly may produce, directly or indirectly, group cohesion and its possible groupthink consequences.

First of all, the existence of conflict in a governmental system that nevertheless has to produce policy outputs may give rise to various kinds of conflict-mitigating techniques. Accommodation and coalition formation are well-known ways in which political and administrative leaders eventually come to bridge the gaps that keep them divided, and succeed in producing more coherence and stability. However, the various conflict-mitigation techniques may backfire and produce conflict-avoiding behavior similar to groupthink, where nobody dares to challenge the tenuous political-administrative consensus once this has been achieved. Groupthink analysts would therefore do well to scrutinize situations in which the group decision-making process includes habits of: non-intervention in members' portfolios or petty subjects; accommodative opinion formation by anticipation of other members' likely stances on a given policy issue; delegation of difficult issues to isolated committees and subcommittees; and secrecy of group deliberations as a technique to mitigate public differences.

Secondly, it may be true that from the overall level of the government or the policymaking process, conflict and division are pervasive. Conflict mitigation techniques may fail to bring accommodation. However, if one shifts the focus to the political and administrative groups and coalitions that operate within one side of the dividing lines, the picture changes dramatically. Applying the notions developed in chapter 7 on the intragroup implications of intergroup conflict, it has been shown that bureaucratic rivalries may trigger and reinforce strong feelings of in-group solidarity and out-group hostility within each of the factions concerned. These cohesive factions try to find ways to assert prominence in the decision process. The techniques used in this respect may be quite conducive to groupthink: secrecy, back channels, eliminating opponents from the decision loop, moral complacency in the face of dubious actions, against out-groups, entrapment in a course of action that the group has been publicly committed to.

In conclusion, the first pathway to groupthink requires a subtle and sharp-edged analysis of the factors contributing and detracting to group cohesiveness. In doing so, analysts will find that few decision cases conform to the scenario envisaged by the first pathway. There is no reason to simply assume group cohesiveness. It is safer to assume the opposite and check for (a) the intra- and intergroup dynamics associated with political-administrative controversy; (b) conflict-mitigating techniques and their unintended side-effects.

Deindividuation. The second, deindividuation-driven, pathway to groupthink appears to be not very relevant in analyzing the behavior high-level decision groups. In this setting, the conditions that give rise to deindividuation (see chapter 4) are seldom, if ever, met. Actors are not anonymous – at least not vis-a-vis one another, and group cohesiveness is tenuous.

On these grounds, it was concluded that the deindividuation perspective can be assigned secondary importance in a political-administrative perspective on groupthink. When studying high-level decision groups as potential victims of groupthink, pathways 1 and 3 (see below) should be the prime instruments of analysis. However, the deindividuation perspective comes back into play when the analyst would want to study groups at lower-levels in the bureaucracy, notably army and police operational units, where the uniform, professional training, and the threatening conflict situation with clearly definable out-groups may contribute to loss of individuality among group members – eventually producing group excesses similar to those committed by the guards in the Zimbardo prison experiment described in chapter 4. In sum, deindividuation is more relevant a focus for (certain settings of) the operational implementation of policy rather than the making of policy by political and administrative leaders and their advisors.

This conclusion has been based on rather impressionistic evidence and reflects the lack of substantive applied research in this field. Hence it could not be shown convincingly that the theoretically sound linkage between deindividuation and groupthink bears no relevance whatsoever to political decision processes. Therefore, it would be premature to simply eliminate the second pathway to groupthink from the model altogether. It is therefore retained, for the time being more as a reminder than as an active component of the model ready for empirical testing in case analyses.

Anticipatory compliance. A radically different conclusion was reached with regard to the third pathway to groupthink, that of anticipatory compliance on the part of individual group members. As illustrated in greater detail in chapter 11, the compliance pathway to groupthink relates very clearly to findings about the behavioral impact of structural and role differentiations (hierarchy and leadership), impinging upon decision-making actors and their interrelationships in complex organizations and governmental settings. The pervasiveness, even at the highest levels of an organization, of formal and informal hierarchies of status, prerogatives, and power, is remarkable. Despite the tendency to go for more collegial modes of cooperation and decision making in organizations, there is a permanent hierarchically molded structure of incentives that induces many actors to comply with the real or perceived stances and preferences of superiors or influential colleagues. Furthermore, many bureaucratic organizations have traditionally operated upon Weberian norms of obedience to rules and regulations and strictly hierarchical principles of organizational action (cf. the armed forces, the police).

In the analysis of chapter 11, these general characteristics of structural differentiation and compliance have been used as a background for an analysis of the way in which high-level governmental decision group may operate on principles of (anticipatory) compliance. Specifically, a set of five interrelated propositions pertaining to this issue has been developed and illustrated using the theoretical work of Kelman and Hamilton (social-psychological), Dunsire (administrative), as well as the more empirically-driven work on chief executive decision making by De Rivera and by George.

In discussing these propositions, attention was paid to the potential impact of organizational or political leaders upon the course and outcomes of the group decision process. Often, they define and delimit the agenda and the kinds of alternatives to be discussed right at the outset of the deliberations by stating their premises. They may control the composition of the decision group, and may thus steer towards a likely outcome of the discussion. Leaders may also narrow the range and depth of the group decision process by the manner in which they conduct the meetings, i.e. by 'opening' and 'closing' the discussion based on personal preferences for certain speakers or viewpoints.

A further illustration of these basic points was provided by an examination of the operation of high-level governmental advisory groups. From the perspective of the advisors, there often exists a clear dilemma between his personal points of view and the demands for loyalty and support to the organization, the official policy, or the chief executive. Combining this with the intricate power relations that exist within these groups and between them and the advisers, George has identified nine possible malfunctions of the advisory process, the majority of which directly relates to the dynamics of anticipatory compliance.

From this review of the literature it becomes quite clear that the compliance pathway to groupthink in government is, indeed, the most salient one of the three that have been presented in the preliminary revised model. The compliance pathway is beset by much less ambiguity than the cohesiveness pathway presented earlier. In conclusion, six facilitating conditions for the occurrence of compliance-based groupthink have been formulated:

1) A chief executive whose status as group leader is firmly accepted by the group members: the more strongly the personal bond between leader and group members, the greater the likelihood of quick compliance with his real or perceived demands.
2) Rules of interaction within the group in which it is accepted unquestioningly that the chief executive sets the agenda and defines the scope of discussion for the predominant policy issues.
3) External conditions that appear to necessitate determined action, enhancing the perceived need for strong leadership from the chief executive.
4) A basic consensus about the general gist of the policy to be pursued

among the advisors/group members, as opposed to a situation dominated by bureau-political factionalism and strife over even the basic assumptions.

5) The group is confronted with external opposition, criticizing the group's course of action, and, in particular, the effectiveness or the legitimacy of the chief executive/group leader.

6) The group as a whole operates in a situation of perceived win-lose conflicts with other groups inside or outside the government.

This set of facilitating conditions identifies a range of situations that are most susceptible to compliance-based patterns of premature or excessive concurrence-seeking by the group members. As such, it can be used as an analytical instrument for the analysis of empirical cases, but it can also be used as a diagnostic instrument, pinpointing potential flaws and pitfalls in the organization and context of the policy decision-making process.

Outcomes

The 'output' model of groupthink specifying the decisional consequences of groupthink patterns of decision making, was developed in chapters 5 and 6 of part II. It entails assertions about the ways in which groupthink may produce instances of excessive risk taking (recklessness), and, in certain kinds of repetitive, multi-decision contexts, entrapment in a failing course of action. In developing these thoughts from the experimental literature within Social Psychology, already some supporting and modificating insights involving the organizational and political-administrative contexts of risk-taking and entrapment were included. There was no need to redo this in part III. Therefore, the output model was not further examined in this part of the study and remains unchanged.

13.3. Groupthink in context: two types of groupthink

The final chapter of the theoretical analysis of groupthink presented in this study is also the most speculative, with, potentially, the most far-reaching implications. Exploring in detail one of the structural parameters of governmental decision-making processes, an attempt was made to develop thoughts about how different modes of accountability affect the behavior of members of decisional groups and the resulting pattern of group deliberation and choice. On the basis of a newly developed conceptual model of accountability and decision-making behavior, two different types of groupthink were discerned:

– collective avoidance (the classical pattern – type I)
– collective overoptimism (the new pattern – type II).

Collective avoidance.

Groupthink type I rests on the following proposition: if members of a decision group perceive the issue confronting them as a problem that may result in failure rather than as an opportunity for success, they will attempt as much as possible to avoid being associated with the decision process concerning the issue. The stronger the perceived likelihood of a major policy failure, the greater the motivation to avoid being associated with it.

In such a setting actors will try to avoid being held individually accountable. If they feel that they are unable to get the group to change its course of action, they can only seek ways to circumvent personal responsibility:
– non-participation or termination of group membership (the exit option);
– hiding within the group (the loyalty option as an attempt to spread responsibility to the collectivity);
– registering dissent for the record (the quasi voice option as a form of covering one's back).

These alternative modes of escaping personal responsibility were illustrated using several case examples. Recent research has indicated that the structure of accountability under which decision makers operate does indeed affect these processes: they are much more likely to happen under a regime of collective accountability than under a regime where personal responsibility for one's share in collective decisions is firmly embedded.

Collective overoptimism.

Groupthink type II rests upon a similar proposition: if members of a decision group perceive the issue confronting them as an opportunity for success rather than a problem that may result in failure, they will be strongly motivated to cooperate with one another in achieving the expected gains. The stronger the perceived likelihood of a major policy success, the greater the motivation to be associated with the group responsible for achieving it.

The second type of groupthink reflects the other side of accountability (rewards instead of punishments), and brings the cohesiveness pathway to groupthink back into the forefront. It does so by stressing the accountability-driven logic of maintaining consensus and a basic 'drive' regarding a policy that is seen by all as a potential opportunity for success. The motivation to stick together on a joint venture likely to bring the participants bureaucratic or political fame and glory may come to override group members' concerns for the substantive quality of the policy, and blind them to potential risks and drawbacks.

It is interesting to note that the distinction between type I and type II groupthink may solve a persistent problem in the original formulation of groupthink. This concerns one of the symptoms of groupthink defined by Janis as the illusion of invulnerability, which was never quite compatible with the picture of groupthink as a stress-triggered defense mechanism. It is much more compatible with the groupthink type II interpretation of collective overoptimism. This calls for a differentiated analysis of groupthink, which is sketched in the next paragraph.

To illustrate the plausibility of this alternative type of groupthink, three policy settings most prone to give rise to type II phenomena have been discussed using case examples:
– political honeymoon periods of new regimes;
– big projects, pet policies requiring large-scale investments;
– military contingency planning.
These are not the only settings where collective overoptimism may affect the decision process. It is up to further researchers to explore this new dimension of groupthink.

13.4. Remodelling groupthink: final revision

The analysis of part III has produced a rather large number of questions, points of discussion, and qualifications with regard to the revised model of groupthink that has emerged from the social-psychological analysis of part II. It is not feasible to try and incorporate each and every point in a final reformulation of the model. This would render the model too complex to be workable at all. The theorist should always be aware of the dilemma between parsimony and practicality on the one hand, and empirical accuracy and precision on the other. All too often, analysts expend the former in favor of the latter, and end up with impressive but unusable models.[1] Here, an attempt has been made to steer a middle course.

In addition, it must be remarked that there exists a wide discrepancy between the kind of well-developed and precise social-psychological research findings that have formed the basis of the revised model at the end of part II, and the more contextually complex, diverse, yet much less conclusive empirical patterns that have emerged from examining the literature on political-administrative decision making, presented in part III. In part, this discrepancy reflects the differences in development and state of the art in these two respective fields. Social Psychology and, within it, studies of group dynamics have been around on a large scale much longer. The use of experimental methods makes for much more cumulative work, and more solid theory development.

However, from another point of view, the balance tips the other way. From the perspective of an analyst interested in the micro-processes of governmental decision making, the sheer simplicity and lack of consideration for contextual factors evident in many social-psychological studies of group processes is often disappointing. Here, empirical studies of strategic policy decisions in public and private sector settings provide rich, if scattered, insights and leads for theorizing about the effect of contextual factors on the course and outcomes of group decision making.

In any case, for a variety of reasons, not all of the qualifications emerging from part III have been taken into account in constructing a final revision of the groupthink model. Later research must show whether these sim-

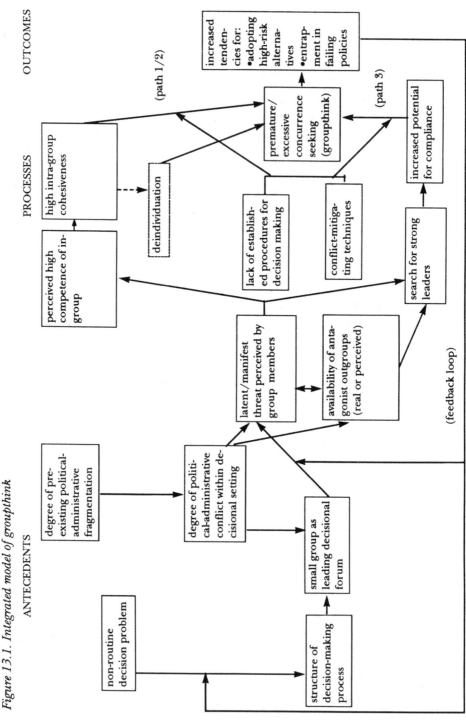

Figure 13.1. Integrated model of groupthink

ANTECEDENTS   PROCESSES   OUTCOMES

204

plifications are unwarranted. Taking into account the most important findings from the political-administrative reexamination of groupthink theory, the following picture emerges (see figure 13.1.).

At this stage, the basic structure of the model needs no further explanation.[2] It is evident that the modifications suggested are highly contextual, further specifying the domains of applicability of groupthink analysis. Also, a feedback loop is included to indicate the dynamic, self-reinforcing character of the processes described. In the model, this implies that a political-administrative analysis of groupthink necessitates a much more sophisticated scanning of the preconditions and situational factors, and the way they impinge upon the structure and process of governmental decision making. This scanning acts as a selective mechanism for groupthink analysis: many historic cases of policy fiascoes will be found not to meet the structural and process requirements presupposed by the groupthink explanation; they will have to be explained by other factors. In the introduction to part IV, this final version of the revised model is operationalized into a set of detailed research questions, that, taken together, provide the analyst with a relatively simple instrument to check for groupthink phenomena in any historical case.[3]

Optimism and pessimism: two types of groupthink. Going beyond this integrated picture of the groupthink phenomenon, the analysis of chapter 12 provides material for speculating about a more differentiated approach. More specifically, it is possible to distinguish between groupthink type I and groupthink type II. Inserting the accountability factor and its perceptual/behavioral implications, figure 13.2. indicates how the two types of groupthink differ:
– different dynamics, depending upon the decision makers' perceptions of the 'manageability' of the issue at hand;
– different 'escape routes', suggesting the need for differentiated techniques for preventing groupthink;
– slightly different symptoms of groupthink.

At this stage, the analysis of optimistic and pessimistic variants of groupthink is in its earliest stages. The models depicted here should, therefore, be regarded only as a first attempt to master the complex dynamics of different patterns of failing group decisions in political-administrative settings. Research using the model should provide more definitive answers about the validity of the model as a diagnostic instrument in analyzing different types of groupthink.

Notes

1. In decision-making analysis, a classic example concerns the model of foreign policy decision making developed by Snyder, Bruck and Sapin (1954).
2. The reader is advised to consult again chapter 8 if necessary.
3. This pressupposes, of course, that the analyst possesses a sufficient amount and quality of data to analyze each of the questions. Groupthink analysis data requirements are relatively high.

Figure 13.2. A speculative analysis of two modes of groupthink

GROUPTHINK TYPE I: COLLECTIVE AVOIDANCE

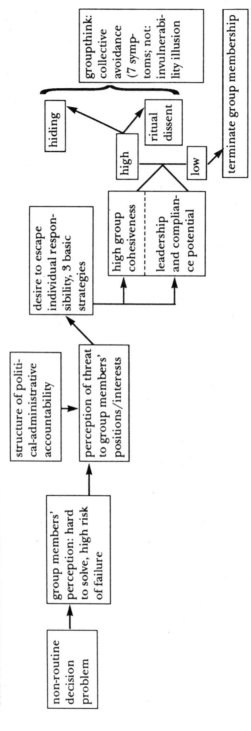

GROUPTHINK TYPE II: COLLECTIVE OVEROPTIMISM

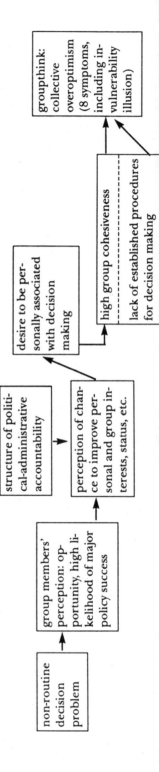

PART IV – GROUPTHINK: AN EMPIRICAL INVESTIGATION

Introduction to Part IV

Investigating groupthink

It has been pointed out earlier that the body of empirical research on groupthink is relatively small. There have been a number of replicatory case studies, some laboratory experiments, and a number of empirical investigations of group phenomena more or less directly related to groupthink. As noted, their results were rather mixed.

Why this lack of empirical work? No doubt one important reason lies in the fact that it is very difficult to design and conduct a rigorous investigation of groupthink. It is a complex concept; the number of variables to be taken into account is so high as to foreclose a really comprehensive experimental design. Furthermore, the causal flow implied in groupthink theory is rather elusive and open to different interpretations. While it is acknowledged that the best way to tackle these problems is to adopt and combine different research strategies, as suggested by Janis, this is difficult to arrange in practice.[1]

On the whole, it can be argued that the technically 'best' and theoretically 'richest' single piece of groupthink research has been Janis' Watergate case study[2]. There are two reasons for this. First of all, unlike his early groupthink studies, this one was conducted and reported following a set of systematic research questions derived from his theoretical model – making the case study work less 'impressionistic'. Secondly, he could benefit from the unique situation of the availability of a huge amount of data concerning the group process – the taped conversations of the President and his assistants. This data base enabled the case study to rely to only a very small extent upon post-hoc selection of second-order material, and instead analyze the group decision-making process as it took place during the taped conversations. As a result of these two factors, the Watergate case study provides an interpretation which is both convincing and easy to replicate, verify, and contend with by other researchers, whereas the original case studies were of necessity more loose, and open to charges of selectiveness and bias in collecting and interpretating the evidence.

The empirical investigation that follows in the next chapter also uses the case study method, but tries to attain a level of rigor comparable to the Watergate case. Lacking the kind of process data available for Watergate in the case study presented here, the main way of achieving rigor is to carefully outline and apply a research scenario that operationalizes the revised interpretation of groupthink theory developed in parts II and III of this study. This involves: (a) making explicit the steps to be taken in analyzing the case, as they follow from the theory; (b) consistently checking the material for both corroborating and disclaiming evidence; (c) keeping a clear view of the possibilities and limitations of the available data base, and reflecting upon the consequences for the analysis presented.

Following the work of, amongst others, George and Yin, it is argued that the case study need not at all be a 'soft' method of research.[3] Especially when the theory under consideration is still at an exploratory stage, indepth case studies are potentially very useful given their heuristic potential. Moreover, by elaborating the case design as such, the level of systematization can be raised considerably – e.g. by quasi-experimentation within the design of the case study (Yin), or by going for a focused comparison of comparable cases (George). In this study, the comparable case method is followed, in the sense that both cases are approached and analyzed using the same set of research questions derived from the theory. This allows for a more or less systematic comparison of findings between the two cases, as well as between each case and the hypotheses suggested by the theory. As the design is based on Janis' own revised design used for his Watergate case study, comparisons to the case are also facilitated. Furthermore, the Hensley and Griffin case study of the Kent State controversy allows for systematic comparison, too.[4]

A research design

In parts II and III of the study, a more or less systematic revision of groupthink theory has been pursued. In the social-psychological examination in part II, groupthink has been examined within a broader context of small-group theory and research. This has resulted in the provisional revised model formulated in chapter ten. Subsequently in part III, the components of this revision were critically monitored from an organizational, politico-administrative perspective. This resulted in additional elaboration of the model, inserting new contextual factors and dynamics, as well as qualifying existing linkages and hypotheses. Taken together, these analytical efforts have produced a preliminary model to be used in the present research. This model has been depicted in chapter thirteen. Its key themes and linkages can be operationalized in the following set of research questions.

Contextual factors and preconditions
1a. What is the nature of the case selected for analysis?
  b. In what sense and to what extent could it be regarded a fiasco?
  c. What is the historical, political, and institutional background of the case?
2. What principal actors were involved?
3. To what extent did all or some of these actors perceive the issue as a difficult, critical, even dangerous challenge?

4. To what extent did all or some of the actors perceive the issue as an opportunity for achieving a resounding (personal, organizational or political) success?
5. Were explicit decisions required to cope with the issue?
6a. Who were involved in the decision-making process?
  b. Was there any single dominant locus of decision?
  c. To what extent were key decisions made by a comparatively stable (in terms of membership), small group?
7a. Given the existence of a core decision group, what other groups did it interact with?
  b. To what extent did the decision group perceive itself to be in conflict with one or more of these other groups?
  c. What were the core group's perceptions of its own effectiveness in attempting to prevail over other groups in its environment?

Process dynamics
8. How was the decision group formed and maintained throughout the process?
9. To what extent was the group highly cohesive?
10. What specific sources of cohesiveness can be discerned? Did they include:
  a. conflict with outgroups (inside and outside the group's own organizational environment - see point 7);
  b. secrecy;
  c. group prestige?
11. What was the hierarchical structure of the group? Were there any group leaders? How many? What leadership styles and practices were common in the group? How were they perceived by the group members?
12. To what extent was the group decision process affected by processes of internalized compliance on the part of group members?
13. To what extent did the group and/or the group members individually anticipate conditions of accountability operating within the organizational, political or administrative context of the decision-making process?
  a. Did this in any way affect their perception of the situation as potentially damaging their individual or collective status?
  b. Did this in any way affect their perception of the situation as a possibility for achieving a major success?
14. Can symptoms of groupthink be discerned? (See the eight symptoms of groupthink – types I and II)

Outcomes
15. Can the decisions reached by the group be perceived as recklessness, e.g. excessive risk taking?
16. If so, how could the decision makers end up taking inordinate risks? (see the factors identified in chapter 5).
17. Can the course and results of the decision process be characterized in terms of entrapment?

18. If so, how could the decision makers become entrapped in their failing course of action? (See the factors identified in chapter 6.)

Reflection
19. To what extent did groupthink provide an adequate (or plausible) explanation of the decision-making process?
20. Did the case analysis suggest any new leads in further developing and sharpening the groupthink model?

Toward case analysis

Admittedly, the set of questions outlined above does not 'solve' each and every problem or subtlety identified in the theoretical analysis. But it does cover all principal analytical themes and qualifications identified in parts I to III of the study. It forces the analyst to put to the test often-neglected matters such as "was the course of events of the case due to a limited number of identifiable decisions?", as well as "was there really one group taking these decisions?"

Despite this list, however, and probably somewhat more than some other research strategies in social science, the case study approach can only be viably employed if the analyst remains very much open to alternative, contrasting interpretations of the case evidence. No list of rigorous questions can enforce this. Much comes down to adequate illustration, the systematic checking of counter evidence, and the plausibility of the argument developed by the analyst. In this sense, the reader is invited to maintain a critical attitude in examining the following case study. This case study, on the U.S.-side of the Iran-Contra affair, was chosen firstly, because it matched the policy context of the bulk of Janis' original case studies: American foreign policy. More specifically, however, I decided to proceed with it after initial explorations because it turned out that the case seemed to provide a clear-cut illustration for some of the key revisions and innovations presented in the theoretical analysis of this study. It was, in other words, a likely candidate for groupthink, be it for other reasons than might be expected if one would employ the original conceptualization by Janis.

The case is analyzed using the set of research questions formulated above. Rather than engaging in a dullish point-by-point exegesis of these questions, I have attempted to build them into a running story. More specifically, the key questions in the order presented above provide the structure of the case chapter. Each of the analytical points of examination is addressed accordingly. In doing so, it will produce a number of leads with regard to groupthink theory is taken up more elaborately in the final chapter.

Notes

1. Janis (1982b).
2. Janis (1982a).
3. Useful accounts of the uses and limitations of case study research can be found in George (1979); Yin (1984); George and McKeown (1985), and Boos and Fisch (1987). For a stimulating discussion of the implications of case study research for theory formation in the area of deterrence, see the theme issue on this subject of World Politics (1989), 2.
4. Hensley and Griffin (1986).

14 – Hostages, arms sales and
Contra funding

14.1. Introduction

Six years after the Carter administration was deeply humiliated by the continuing captivity of American embassy personnel in revolutionary Tehran, American hostages were again both the trigger and the focal point of dramatically failing American policy initiatives towards Iran. Soon after the first revelations in the fall of 1986, a new policy scandal came to light: the Iran-Contra affair, or, with pointed cynicism, *Irangate* (drawing a parallel between the Iran-Contra affair and the Watergate scandal which led to the forced resignation of President Nixon). Irangate is a brief denominator for secretive, deceptive, and partly illegal practices of officials and agencies within the Reagan administration in their efforts to obtain the release of American hostages held in Lebanon by Iran-backed extremists, and to use the funds from these transactions to support the Contra rebels in Nicaragua.

The focus of this case study lies with the genesis of the process: how could it happen? How could the United States suffer a major embarrassment over a middle-sized country somewhere in the Middle East? And how could it do so only five years since this same country had brought an entire administration virtually to its knees? More specifically, this chapter attempts to assess the explanatory value of the revised model of groupthink in a policy setting which closely resembles the 'standard Janis' situation: U.S. foreign policy, a crisis atmosphere (stress), a fiasco, widespread criticism of the decision-making process.

The material for this case study comes from the voluminous reports and – when available – testimonies of key participants produced during the various investigations of the affair: the Tower Commission, and the Congressional Select Committees on the Iran-Contra Affair.[1] Furthermore, a press archive containing all articles published on the affair by Time, Newsweek, and the New York Times was compiled. Thirdly, a number of journalistic and academic accounts of the affair have been consulted.[2] Finally, material from autobiographies of some of the key players, as well as from Oliver North's published testimony has been included.[3] It is obvious that this data base, although unusually rich when compared to the material that some other students of foreign affairs have to work with, probably does not cover each and every fact or detail pertaining to the case. Much valuable material has been lost in the early stages of the public enquiry, when records were destroyed by key participants in an (aborted) cover-up attempt. And certain key documents remain confidential for reasons of national security. In summary, most of the facts and their interpretation as reported in this study can be given with a fair amount of confidence; but at the same time there are some uncertainties and gaps in public knowledge about the events which should be taken into account.

This chapter first presents a general background of the Iran-Contra episode and the main conclusions about the policymaking process reached by various investigative bodies. Then, the situational, political and administrative setting of the decision-making process is outlined. The analysis starts in section 14.4., where the development of the structure of the decision-making process over time is examined, in order to check whether the main decisions in the Iran-Contra episode were taken by a small, informal group. Nine phases are distinguished from May 1985 to February 1986, when a basic pattern of decision had been set; the dramatic events that followed were, in a sense, the inevitable consequence of the way in which policymaking was conducted. In section 14.5., the decision-making process is analyzed using the perspective of the alternative pathways to groupthink, after which the symptoms of groupthink are discussed in greater detail. The outcomes of decision are examined from the perspective of the output model of groupthink, focusing on risk taking and entrapment, in section 14.7., to be followed by the conclusions of this case study.

14.2. Facts, interpretations and comparisons: a first assessment

The initiative: a long shot

Basically, the 'Iran initiative' grew from a complex series of informal consultations between public and private agents from various countries. It began partly as an attempt to break through the stalemated and highly tense relations between the United States and the new Islamic regime in Tehran, which despised the U.S. as supporter of the Pahlavi regime of the Shah, and of Iran's enemy in the Gulf War, Iraq. At the same time, for the Americans, the short-term objectives included obtaining the release of hostages held in Lebanon by Iran-backed extremist groups.

At the core of the initiative lay repeated weapons deliveries from the United States to Iran, either directly or through Israel, involving a wide range of private business firms and middlemen, back channels, negotiating deals, and controversy within the Reagan administration. The key actors on the U.S. side guiding the initiative were National Security Advisor McFarlane, and his successor admiral Poindexter (December 1985), NSC staffer lieutenant colonel Oliver North, the Director of Central Intelligence Casey, a retired U.S. general turned arms merchant Secord and his business associ-

ates, and – at a distance – the President. As the initiative unravelled, its scope and focus began to change:
- the original policy and strategic backgrounds of the opening toward Iran faded into the background, as the overarching objective of the arms deliveries became getting the hostages out;
- what started out as an indirect link using third countries such as Israel became a direct linkage between the U.S. and Iran;
- the Iran initiative became linked to another avenue of clandestine policy-making, namely the continuing financial and military support for the Contra rebels in Nicaragua (which was officially prohibited by the First and Second Boland amendments of the Congress); the linkage was established by channelling the profits from the clandestine arms sales to Iran to the Contra rebels through a complex network of international banking transactions.

At the same time, there were a number of stable factors:
- the stated policies of the United States Government not only denied U.S. involvement in either affair, but actively condemned the selling of arms to Iran or the making of deals with terrorists of any kind;
- the entire Iran operation was shredded in strict secrecy, not in the least because some of the major U.S. policy makers in the Defense and Foreign Policy areas were strenuously opposed to selling arms to Iran;
- despite this constellation and turn of events, Presidential support for both the Iran and Contra-funding operations continued unwavered (although the precise extent of Presidential foreknowledge and active involvement remains unclear).

The outcome: a fiasco

It may be claimed that two hostages were released on account of the development of the Iran initiative. However, the others remained in custody. Moreover, three more hostages were seized in the fall of 1986. And the initiative began to unravel quickly after, on November 3, 1986, the Lebanese magazine Al-Shiraa disclosed that U.S. arms sales to Iran, as well as a clandestine trip to Tehran undertaken by McFarlane in May 1986. The American press and Congress started to investigate the affair.

The main actors within the NSC, Poindexter and North, initially tried to cover up the true nature and extent of U.S. involvement, as well as evidence about the role of the president. DCI Casey did likewise, stonewalling congressional Intelligence Committees asking information about CIA involvement. The president ordered an investigation of the affair by Attorney General Meese. His work was compromised when it was revealed that the investigation had been 'slowed down' at a crucial moment. In the end, the president appointed a Special Review Board headed by former Senator John Tower to make a detailed assessment of the affair. The so-called Tower Report was published in February 1987. It was highly critical of the Iran policy and the decision-making process that had produced it.

In the meantime, Lawrence J. Walsh had been appointed Special Prosecutor in the Iran-Contra affair, to investigate whether illegalities were involved, and who ought to be prosecuted in this connection. Also, Poindexter, North and – indirectly – the Chief of the White House Staff Regan were fired or resigned following the disclosures. Following the disclosures, McFarlane attempted to commit suicide, allegedly because he could not face the disgrace of having served his president so badly. DCI Casey died of a brain tumor on May 6, 1987, just before he was to testify before a joint Congressional Investigation Committee, which had started conducting hearings a day earlier. The Congressional Report was published in November 1987. It was even more critical in tone of the administration than the Tower Report. In particular, the majority report emphasized the disdain for law and parliamentary procedures that were said to pervade the Iran-Contra period. While attacking him for his passive attitude, the report concluded that there was insufficient evidence to officially condemn the president's conduct. Oliver North became somewhat of a folk hero of conservative America due to his high-profile performances during congressional and judicial proceedings. He was later given a symbolic sentence. In April 1990, John Pointdexter was found guilty by a jury on five points related to deception and misinformation of Congress with regard to the Iran-Contra affair.

It is very hard not to consider the outcomes of the Iran-Contra affair a major policy fiasco. Not only did it fail to attain the 'opportunistic' and 'strategic' objectives which the policy makers had set themselves (hostages were not released as planned, in fact, more were taken; and no opening to Iranian 'moderates' was obtained), it also compromised an administration otherwise regarded as relatively successful. It hurt the image of the president. It raised serious questions about the extent of covert and illegal activities going on under the guise of official U.S. policies. It called attention to the inordinate amount of discretion and leeway offered to and seized by lower-level officials such as North.

Unlike most of the case studies by Janis, the Iran-Contra affair did not directly result in (avoidable) military violence and/or U.S. military defeat. But indirectly, the affair was responsible for considerable mischief. The weapons delivered to Iran contributed to the continuation of the bloody war between Iran and Iraq. The funds diverted to the Contras implied support for further domestic violence and insurgency throughout Nicaragua. And it did little to diminish the agony of the American hostages in Lebanon and their families: American hostages continued to be held in captivity in the Middle East; some have been imprisoned for more than four years at the time of writing.

Furthermore, the initiative did not bring about a relaxation of tensions in the Middle East, and weakened U.S. international prestige among its allies and other nations. Nor did it preclude the slow but steady improvement in Iranian-Soviet relations, as witnessed by President Khameini's visit to the Soviet Union in June 1989. By all counts, therefore, the Iran-Contra affair must be considered a policy failure. This makes it all the more interesting to understand how and why it could happen.

Tower Report. In its report based on extensive interviews with 49 people including most of the key actors as well as former foreign policy makers and advisors, the Tower board left no room for doubt that the initiative was the product of a flawed decision-making process. More specifically, several points were mentioned with regard to the arms transfers to Iran:

- the process was too informal: unprepared and unminuted meetings leaving room for ambiguity and diverse interpretations among the participants as to what had been agreed;
- the initiative was never subjected to a rigorous review below the cabinet level: the concern with secrecy impeded a full discussion of the policy among experts within the executive agencies ordinarily involved in the making of foreign policy, such as the State and Defense Departments – the initiative was monopolized at the sub-cabinet level by the NSC staff;
- the opportunity for a full hearing before the president was inadequate: key presidential decisions concerning the Iran initiative were either taken in small sessions with a highly selective attendance (mostly NSC only), or made post-hoc by the president in the form of signing Findings authorizing actions already taken – in 17 months only two or three cabinet-level reviews took place.[4]

Further, the Tower Commission criticized the 'unprofessional' implementation of the initiative, especially the fact that the entire enterprise was led almost single-handedly by North without the back-up information, expertise and resources normally available to foreign policy implementors. The questionable legality and the ensuing need for total secrecy also prevented substantive CIA involvement in implementation, and were partly the cause of the non-notification of Congress also criticized by the Tower Commission. The implementation difficulties were compounded by the reliance upon a variety of private businessmen and firms to implement sensitive parts of government policy.

Another major component of the Tower analysis concerned the failure of responsibilities. Describing the "personal management style" of the President and noting that it places "an especially heavy responsibility on his key advisors", the Tower board discussed the failure to meet these responsibilities for caution and guardianship of the policy process for each of the key authorities involved: the National Security advisor (effectively the head of the National Security Council staff – NSC staff), the Chief of Staff, the DCI, and the secretaries of State and Defense.

In its recommendations, the Tower commission particularly stressed the need to reform the National Security Council machinery: its legal basis, its organization, its operation within the interagency framework of foreign policy, its linkage to the president and the CIA, and its role in covert actions. Further recommendations concerned the need to reform congressional oversight of secret operations and the imperative to prevent private intermediaries from dominating policy implementation and oversight.

Congressional Report. In the Report of the Congressional Select Committees (headed by Senator Inouye and Representative Hamilton), largely the same line of reasoning was followed. Again, emphasis was laid upon flaws in the policy process. The keywords around which the Congressional majority's analysis evolved were as follows: confusion and disarray at the highest levels of government, overemphasis on secrecy leading to dishonesty of executive officers in front of Congress and the general public, privatization of foreign policy in the hands of arms dealers, the withholding of information resulting in a lack of accountability, abuses of the intelligence apparatus, and a general disdain for law.[5] The Report, first and foremost a political statement, struck a less 'analytical' and more 'condemnatory' tone.

In its overall analysis, the Report signalled a number of legal and Constitutional issues concerning the making of covert action in a democratic political system (and the misuse that was made of Presidential Covert Action Findings in this respect), the powers of Congress and the president with regard to the making of foreign policy (emphasizing the necessity of joint action rather than executive primacy and soloism), and the rule of law.

The 27 recommendations of the Congressional Report reflect these concerns. Detailed guidelines for the future use and limitations of Presidential Findings were presented. The NSC was recommended to discontinue its operational activities. Furthermore, the Report stressed the need for reporting to Congress all covert arms transfers, as well as giving it a periodic update on NSC activities in general.

These two official reports provide an idea about the ways of thinking about the genesis of the Iran-Contra initiatives that prevailed in government circles in and around Washington (it should be noted that a number of reputed academics assisted both groups in compiling the reports).

What is lacking in these reports, however, is a more interpretive, generic account of *why* all these failures in the policy process occurred and *how* they affected the quality of policy making. No attempt has been made to seek to compare the sketchy explanations provided in both reports to explanatory frameworks available in the literature on U.S. foreign policy in general. The groupthink interpretation is only one amongst other hypotheses that might be employed and tested in this respect.

14.3. The setting: a critical episode

When the Reagan administration took office in February 1981, the United States was only just recovering from the dramatic and drawn-out crisis surrounding the hostages in Iran. It was evident to the new administration, as it was to all Americans, that the Iran issue had broken the back of Carter's presidency. It was considered imperative that the Reagan administration would avoid getting entangled in a similar quagmire. This made both 'Iran' and 'anti-terrorism policies' prominent issues on the Reagan foreign policy agenda.

In both instances, the basic attitude adopted was one of toughness: the

U.S. arms embargo was extended, and in the official rhetoric, condemnation of international terrorism went hand in hand with repeated assurances that the United States would now refuse to make any concessions or deals under terrorist blackmail.

Lebanon crisis. These separate policy avenues again became intertwined when it appeared that Iran played an important role in supporting anti-U.S. terrorism. The scene was war-torn Lebanon. The trigger was the Israeli invasion of southern Lebanon in June 1982. The actors were extremist Shiite groups supported by Iran, such as the Islamic Jihad and the Hezbollah party. The victims were American citizens living in Beirut. The objectives were to force the U.S. to relinquish its support of the Israeli actions.

The initial U.S. response to the quickly escalating political and military situation was to send the Marines as a self-appointed peace-keeping force. This worked well in the beginning, until they too became enmeshed in the complexities of factionalist strife throughout Beirut. Throughout 1983, American lives and interests came under terrorist attack. In particular, suicidal car-bomb attacks took a heavy toll: the destruction of the U.S. embassy in Beirut (April 1983, 63 deaths), and an attack on the U.S. Marines compound in Beirut (October 1983, 241 deaths).[6] Especially the latter attack came as a severe blow to the Reagan administration and its aspirations in the Middle East 'peace process'.

The wave of attacks spread geographically. In December, the U.S. embassy in Kuwait suffered a series of bombing attacks. The policy machinery responded. On January 20, 1984, the State Department declared Iran a supporter of international terrorism.

Kidnappings. But more was yet to come. On March 7, 1984, Jeremy Levin, Beirut Bureau Chief for the CNN television network was seized, followed by the CIA's Chief of Beirut station William Buckley on March 14. Buckley's abduction came as a personal blow to CIA director Casey, who felt humiliated not only by the seizure but also by the fact that under the official 'no deals' policy, he could do so little for one of his key men who was probably being tortured by his captors.[7]

The kidnappings continued on May 8, when the Reverend Benjamin Weir was seized. After a pause during the second half of 1984, four more Americans were taken hostage in the first six months of 1985 (Jenco, Anderson, Jacobsen, Sutherland). A new climax came when on June 14, 1985, Shiite terrorists hijacked a TWA flight from Athens to Rome, murdered an american Navy diver aboard the plane, and flew all through the Middle East for the next fourteen days.

Terrorism crisis: presidential perspective

The key question to be answered is how this series of events influenced the perceptions and state of mind of U.S. policy makers, in particular the president. Did president Reagan perceive the hostage issue as a crisis? Did it engender psychological stress? If so, how did it affect his thinking about U.S. counter-policies?

While there is little hard evidence to go on in answering these questions, it shall nevertheless be argued that the affair did indeed trigger perceptions of threat and urgency in the president, as well as a strong degree of personal concern for the well being of the hostages and their families. It is surmised here that the degree of anxiety over the hostage issue reached a peak level during May-June 1985 – just before the initial decision to condone arms transfers to Iran was made. Three inferences are cited as support for these claims.

Firstly, Reagan and his political advisors had seen first-hand what the hostage crisis had done to his predecessor. Therefore, when the hostage takings and other acts of terrorism started to develop, the tendency to draw analogies with the Carter era was strongly manifest. The implications from these analogies were negative: avoid the image of impotence and inaction that descended over the Carter presidency when the hostage crisis in Tehran dragged on and on. Sick described of the tremendous pressures upon the president – partly self-imposed – to 'do something' that can arise in these sort of situations.[8] Knowing what patience had resulted in during the 1980-1981 hostage crisis, Reagan must have been reasoning that time was limited.

Secondly, several analysts of presidential decision making during terrorist events have argued that, for a variety of reasons, presidents have a strong tendency to personalize (domesticate) hostage situations, i.e. to feel a personal responsibility for the fate of the hostages.[9] This is reinforced by dramatic meetings with hostages' families. In this way, the hostages become persons instead of mere names or pawns in a broader policy arena. This raises the burden of decision upon the president tremendously. Note that, again, the pressure is at least partly self-imposed by the president in taking a specific interpretation of his role as chief policy maker.

Thirdly, the continuing drama of the TWA hijack has acted as a final stroke upon an already plagued chief executive, in part also haunted by the comparatively recent, dramatic failure of forceful military intervention (the fiasco of the deployment of Marines and the bloody attack on their barracks). The extensive media coverage of the hijacking, the execution of an American Navy diver aboard, the dramatic conversations with the pilot: they all raised the emotional stress and frustration of the president in connection with 'terrorism' (Reagan went to mourn at the grave of the killed diver Robert Dean Stethem just before greeting the surviving hostages at Andrews Air Force base, promising his sister that those guilty of his death would be punished; at about the same time, he met with the families of the Beirut hostages).[10]

The net effect of the sequence of events and developments, along with the growing anxieties in American public opinion about terrorism and the hostages issue, upon the president's predispositions towards the entire issue of Islamic terrorism was as follows:

- it raised the salience of the issue in his mind, considering it a major threat to American policies and reputation in the area, as well as a potential threat to his own presidency;
- it created a sense of urgency;
- it was a source of intense frustration and anger, mixed with feelings of impotence;
- it led to a great eagerness to try 'anything' to get the hostages out, including unconventional moves;
- it raised his willingness to follow the advice of those who offered him ways of resolving the issue.

Terrorism crisis: policy perspective

The issue of Iran-supported terrorism turned into a rather major policy dilemma for the Reagan administration. First of all, the official, stated policies of the United States government were unambiguous in their condemnation of anything else but a straight, non-compromising attitude vis-à-vis both Iran as well as international terrorists and their donors at large: no deals.

During the early eighties, the Reagan administration had continuously attempted to discourage third countries from supplying Iran with arms. Iran must not be allowed to crush Iraq in the Gulf War. This policy was extended and formalized in Operation Staunch, launched in December 1983. The main goal was to try and develop a broad coalition of countries that would implement and encourage others to join in a total arms sales embargo against Iran. The operation was not very effective: individual countries free-rided upon the U.S. initiative, and the Iranians also bought a large quantity of arms through private channels (international arms dealers).

The departments of State and Defense both propagated and supported the official line of the administration. From a geopolitical perspective, the Gulf War was extremely sensitive, because it could trigger major instabilities and political realignments throughout the Middle East. It would certainly not advance the political and military interests of the United States to see Iran prevail over Iraq, although both countries were basically hostile to the U.S. (but Iran decisively more actively and dangerously so). With regard to terrorism, secretary of State Shultz was bent on avoiding the plight of his predecessor Vance, whose moderateness, diplomatic decency, and indecisiveness had not only extended the Tehran hostage crisis, but also brought about his demise from the Carter administration. Shultz's position within the administration was sufficiently vulnerable as it was. An enlightened stance toward Iran or international terrorism was simply not a viable option.

The tough policies of the government met with the active support and approval of the Congress. After Tehran, the bloody bombings in Beirut, the series of hostage-takings and the continuing anti-U.S. rhetoric emanating from Iran, few Congressmen were prepared to reconsider the official policies from a more moderate or flexible point of view. An official change of policy was out of the question. Like the president, Congress was aware that the terrorism and Iran issues were potential political dynamite, in which even the appearance of 'softness' and 'passivity' must be avoided at all costs.

From crisis to opportunity: the NSC staff. The abduction of especially Buckley was not only a personal blow to Casey but an institutional threat to CIA operations officers scattered around the world:

> "For DDO [Deputy Director for Operations, PtH] Clair George, who had been the Beirut station chief from 1975 to 1976, the Buckley kidnappingrevived bad dreams. During his time in Beirut, two U.S. government officials had been abducted and held hostage for four months before being released. He had lived that agony. George had turned the DO inside out to save Buckley. It was not only that he wanted Buckley back; the effort was a signal to thousands of DO officers abroad that the CIA would do just about anything to rescue one of its own. (....)
> 'It was time to hit back. But the Lebanese [right-wing christian militants supported by the CIA, PtH] was proving to be trouble. They couldn't be controlled; they were willing to commit murder, very willing. Casey's own CIA people began slowing down. No one inside the agency wanted to step out front."[11]

Therefore, other means of action would have to be sought. For retaliation purposes, the CIA, through the assistance of Arab allies, was instrumental in directing Lebanese groups to do some counter-bombing aiming at the elimination of known terrorist leaders. These efforts were not only illegal under the strict guidelines for CIA operations, they were also largely unsuccessful. Besides, they did not bring about the release of any hostages. DCI Casey wanted action but could not use his own agency to do so.

In this constellation, certain developments within the NSC staff could not have come at a better time for Casey, who wanted things done but found his subordinates too much numbed and indoctrinated by extended congressional oversight and by the 'moralism' of his predecessor Stansfield Turner, to be prepared to develop bold initiatives and get really tough in covert action.

During the early years of the Reagan administration, the National Security Council and its staff had led a comparatively marginal existence. Initially, the president wanted the NSC reduced to its original option-assessment and advisory roles. Policy was to be made by the president and through the State and Defense departments. Reagan's first National Security Advisor, Richard Allen, was kept from direct contact with the president and had to report through his counselor Meese. This was done to prevent the endless turf battles between the NSC and the State Department, which had often crippled foreign policy during the Nixon and Carter years.[12]

This seriously affected the morale of NSC staffers.[13] They were kept away from crucial meetings, and did not carry any weight in the bureaucratic give and take. The situation improved markedly when Allen was replaced by William Clark, a personal friend of the president, with direct and frequent access to the White House. The bureaucratic status of the NSC was enhanced. But its foundation turned out to be narrow, because when Clark left, the NSC had to struggle to claim its position. Clark's successor McFarlane, while being more of an expert in foreign policy than Clark, lacked his ties to the president and personal charisma. The NSC, therefore, was constantly on the look-out for opportunities to assert itself and regain its pivotal role in the making of foreign policy (the earlier curtailment of the NSC had served only to displace not to delimit bureaucratic battles, which were then raging between the departments of State and Defense; so the ratio of keeping the NSC small had lost its appeal in the White House anyhow).[14]

This was roughly the situation of the NSC when the Iran-supported, Lebanese terrorism issue reappeared on the agenda of the government in the fall of 1983. At the same time, the NSC had assumed a key position in another arena involving the 'circumvention' of official policies: Latin America, especially the Nicaraguan civil war. The Reagan administration was composed of staunch supporters of the anti-Sandinista Contra rebels. The rebels were perceived to be freedom fighters for democracy, resisting the move towards totalitarian communism that was allegedly manifest from the development of the Sandinista regime which had taken over the country since the ouster of the right-wing dictator Somoza. Conservative America feared "another Cuba", and vociferously opposed it.[15]

Congress, however, feared "another Vietnam" more than another Cuba and wanted to avoid the U.S. being dragged into another bloody and costly war. Also, liberals held a much different view of the Ortega government, and denied it to be a communist puppet regime. In the spirit of this mood, Congress had approved the so-called Boland amendments, forbidding the CIA, the Department of Defense, or "any other agency or entity of the United States involved in intelligence activities" to engage in any activities supporting the Contra rebels. The Second Boland Amendment was passed in October 1984, prohibiting any U.S. military aid from October 3, 1984 to December 19, 1985.

The congressional move was a severe political setback for an administration that had since long committed itself to the fate of the Contras. Given this degree of involvement, the policy makers did not wish to comply with the newly approved law. They sought ways to get around it, and found two.[16] The first was by privatizing U.S. aid through private fundraisers – who could count on more than the vocal support of the administration. The other was to bend the interpretation of the law and suggest that it did not apply to the NSC (despite the fact that the NSC, had explicitly been given a broad range of responsibilities in the development of intelligence activities).

The NSC subsequently assumed the task of keeping the Contras alive by mobilizing third countries to donate money in their support, and channel these contributions to the recipients. Within the NSC, both National Security advisor McFarlane and some of his aides were actively involved in these efforts.[17] They were not concerned by the fact that they were acting against the parliamentary will and the letter and spirit of the Boland Amendment. They, instead, chose to believe that it was the President's will that ought ultimately to determine the course of U.S. foreign policy; and president Reagan was an enthusiastic supporter of the Contra cause. The same went for DCI Casey, who was very eager that the Contra aid continue, and was frustrated that he could not get his own people to work at it. Also, this turn of events conveniently brought new prominence to the NSC, which was allowed not only to make but also to implement the secret Nicaragua policies almost autonomously.

The task of doing so increasingly fell to Lieutenant Colonel Oliver North, assigned as a deputy director of the Political-Military Division of the NSC staff. In a short time, he had developed an entire network of private operatives and donor countries to sustain the Contras. In fact, his room 392 in the old Executive Office Building had become an ad-hoc nerve center for a variety of covert operations taking place parallel to and beyond those of the regular intelligence agencies.[18] One of his key 'agents' was the retired Major General Richard V. Secord, who eventually was involved in setting up the so-called Enterprise organization, specifically to this end.[19] In his efforts, North was heavily guided by DCI Casey, whom he regarded with the utmost esteem. In fact, Casey more or less acted as North's 'case officer.'[20] Casey's unwavering support kept North on the track even when his boss McFarlane began to come around to the view that the NSC was covered by the Boland Amendment after all and ought to discontinue its activities. McFarlane eventually resigned and was replaced by his deputy, admiral John Poindexter, who harbored far less inhibitions with regard to Contra aid.

In this setting, then, it was almost inevitable that the NSC was to become the main source of the 'reassessment' and subsequent redesign of the government's Iran and counter-terrorism policies. Given his aptitude and energy in setting up the Contra aid-operation, it was only natural that the prime mover within the NSC with regard to the Iran initiative would eventually come to be Oliver North.

It is interesting to note, however, that the extent of direct U.S. involvement in the initiative, as well as North's stepping into it, were greatly enhanced as a result of the 'mini crisis' surrounding a shipment of HAWK missiles to Iran in November 1985. This was, indeed, a very stressful episode, after which it seemed there was no alternative but to make it a U.S.-run operation with Israeli support, instead of continuing the reverse pattern that did not run smoothly.[21]

14.4. Group decision making: the formation of an inner circle

Examining the structure of decision making with regard to the Iran initiative, it is important to differentiate between the strategic decision-making process in and around the White House about whether (and to what extent) to probe the policy of dealing with Iran, and the operational decision-making process regarding the actual implementation of the initiative. While it is hard to draw a perfect line between the two, they were nevertheless fundamentally different. Strategic decision making took place at the highest levels of the Reagan administration, while the actual conduct of the operation involved a large and diverse number of civil servants, bureaucrats, private citizens, soldiers, both from the U.S. and foreign countries. Lt. Col. North was the linking pin between these two arenas of decision making, as provider of input to the top decision makers (he wrote notoriously lengthy memos to that effect), and as key coordinator of the implementation of the initiative.

Although the importance of the operational side of the Iran-Contra affair can hardly be underestimated, the focus of this decision-making analysis lies nevertheless with the key strategic decisions which basically shaped and determined U.S. engagement. It is here that the formation of an inner circle (or in Draper's more pejorative terminology, a "junta") can be observed.[22] It is here, therefore, that a groupthink analysis could be useful in principle.

A controversial idea

Only three years after the termination of the embassy hostage crisis, the very idea to move toward more friendly relationships with Iran, was highly unusual. The suggestion that, as a means of enhancing this rapproachment, American arms should be transferred to Iran, was outright controversial. The day to day managers of American foreign and security policies, Secretaries Shultz (Foreign Policy) and Weinberger (Defense) and their immediate entourage, were certain to oppose any such ideas. Despite their continuous and often bitter disagreements, they had been the chief architects of the official U.S. policy of continued hostility toward Iran, as well as the policy of taking action against international terrorism and the regimes that supported it. Even when informed that the new Iran initiative was designed to look beyond the Khomeini era and start to support 'moderate elements' within the Iranian regime as an investment in the future, the foreign policy professionals were not convinced. The briefs they had been receiving about the internal politics of Iran, indicated just one thing: whatever it was that was going on there, U.S. officials simply lacked adequate information about it; there was no way to tell whether there were any moderates, and, if so, who were the right persons to approach.

In this light, it was hardly surprising that, upon receiving an NSC policy paper by Donald Fortier and Howard Teicher arguing the delivery of Western arms to Iran to prevent it from becoming a Soviet satellite (June 1985), Secretary of Defense Weinberger remarked to his military advisor General Powell: "This is almost too absurd to comment on."[23]

The development of the strategic decision-making process can be characterized as the outcome of a bureau-political battle between different groups and factions. This test of wills ultimately determined who were involved in making the decisions and, consequently, what was to be decided. Its outcome was, indeed, the formation of a small, informal, and relatively isolated group at the core of the decision-making process. In other words, the facts of the Iran-contra affair as they are known today appear to bear out the preliminary condition of the revised model of groupthink: the existence of one clearly definable decision group.

It is now indicated how this came about. A number of stages in the shaping of the decision process can be discerned.[24]

Stage 1: Initial probes

The first specific act with regard to the initiative that indicated the likelihood of it engendering controversy within the administration, occurred in early May, 1985. Ghorbanifar, his colleague and competing lobbyist and arms merchant Kashoggi, and several Israeli officials had been dropping feelers about the possibility of altering U.S. Iran policies for some time. As indicated earlier, these initiatives were looked at favorably within the NSC staff. NSC advisor McFarlane eventually decided to send a new and energetic NSC staff member, Michael Ledeen, on a private mission to the Israeli Prime Minister Peres to find out Israel's knowledge and opinions on Iran.

The trip itself was not very successful, although it was the first time that the Israelis suggested delivering arms to Iran with U.S. approval. Its significance, in retrospect, came from the way it was staged. It was organized without prior knowledge from the State Department. The Department nor the U.S. ambassador in Israel were informed in advance by McFarlane. They subsequently protested this NSC soloism, seizing the opportunity to indicate their suspicion of the affair, claiming that care should be taken to understand that with regard to Iran, Israel might be pursuing its own agenda independently from the U.S.

Stage 2: Opposition

The contours of the rift within the Reagan administration began to show more clearly when the above-mentioned memo by Fortier and Teicher was circulated to the Defense and State Departments, and the CIA. As indicated, Weinberger was both stunned and irritated over the implied policy change. He was opposed to easing the restrictions on arms sales to Iran, and was highly skeptical about the idea of doing business with so-called 'moderates' within Iran. Secretary of State Shultz was of the same opinion. DCI Casey, however, came out in favor of the ideas in the memo, in particular its concern with preventing the Soviet Union to increase its influence on Iran. McFarlane, not surprisingly, sided with Casey in supporting the initiative. At this point, the parties were stalemated, and the memo seemed to die an easy death. This episode established a pattern of advocates and opponents that was to become more pronounced over time. The lines were beginning to get drawn.

Stage 3: First shipment

The initiative did not die down. As remarked in the Tower Report, events in the Middle East kept the NSC staff's ideas alive, basically: the kidnappings, the many violent incidents, and the TWA hijack magnified the perceived need for a policy reassessment.[25] The two basic objectives, the strategic opening to Iran and the release of American hostages held by Iran-backed groups, were too salient to some of the key officials in the administration, to allow the initiative to simply wither away. As a consequence of the Ledeen-Peres contacts and the implicit or explicit approval of McFarlane, a first shipment of U.S. made arms (508 TOW missiles) was sold from Israel to Iran, of course in the utmost secrecy.

As Israel could not have done so without explicit U.S. approval given by the President, it appears that the United States was already directly and legally involved in the sales of arms to Iran as early as August 1985. At the same time, during the various investigations no clear answer was found to the question of whether Reagan actually approved the shipment. The President first agreed that he had done so, later denied it, and finally said he could not remember. Yet McFarlane had a very clear recollection. He had said to the President: "Mr. President, as you know, your Secretaries of State and Defense are opposed to this." According to McFarlane, the President had said he understood that, but had decided to go ahead with it. In addition, North was put in charge of the implementation of U.S. attempts to free the hostages and negotiate with Iran, adding to his already voluminous workload (Nicaraguan Contras support).

In this third stage, therefore, the rift over Iran was acknowledged at the highest level of the administration. Even more so, the President began to choose sides: he supported the NSC (and the CIA) in proceeding with the covert (and clandestine) policy of arms sales to Iran. Yet at this point, the U.S. was committed only to a back-up role in replenishing Israeli stocks of U.S. weapons.

Stage 4: North steps in

The commitment was strengthened and made more direct, however, by a series of events surrounding the second transport of arms in November 1985. First of all, the Israelis again insisted upon a U.S. guarantee of replacing Israeli stocks. Secondly, it was to be made clear to the Iranians that this deal was one of trading arms for hostages: the missiles (Hawks) were to be delivered not until five American hostages had reported to the U.S. embassy in Beirut.

The deal was to be made via Portugal, but Israeli middlemen had forgotten to get Portugese customs clearance. Also, the shipment had originally been planned to proceed in a regular and marked Israeli aircraft, not the most appropriate means of transport to Iran.

As time was running out for the deal to be successfully completed (the large Iranian distrust toward the Americans and Israelis necessitated the development of very strict time schedules. Confronted with the risk of the transaction breaking down, North decided to go higher up. He alerted

McFarlane, who was in Geneva assisting the President during the summit with Soviet leader Gorbachev. Meanwhile, the Israelis called their Defense minister Rabin in New York.

Pressure was put on the Portuguese authorities not to delay this transport of 'oil drilling equipment' (maybe a more accurate description was given). But Portuguese intransigence continued. To solve the problems with the deal, North alerted Secord, a key actor in the Contra assistance operation, who had a long experience in this line of work. Further, he called the CIA to furnish one of their 'proprietary' aircraft (i.e., a plane from a company that was allegedly private but in fact owned or controlled by the CIA). Ultimately, the transport proceeded directly from Israel to Iran in that aircraft. Even then, the operation was a disaster: only 18 out of 80 promised Hawks were on board (the plane was too small), and they were the wrong type of Hawk. The Iranians were outraged, and cut the deal. No hostages were released.

Despite this lack of success, U.S. commitment increased, but for different reasons. What happened was that the deputy director of the CIA, John McMahon found out about CIA involvement in the November 1985 transport soon after it had taken place. As DCI Casey was out of town at the moment, McMahon decided that what the CIA had done (lending a hand in a cover operation) was illegal under the Hughes-Ryan Amendment to the Foreign Assistance Act, unless the President issued a finding stating that the operation was in the interest of U.S. national security. He, therefore, called in CIA General Counsel Sporkin to draft such a finding, which would serve as a post-hoc legitimation.

This finding, drafted in consultation with Casey after his return, was a remarkable document. First of all, it explicitly established U.S. involvement in arms deliveries to Iran – in direct contrast to official U.S. policies, as well as implying the making of deals with terrorists. But also, the finding explicitly instructed the DCI not to brief the Congress on what had transpired, until after the President had decided to do so.

This latter clause was politically significant. Not only did it indicate that secrecy and security were deemed more important than the following of regular parliamentary procedures, it also showed that, again, potential opponents to the initiative were kept in the dark by its key propagators – in this case DCI Casey. Casey had already had serious trouble with Congress about his reluctance to forward crucial information about CIA operations, and wanted the matter to be kept strictly secret, probably realizing that opposition to the arms deliveries would be immense. The wording of the finding took care of that. Outgroups were to be kept 'out'. (The finding was allegedly signed by the President on December 5 but later destroyed by McFarlane's successor at the NSC, Admiral Poindexter.)

Stage 5: Defense and State find out
At about the same time, Secretary of Defense Weinberger was informed of an intelligence report mentioning negotiations between high-ranking American and Iranian officials, including the topic of 'arms'. Weinberger

was outraged, particularly when he heard that he was not even supposed to have seen the report by his own Defense Intelligence Agency in the first place – it had been sent off to him by accident. Furthermore, the DIA had heard the news not from American but from foreign sources!

Consulting Shultz, he learned that the State Department had been by-passed, too. Shultz had also heard only bits and pieces from various, partly accidental, sources. Probing further, it turned out that the decision to circumvent the Secretaries of State and Defense originated in the White House. He had one of his undersecretaries find out who was conducting the negotiations. This quickly lead to Oliver North.

Weinberger's furor was undiminished. Never before had the President deliberately decided to by-pass his trusted friend and associate, as well as Shultz. He too discerned the formation of a core group erecting an informal and secretive policy circuit. He wanted an explanation, and demanded a meeting of the members of the National Security Council.

Stage 6: A big meeting
On December 7, the meeting requested by Weinberger proceeded in the presidential quarters. Present were Reagan, Shultz, Weinberger, McMahon (Deputy DCI), Chief of Staff Regan, McFarlane, and his deputy Poindexter.[26] It was the first full dress confrontation between the two ad-hoc coalitions that were beginning to emerge. But it did not bring a clear resolution of the issue. Nor did it change the pattern of small-group decision making by principals from the NSC, the CIA, and the President, that had, by now, settled in.

The meeting was conducted on the basis of a lengthy memo by North reporting the basic rationale for the initiative as well as a summary of events. Furthermore, it proposed that the U.S. should allow the Israelis to immediately sell the Iranians another 3300 TOW's and 50 improved Hawk missiles, replenishing their stocks afterward. This would result in the freeing of the five americans held hostage in Beirut. As Iranians, Israelis and Secord had already agreed to meet on the sale, a quick decision was required, according to North.

Not surprisingly, Shultz and Weinberger vehemently opposed any such deal. In fact, they were opposed to the entire initiative. Not only did it go against the stated policies of the U.S. and did it violate the law, it was also doomed to be a failure. Although, at present, there is no information available about the content of the speeches made during the meeting, Shultz and Weinberger's comments were no doubt influenced by their recall of the mistake of the Carter administration in pretending to understand and to be able to control the internal dynamics of Iranian politics. Carter had not wanted to understand that the hostages would not be freed until the internal political turmoil in post-revolutionary Iran would have subsided, no matter what the U.S. did. The advocates of the Iran initiative failed to see the tenacity of their assumptions about the possibilities of a dialogue with Iranian moderates.

Upon hearing these arguments, the President seems to have been evasive. He did decide to send McFarlane to Secord, Ghorbanifar and the others to inform them of a change in U.S. policy: no more arms would be delivered, but other means would be attempted to achieve a political dialogue. On this count, Weinberger was content, leaving the meeting with the distinct impression that he and Shultz had succeeded in terminating the initiative. However, the ambiguity of the President's attitude is revealed by the fact that Secretary Shultz perceived it differently. He came away feeling that the President was annoyed by Shultz and Weinberger's opposition, determined as he was to set the hostages free (remember again the stressful context that had developed around the hostage issue within the United States). The President wanted to "do something, anything" to get the hostages out, and now his two Secretaries were trying to block the only feasible route to short-term success.

Stage 7: The initiative survives
Shultz' impression was correct. Moreover, the President was not about to change his course in earnest, nor were the NSC elite and their supporters in the CIA. This was evident when McFarlane reported a bad reaction from Ghorbanifar and the others to his announcement that the arms deal was off. Instead, Ghorbanifar had wanted to talk only about specified numbers of TOW missiles for each hostage.

Much of what was decided in the days after the London-meeting depended upon the question whether or not the Americans could trust Ghorbanifar. Ledeen urged, with North's approval, the CIA to arrange a new evaluation of Ghorbanifar. An interview with him convinced the CIA Iranian desk chief of Ghorbanifar's untruthfulness. It was decided that Ghorbanifar should be given a polygraph test.

With McFarlane out and Poindexter newly installed, North became the driving force behind the initiative, despite his subordinate rank. North was very unhappy with McFarlane's negative comments during and after the London meeting with Ghorbanifar. He wrote an 'eyes only' memorandum to McFarlane and Poindexter, called *Next Steps*. In this memorandum, North described four options that he saw as necessary: the arms-for-hostages swap discussed in London; an Israeli delivery of 400 to 500 TOWs to Iran to restore 'good faith'; a military raid; and the 'do nothing' approach.

North also described a fifth possible option: the U.S. could, with an appropriate covert action Finding, commence making direct deliveries, using Secord to control Ghorbanifar and manage the delivery operations.

In mid-December 1985 Amiram Nir, advisor on terrorism to the Prime Minister of Israel, Shimon Peres, proposed the following: the Israelis would ship 4,000 'unimproved TOW's' to Iran; after the delivery of the first 500 all five American hostages would be released; simultaneously, the Israeli Southern Lebanon Army would release 20-30 Hezbollah prisoners. If the American hostages were released, Israel would ship the other 3,500 TOW's, having Iran confirm that it would stop supporting terrorism and new hostage seizures. The US would have to replace the TOW's only in case the hostages were released. Another feature of Nir's proposal was the generating of profits from the Iran arms sales that could be used for other projects, something which Nir and North had talked about earlier (in November '85).

If the US favored the Nir-proposal for revitalizing the Iranian initiative, obtaining a new covert action Finding signed by the President would be essential. CIA council Sporkin prepared a Finding that would enable the US to commence direct deliveries to Iran. In particular also, the finding especially enabled Casey, who was supposed to be in charge of any US covert action, to refrain from reporting to Congress about the deliveries.

The draft version for covert action was ready on January 6, 1986, having been scrutinized by both North and Poindexter, and was signed by the President that same day.[27]

Stage 8: The President makes a choice
The next day, another full NSC meeting was held. That meeting on January 7, 1986 was the final turning point. Present at the meeting were the President, Vice President Bush, Shultz, Weinberger, Regan, Casey, Poindexter and Attorney General Meese. Weinberger and Shultz continued to object strenuously, while all the others favored the plan or were neutral. However, no mention was made of the proposed Finding that was already signed by the President.

Meese proposed a new line of action: the CIA could legally sell weapons, obtained from the Defense Department, to third countries, under the Economy Act. Using this mechanism would render obsolete Weinberger's legal objections to he continuation of the arms deliveries.

The atmosphere at the meeting was awkward. It became quite clear that Schultz and Weinberger stood alone in their opposition. Weinberger recounted his disenchantment before the Tower Board:

"The only time I got the impression the President was for this thing was in January, (...), and at the time it became very apparent to me that the cause I was supporting was lost and that the President was for it."[28]

A slightly changed version of the Finding was signed by the President on January 17. At about that time, Weinberger was informed in no uncertain terms by Poindexter, on behalf of the President, that a decision has been reached, and that the Department of Defense was obliged to deliver the required numbers of arms, and to do so very discreetly. It was clear that further bureaucratic obstruction was useless. For Weinberger, a long-time friend and associate of Reagan, the outcome of this decision and the way of was communicated to him, must have been quite painful.[29] At the same time, Schultz never even heard of the fact that the plan was actually going to be implemented.

Meanwhile, operational planning was restructured to implement the new policy. The fact that one of the key pawns in the game was Manucher Ghorbanifar was not considered a problem. In mid january, Ghorbanifar returned to Washington for his new polygraph test. The conclusion was that "Ghorbanifar is a fabricator who has deliberately deceived the U.S. Government concerning his information and activities."[30] Yet although this harsh assessment led to internal CIA instructions not to deal with Ghorbanifar, the proponents of the initiative at the NSC (as well as Casey) discounted the report.

Stage 9: the cards are drawn
Thus passed the final phase of the formation of the inner group. The key factor was the conversion of differences into a division of power: those on one side were now given a licence to act and those on the other side were not even permitted to know what actions were being taken.

The President's signing of the Finding marked the beginning of direct U.S. control over the Iran arms sales initiative. On February 17, 1986, the U.S. sent 500 TOW's to Israel for shipment to Iran, followed by another 500 on February 27. Altogether, 2,004 TOW's were sent to Iran. However, no hostages were released. Instead, one hostage was killed on April 17 in retaliation for the American bombing of Libya two days before.

The key goals set forth in the Finding were not achieved. Yet, as North did not hesitate to point out to his fellow operators and his superiors, the arms sales were successful in that the Iranians were willing to pay substantially more for the military goods than they cost. These profits were diverted to be used in supporting the battle of the Contras in Nicaragua. In order to achieve this, North had set up a complex web of financial transactions through European and other accounts. In this way, the Iran initiative became a no-lose policy: with the transfer of money to the Contras there would always be an incentive to continue.

Meanwhile, on the negotiating front, things were very difficult after the February shipments had failed to produce results. However, after long and difficult talks, it was agreed that former NSC advisor McFarlane would head an American delegation including North and Nir (who passed as an American) to Tehran. The Americans were lead to believe this would be a major step in normalizing American-Iranian relations.

On May 25, 1986, McFarlane set foot on Iranian soil hoping for a steady release of all the hostages. He had one out of four pallets of Hawk spare parts originally demanded by the Iranians with him as a goodwill gesture. He also carried as gifts a hand-inscribed bible from President Reagan, and a piece of kosher chocolate cake. The meetings turned out to be an unmitigated disaster: none of the high-level Iranian officials that he had been led to expect, were available to see McFarlane. Talking with Americans, especially high-level policy makers was still a dangerous feat in post-revolutionary Iran. Moreover, the Iranians were angry that the Americans had not brought all of the spare parts. There was a chain of misunderstandings, and distrust mounted. Frustrated, McFarlane decided to leave on May 29. In the end, no hostage was released. The initiative lay in ruins.

However, it resurged again when on July 26, one hostage (Jenco) was released. The core group saw this as proof that Ghorbanifar could deliver after all. In the early Fall, an alternative channel of communication with alleged Iranian leaders was opened through the efforts of Albert Hakim, Ghorbanifar's countryman and competing arms merchant. It lead to new euphoria North et al.: at last, things would work out well. Meetings took place in September in Washington and in October in Frankfurt, first on the 6th and later on the 26th. After a new round of deliveries, one further hostage, dr. Jacobsen, was released on November 2. By then, the initiative had begun to unravel. The 'Second Channel' did not produce any other results.

Conclusion: The Iran decision group

Reviewing the structure of decision making during the critical period in which the arms transports and related activities took place, the evidence suggests that the key strategic decisions were, indeed, taken by a small, basically informal group of officials. In this sense, the case of the Iran-Contra affair appears to be an appropriate candidate for groupthink analysis.

Who were in this group? First of all, it should be remarked that there were very few occasions at which the group as a whole would actually meet. Rather, the members of the group were interacting intensively on a bilateral basis. The format and operation of the group were determined by a number of factors which are discussed at greater length shortly. However, the most important binding mechanism lay in the mutual agreement on the Iran initiative – although the actors had different reasons for pursuing it. By this standard, actors were 'in' or 'out'. The decision process was simply channeled so as to leave only supporters of the initiative at the helm of events.

The small amount of collective meetings throughout the episode makes the issue of determining the boundaries of the group a matter interpretation rather than simple assessment. Upon examining all the available evidence, however, the following officials can be said to have constituted the core group responsible for the Iran initiative: President Reagan, NSC advisor McFarlane and his successor Poindexter, DCI Casey, and North, with a small number of other NSC staff as fringe members supporting the group.[32]

The triangle of McFarlane (but even more Poindexter) – Casey – North constituted the core of the group developing the various steps, in concert with the numerous third parties involved on the operational side of the process and the contacts with the Iranians.

Although the specific knowledge and role of the President during the developmental period can, at present, not be ascertained with precision, it is hard to escape the conclusion that he helped shape the (bureau)political climate and the collective assumptions and priorities underlying the initiative. Actively and passively, he encouraged the core group to proceed. At a number of occasions, he explicitly supported the group vis a vis its bureaucratic opponents. He allowed the informal circuit to grow and by-pass the regular actors of American foreign policy. Content with only a very superficial knowledge of the details, he made it clear that for himself, the goal of setting free the hostages justified the means of delivering arms to Iran; he wanted it done, and was not too interested in how it was done. The members of his group understood and supported the Presidential agenda (particularly Casey), and considered themselves at liberty to proceed with their secret activities. With regard to the diversion of funds from the Iran project to the Nicaraguan Contras, the situation was similar, although the extent of presidential involvement in the diversion decisions seems to have been kept at a minimum by his subordinates.[33]

14.5. Groupthink dynamics

Dave McCurdy, the Oklahoma Democrat, asked: "Who managed the operation, Mr. Casey?"
"I think we were all in it. It was a team."
Who headed the team? Who called the shots? Was it Poindexter or Casey?"
Casey replied: "I think it was the President."[34]

Having established the basic course of developments and the structure of decision making with regard to the Iran initiative, it is time to analyze the group decision process in greater detail to assess whether the dynamics of groupthink as outlined in the revised model were present. Following the revised model, the analysis focuses on group cohesiveness and anticipatory compliance as the two basic process dynamics leading to groupthink. Furthermore, it also takes into account the distinction between type I and type II groupthink. Subsequently, the symptoms of groupthink are discussed.

Group cohesiveness: an ad-hoc coalition

Was the Iran group cohesive? What kinds of binding factors were operating? How did the group withstand pressures to disintegrate or terminate its activities? When did it fall apart?
    The Iran decision group was actually a sub-group formed within the more formal framework of the National Security Council. It was an ad-hoc coalition, which took shape on the basis of elimination and selection: only those who supported the initiative ultimately remained part of the decision-making process. The coalition was bound together by a number of factors.

Solidarity. The core group fully sympathized with the President's urge to get the hostages out. They observed the stress the hostage crisis generated in the President, evidenced by his constantly returning to the hostage problem during meetings. They understood the urgency he felt in accomplishing this goal; they were also aware that the President would condone almost any means that would be used to achieve this goal, or were led to believe so (as was North by his superiors).

The Cause. At the time, the NSC staff was highly ideologically motivated. Especially North but to a lesser extent also McFarlane and, within the CIA,

Casey, were strongly committed to anti-communist policies. Preventing the spread of communism in Iran and diminishing Soviet influence there were highly salient policy objectives to these actors; even though in practice, they might have been secondary to the short-term goal of liberating the hostages. An exemplary indication of the ideologically-motivated affection between group members can be found in a memo from ex-national security advisor McFarlane to North. In response to North's reports of the likely release of a hostage and the prospect of a first Iran-U.S. meeting, McFarlane commented as follows:

> "Roger Ollie. Well done – if the world only knew how many times you have kept a semblance of integrity and gumption to U.S. policy, they would make you Secretary of State. But they can't know and would complain if they did – such is the state of democracy in the late 20th century."[35]

Not only did McFarlane in this note reconfirm the group ties, he also denounced the outside world, that did not understand or appreciate the group's heroic work.

During the later stages of the Iran initiative, the diversion idea was particularly appealing to North, who had been a fanatic, if covertly operating supporter of the Contra cause. In this manner, the Iran initiative became an opportunity to kill two flies in one stroke.

While the Secretaries of State and Defense broadly subscribed to these ideological viewpoints, their opposition to the initiative and subsequent exclusion from the core group followed from their taking into closer consideration the broader geopolitical implications of the initiative. They were especially concerned with the adverse consequences for American standing in the Middle East and elsewhere, which would emerge when the initiative would become public.

Despite these broader ideological stimuli, it was clear among the members of the core group that the liberation of the hostages was the primordial consideration in the mind of the President in supporting the initiative. The fact that it required trading arms for hostages, in this respect, was an unpleasant reality that was carefully hidden:

> "And you would have to be a fool not to see that, whatever our intentions were, the reality was apparently arms for hostages."[36]

Secrecy. From an operational necessity, the need to maintain secrecy became an instrument for differentiating between who were in the core group and the marginalized outsiders. Secret knowledge determined one's status. The emphasis on the need to maintain secrecy legitimized the exclusion of outgroups. Group deliberations were pervaded by a fear of leaks. According to the Congressional Report, secrecy became an obsession.[37] The Tower Review board arrived at a similar judgment, stating that:

"Because of the obsession with secrecy, interagency consideration of the initiative was limited to the cabinet level. With the exception of the NSC staff and, after January 17, 1986, a handful of CIA officials, the rest of the executive departments and agencies were largely excluded. As a consequence, the initiative was never vetoed at the staff level. This deprived those responsible for the initiative of considerable expertise – on the situation in Iran; on the difficulties of dealing with terrorists; on the mechanics of conducting a diplomatic opening. It also kept the plan from receiving a tough, critical review."[38]

Another apparent reason for secrecy stemmed from the application of historical analogies by the participants. In particular, the Carter period served as a negative anchor and source of 'don'ts' for the current policies:

"But the real thing that was driving this was that there was in early '86, late '85, a lot of pressure from the hostage families to meet with the President and there were articles in the press about the forgotten hostages, and there were a lot of things being said about the U.S. government isn't doing anything, not doing anything. And, of course, what is being done we are desperately trying to keep secret. And there is a lot of fear about the yellow ribbons going back up and that this President would have the same problems that the last President had with Iranian hostages."[39]

Interestingly, the Iranians were similarly influenced by unpleasant analogies. For instance, the Iranian contacts during the meetings with McFarlane and others stressed again and again that back in 1980, a mere talk with then NSC advisor Brzezinski had brought down Prime Minister Bazargan; therefore, the present contacts were to be seen as a heroic and risky initiative on the part of themselves. [40]

Congress was perceived to be part of the outsiders that were potentially damaging. It was therefore to be kept in the dark. CIA counsel Sporkin took great pains in drafting the Findings of December 1985 and January 1986, to ensure that this policy of information minimalization would be legitimized by Presidential decree.

The need to maintain secrecy also involved the group decision-making process itself. In this respect, the following observation by Attorney General Meese referring to the January 7, 1986 NSC meeting, is revealing:

"One of the difficulties that I have and that I suspect others may have, is that I considered this so highly sensitive and classified that I took almost no notes at any time during the thing because I didn't want to reduce anything to paper. I talked with no one about it (....)."[41]

Throughout, the emphasis on secrecy contributed to the extreme informality of the decision process, and promoted ambiguity about what was being agreed. In this manner, all participants could form their own particular interpretations of the meeting, while the core group could proceed unhindered.

Bureaucratic opportunism and interdependency. Ideology and solidarity were not the only factors shaping the coalition. The key actors also had definite interests, which, for various reasons, were served by teaming up in favor of the initiative. This is evident from the review of the context of decision making presented above. The President wanted, first and foremost, to free the hostages, and he was attracted to anyone inside or outside the administration who might deliver. The NSC Staff regarded the initiative as an opportunity to regain the territory and bureaucratic momentum it had been lacking ever since the beginning of the Reagan administration. In particular, the Iran initiative provided the NSC with an opportunity to circumvent the State and Defense Departments not only in the making of policy, but also in its implementation. DCI Casey, finally, needed the NSC Staff to implement the policy which he heavily supported on ideological grounds as well on the basis of his perception of the desires of his old his friend (the President). He needed the NSC Staff because his own agency was either legally prevented (Boland amendment about Contra Aid) or institutionally hesitant (the CIA in the post-Turner era) to undertake this kind of covert action.[42]

Cohesiveness: conclusion. The cohesiveness of the decision group, therefore, was the result of a combination of 'ideological' and pragmatic considerations. It was partly based on affection between group members (North-Casey, CaseyReagan), but above all premised on interdependence. Finally, group cohesiveness was in part the result of spontaneous processes, but also brought about by specific efforts on the part of some members (exclusion of outgroups, selective presentation of available information).

This rather complex and solid basis for the group enabled it to withstand considerable pressure to abandon the policy throughout the late summer of 1986, and following the first public disclosures in the late fall. This explains in part the aborted cover-up by North and Poindexter. Faced with public disclosure of the initiative, their first instinct was not to save themselves but rather to contain the damage to the operation itself, but in particular to the President. The frantic paper-shredding sessions and the compilation of various chronologies were motivated by these desires. The President, in turn, when faced with public and congressional indignation, could not but embark upon a policy of 'getting out the truth'; but, to find the truth, he appointed the Attorney General, a personal friend and co-worker highly sympathetic to the Reagan foreign policy in general – and also involved in meetings about the Iran initiative long before the news broke. Not surprisingly, Meese's investigation slowed down when he learned the details of the case. His caution allowed the key actors more time to cover their tracks.

Even after the inevitable had happened and the key facts were made public, signs of continued 'we-ness' among the group members were evident from their public statements. While Poindexter and particularly North were full of glowing statements about the basic values of American democracy and the fight against communism, they were also very emphatic in their continued admiration for and loyalty to their president. In turn, Reagan refused to condemn North and instead called him a national hero. In this respect, the Iran group dissembled the Watergate group which rapidly disintegrated when the news began breaking (Dean's defection, Nixon's dissociation from Haldeman and Ehrlichman). Indeed, it reminds more of admiral Kimmel's group at Pearl Harbour, whose members continued to express their affection and admiration for their leader when testifying about the fiasco.[43]

Conformity, leadership, and responsibility

The revised model of groupthink provides a second perspective in analyzing groupthink processes: 'closed' leadership styles and (anticipatory) compliance among group members. Did these mechanisms play a role in the case of the decision-making process concerning the Iran initiative? It shall be argued here that they did. Indeed, it is suggested here that in order to understand the dynamics of *Irangate*, it is necessary to understand the dynamics of leadership and compliance in the decision group, in addition to examining group cohesiveness and its possible effects.

Promotional leadership: "The President wants it." In many reports about the Iran-Contra affair much emphasis was placed upon President Reagan's management style of delegation and leaving most of the conduct of policy to his associates. It was alleged that because of this lack of solid leadership, the initiative was allowed to go on unchecked far too long. In graphic detail, it was reported that the President signed some of the key "Findings" authorizing the arms deals inadvertently or absent-mindedly. In summary, an image was created in which a well-intending but not fully competent President was manipulated by some of his key advisors that should have known better. The Tower Commission, for instance, stated that:

> "President Reagan's personal management style places an especially heavy responsibility on his key advisors. Knowing his style, they should have been particularly mindful of the need for special attention to the manner in which this arms sale initiative developed and proceeded. On this score, neither the National Security advisor nor the other NSC principals deserve high marks."[44]

As a consequence, the policymaking system of these NSC is said to have failed.

While there is no doubt value in this analysis, it does not seem to catch fully the impact of Reagan's leadership style. In effect, from a somewhat different perspective one might say that the system did not fail at all. In fact, it implemented the basic desires and objectives of the President. It failed in the sense that it did not lead to a review of the preferred course of action, develop alternative solutions, and work towards restraint. It is, however, questionable whether these latter functions can be realistically 'designed-in' in the NSC system, as the Tower recommendations seem to imply. More pointedly, the above analysis probably does not grab the full extent and impact of Reagan's involvement.[45]

Reexamining the patterns of leadership in the Iran decision-making process, the following questions emerge: Who were the group leaders? What were their policy preferences? To what extent did they steer the process of deliberation and choice toward these preferences?

Presidential leadership. There were two 'leaders' in the Iran group. First of all, there was President Reagan. Formally, the NSC system is designed according to his desires and viewpoints. With regard to the development of the Iran initiative, Reagan's leadership of the NSC was not at all only superficial and delegatory. In fact, he made a number of key choices which shaped the basic course of action that emerged.

By far the most important bias that he imposed upon the process was his explicit support of the initiative. This enabled the proponents of the arms deals to withstand the opposition from the two secretaries. Indeed, during the January 7, 1986, meeting of the NSC principals, the President made it very clear that he was all in favor of pursuing it further. He subsequently allowed Shultz and Weinberger to be cut out of the decision process altogether, and did not object when it was proposed that Congress should not be informed of the developments with regard to Iran.

In doing so, the President was instrumental in narrowing down not only the feasible options under consideration, but also the range of actors to be further involved in the decision-making process. Had Reagan not chosen so explicitly at such an early stage, the bureaucratic pulling and hauling could never have been resolved so quickly and unilaterally; a more bipartisan, adversarial policy process would have developed, and better use could have been made of the NSC system. It would have prevented, if anything, the amateurism of NSC staff members in implementing the initiative using a strange mix of public officials and private actors, some of dubious reputation.

However, as many of his predecessors (notably Richard M. Nixon as one of them), Reagan felt highly uncomfortable with disagreement among his advisors in his own presence. He strongly preferred harmony and consensus when deliberating about policy decisions. As these did not exist in the Iran case, they had to be engineered. This was accomplished by removing the known opponents to the initiative from the range of participants in the decision-making process. It was typical that the two secretaries did not receive this message from Reagan personally. He had it done through operatives, in this case Poindexter, who bluntly informed Weinberger by telephone in mid-January that the President had decided that there was no room for argument anymore; a definitive Finding had been signed, Poindexter said, and Weinberger simply had to obey presidential orders and deliver the requested TOW's to the CIA for further delivery to Iran. To Weinberger, a long-time personal friend and associate of Reagan, this was humiliating.

Part of this conduct can be explained by the President's strong personal commitment to the fate of the hostages and their speedy liberation. On several occasions he made it clear that it was one of his chief worries; he wanted a solution, a soon as possible. This Presidential position was, of course, well-known among his associates. This put the proponents of the initiative in a very strong position. The supporters had at least something to offer, while the opponents (State, Defense secretaries) had to reason against a course of action known to have the President's sympathy without offering any short-term alternatives – and both parties knew this to be the case. In other words, Shultz and Weinberger probably saw little benefit in continuing to argue their objections in front of a president with his mind already made up. Stubbornly resisting the arms deliveries would probably not prevent the premature 'closure' of the decision-making process: The initiative would continue with or without their support. Furthermore, resistance was likely to severe their relations with the President. Already Secretary of State Shultz sensed irritation with the President over his and Weinberger's resistance at the January 7 meeting. This was a president who wanted a policy approved, and who was not prepared to argue about it at length.[46]

Leader behind the scenes. There was a second leader figure operating in the decision process, in particular within the core group who managed the Iran initiative. It was DCI Casey. In his book on Casey and the CIA, Woodward describes at length the way in which Casey practically 'ran' Oliver North as an agent. In doing so, he indirectly managed the implementation of the initiative; to what extent he did so upon Presidential request will never be clear. In any case, North was an invaluable operative for Casey, whose own agency had to be kept out of the operation as much as possible (Casey even by-passed and misinformed most of his own CIA staff). Consider the following observations:

> "More and more, Lieutenant Colonel North found himself making that short trek from his own office to Casey's. Casey was not a boss but a soulmate. The DCI had evolved into a father figure, an intimate and adviser. He had become a guiding hand, almost a case officer for North. (....)
> As North's activities became increasingly risky and compartmented, Casey was one of the few who knew. North found Casey's advice invaluable; he knew how to get things done and did not hesitate. (....)
> North explained to the DCI that he and the Israelis had devised the diversion scheme to funnel the profits from the Iranian arms sales to the Contras. Casey was effusive, immediately grasping the irony. Iran had earlier tried to ship arms to the Sandinistas and had provided them with some $100 million in oil credits over the years. To get the Ayatollah to fund the Contras was a strategic coup, a 'sting' of unimagined proportions: having an enemy fund a friend. The DCI labeled this 'the ultimate covert operation'.

North's world became more and more confined. The most secret System IV channel for NSC intelligence documents was not considered safe, his paperwork was 'non-logged', he dealt with 'out-of-system' documents. But he could talk freely with the DCI, who was the Godfather of both the Iran and the Contra supply operations."[47]

These observations underline not only the subtle leadership role of Casey but also the shared sense of mission, the feeling of triumph and optimism that pervaded the core group during key stages of the Iran operation.

Compliance: "The President approved it." It is significant to note that most of the members of the core group were either military men or officials with a military background (Poindexter and North were career military, Casey and McFarlane had military backgrounds). Especially North and Poindexter were unexperienced politically. They tended to view the President more as their commander-in-chief than as a political official operating in an elaborate system of checks and balances. Their loyalty to the President stemmed from this military perception. During the congressional hearings, North, for instance, remarked: "And if the commander-in-chief tells this lieutenant colonel to go stand in the corner and sit on his head, I will do so."[48] In a way, this quotation reminds one of the "agenetic state" put forward by Milgram to explain the destructive obedience of a large number of the subjects in his experiments.[49] As suggested above, North held Casey in a comparably high esteem:

> "If Casey told him what to think and what to do, North had every reason to believe that the older man knew best and, above all, knew what the President wanted. (....)
> Yet North was not an ordinary military timeserver; he had a touch of fantasy in his makeup that made him overdo, overestimate, and overstate. North was a strange combination of the naive, the driven, the fanatical, and the self-deceived, with a little of the background and guile necessary for clandestine operations in Central America or the Middle East. He was a soldier in a civilian setting, refighting an old war in new and different circumstances. He was more than anything else a latter-day American innocent abroad."[50]

This image was confirmed when North, testifying during the hearings gave his own particular version of the United States' political system as laid down in the Constitution:

> "I deeply believe that the President of the United States is also an elected official of this land. And by the Constitution, as I understand it, he is the person charged with making and carrying out the foreign policy of this country. I believed from the moment I was engaged in this activity in 1984, that this was in furtherance of the foreign policy established by the President. I still believe that."[51]

Similarly, NSC advisor Poindexter reduced the American political system of checks and balances to presidential supremacy, indicating his perceptions of leadership and authority. Specifically, he stated that:

"My objective all along was to withhold from Congress exactly what the NSC staff was doing in carrying out the President's policy."[52]

In other words, as what they did reflected the commands, wishes, or intentions of the President, both North and Poindexter believed that, by definition, their acts were legitimate – morally if not legally. While strictly adhering to presidential leadership, their disdain for Congress and other political institutions came to the fore.[53] Poindexter remarked about his policy not to inform Congress that he simply did not want any *outside* interference. The third member of the core group, DCI Casey, had already gained notoriety for a similarly crude policy of information restriction.[54]

It is significant to note that for this process of leadership and compliance to work, explicit commands were not always needed. What was needed was the *belief* that what was being done was supported by the President. For instance, when the initiative was at a low ebb during the difficult period of negotiating for the McFarlane trip to Tehran (Spring 1986), it was recalled by the CIA's Chief of the Near East division, that,

"We [the U.S., PtH] had delivered our missiles and the shoe was on their [e.g., the Iranian] feet, but they were acting like the shoe was still on our foot. (....)
So, you know, it's a bag of worms. I was present when North briefed Poindexter after that meeting, and Poindexter at that point was fed up and wanted to just cut it off entirely, forget it. It wasn't going anywhere. (....)
There was a lot of discussion essentially to try to figure out a way to get Ghorbanifar out of it and, North, who you must have sensed by now is a man of a lot of energy and a lot of determination, essentially kept it alive because of the President's personal and emotional interest in getting the hostages out..."[55]

This testimony suggests two things. First, it indicates the degree of mental support and cohesiveness that existed within the core group, where one group member would support and sustain another in continuing with the project. More importantly here, however, it indicates to what extent the eagerness to please the leader pervaded the thoughts and actions of the group members – even without explicit commands or instructions being given at the time.

Deniability. Similar to the Watergate case, the actions of the group were premised as much on the unspoken beliefs and assumptions just as much as on what was actually said. For example, Poindexter led North to believe that the diversion of funds from the Iran arms deals to the Nicaraguan Contras was approved by the President – when in fact it was (probably) not. This, Poindexter felt, was necessary to offset any doubts or misgivings that North may have had in overseeing this explicitly illegal act. It is reminiscent of Haldeman and Ehrlichmann smoothening John Dean in his early career as main actor in the cover-up for President Nixon.[56]

This system of holding back information in the hierarchical line also worked the other way around. According to his testimony, Poindexter also did not tell the President of the diversion decision. He had two reasons for this. Firstly, he believed that the President would have approved it anyhow when told. Secondly, he wanted to give the President 'deniability', i.e., he wanted to protect the President from potentially embarrassing knowledge about the illegal diversion if it ever became public.[57]

Again like during the Watergate conspiracy and other questionable activities of the Nixon group, deniability replaced accountability. The whole operation was approached in a seemingly 'technocratic' manner. The chief concern was that the President's (unspoken or broadly worded) desires and policy proposals were implemented, although this might imply engaging in criminal actions, while at the same time the President himself was to be protected from potential embarrassment. Therefore, the very culture of the core group rested upon this specific form of anticipatory compliance to its leader, the President.

Type I or type II groupthink: coping with accountability

In the revised model of groupthink, an important place has been accorded to structures of accountability, and the way they are perceived by participants, as factors that influence the group decision process. In particular, a distinction has been made between 'pessimistic' (collective avoidance – type I) and 'optimistic' (collective overoptimism – type II) variants of groupthink. The case of the Iran initiative provides a suitable and yet very complex context to analyze the impact of accountability structures and perceptions. It is suitable because it was a fiasco, which involved the commitment of illegal actions by officials close to the pinnacle of government. This raises obvious questions as to how and why this could happen. Also, the perspective of accountability might help explain the actions of some of the key officials outside the core group who did not participate in these activities. The case is difficult to analyze, however, because it is rather hard to assess how optimistic and pessimistic the participants were throughout the different stages of the project, and to what extent they anticipated the fact that they were accountable for what they did. A close reading of the available evidence suggests that there were elements of optimism as well as pessimism in the core group.

Pessimism: mitigating catastrophe. President Reagan's willingness to pursue the Iran initiative stemmed from his strong personal concern about the fate of the hostages. This was reinforced considerably by a series of meetings with the hostages' families since June 1985. Also, the President believed that a failure to set free the hostages would seriously hurt his stance as President. Elected and reelected on a platform of 'toughness' in foreign affairs, Reagan could ill afford this continued challenge by Islamic fundamentalists. The long duration of the hostage crisis – new hostages were taken even during the months that the initiative was enthusiastically pursued – contributed to the frustration. According to several participants, there was a definite willingness on the part of the President to try anything, even if it had only a remote chance of success, or if it was at odds with official policies and national laws.

It is with this state of mind that Reagan conducted his Iran policy: a mixture of anxiety and hope for a speedy solution to the hostage crisis. In this respect, it was natural that, in his view, the short-term ends of the Iran initiative came to be a sufficient justification of the means. Reagan conveyed this attitude to his subordinates, particularly at the NSC staff, by returning to the hostage issue time and again during briefings and other meetings.

Optimism: a daring scheme. Casey and other key actors viewed the Iran initiative more optimistically. To NSC staff members such as North and Ledeen, the Iran initiative was an opportunity rather than a potential fiasco. Because of the eventual 'non-involvement' of the regular institutions implementing U.S. foreign policy, the NSC was given more or less a blank check. This enhanced the status within the administration of this much plagued organization. When, subsequently, North was handed the idea (either by Peres' advisor Nir, or by Ghorbanifar) of transferring the profits from the arms sales to the Nicaraguan Contras, the Iran project gained a definite, if devious, attractiveness (recall Casey's delight over North's revelation that he had managed to have Khomeini help funding the Contras without even knowing it).

For Casey, apart from his initial personal commitment to his captured CIA colleague Buckley (which diminished when it became known that Buckley had died in captivity), the long-term goal of checking Soviet expansiveness in the region was an important stimulus. Knowing that his own agency was unable to accomplish it, taking the indirect track via the activists on the NSC staff was an acceptable solution for Casey. Establishing tight links to North, Casey fueled the prevailing enthusiasm at the NSC staff level, even to the point where North and others came to oppose their boss McFarlane when he recommended terminating the connections with Ghorbanifar (who to North et al. could not be missed) in December 1985 (just before MacFarlane's resignation as security advisor).

The optimism pervading the initial stages of the operation was mitigated by several setbacks and misunderstandings, with the failed visit to Tehran in May as a negative peak. However, these setbacks could not break the drive of the energetic North and co. As illustrated earlier, the members of the core group supported each other during these difficult moments. On the way back from Tehran, North tried to console the disappointed McFarlane by saying that, at least, the money from the arms sales to the

Iranians would be used to provide the Contras with much needed support.

More fundamentally, optimism was maintained by a strong belief that the power of the presidency was behind the initiative. The White House's unconcern with 'operational' dilemmas and complications prevented the group from seriously considering problems which could have led to a far less optimistic assessment of the odds, such as: the unreliability of Ghorbanifar; the uncertainty about the internal political power structure in Iran; the uncertainty about the extent of Iranian control over the Lebanese hostage takers; the dubious legality of the diversion of funds to the Contras; the risks of leaks by disgruntled operatives inside and outside the administration; the great reliance upon private actors and agencies with distinct commercial interests; and the uncertainty about the role of the Israelis.

Therefore: type I or type II groupthink? It is concluded here that the core group and the decision-making process as a whole (scattered as it was), were more likely to suffer from the kind of overoptimism pervading a group working on what promises to be a resounding success (type II), than from the collective defensive avoidance typical for the stress-induced from of groupthink (type I).

Reagan's stressful and, in essence, defensively motivated striving for the liberation of the hostages did affect the genesis and basic course of the project. But it did not do so to the extent that the entire group shared his narrow perception of the odds. The day-to-day managers of the Iran initiative, on the other hand, were driven by a much more favorably colored picture. Particularly North was an unrelenting optimist.

Despite this fact, the actions of key players such as Poindexter were, to a certain extent, influenced by their anticipation of problems of accountability. Although Poindexter and North privately believed the initiative and diversion were wholly justifiable, Poindexter in particular did grasp that other political actors might hold a different perspective. Alerted by concerns of, amongst others, CIA professionals like McMahon, George, and Sporkin, he was aware of the fact that public disclosure of the facts would raise serious criticisms in Congress and the press. Typically, however, this realization did not bring Poindexter to favor timely notification (and coaptation) of congressional leaders. Instead it inspired a further emphasis on secrecy, 'compartmentalization', and 'deniability': narrowing down the circle of those allowed to know, withholding the complete picture from anyone, shutting off the President from potentially incriminating knowledge by not informing him of key parts of the plan as it developed.

Poindexter took a rather narrow, technocratic view of responsibility: only those who knew could be held responsible. He overlooked the fact that in the public or political eye, responsibility is judged by different standards. The fact that the President, for instance, did not know everything might protect him from legal liability, but not from moral and political indignation about his helping to create a climate in which these acts were deemed allowable, lack of leadership, and negligence in monitoring and controlling his subordinates.

A similarly narrow view of the potential significance of (post-hoc) account-ability mechanisms was evident from the off-handed and self-serving method of seeking legal advice that had already been established during the Contra support operation. The way in which the group had it established that the NSC was not covered by the restrictive measures of the Boland Amendment, illustrates this: rationalizations, using third-rate, inexperienced counselors while by-passing regular legal advisors.[58]

During later stages of the Iran initiative, the mood of the key players on the American side constantly vacillated between exuberant optimism and great frustration over short-term setbacks. For instance, the failure of the May 1986 mission to Tehran was reflected in the President's decision to (re)commence military contingency planning for a possible rescue operation in Lebanon.[59] The opening of the so-called Second Channel and Father Jenco's release redrew the balance (July 1986): the group was suddenly eager to believe that the Tehran meeting had started to pay off after all.[60] Yet again there were pessimist undertones looming. Because right after Jenco's release, North and others emphasized that without a speedy American follow-up, hostages might be killed.[61]

The self-marginalization of dissenters: anticipating failure. One of the chief criticisms afterwards raised with respect to Secretaries Shultz and Weinberger was that they allowed themselves to be cut out of the decisionmaking process all too easily.[62] They knew that something was going on. Through their own institutional channels they could have obtained sufficient information about the affair to know that it did not come to an end in January 1986 – and they probably did. However, they did not utilize their positions to oppose more effectively the Iran project. Instead, they took a formalistic point of view and requested only to be informed of the essentials required for them to do their job. The Tower commission put it as follows:

> "Secretary Shultz and Secretary Weinberger in particular distanced themselves from the march of events. Secretary Shultz specifically requested to be informed only as necessary to perform his job. Secretary Weinberger had access through intelligence to details about the operation. Their obligation was to give the President their full support and continued advice with respect to the program or, if they could not in conscience do that, to so inform the President. Instead, they simply distanced themselves from the program. They protected the record as to their own positions on this issue. They were not energetic in attempting to protect the President from the consequences of his personal commitment to freeing the hostages."[63]

The question is *why* they acted as they did. Earlier on, it was noted that one of the reasons was that the two Secretaries sensed that they could never win the argument because the President would support the project anyhow. Other than continuing to argue about it, they could try to sabotage its implementation (as Weinberger attempted by objecting to the transfer of TOW's from Defense to the CIA, only to be rebuffed by Poindexter instructing him to do proceed with the delivery), or they could leak it to the press. Both of these strategies were unattractive, because they would almost certainly engender highly unfavorable reactions from their superior in the White House, the President. Hence, anticipatory compliance in the case of these two dissident ex-group members induced them to be passive and complacent.

Experienced enough, however, to know that the initiative would stand not more than a remote chance of being successful and/or to remain secret long enough, both Shultz and Weinberger must have realized that, one day, they would be questioned about their part in the initiative. This provided them with another motive for dissociation. Consequently, from the earliest possible phases of the project, Shultz and Weinberger went on record registering their opposition to the proposed 'opening to Iran'. When, subsequently, they were cut out of the decision process, they were content to leave it at that. Realizing that the course was set for failure and ultimate disclosure, they preferred not to know the details. Implicitly, the two Secretaries seemed therefore to adhere to the same kind of limited notion of responsibility as Poindexter did in compartmentalizing the operation. In both cases, these strategic actions were taken in anticipation of the operation of accountability structures.

14.6. Symptoms of groupthink

Symptoms of groupthink (I): overestimation of the group

Did a shared illusion of invulnerability pervade the group's deliberations?
Given the prevailing enthusiasm in the core group during the early stages (September 1985-February 1986), it is not surprising to find several indications of overoptimism in the communications between its members. Optimism about both the 'rightness' of the project and its chances of success led them to quickly discount or downplay the risks of the operation, particularly the possible adverse consequences of public disclosure. Reflecting on his failed attempt to criticize the initiative during the January 6, 1986 meeting, Secretary Shultz told the Tower Board that,

> "[Concerning the] nature of the risks (....) when – I would say 'when', not 'if' – it came forward publicly, the description [by the proponents of the initiative, PtH] always was that Israel was going to be the conduit, and, therefore, it would be deniable, and we'd just say well, we don't know anything about it, and it's something Israel is doing, and so on. All of this was argued with, that it wouldn't work."[64]

But Shultz failed to obtain any leverage. In fact, the security issue was dismissed quickly, and disappeared from the agenda for many months. It did not reappear until September 1986, when CIA official Clive Allen wrote a lengthy memo expressing his concerns that the operation was spinning out of control.[65] In the intervening months, the group was totally complacent on this point, despite engaging in an ever more complex and risky covert operation. This attitude also pervaded their dealings with regard to the Contra diversion:

> "Poindexter admitted knowing that public revelation of the diversion's approval by him would result in his leaving the Administration, although he said that he 'probably underestimated' the effect public knowledge of the operation would eventually have on the Administration."[66]

Where did this sense of invulnerability originate? As already noted, part of the explanation lies with the 'idiosyncratic' interpretation of the structures of power and accountability in the United States that the group members adhered to. In addition, some of the key members of the group were strengthened by recent successes. North, for instance, had accomplished quite a lot in keeping the Contras alive before being called in to manage the Iran project. He had run the Contra support operation in a similar way, using private businessmen and firms, third countries, informal meetings and complex transactions. From his point of view, there was no reason why the same methods could not also be applied to the hostage problem.

Similarly, Casey had been quite successful in pursuing his mission of reviving the CIA's covert operations activities. In doing so, he had encountered and survived a number of congressional storms and press outrages. This included the indignation about the CIA's role in the mining of Nicaraguan harbors. Each time he knew how to placate the representatives and senators while hardly losing his freedom to maneuver. In fact, the episodes reinforced his private opinion that congressional oversight should not be taken too seriously. These experiences may have led him too, to overestimate his and the other group members' capacities to manage the Iran operation, as well as the impact of future publicity about it.

Are there signs of a shared belief in the inherent morality of the group?
The decision makers in the Iran group were all ideologies, though each in his own manner. North in particular had always considered himself a warrior for democracy in Nicaragua. So had, in a more detached manner, Casey and McFarlane. They were part of an administration with a highly ideologically loaded foreign policy. A key characteristic of this policy was its explicit identification of 'enemies': the 'evil empire' of the Soviet Union; 'project Democracy' in Latin America to eliminate 'communist dictatorship' of the Sandinistas. By viewing the world in terms of good and bad, it was not surprising that, vis-à-vis enemies, a strong in-group sense of moral superiority existed among members of the Reagan administration. This included key officials such as Shultz, Weinberger, Perle, Burt, and Kirkpatrick.

Moreover, in the case of the hostage crisis, the opponents were terrorists;

and they were terrorists backed by Iran. At the time, Iran was probably among the five states that generated a maximum amount of hostility in the thoughts and rhetoric of U.S. government officials (others were the Soviet Union, Libya, and Cuba). The historical legacy of the Carter administration's mishandling of the final phases of the Shah's regime, as well as the Tehran hostage crisis, had left its marks upon the Reagan foreign policy elite. Islamic fundamentalism was feared because of its inherent expansionism, and its main propagator, the Khomeini regime, was feared because of its cruelty and arrogance. Although the United States remained neutral in the Iran-Iraq war, if a choice had to be made, it would be in favor of Iraq as the lesser evil. Within this context, the Iran-supported terrorism of the Hezbollah extremists in Lebanon was considered morally repulsive and highly frustrating, because there was little the U.S. could do about it. Hence, the Reagan administration had declared a war against international terrorism, in particular Arab terrorism.

Against this background of a self-proclaimed, American-style 'Jihad' against state-sponsored Islamic terrorism, it was clear to the members of the core group who was right and who was wrong. The moral superiority of the U.S. was self-evident. Furthermore, the key decision makers on the U.S. side believed that in order to accomplish the two ends of liberating the hostages and bringing about political change in Iran, unconventional means were not only allowable, but probably necessary – even if it included dealing directly with forces within Iran and selling weapons to an acknowledged enemy of the United States.

In its secretive deliberations, the group also appeared to believe that they were the only ones who saw these things in the right perspective. Congress in particular was considered weak, ill-informed, and too liberal. Therefore, the group had to do it all by itself. The fact that it was opposed by otherwise like-minded officials such as Shultz and Weinberger was considered a setback, but could not really shake the sense of moral righteousness of the inner circle around Reagan.

Symptoms of groupthink (II): Closed-mindedness

Are there manifestations of collective rationalizations?
The moral confidence of the proponents of the Iran initiative suffered from a number of nagging doubts. These were basically of four kinds:
- the fact that trading arms for hostages stood in flagrant contrast to the official U.S. policies on combatting terrorism;
- the fact that delivering weapons to Iran was at odds with the official U.S. policy of neutrality in the Iran-Iraq war, a policy which the U.S. also emphatically advocated with its allies (besides, the weapons delivered as a consequence of the initiative were likely to kill a vast number of times the amount of hostages that were to be freed);
- the fact that parts of the entire project, particularly the diversion of funds to the Contras, implied violations of U.S. law;

– the fact that the entire project proceeded in utmost secrecy, by-passing many of the institutions and officials formally entitled to timely knowledge of and participation in decision making.

How did the members of the core group cope with these doubts? The answer is that they rationalized away most of these implicit objections to what they were doing. Again and again, the discrepancy of trading arms for hostages in the face of official rhetoric calling for an uncompromising attitude towards terrorists and their supporters, was made invisible by putting the emphasis upon the 'strategic' dimensions of the initiative (i.e., the objective of bringing about a political dialogue with Iranian moderates in anticipation of an internal political power struggle). This strategic dimension was thought to make up for the fact that the core of the deal was trading arms in exchange for the liberation of hostages. And it could not be doubted that this was indeed the core of the matter.[67]

This reality was circumvented by the group. Even while talking to the Tower Board after the collapse of the initiative, the President continued to deny that it was arms for hostages:

> "The President made the point to the board that arms were not given to Iran but sold, and that the purpose was to improve the stature within Iran of particular elements seeking ties to the Iranian military. The President distinguished between selling to someone believed to be able to exert influence with respect to the hostages and dealing directly with kidnappers. The President told the Board that only the latter would 'make it pay' to take hostages."[68]

The rationalized facade of a wider political objective was also kept up with the Iranians, who themselves were probably more eager for the weapons than for any substantive political talks. During his acrimonious visit to Tehran, McFarlane justified his presence as follows:

> "A bridge of confidence is a useful metaphor. I have come as an expression of good will. In addition to my own presence, we put items on the aircraft which can be brought forward. The corresponding act on your side, a humanitarian gesture, involves the release of our people. While separate and not related, these acts do contribute to mutual confidence."[69]

In sum, with regard to the first area of doubt, the dominant rationalization adhered to by the members of the core group went something like this: "This is a policy initiative serving our broader geopolitical and regional interests rather than merely and solely being an opportunistic move to free American hostages because the President wants it for humanitarian and domestic political reasons." Time and again, this line of defense was used by the members of the core group to assure themselves that what they were doing was right.

The reality of violating the official neutrality policy (and thereby deceiving American allies) was evaded by another simplistic assertion. It read as follows: "The weapons and intelligence estimates that we deliver to the Iranians will not win the war for them, therefore they do not conflict with our policy of neutrality." For instance, it took the Deputy Director of the CIA McMahon frantic persuading and bargaining to induce Poindexter, Casey, and North agree to limit the amount and quality of information about the Iran-Iraq front that they were going to provide to the Iranians as an incentive.[70] They were largely unimpressed by his claims that giving all could have "cataclysmic results." They preferred to downplay the risks of their proposed course of action. Stating his objections to Poindexter, McMahon was rebuffed:

> "I objected to that. Poindexter didn't take me on. He didn't challenge that at all, but he said: We have an opportunity that we should not miss, and we ought to proceed to explore it; and if it doesn't work, all we've lost is a little intelligence and 1,000 TOW missiles; and if it does work, then maybe we can change a lot of things in the Mideast."[71]

Similarly, the group turned a blind eye to the fact that thousands of TOW's and large numbers of HAWK's would kill a great number of people, and that these weapons were sold to obtain the release of fewer than ten Americans held hostage. That they did not even try to rationalize; they never mentioned it. Probably Islamic lives did not count when compared to American lives. Another example concerns the selective processing of juridical advice with regard to the legal problems involved in the operation.[72]

Finally, to resolve any possible doubts that might exist concerning the excessive secrecy and the non-notification of Congress, the group members shared the assumption that secrecy was a necessary precondition for the project to work. It must be granted that, given the volatility of the domestic political situation in Iran, external secrecy was of great significance. However, the group apparently reasoned that informing the House and Senate committees on Intelligence would automatically result in public disclosure. In other words, the group presumed that congressional members could not keep a secret.

With secrecy occupying a central place in the line of reasoning employed by the group, 'reliability' became a key criterion for evaluating those who were in any way involved in the decision-making process. But reliability was judged by dubious standards, which sometimes had to be stretched considerably in order to fit the desired outcomes of the reliability assessments. For example, there were repeated signals that Ghorbanifar, the seemingly indispensable middleman between Americans, Israelis, and Iranians, was untrustworthy. The CIA had advised all its branches not to deal with him following the negative results from a polygraph test taken by Ghorbanifar; he was dismissed as a compulsive liar. The members of the core group, however, needed Ghorbanifar because until the late summer of 1986 he was their only point of contact with the Iranians. They thought they had no one else to turn to. How did they resolve this inconsistency between their needs and the negative judgments about Ghorbanifar by the intelligence professionals? A new test was taken. The results were devastating: the only thing Ghorbanifar had not lied about was his own name. The rest was all fabrications. How did the core group react? Again, they rationalized:

> "After the test, a CIA officer reported in a memorandum to Casey, McMahon and Clair George: 'Ghorbanifar is a fabricator who has deliberately deceived the U.S. government and activities. It is recommended that the Agency have no dealing whatsoever with Ghorbanifar. (....)
> Ghorbanifar's polygraph failure, however, did nothing to squelch his relationship with Casey and the NSC staff. Indeed, North – who 'wanted' Ghorbanifar to pass – had braced himself for a negative result. He told Ledeen beforehand that the CIA would make sure Ghorbanifar flunked because they did not want to work with him. Casey, notwithstanding Clair George's advice to terminate the Ghorbanifar relationship, found a way to deal with Ghorbanifar outside the normal Operations Directorate headed by George."[73]

Bad news was neglected or misinterpreted. No precautionary action was taken. Instead, the core group isolated itself a little more by again bypassing some of the regular professional channels.

Did the group rely on crude stereotypes?
Many decisions and actions taken by the core group can be understood within the context of various patterns of intergroup conflict. First of all, the core group was molded by people with converging perceptions of international conflict: the struggle against Arab terrorism, Communist and Islamic expansionism, and – also important in the Iran affair – the struggle between good and bad in Nicaragua. These perceptions implied a number of 'out-groups': the Hezbollah terrorists, the Khomeini regime, the Sandinista government.

The group's perceptions of the authorities in Tehran were biased by negative stereotypes leading to intense hostility and mistrust, while the mysterious group of 'realists' portrayed by Ghorbanifar and allegedly lead by the speaker of Parliament Rafsanjani were more favorably looked upon. The very simplicity of American perceptions is best evidenced by the idea of having the President inscribe a Bible to be handed to the Iranians during one of the meetings; this was done to soften up the Iranians by conveying the impression that America too was being ruled by a religious man.

At the same time, both the Frankfurt and Tehran sessions between Americans and Iranians failed because of mutual distrust and suspicion between the two groups. It was typical for McFarlane, frustrated about the lack of results from the Frankfurt meeting in February 1986, to reconfirm the group's own righteousness by stereotyping all the others as crooks:

"Ghorba[nifar] is basically a selfserving mischief maker. Of course the trouble is that, as far as we know, so is the entire lot of those we are dealing with."[74]

Intergroup conflict in the Iran initiative had a second, more subtle dimension: the gap between proponents and critics of the project. It has been argued that the very 'formation' of the core group can only be understood by considering the bureau-political disagreements and coalitions that transpired over the initiative. In particular, there was opposition from State (Shultz), Defense (Weinberger) and part of the CIA (McMahon initially, Clair George, and others). After the critics had lost the battle for the President's support, they were instantly marginalized. Weinberger in particular was deemed a saboteur by the members of the core group. In one of his secret communications to Poindexter, North approvingly reported Casey's assessments in a meeting on January 14, 1986:

"Casey's view is that Cap [Weinberger] will continue to create roadblocks until he is told by you that the President wants this to move NOW and that Cap will have to make it work. Casey points out that we have now gone through three different methodologies in an effort to satisfy Cap's concerns and that no matter what we do there is always a new objection."[75]

A few days later, Poindexter phoned Weinberger to tell him of the President's order to deliver the missiles from the Defense Department to the CIA in order to proceed with the Iran sales; the 'saboteur' had been outflanked.

Symptoms of groupthink (III): Pressures to Uniformity

Are there signs that potential disagreements were being suppressed through self-censorship and the maintenance of an illusion of unanimity?
At this point, the limitations and problems of distinguishing between the various symptoms of groupthink come to the fore. In discussing the previous four symptoms, many phenomena were presented which, with the same ease, could also plausibly be couched in terms of self-censorship and maintaining an illusion of unanimity. The lack of direct data about the discussions between group members makes it difficult to bear out these different interpretations. For example, Poindexter's role in not telling the President about the Contra diversion, and not telling North that the President did not know could arguably be characterized as efforts to maintain an illusion of unanimity with regard to a highly sensitive aspect of the entire operation. The same goes for President Reagan's 'management style', i.e., his striving for consensus and good spirits among his advisors without bothering about details.

More remarkable is the fact that, within the core group, there was no *illusion* of unanimity with regard to the basic issues of the Iran project; unanimity was real. At the same time, this unanimity could only be achieved by purposefully cutting out of the decision-making arena opponents of the plan. By narrowing down the range of actors to the very basic minimum, unanimity was prefabricated; its maintenance was no problem as long as the initiative remained secret. Only when the news started leaking, the core group started to fall apart – at least in public – although initially, Poindexter and North in their compliant role as soldiers for a good Cause seem to have had no trouble sacrificing their own careers for the sake of protecting the President.

With regard to self-censorship, the most interesting group member to concentrate on would be the ex-National Security Advisor McFarlane. Initially an enthusiastic supporter of the reorientation of U.S. policies toward Iran, he began to have more and more reservations as the initiative increasingly spiralled toward arms for hostages. In September 1985 he was still prepared to lie to Congress about the NSC's involvement in the Contra resupply efforts, despite the Boland amendment. Later on, he decided that the prohibitions of the Boland amendment did apply to the NSC too, and recommended decreasing NSC staff involvement in the operation. Similarly with regard to the Iran initiative, McFarlane felt very uncomfortable with the fact that the success of the initiative to a large extent depended upon the activities of unreliable middlemen. In particular, following a series of meetings with him, McFarlane greatly distrusted Ghorbanifar. Having stepped down as National Security Advisor in December 4, he no longer bore formal responsibility for U.S. action in these areas, and continued to perform a substantive role in the negotiations with the Iranians when called upon by the remaining members of the core group. Stepping into this new role, McFarlane seems to have refrained from further discussing his doubts. In this sense, he may have engaged in self-censorship.

Did the group put direct pressure on dissenters?
As has been shown in analyzing the role of anticipatory compliance and leadership, there was very little need to pressure participants in the decisionmaking process to coincide with the rest of the group. The only sessions where these kinds of arguments have taken place were the December 1985 and January 1986 NSC sessions where Shultz and Weinberger argued their case. The net result of that was that they were eliminated from the group.

Following the January meeting, a direct sale of TOW's to Iran necessitated the involvement of the Defense Department. Although here too, strict secrecy was observed and regular procedures were by-passed as much as possible, Secretary Weinberger made an attempt to forestall the transaction by obstructing its implementation. After some discussion within the core group, he received – via Poindexter – direct presidential orders to cooperate. This was a rare example of direct pressure, but it was not pressure to conform to any opinion whatsoever, it was simply a command for action which was to be obeyed.

256

In general, however, the game was played with much more subtlety. Despite its odd, multi-layered composition and lack of plenary meetings, the core group remained intact all the way up to October 1985, when disclosure ensued. Even if an operative such as North had occasional doubts (which he had very few), he would have relied on the hierarchical justification of his actions, which was readily available. There was no need, except for the maintenance of the belief that everything that was being done was condoned by the President, for others to engage in open pressure. The preferred strategy in such cases was different: marginalization and exclusion.

Did group members serve as mindguards protecting the group consensus from facing controversial issues?
In this vein, DCI Casey's handling of some of the more recalcitrant members of his own staff can be brought to attention. Rather than pressuring his Deputy Director for Operations Clair George in divulging his doubts about the use of Secord and, in particular, Ghorbanifar for the project, Casey simply removed them from the inner circle involved in the implementation of the project.

> "Prior to the signing of the January 17 Finding, George advised North of the failed polygraph test results. He also recalled warning Casey against dealing with Ghorbanifar, but 'before I could go through one more fight about Mr. Ghorbanifar, [the CIA] received a Presidential order which (....) ended up meaning we were dealing with Mr. Ghorbanifar.' Eventually, Casey designated Charles Allen to oversee Ghorbanifar's activities."[76]

No doubt the 'Presidential Order' originated with, or was approved by Casey. The next step was to remove George as much as possible from the knowledgeable few. Similar strategies were pursued by Casey to keep other soft-liners such as McMahon at bay. In doing so, he shielded the group from being forced to consider critical questions raised by covert operations professionals that might have shattered the prevailing optimism about the initiative, or may have lead the group to question the moral dimensions of their project. The manipulation of legal advice and the outflanking of regular counselors in favor of less experienced and/or already committed advisors (Sciaroni and Sporkin, respectively) can be viewed in a similar vein.

In fact, mindguarding was more or less institutionalized within the group. The culture of secrecy which was prominent brought about a situation in which information was distributed on a very limited scale: the dynamics of 'need to know.' This was not only used as a tool to obtain compliance from persons or institutions that would otherwise pose problems (such as the Army in organizing the delivery of TOW's in January 1986).[77] It was instrumental also in prohibiting alternative perspectives from reaching the group.

Interestingly, mindguard roles seem to have been predominantly played by fringe members of the group, i.e., various middlemen and interlocutors who had an autonomous stake in the well-being of the arms trans-actions. Ghorbanifar, Secord, Nir, and Hakim, to name but the most impor-tant ones, were all either financially, politically, or physically committed to the project. They had every interest to see it proceed smoothly, even to the point of manipulating both of the key parties (Americans and Iranians) to remain optimistic about the chances of success. Particularly Ghorbanifar excelled at this. But the Israelis, too, contributed significantly to getting the U.S. to participate in the project. With continuous promises of impending releases of hostages and promising links to Iranian leaders interested in a political dialogue, North, Poindexter, McFarlane, Casey, and the President were persuaded to get in and stay in on the deals. Downplaying setbacks, ignoring the wide gulf between the two principal parties' perceptions and expectations, and occasionally lying about intentions, times, numbers, places, and finances were all part of that strategy.

And the core group was eager to believe it all. The President in particu-lar was susceptible to even the faintest rays of hope about the release of American hostages. But, remarkably, so did Casey, who generally was much more cynical and cunning in these areas. Casey was fixated on the fact that, despite his treachery, Ghorbanifar was the sole link to Iran or otherwise that had ever produced the release of any hostage. To him, something was better than nothing, as long as there were no alternatives. The fact that, in reasoning like that, he allowed himself and the others to become depen-dent upon this channel, was apparently offset by the (carefully nourished) hope and expectation that more hostages might come out.

In retrospect, a hopeful assertion such as the one quoted below seems hopelessly naive, but does reflect the prevailing attempts of group members to talk each other into perseverance:

> "I believe we have succeeded. Deposit being made tomorrow (today is a bank holiday in Switzerland). Release of [all] hostages set for 19 May in sequence you have specified. Specific date to be determined by how quickly we can assemble requisite parts [e.g. deliver arms, PtH]. Thank God – he answers prayers."[78]

14.7. The outcomes of decision

The Iran initiative must be qualified as a fiasco by almost every conceivable standard. In the decision-making process many norms of orderly procedure and democratic governance were violated, as discussed above. The out-comes of decision were equally negative.

Firstly, although two hostages were released as a consequence of the ini-tiative, others remained in captivity. What is more: additional hostages were taken during the course of the initiative. Secondly, the 'strategic' objectives of the initiative were not attained; more likely, it ultimately played into the hands of the most radical anti-American groups within Iran. Thirdly, the exposure of the project did not only uncover illegal practices, amateurism, lack of coordination, and factionalism within the U.S. government, it also seriously hurt the image of the Reagan presidency abroad, where allied governments were annoyed by American soloism and deceptiveness, and embarrassed by the administrative incompetence of their major ally. At home, finally, the Iran scandal brought back nasty (if miraculously temporary) memories of Watergate.

At the close of this groupthink study of the Iran-Contra affair, it is useful to examine in greater detail the substance of the policies pursued, as they were produced by a groupthink-like decision-making process. The revised model of groupthink suggests two kinds of expectations in this respect. First, it posits that the low-quality policies resulting from groupthink are due to excessive risk taking fostered by groupthink modes of deliberation. Secondly, the model claims that if groupthink processes occur in groups operating in multi-decision situations, they are likely to become entrapped in a failing course of action. These two claims are examined below.

Ignoring the risks of a long shot

In the revised model of groupthink it is contended that decision groups operating in a groupthink mode are prone to excessive risk taking and recklessness. One of the principal reasons for this is that in a groupthink process, decision makers tend to misperceive or ignore altogether the risk dimensions of their actions. Especially in Type II groupthink, collective illusions of invulnerability drive the group toward exceedingly grandiose schemes without adequate attention for their possible drawbacks. To what extent did this mode of thinking occur among the core group responsible for the Iran initiative?

To be sure, the Iran initiative was fraught with risks. At stake were the lives of hostages, held by extremists unlikely to show mercy when they perceived that killing one or more Americans suited their political ends. Secondly, it was uncertain whether the Iranians were willing and able to control the Lebanese captors. For instance, at various moments during the Spring of 1986, there were repeated signs that the American hostages might be 'sold' to Libya, which wanted to exploit the hostages for blackmailing or humiliating the U.S. government. Thirdly, there was the persistent uncertainty about whom the Americans were dealing with in Iran, and the risk of disturbing its internal balance of power, with unpredictable, yet mostly gloomy consequences for the hostages as well as the stability of the region. Furthermore, there was the risk that American arms and intelligence support delivered to Iran would cause a break in the stalemated Iran-Iraq war; this was not considered in the interest of the United States and its allies.

However, by far the greatest risk concerned *OpSec,* the military-style jargon for Operational Security, i.e., the risk that news of the initiative toward Iran would spread beyond the few key officials involved. Premature public disclosure would compromise the initiative and endanger the lives of the hostages, it was reasoned. Moreover, it would reveal that the Reagan administration had been seriously divided over the initiative, that it had not informed Congress about what was going on, that – by implication – it had pursued an informal policy fully at odds with the official line against terrorists and their supporters, as well as with the arms embargo against Iran. The most embarrassing news, however, would be the fact that money gained by the Iranian arms deals was being secretly diverted to the Nicaraguan Contras; such a form of direct U.S. government support was explicitly forbidden under the second Boland amendment.

In summary, the risks (the potential adverse consequences) of the operation were numerous and important. Apparently, this did not suffice to stop the core group from pursuing it. Were they blind to the harmful effects that might result from their actions?

There is no easy answer to this question. Reviewing the evidence contained in the testimonies and reports, a mixed picture emerges. It has already been noted that in the core group, many of the operational risks were played down, notably the risk of public disclosure and its negative impact. During the early stages of the decision-making process, the group's self-confidence and hope that the initiative would bring results quickly outweighed all concerns brought forward by Shultz and Poindexter. Similarly, CIA specialists' assertions as well as McFarlane's own negative impressions concerning the reliability of Ghorbanifar and the risks to the project this entailed, were discounted. Expecting the release of the hostages within a few weeks, the members of the core group saw only advantages to the plan, and thought the security concerns to be irrelevant.

But as the project dragged on without the release of all the hostages, this most blatant one-sided optimism could no longer be maintained. Complications became apparent: the uncertain extent of Iranian control over Hezbollah, the Libya factor, the threat of executions of hostages, the possibility of leaks by Iranian factions or disgruntled private middlemen cut out of the deal. These concerns could not be ignored altogether.

Reviewing the correspondence between members of the core group as well as other evidence, it becomes clear that they did consider some of the risks involved in continuing the operation. Their reaction was basically twofold. Firstly, they assessed the risks of the operation and traded them off against the apparent risks of slowing down, altering or altogether discontinuing the operation. Such assessments invariably led to the conclusion that the short term risks of harm to the hostages that would result from a change in the course of the initiative were so big that it was imperative to go on, and indeed, to move as quickly as possible. The following message from North to Poindexter is illustrative of this line of reasoning:

"I believe that we are, at this point, barring unforseen [sic] developments in London or Tel Aviv, too far along with the Iranians to risk turning back now. If we do not at least one more try at this point, we stand a good chance of condemning some or all to death and a renewed wave of Islamic Jihad terrorism. While the risks of proceeding are significant, the risks of not trying one last time are even greater."[79]

Note that this message was written on December 4, 1985. The seemingly inescapable logic of trying "one more time" was sufficient to enable the initiative to survive for many months beyond that point. Similarly, during the January 7 meeting on the initiative, one of the 'fringe' participants, Attorney General Meese, fell for the same kind of argument:

"I think what most influenced me was the idea that we would be taking – that the risks would be fairly short-term because if it did not work, we would be able to stop it; if this didn't produce results after, say, the first foray, that the thing would be stopped. There was quite a bit of discussion about that, that this would be in stages so that it could be stopped. We knew, in retrospect, that it did not work out that way. But that was one of the things that made it, while a close call, acceptable, as far as I was concerned."[80]

Evidently the members of the core group not only convinced themselves that they were in control of events as far as managing the risks of the operation were concerned, with the same reassurances, they also persuaded others to accept the proposed course of action at the few more or less plenary sessions that were devoted to the subject.

The consideration of threats to *OpSec* lead the key proponents of the initiative to further tighten the secrecy of the entire operation. Poindexter in particular was the driving force behind the efforts to limit the number of people who knew what was going on. On several occasions he proposed to cut out potential sources of trouble within the administration in order to minimize the chances of leaks. However, he never personally succumbed to arguments about risks. Poindexter's rare moments of despair about the initiative, when he indeed argued that it should be stopped, arose, rather, out of frustration over Iranian capriciousness and the lack of substantive results.

Discussion of risks apparently never made it up to the group leader. The President was only concerned with the substantive gains that the initiative might bring, notably the hostages' release. Uninterested in the details of the operation altogether, Reagan did not probe his subordinates about risks or drawbacks. In their turn, Poindexter, Casey, and North had an interest in shielding the President from any source of doubt about the project. It is interesting to note that the opponents of the plan, such as Secretary Shultz never used the risk dimension in arguing against the initiative before the President. Did this reflect the President's more general disinterest in any 'operational' issues of White House policies? Or should it be interpreted as a sign that talking about risks was anathema to the predominant culture of gung-ho toughness (as in Nixon's Watergate group)? It is hard to tell. Consider, however, the following observation by Chief of Staff Regan, again describing the January sessions:

"In response to a question about the degree of discussion of the risks,

Regan noted: 'The President was told, but by no means was it really teed up for him of what the downside risk would be as far as American public opinion was concerned. There was no sampling. No one attempted to do this. The NSC certainly didn't in any paper or discussion say that. I don't believe the State Department in its presentation arguing against this really brought out the sensitivity of this. None of us was aware of that, I regret to say.'"[81]

In sum, therefore, it can be concluded that while a broad range of risks was identified by various participants during various stages of the operation, considerations of risk did not exert any influence as far as the course of the top-level decision-making process about the initiative was concerned. They were brought up occasionally in private communications between North, Poindexter, Casey, and McFarlane, as well as being raised by experienced CIA officers, but in these cases, the members of the core group would always fall back on the trade off between short-term and long- term risks and benefits of the project. In their view, the potential gains always made up for the risks of drawbacks. This was reinforced by the group members' adherence to a relatively limited time horizon. They would always be concerned only with the 'next step', which tended to be seen also as the 'final step': the logic of just one more effort. It was not until late September 1986, after another fresh start by opening up the Second Channel with a relative of the Ayatollah Khomeini did not produce the desired results, that concerned CIA officials were beginning to get any grip on their boss DCI Casey, who subsequently started to urge North to begin clearing his tracks in anticipation of a disclosure.

At the operational level, risks of disclosure were used to legitimize an extraordinary emphasis on intra-Administration secrecy, compartmentalization, and deniability. This was done while at the same time, many individuals outside the administration and the United States were aware of important elements of what was going on, as well as numerous lower-level Army and CIA operatives who were involved in the implementation of the arms deals in various capacities.

Prisoners of the process: another avoidable quagmire

"While acknowledge 'a high degree of risk' in continuing the operation, North emphasized, 'we are now so down the road that stopping what has been started could have even more serious repercussions'."[82]

The analysis of risk taking has already provided numerous indications of how the decision makers became more committed to the initiative as time went by; on the basis of their biased assessments of the risks involved in continuing or stopping, they each time decided to pursue the arms deals. This provides a first indication of the extent to which the the Iran-Contra episode can be viewed as an example of entrapment. A more systematic account can be given, however, by using the framework presented in chapter eight.

Context. First of all, the structure of the decision-making situation perfectly matches the entrapment ideal-type. The Iran initiative comprised a number of interrelated decisions, that can be viewed as a series of investments designed to reach a 'big' goal, i.e., the liberation of all American hostages in Lebanon (as well as the strategic opening toward Iran). Originally thought to be a swift all-in-one type of deal, the project incrementalized almost directly. While two hostages were released during the course of the project, this was insufficient to consider the original goal to have been reached. In other words, particularly when, at a certain point, new hostages were taken.

The decision makers found themselves in a situation where the conflict over what to do increased with every new major step (a new delivery). The apparent deviousness of the Iranian contacts and the setbacks that occurred in the many hopeful arms-trade scenarios designed by North and co, seemed to indicate that going on was not very useful. On the other hand, the plight of the remaining hostages continued, as well as the President's urge to get them out. In this dilemma-like situation, the members of the core group chose to persevere in their efforts – only to further complicate the situation and enhance the risks of disclosure or other mischief.

> "The August-September 1985 TOW transaction set the pattern for the entire Iran initiative:
> – A promise by the Iranians to release the hostages in exchange for an agreed quantity of weapons.
> – The breach of that promise after delivery of the weapons [although the U.S. did not always deliver what had been agreed to, PtH].
> – The delivery of more weapons in response to new demands by the Iranians.
> – The release of a single hostage as an enticement to further arms transfers."[83]

Managing setbacks. What ended up as entrapment was produced in a process full of push and pull factors, optimism and despairs, small successes and 'temporary' setbacks. The available evidence provides marked examples of this going back and forth. The lack of results from the November 1985 HAWK shipment was explained by the fact that the Iranians were angry because they had received outdated missiles. In mid-February, 500 TOW's were shipped to Iran, to be followed by another 500 following the meeting with the key Iranian contact in Frankfurt. Again, nothing of substance was reached – only a promise of more meetings with the Iranians. The explanation, this time, was found in part in the apparent distrust among the Iranians; but for the most part, this lack of progress was made understandable by the general assertion that "these things simply take time". More difficult to accept was the dramatic failure of the McFarlane mission to Tehran in May 1986. This was a period when the initiative was really in danger of falling apart. The President and his advisors were beginning to rethink American policy: there was talk of resuming military contingency planning. For various reasons, the initiative survived after all. It was with great relief therefore, that Father Jenco's release on July 26 was greeted. It was immediately regarded as a direct consequence of the May trip: so 'Tehran' was a success after all, and Ghorbanifar, though devious, was able to produce results if carefully induced to do so.[84]

This good news provided new fuel to surmount the stalling and the setbacks that occurred in the late Summer and Fall of 1986, particularly because in the course of August, a new Iranian channel emerged, independent of Ghorbanifar and thus unburdened by the mixed feelings about the past transactions. This renewed energy was strong enough to survive new hostage seizures (Reed, Tracy), as well as increasing signs that the initiative was getting more and more exposed.

Despite all that, even the most driven proponent of the initiative, Oliver North, had finally began to despair in late October. Writing to Poindexter on October 29, when the final curtain had begun to fall, he indicated his exhaustion:

"This is the damnest operation I have ever seen. Pls. let me go on to other things. We very much like to give RR two hostages that he can take credit for and stop worrying about these other things."[85]

Triggers. Apart from the dynamics of groupthink, several other factors enabled the development of entrapment in the Iran project. Indeed, the entrapment perspective provides a logical angle for analyzing the role of the interlocutors, third parties and intermediaries that were involved in conducting the arms transfers. More specifically, it is surmised that some of them were instrumental in 'framing' the decision situation as perceived by the American government officials: Israeli officials, Ghorbanifar, Hakim, Secord, and others. In particular Ghorbanifar had a vested interest in seeing the operation continue. Moreover, the Iranians themselves wanted U.S. weapons, intelligence, and other expert assistance.

All of these parties had to assure themselves of continued American participation. To achieve it, a variety of incentives was used. The comprised of positive stimuli, such as optimistic information about high-level Iranian officials' involvement in the opening towards the United States, Iranian willingness and ability to secure the release of the hostages, and Iranian fears of the Soviet Union as a solid motive for them to seek re-approachment with the U.S.. One example of this was Ghorbanifar's repeated suggestions to North about the possibility to use excess funds from the Iran arms deals to support the Contras. This was a shrewd suggestion, as it added another ratio for proceeding with the arms sales, independent of the political (in)effectiveness of the sales vis-a-vis the Iranian/Lebanese scene. Note that the same suggestion was also put forward discreetly by the Israelian official Nir.

The Israelis pursued their own agenda with regard to the arms sales. Their primary interest was to secure a stalemate in the Iran-Iraq war, or at least prevent an Iraqi victory. In fact, they did not really hide their own objectives from the Americans, whose participation they initially needed to supply their own stockpiles of weaponry used to make the initial deliveries to Iran. Secondly, there were two Israelis missing in Tehran who were also held hostage. Also, Ghorbanifar was associated with the Israelis, and they wanted to keep this relationship going, because of Ghorbanifar's apparent access to the political leadership in Tehran. Consequently, the Israelis joined the other middlemen in promoting the project.

Prime minister Peres' foreign policy aides Kimche and Nir were a constant source of optimistic information, and would pledge their support for the project at every opportunity. Peres himself was involved in the efforts, as evidenced by the following briefing memo from North to Poindexter:

> "Several weeks ago, Peres expressed concern that the U.S. may be contemplating termination of current efforts with Iran. The Israelis view the hostage issue as a 'hurdle' which must be crossed enroute [sic] to a broadened strategic relationship with the Iranian government. It is likely that Peres will seek assurances that the U.S. will indeed continue with the current joint initiative. (....) "[86]

Note that this memo was written as late as mid-September 1986, when the initiative had been dragging on for more than a year with disappointing results (from the American point of view).

At other times, negative stimuli such as (indirect) threats were sent by way of indicating the potential costs of unsatisfactory or terminated U.S. involvement. These included threats to kill the hostages or to sell them to Libya, Similarly, Ghorbanifar threatened with reprisals when the Americans signalled they were giving up, or when he believed that he was being cut out of the process; his knowledge of the covert policies pursued by the U.S. government alone gave him a trump card in this respect. Also, he exploited his carefully advertised monopoly on contacts within the Iranian government: he was all the Americans could turn to in seeking an opening to Iran (before they opened up the second channel; note that it is unknown whether this second channel was really a different one – at least once, the same Iranians who had been spotted earlier through the original channel with Ghorbanifar, showed up in second channel contacts).

The American most closely exposed to all these subtle and less subtle cues was North. It was not surprising, therefore, given his own degree of commitment to the project, that he would relay these threats in his memos and conversations with the other group members. Phrases such as the following were not uncommon:

> "[I]t is entirely possible that if nothing is received, [the Second Iranian] will be killed by his opponents in Tehran, Ghorbanifar will be killed by his creditors (....) and one American hostage will probably be killed in order to demonstrate displeasure."[87]

Unwittingly or purposeful, these actors were instrumental in framing the decision situation for the Americans so as to favor the odds for continuing to invest in the project. Combined with the group dynamics of the inner circle around Reagan and Casey, the entrapment character of the Iran-Contra affair becomes somewhat more understandable.

14.8. Arms for hostages in perspective: conclusions

In terms of causation, there is no single person solely responsible for the dramatically flawed U.S. initiative towards Iran, the trading of arms for hostages, and the diversion of money gained in this operation to the Nicaraguan Contras. Equally, there is no single analytical explanation that accounts for all that has transpired during the Iran-Contra affair. Despite all the secrecy, there were many officials and other participants involved, the initiative proceeded in a complex interorganizational and international setting, it went through different stages and 'moods' during the sixteen or seventeen months of its operation. The alternative interpretations briefly outlined at the beginning of this chapter may all contribute specific components of the explanation of "how it could happen". At this point, there is no way of knowing which of these fits 'best', or how they should be combined to provide a single, integrated explanation.

The main issue here is whether the groupthink perspective has anything to offer in explaining the Iran-Contra affair. Secondly, this case study provides us with an opportunity to begin to assess the value of the revised model of groupthink that has emerged from the theoretical parts of this study.

Groupthink?

Using the case study method to explore the explanatory potential of a conceptual model or theoretical framework requires, above all, a high degree of honesty and impartiality on the part of the analyst. He possesses a wide discretion in selecting and organizing the historical facts into his description and analysis. The temptation to find what one needs to find in order to fit the model is always there. This is not simply a matter of purposeful manipulation. It is much more subtle: the analytical perspective one is 'testing' at the same time provides a logical reference point in interpreting the evidence. The facts that fit the model will inevitable assume more importance than others, for which the analysts has no immediate interpretive purpose.

To what extent did this happen in the present case study of the Iran initiative? In other words, to what extent should the emergent conclusion that groupthink played an important role in bringing about the Iran-Contra affair be mitigated?

On balance, a number of doubtful sports in the analysis can be discerned. First of all, the supposition of a 'group' leading the Iran initiative is plausible, but weakened by the fact that the group as a whole rarely ever met. The Iran group was a group because at an interpersonal, bilateral level, its members were close; furthermore, they shared a common goal and had identical perceptions of what policies ought to be pursued; and finally, the members of the core group did know one another very well from other areas of joint covert activities (Contra support). Yet, they did not interact as a collectively.

Secondly, the specific position of the President within the group remains rather uncertain, due to lack of solid evidence as well as contradictory testimonies on the part of key participants. The solution adopted in this study – the President as a 'leader in the background condoning and inspiring the core group's actions – seems plausible, but this does not exhaust the possibility of other interpretations.

Thirdly, the cohesiveness of the group seems to have been considerable, due to the set of factors outlined in detail in the analysis. But there are serious questions to be asked about whether group cohesiveness was consistently high throughout the entire episode. For instance, McFarlane's resignation as NSG advisor placed him outside the mainstream of events, although he remained connected with North and Poindexter through the PROF note system (i.e. the private, secured computer link-up between the key actors). McFarlane, too, seemed to have been somewhat more doubtful about the initiative, in particular about the heavy reliance on what he considered to be a despicable figure such as Ghorbanifar. His successor Poindexter was more determined and, when necessary, cunning. However, this included a fanatic desire for secrecy which led him to even exclude a figure as Casey from certain developments. For instance, Poindexter urged North not to tell Casey about the diversion. North did it anyway. In other words, Poindexter's radical way of protecting *OpSec* occasionally brought him to favor tactics that were at odds with maintaining high group cohesiveness.

Finally, there is a problem with assessing the importance of individuals outside the U.S. government in shaping the decision-making process concerning the Iran initiative. For instance, the direct intervention of Israeli Prime Minister Peres and his closest advisors throughout the early months may have served to convince the President that the initiative was a sound one. Furthermore, the Israelis served as a crucial interface between the Americans and Ghorbanifar. In other words, throughout the Iran initiative the Israelis, for reasons that were not completely congruent with those of the Americans, strongly backed the project and assisted in convincing U.S. decision makers. Similarly, the entire network of businessmen also involved in the Contra supply operation had a persuasive influence on key officials such as North and Ledeen. As discussed above, all of these participants served as environmental cues for the group. It is hard to tell which came first: the core group decisions about approaching Iran, or the diverse but comprehensive efforts to get the U.S. to hop on a train that was already in motion.

Taken together, these potential sources of 'anomalies', as well as the (temporarily) persisting uncertainty about the very facts of the working of the core group, may form the core of a case against the groupthink explanation of the Iran-Contra affair. In the present case analysis, some of these points have received little attention. It is up to analysts with different perspectives and, hopefully, more relevant facts to put the groupthink explanation through a more stringent test.

Groups in context

In the context of the case of the Iran initiative, the revised model of groupthink provides the analyst with a more subtle and realistic frame of reference than the original conceptualization. In particular, it allows for a better analysis of the organizational and political factors involved in the formation, maintenance, performance, and disintegration of decision groups in a governmental setting. Even more so than Janis' thorough analysis of the locus of decision with regard to the Watergate case, the revised model forces the analyst to thoroughly scan the historical and organizational context.

The model alerts the analyst to the fact that the very existence of intergroup conflict within the government may be a source of the development of factional cohesiveness. Therewith, the revised model provides an almost ideal-typical account of what happened in the early months of the Iran initiative: the redrawing of the group's boundaries in an ongoing process of meetings and arguments back and forth – with the end result of an inner circle at the heart of the policy, and a large, amorphous collection of opponents cut out of the decision process. By examining this context of group formation, the revised model allows for a careful analysis of the various sources of group cohesiveness that emerge in the process – both socio-emotional and interdependence-based. Furthermore, stressing the intergroup context of groupthink makes more logical certain seemingly extraordinary phenomena as the desire for secrecy.

The most important innovative element of the revised model concerns its construction of an alternative (or additional) path towards groupthink, i.e., the effects of leadership styles and anticipatory compliance among members. More explicitly than Janis' original account, this allows the analyst to explore the complex and subtle relationships that exist within the kinds of ad-hoc coalitions such as the group that pulled the Iran initiative.

In the case study, this alternative path has proven to be very useful. It fitted the odd composition of the group, which covered widely different ranks in the administrative hierarchy. The stress-induced, subtle and only partially willful leadership exerted by the President triggered his subordinates in the core group into pursuing their ideas, and adhering to them despite drawbacks. Although the Iran initiative itself cannot be called a crisis, it did arise from a crisis atmosphere particularly manifest at the level of the President and his closest associates: the hostage issue as a potential threat to the President and his foreign policy and domestic popularity, as well as an emotionally tense episode for a President who deeply sympathized with the families of the victims. Furthermore, there were critical moments during the course of initiative, such as the crisis surrounding the November 1985 transaction when North and the CIA had to intervene to prevent a fiasco.

In such a setting, the sense of loyalty and duty experienced by military minds as McFarlane, North and Poindexter has been of key importance. Adhering to a highly simplistic and 'imperial' view of the power and legitimacy of the presidency, they felt they were backed by superiors in undertaking what they did. The revised model of groupthink offers the conceptual framework to spot these dynamics and put them in perspective.

Finally, the output side of the revised model has produced convincing results in the case analysis. In particular the analysis of entrapment illuminates in a more reflective manner the overall course of the decision process and the ways in which the group members became entangled in an initiative they could no longer fully control.

It is important to note that despite these apparently useful features, the case study revealed some of the weaker spots of the revised model. In particular the eight symptoms of groupthink adopted from the Janis model yet await further analytical scrutiny as well as a cogent operationalization. In the analysis, it was difficult to distinguish the specific function and meaning of the eight symptoms in interpreting the facts of the case. Many phenomena observed in the decision process concerning the Iran initiative could arguably be presented as examples of two or more different symptoms. Without further specification, this part of the analysis remains the least rigid, allowing for considerable discretion on the part of the analyst. Hence an additional task for groupthink analysts presents itself.

Notes

1. Tower Report (1987); Congressional Report (1988).
2. Among the majour sources are: Armstrong et al. (eds 1987); Cockburn (1987); Draper (1987a); Draper (1987b); Draper (1987c); Woodward (1987); Bill (1988); Mayer and McManus (1988); Segev (1988); Smith (1988); Taheri (1988).
3. For instance, Regan (1988); North (1988).
4. Tower Report (1987), pp.62-87.
5. Congressional Report (1988), pp.21-34, 333-362.
6. Gabriel (1985).
7. Woodward (1987), pp.394-395; Congressional Report (1988), p.142; Mayer and McManus (1988), pp. 156-163.
8. Woodward (1987), pp.394-395; Congressional Report (1988), p.142; Mayer and McManus (1988), pp. 156-163.
9. Hermann and Hermann (1988); Sick (1988).
10. Mayer and McManus (1988), pp. 161-165.
11. Woodward (1987), p.395.

12. Barrett (1982), Smith (1988).
13. See ex-NSC staffer Kemp in the Washington Post, 10 December 1986; see also Armstrong et al. (1987), pp.1-76.
14. Tower Report (1987), part II, appendix B, section 1.
15. Etheredge (1985), Mayer and McManus (1988), pp.109-136.
16. Draper (1987a), pp.48-50.
17. Executive Order 12333.
18. Mayer and McManus (1988), p.129.
19. Dongressional Report (1988), pp.40-125; Tower Report (1987), appendix B, section II.
20. Woodward (1987), p.466.
21. Tower Report (1987), pp.154-164.
22. Draper (1987a,b).
23. Draper (1987), p.52.
24. This chronology does not aspire to be comprehensive in any way. Only those facts that are relevant to understand the developing structure of the decision-making process are presented. This implies, for instance, that less attention is paid to the final months of the initiative, when events unfolded within a relatively stabilized decisional context. For key chronological accounts, see Armstrong (1987); Tower Report (1987); Congressional Report (1988).
25. Tower Report (1987), pp.121-122.
26. Tower Report (1987), pp.182-188.
27. According to some sources, he did so rather inadvertently, see Regan's testimony before the Tower board, Tower Report (1987), p.219.
28. Tower Report, pp.227-228.
29. Draper (1987a), p.58.
30. Tower Report (1987), p.254.
31. Draper (1987b), p.50.
32. Draper (1987c), p.67.
33. Congressional Report (1988), pp.235-236.
34. Woodward (1987), p. 492, describing a closed hearing by the House Intelligence Committee, November 19, 1986.
35. Tower Report (1987), p.254.
36. McFarlane, in Tower Report (1987), p.152.
37. Congressional Report (1988), p.24.
38. Tower Report (1987), p.68.
39. Chief of the Near East and South Asian Division in the Operations Directorate, CIA, Tower Report (1987), p.298.
40. Tower Report (1987), p.298.
41. Meese, in Tower Report (1987), p.220.
42. Woodward (1987) provides an elaborate description of the extreme cautiousness and reluctance to engage in any convert operations on the part of leading CIA officials when Casey came to head the Agency.
43. For these two examples, consult the case studies in Janis (1982a).
44. Tower Report (1987), p.80.
45. Draper (1987a), p.58.
46. Schultz, in Tower Report (1987), pp.224-225.
47. Woodward (1987), pp.466-467.
48. Draper (1987a), p.69. See also North (1987).
49. Milgram (1974).
50. Draper (1987), pp.69-70.

51. North (1987).
52. Poindexter, Joint Hearings Congress Select Committee, July 17, 1987.
53. Congressional Report (1987), pp.24-32.
54. Woodward (1987), pp.293-284, 319-338.
55. Chief of the Near East and South Asian Division, Operations directorate, CIA, in Tower Report (1987), pp.260-261.
56. Janis (1982a), pp.211-241.
57. See, however, the qualifications on this point presented in thte Congressional Report, pp. 235-236.
58. Draper (1987a), pp.49-50.
59. Tower Report (1987), pp. 361-365.
60. Tower Report (1987), pp. 373-393.
61. Tower Report (1987), pp. 378-382.
62. Tower Report (1987), pp.80-83, Draper (1987c), pp.72-74.
63. Tower Report (1987), p.82.
64. Shultz, in Tower Report (1987), p.225.
65. Allen, in Tower Report (1987), pp.428 ff.
66. Congressional Report (1988), p.169.
67. Consider again McFarlane's expression that one would have to be a fool not see that the initiative was all about arms for hostages, Tower Report, p.152.
68. Reagan paraphrased in Tower Report (1987), p.39.
69. McFarlane, in Tower Report (1987), p.304.
70. Note that, at the same time, the Americans also passed on information about the war to Iraq.
71. McMahon, in Tower Report (1987), p.240.
72. Draper (1987a), pp.49-50; Congressional Report (1988), pp.347-361.
73. Congressional Report (1988), p.181.
74. McFarlane, in Tower Report (1987), p.262.
75. North, in: Tower Report (1987), p.232.
76. Congressional Report (1988), p.186.
77. Congressional Report (1988), pp.187-188.
78. North to Poindexter on May 6, 1986, Congressional Report (1988), p.203.
79. Armstrong et al. (eds 1987), p.203.
80. Meese, in Armstrong et. al. (eds 1987), p.245.
81. Regan, in Armstrong (1987), p.248.
82. Congressional Report (1988), p.171.
83. Congressional Report (1988), p.153.
84. Tower Report (1987), pp.372-376.
85. Tower Report (1987), p.435.
86. Tower Report (1987), p.400.
87. Congressional Report (1988), p.216.

15 – Conclusions

15.1. Introduction

"This was the day of the big Cabinet meeting on my public-housing programme. Harold and I agreed later that it was far the most important and far the best Cabinet of this Labor Government. At long last we did take decisions; and for the first time Harold Wilson came out as a leader – a man who wasn't just content to sit back in the chair and see what happened but was prepared to make sure that things happened the way he wanted. (...) Harold's speech completely cut away the ground under the opposition. Nobody spoke against us. The First Secretary helped us along, and within an hour the issue had been settled. Afterwards Harold said to me, 'Well, aren't you pleased? That's the best meeting we've had. I enjoyed it.'"[1]

(...) "So what this comes to is that there are two ways in which officialdom impresses its views on Ministers. The first pressure comes from inside the Department where officials try to make one see things in a departmental way. Ministers tend to have *only* a departmental briefing. The second pressure is inter-departmental, coming when the official committee brings its inter-departmental cohesive view to bear on the Ministers in a single official policy paper. (....) And this is where one's relationships with the P.M. are so all-important. If one doesn't have his backing, or at least the Chancellor's or the First Secretary's, the chance of winning against the official view is absolutely nil.

"But though Cabinet Ministers have this enormous limitation on their power of decision-taking, still their standing is infinitely superior compared with that of the non-Cabinet minister (....) I am sure they find it much more difficult to impose their views on their civil servants. Because though the discussions of the Cabinet Committees and Cabinet very often don't have much reality and are simply rehearsing departmental points of view, nevertheless we Cabinet Ministers do have status within Whitehall, in Parliament and in the nation at large."[2]

(...) "Cabinet drooled on till 12.15. Then we were thrown out because the Defence Committee was there, waiting outside the door with George Wigg. As I walked out I became more and more aware of how fictitious Cabinet government really is. The big issue to be decided concerned, of course, Rhodesia and the action to be taken about the tankers which were breaking the blockade by coming through the Mozambique Channel. So at this point the Cabinet is sent out of the room and the Chiefs of Staff come in. It's the Defence Committee who manage Rhodesia. But at least that consists of half the cabinet, whereas the committee which is secretly preparing the budget consists only of Harold, George, and Jim. So the two main decisions to be taken in defence and finance are entirely lifted out of the hands of the Cabinet. The rest of us are totally excluded."[3]

(...) "At long last Barbara and I were to see Harold at 9.30. He started off straight away by saying he was going to let us have an inner Cabinet of seven (....) I said, 'It all depends who is on it. Is Callaghan in or out?' 'What do you think?', he said, and Barbara and I both answered, 'If it is going to be a real group, an inner Cabinet of likeminded people fighting to win and fighting to build you up, Harold, then it is no good having Callaghan. This is an acid test of your intentions.' He made it quite clear that he agreed with us and that Callaghan should be excluded."[4]

The context of the present study is not England in the second half of the Sixties, nor does the English cabinet under Harold Wilson provide a pure model for the broad variety of high-level governmental decision groups that have been discussed. Nevertheless, the quotations from Richard Crossman's cabinet diaries do exemplify key issues and problems of small-group policy decision making analyzed in this study on groupthink in government. Crossman's observations can be interpreted in terms of more general problems of group decision making in government:
– the need for and the potentialities of group leaders to enhance the group's capacity to make decisions; yet at the same time, the first quote indicates that over-assertive leadership can indeed manufacture the kind of quick consensus 'without' opposition that risks producing ill-considered policies (cf. groupthink through anticipatory compliance);
– the relative impotence of single decision groups, even if they technically hold top-level positions, to assert control over policy decision-making processes that involve a myriad of other actors and agencies within and around the government bureaucracy;
– the subtle power differences between various members of a group in asserting executive leadership over their departmental and other constituencies, which in turn affects their status and importance within the group itself;
– the constant jockeying for influential positions within the decisional loop on any given issue, while simultaneously aspirants try to exclude known opponents from these positions;
– the subtle dynamics of the formation, composition, reshuffling, and operation of inner circles within the context of a broader body of collective decision making;
– and the crucial implications all this may have for group cohesiveness, consensus formation, and the breadth of viewpoints being considered.

Moreover, taken together, the four quotations also reveal how Crossman's personal perceptions and assessments of the Cabinet were constantly vacillating between the extremes of optimism and self-confidence on the one hand, and a sense of impotence and frustration on the other. This in itself is an important indication of how difficult it is to study groups in their context: not only the 'objective' parameters of the organizational and political environment are subject to constant changes, but also the perception and interpretation of these dynamics by members of the group.

This is not the place to discuss the fundamental question of the appropriate extent of using committees in the making of government policy. Although different political communities differ in this respect in their formal blueprints of the governmental process, the empirical reality of small groups being involved in decision making on many key policy issues is hard to escape.[5] So whichever normative position one may adhere to, there is a persistent need to study the working of small groups in the policymaking process, and to try and develop ways of maximizing the potentialities of small groups and minimizing the risks and drawbacks of distorted group decision-making processes.

In this sense, then, the analysis of groupthink can be put to practical use in improving the quality of government. Awareness of the dangers of groupthink can assist decision makers in preventing themselves and the groups they belong to from stumbling into avoidable fiascoes produced by premature and excessive concurrence-seeking.[6] In order to be able to adequately suggest ways to prevent groupthink and spelling out some of their implications for designing and managing policymaking systems, however, it is necessary to clearly assess what has been learned, and to evaluate groupthink analysis itself.

At the outset of this study, four main research questions have been formulated. These pertained to: (a) the theoretical status of groupthink within the broader field of group dynamics; (b) groupthink as applied to governmental decision making; (c) the development of a revised model of groupthink, incorporating findings from both social-psychological and political-administrative strands of theorizing and research; (d) groupthink as an explanation for policy fiascoes.

In this final chapter, it is now time to recapitulate the main findings of this study and to provide answers to the key research questions. Furthermore, an agenda for further research on groupthink will be outlined. Then it becomes possible to discuss methods for preventing or mitigating groupthink in government policymaking and their broader implications.

15.2. Groupthink and group dynamics

In its original version, the notion of groupthink has been developed as a rather idiosyncratic explanatory model. In developing the basic groupthink hypothesis – which claims that under conditions of stress-inducing external threat small, cohesive policymaking groups may engage in concurrence-seeking to such an extent that it impedes their capacity for making effective decisions – Janis has used only part of the mainstream literature on group dynamics, supplementing it with his own research experiences on individual and collective decision making under stress. In fact, the genesis of the groupthink hypothesis goes back in part to Janis' original field of psychoanalysis, more than to mainstream social psychology.[7]

Therefore, in part II of this study, it has been attempted to explore the possible linkages between groupthink and empirically further developed group phenomena. In its turn, however, the survey of part II has been selective: five topics have been selected for analysis on the basis of available leads and suggestions about possible similarities that were found in the literature: peer pressures to uniformity within cohesive groups, anticipatory compliance occurring in hierarchically structured groups under external pressure, deindividuation, group polarization (notably excessive risk taking), and entrapment.

They were selected here because they are frequently, like groupthink, associated with 'detrimental effects of groups upon individuals' or 'defective group decision making.'[8] While each of these five phenomena have indeed been useful in enhancing the theoretical and empirical understanding of groupthink, they do not exhaust the possibility that other, related theories and research areas can shed further light on the antecedents, processes and effects of groupthink. Among possible candidates for further scrutiny and comparison with groupthink are: social facilitation, social impact theory, and the enhancement hypothesis.[9]

Meanwhile, the analysis of part II has resulted in the preliminary revised model of groupthink summarized fully in chapter 8. The model suggests that many of the preconditions for groupthink as outlined by Janis actually trigger either of three of the above-mentioned group processes, which, in turn, lead to the premature/extreme concurrence-seeking that is characteristic of groupthink. These three process dynamics have been conceived of in the model as alternative pathways to groupthink: a cohesiveness path (closely resembling Janis' original hypothesis), a deindividuation path (with cohesiveness as a crucial precondition but adding a new and more forceful dimension of the group process), and a compliance path (which is manifestly different from any previous conceptualization of groupthink).

In addition to specifying the process dynamics, i.e., linking the situational antecedents to the behavioral tendency of concurrence-seeking among group members, the concepts of risk taking and entrapment were incorporated in the revised model to illuminate the decisional outputs that are likely to result from groupthink.

Decision groups affected by groupthink tend to take high, if not excessive, risks. This occurs in part because groupthink blinds the group members to the risk dimension of their actions. When the situation is structured so as to require a repeated, interrelated decisions and the continual reaffirmation of initial commitments, decision groups affected by groupthink are likely to become entrapped in increasingly ineffective policy cycles. The firm belief in the group and the devaluation of dissenters and outside opponents heightens the members' psychological commitment to the group's initial course of action. Strong, if not necessarily overtly expressed, pressures to maintain consensus make it increasingly difficult for group members to voice criticisms and try to break through the self-reinforcing cycle.

The final feature of the revised model pertains to a social-psychological analysis of the *preconditions* for groupthink.[10] In effect, in chapter 7 the scope of inquiry was broadened and extended beyond intra-group processes. Breaking through this conceptual barrier proved particularly useful in trying to establish with greater precision under what conditions the different paths to groupthink are most likely to develop. More specifically, one crucial common denominator was found: the intergroup context in which the decision groups under study actually operate.

The literature on intergroup relations and how these affect intragroup processes was examined. The key findings were compared with the various components of groupthink theory. From this exercise emerged the clear picture that a state of intergroup conflict is a crucial antecedent to groupthink. Many of the process dynamics and defining characteristics of groupthink are among the known intragroup consequences of intergroup conflict: increased cohesiveness and over-evaluation of the in-group, increased desire for strong leadership and unquestioned compliance with leaders, and stereotyped images of outgroups.[11] It was, therefore, concluded that it is crucial to understand groupthink as a contextual phenomenon, i.e. viewing group decision making in its wider intergroup, organizational and political context. This social context as precondition for groupthink tendencies stands out in the preliminary revised model.

What all these considerations and findings have amounted to is presented in chapter 8. It need not be repeated here. At this point, it suffices to simply underline the usefulness of a broader social-psychological analysis of groupthink. Although, originally, groupthink was rather an 'odd man out' within the field, it has now been established that it fits in with a number of mainstream avenues of theory and research. This has resulted in a contextually-driven, contingent, and multiple-path understanding of the preconditions, process dynamics, and decisional consequences of groupthink.

15.3. Groupthink in government: theoretical and empirical scrutiny

Yet the investigation of groupthink did not halt with the formulation of the preliminary revised model. The original focus of the present study was to examine the claim that groupthink was among the primary causes for some major policy fiascoes. This implies that the social-psychological model of groupthink can be used to explain instances of governmental decision making. In part III, this claim was examined using the theoretical and empirical literature on organizational and political-administrative decision making. In effect, this implied moving from a mono-disciplinary to a multi-disciplinary perspective. The results of the political-administrative reexamination of the revised model have been described in chapter 13. It has amounted in a further revision of the model, which, consequently, in its final version has assumed an interdisciplinary status.

The main findings of this reexamination can briefly be summarized as follows.

– The fact that groupthink can only affect the policymaking process if a single, small group is the dominant locus of decision making limits the applicability of the groupthink explanation of policy fiascoes quite considerably. In any given historical case, it is necessary to determine the structure of decision making, contemplating the role of the small group in relation to other fora of organizational and interorganizational action. Depending upon the outcomes of such an examination, the groupthink explanation may or may not be explored further.

– In this respect, an examination of empirically oriented studies of organizational and governmental decision making suggests that the better chances of single group decision making are to be found in non-routine problem situations involving high-level actors, such as long-term policy planning, crisis management, issues requiring confidential treatment, investigation committees.

– Applying the cohesiveness pathway to groupthink as identified in the social-psychological model to government decision making requires extremely careful analysis. In many cases, government decision groups are fraught with division and conflict rather than interpersonal harmony and shared assumptions between their members. This is because the members of the group often come from different organizational or political factions with conflicting views and interests, playing the game of bureau-political pulling and hauling. However, at the same time, the very pervasiveness of competition and conflict between actors in the decisional process may trigger ad-hoc coalitions, informal in-groups, and other closely-knit subgroups which may come to dominate the course of policy beyond or beneath the formal decisional body. Similarly, several common techniques of conflict mitigation and bargaining between group members may also contribute to a subtle kind of assumed consensus similar to the cohesiveness pathway to groupthink.

– Little empirical research was available to check the salience of the deindividuation pathway to groupthink within the context of political-administrative decision making; therefore, no solid conclusions could be drawn regarding this part of the social-psychological model.

– The third pathway to groupthink stressing the role of anticipatory compliance seems to be the most relevant in governmental settings, although, again, one should be keen to realize the limits of its applicability. This happens, for instance, when overt pressures for compliance come to dominate the decision process rather than the more subtle and self-induced anticipatory compliance on the part of group members.[12] The political-administrative interpretation of how anticipatory compliance among members of a policymaking group may lead to groupthink has been presented in five interrelated propositions.

– In a speculative exploration of the political-administrative preconditions of groupthink, it has been found that the structure of accountability under which (members of) decision groups operate can play an important role in determining their attitudes toward the issues they and their fellow group members are involved in. Ultimately, then, different accountability structures as perceived and interpreted by group members can affect the course and outcomes of group decision making. In particular, the distinction between individual and collective accountability is relevant, because it helps to determine whether group members share a common fate, or whether they are induced to dissociate from the group.

– Exploring the implications of this line of thought, a distinction was made between two types of groupthink, based on perceived accountability implications of group action: collective avoidance (type I – the classical mode of groupthink under threat) and collective overoptimism (type II – occurring when members of the group perceive the issue confronting them as an opportunity rather than a threat, and operate under a structure of accountability which makes it profitable for them to be responsible). Examples of collective overoptimism can be found in political honeymoon periods (cf. Bay of Pigs case), big project investments (cf. Kent State Gymnasium case), and military contingency planning (cf. Iran rescue mission case). The implications of distinguishing between optimist and pessimist variants of groupthink need to be explored more fully. The distinction does suggest that it may become possible to distinguish with greater precision different types of preconditions, antecedents, and processes of groupthink.

The qualifications and amendments emerging in part III have been used in a final revised model of groupthink presented in par. 13.4. This model has guided the empirical analysis of this study that is summarized in the next paragraph.

15.4. Using the revised model: empirical findings

In part IV of this study, the revised model of groupthink was used in analyzing the Iran-Contra affair. From this case study emerges a number of plausible inferences, illustrated but not yet fully tested by the application of the revised model to reconstruct and analyze historical decision-making processes.

As far as can be presently ascertained, groupthink seems to have played a major part in U.S. decision making concerning the revision of its policies vis-a-vis Iran and the Lebanon hostage crisis in the period of May 1985-November 1986.[13] Virtually all of the preconditions and process dynamics of the revised model were encountered in the available case evidence.

First of all, there was indeed a *high-level, informal small group* of actors

279

within the Reagan administration whose members alone and in concert were taking the key strategic decisions that started the initiative and kept it going. Multiple sources of case evidence point to the following key actors constituting the heart of the initiative: the President, National Security advisor McFarlane and his deputy and successor Poindexter, the Director of Central Intelligence Casey, and National Security Council Staff member North. Other officials that, given their formal position, could be expected to take part in decision making (such as the Secretaries of State and Defense and certain Congressional leaders), did not participate at all or were reduced to a marginal role.

Secondly, the *intergroup context* of the Iran initiative conformed closely to the model's provisions. The core group perceived itself to be battling against various other groups: the Lebanese extremists that kept American hostages; the radical leadership of the Islamic Republic of Iran; the Soviet leadership that was thought to be engaged in attempts to gain more influence in Iran; the Sandinista government of Nicaragua held to be pro-Communist and being the key target for the Contra rebels supported by the United States. In addition, key members of the group were also perceiving various outgroups within the United States and the U.S. government that they thought were opposed to the group's ends: liberals dominating the press and the media circuit calling for an end to Contra support; Congress which had passed the Boland amendments putting the lid on Contra-Aid, and which was seen to be overly critical and unreliable to keep secrets when it came to covert CIA operations; the regular foreign, defense and intelligence bureaucracies which were hostile to the substance of the Iran-Contra initiative, as well as against the idea of it being implemented by the NSC. Consequently, the initiative was conducted largely 'underground' in great secrecy, while the known opponents against it were gradually eased out of the decision process.

Thirdly, there were marked examples of both *cohesiveness and compliance dynamics* operating in the core group. The need to stick together in the face of so many hostile out-groups was reinforced by a shared ideology and a strong sense of the moral righteousness of the in-group and its adventurous policies. The hierarchical differentiation of the core group (ranging from the Chief Executive via senior figures such as Casey and McFarlane to middle-level bureaucratic entrepreneurs as North) was reinforced by the military-type of perceptions of leadership and loyalty prevalent among all group members other than the President. The doctrine of 'plausible deniability' where National Security Advisor Poindexter considered it only normal that he would be the 'fall guy' for a President which could continue to publicly claim ignorance of policies that he in fact had condoned, was a typical example of the 'can-do' mentality that pervaded the group.

Fourthly, the Iran-Contra case provided an illustration of the *output dynamics* of the revised model: excessive risk taking, and, in repetitive decision situations, the tendency to become entrapped in a spiral of ineffective policies. With regard to risk taking, the group members' rationalizing away of the extremely high risks of disclosure of the entire operation, supports the idea developed here that groupthink produces excessive risk taking precisely because the group members are blind towards the risk dimensions of their actions. The constant need to reaffirm American commitments to proceed with the arms for hostages exchanges in the face of highly disappointing results indicates entrapment. Entrapment was strengthened by actors in and around the core group with a vested interest or personal sense of mission in the initiative, that were 'framing' the options and choices, notably arms merchant Ghorbanifar and North. Consequently, time and again, commitments were renewed because so much had been invested already and the alleged costs of stopping would be unacceptable.

Fifthly, the Iran case illustrates the basic validity of differentiating between *optimistic and pessimistic variants* of groupthink. It was argued that while President Reagan's support for the initiative sprang from internalized stress and strong external pressure to produce results in the hostage crisis (to a certain extent, this was also the case for Casey), other actors, notably North, perceived the initiative as an important opportunity for personal and institutional (NSC) advancement.

Finally, the case study of Irangate has provided a number of promising leads for further research on groupthink:

- the extreme importance of *secrecy* in isolating the groups from its organizational and political environment, and the ways in which security considerations are actually used as an instrument by some of the actors to exclude political and bureaucratic opponents from the decisional loop, and to forego normal procedures and constitutionally envisages checks and balances;
- the need for sophisticated analysis in determining the *boundaries* of informal decisional groups, in particular the subtle mechanisms by which actors from different hierarchical levels can become a tight nucleus; the same goes for actors from different bureaucratic agencies constituting ad-hoc coalitions, pitted against yet other groups in the bureau-political setting.

The causes of policy fiascoes revisited

In his case study analyses, Janis has always been quite careful not to fall into the trap of presenting groupthink as the sole and final explanation of any of the fiascoes he described. Yet at the same time, one can find numerous examples of mono-causality among analysts employing the groupthink explanation to account for historical cases.

The analysis of the present study suggests that groupthink is a significant, but limited threat to the quality of policymaking. It is significant in the sense that if policy decision groups working on major, non-routine, controversial policy issues do fall prey to groupthink tendencies, there is a great risk that they will go for decisions that are ill-considered and reckless. This comes out very clear from the revised model. However, it has also become clear that the threat posed by groupthink is limited, in the sense that the set of preconditions of groupthink as depicted in the model makes that only a modest number of policy decision processes actually meet this description.

Parallel to the groupthink interpretation of policy fiascoes should be developed alternative explanatory frameworks. Among the primary candidates for such alternative frameworks may be the following:
– agenda overload and selective inattention;[14]
– stumbling into disaster: disjointed incrementalism;[15]
– bureau-politism;[16]
– motivated failure: incapable or devious leaders;[17]
– inadequate learning processes;[18]
– mismanagement of technology.[19]

15.5. A research agenda

Staying within the more limited framework of groupthink analysis, the results of the present study suggest various avenues of future research. These need to pursued vigorously in order to further move groupthink from its present unwarranted popularity resulting in vulgarized applications and 'quick-and-easy' analyses, to the status it deserves, namely to a conceptually and empirically well-founded, contextually sound, and cautiously used explanatory framework.

Enhance the interdisciplinary knowledge base of groupthink analysis
This study has made a first attempt to widen the theoretical basis of groupthink from an almost completely group dynamic (and within group dynamics, focused largely on cohesiveness) to a more integrated model, drawing on both social-psychological and political-administrative concepts, theories, and research findings. As pointed out in section 15.2. the present survey of the literature has by no means exhausted the possibilities of exploring and refining existing and alternative linkages between preconditions, dynamics, and outcomes of groupthink within the group-dynamic literature. Going beyond group dynamics, there is a need to investigate the cognitive and motivational ramifications of groupthink as it impacts upon the thoughts and actions of group members. Research in this vein may result in more informed answers to the question of what individuals are most likely to the dangers of extreme concurrence-seeking in decision-making groups.

From the meso-perspective of organization studies and government policy making, efforts should be put into identifying more clearly the contextual factors promoting concurrence-seeking. This would include further analyses of the structural and cultural determinants of conformist versus independent thinking in organizational and political-administrative settings. Similarly, this could amount to a typology of 'vulnerability' to groupthink.

Engage in in-depth analyses and elaborations of various components of the revised model of groupthink
The present revised model of groupthink is quite complex. It contains quite a number of antecedents, and specifies in a certain detail the relationships among variables. Many of the components of the model were derived from

an examination of the relevant literatures (f.i. on intergroup relations, risk taking, deindividuation). Yet these various components of the model have not been tested directly in connection with groupthink. Among the topics to be scrutinized by empirical research in controlled settings are the following:

- the effects of the intergroup context of decision making on the intragroup interaction, notably the issue of how group members actually perceive the intergroup context (do they all perceive similar in-group out-group distinctions, or may members coming from different institutional or political backgrounds have different identifications?), its effects upon cohesiveness (when does intergroup conflict lead to higher intragroup cohesiveness, and when not?), and how it affects patterns of leadership and compliance;
- the relations between the different pathways to groupthink and the symptoms of groupthink, specifying further also the optimistic-pessimistic distinction (groupthink type I and groupthink type II: what are the similarities and differences?);
- a more elaborate evaluation of the third pathway towards groupthink, deindividuation, and its contextual parameters; based on the results of further analysis, a final choice may be made as to the inclusion of deindividuation in the revised model.

Broaden the reservoir of case analyses using sophisticated models of groupthink
The reservoir of solid case study analyses of groupthink is still rather small. It is important to broaden the case material to include diverse decision groups (middle and high-level, advisory and authoritative, intra-organizational and interdepartmental), policy areas (supplementing foreign with domestic issues, and within the domestic sphere issues ranging from infrastructural planning to police operations), types of decision problems (consensual versus conflictive issues, technically defined versus politically defined problems), and organizational and political contexts (different structural arrangements, leadership patterns).

Furthermore, it may be worthwhile to move from single case analyses toward more comparative, multi-case designs; in this respect, however, one should be aware of the potential trade-off between analytical rigor and inter-case comparability: multiple-case analyses should not boil down to superficial analysis of each of the individual cases concerned.

Within the case study methodology, groupthink researchers must remain acutely aware of the problem of data availability. There is no use in pursuing a groupthink analysis of a historical case without being able to consult multiple sources of data, preferably including first-hand accounts if not minutes and sound recordings, of group meetings. In this respect, both cases in the present study constitute just about the bottom end of the continuum, whereas the Watergate case approaches the optimal situation.

Diversify groupthink research methodology
Given the need for scrutinizing specified components of the revised model,

and considering the problems of data availability and specifying cause-and-effect relationships when employing the case study method, it is necessary that groupthink research takes a multi-methodological approach. This means that case studies should be supplemented with laboratory experiments, field experiments and role-playing simulations. For these more controlled types of research methodologies to be effective, however, research designs should be developed in such a way as to incorporate as much of the contextual preconditions of groupthink as possible. Some of the previous groupthink experiments have failed to do so, detracting from their usefulness.[20]

15.6. From analysis to policy practice: preventing groupthink

The ultimate goal of this analysis is to provide policy-relevant prescriptions on how to prevent groupthink.[21] Thinking about practices that may help to prevent extreme concurrence-seeking in the making of major policy decisions, one is quickly struck by the complexity of making sound policy recommendations. A key problem concerns the multiplicity of criteria for evaluating the quality of decision making; this implies that policy recommendations have to balance out between different desirabilities in decision making, which do not always overlap.

In fact, the problem of achieving high-quality decision making involves a trade-off between three types of criteria:
– the need to achieve adequate solutions to the problems at hand;
– the need to gain support for decisions, i.e. the need to arrive at solutions acceptable to various constituencies (implementing agencies, different categories of recipients of decisions – winners, losers, third parties);
– the need for prudent management of decision-making resources: given the limited availability of time, manpower, expertise, and other resources, decision makers cannot afford to spend too much of these on a single problem; therefore, decision-making procedures will also have to stand the test of economy and efficiency.[22]

Improving group decision making

There have been many attempts to lay down procedures that can serve to improve the quality of group decision making. Many of these have focused on influencing the group process itself. Many of these prescriptive devices actually produce results in the context of laboratory experiments and problem-solving exercises. A common denominator of many of these devices is that they attempt to restore some procedural order upon the group process. Anarchy in the group process is being substituted by analytical steps and procedures required to effectively use the combined resources of group members in finding adequate solutions. The quality of decision making is enhanced by rationalizing the process. Among the many devices mentioned in the literature are the Nominal Group technique, Delphi methods, sensible group leadership, brainstorming, structured problem solving, and dialectical inquiry. [23]

The problem with many of these techniques is that they neglect the organizational and political context of group action. In particular, most of these devices do not take into account the problem of differential power of group members as it follows from their position within the wider policy setting. Also, they do not pay attention to the different objectives and standards employed by group members, which, again, follow from their organizational and political affiliations outside the group itself. Therefore, while adequate for groups working in relative isolation and in non-politicized contexts, many of these analytical techniques may short-circuit when decision groups operate in more turbulent settings where conflict and bargaining may take over from rational analysis as the leading principle in group members' expectations and behavior. [24]

The most sophisticated attempt to provide for a general set of decision procedures (one might also call it a system for managing the decision process) for improving the quality of collective policymaking is known as 'multiple advocacy', and has been presented most prominently by George.[25]

It is an attempt to channel the disagreement and conflicting viewpoints generated and perpetuated by bureaupolitics into a productive mobilization and weighing of alternative options leading to balanced policy decisions. In order to function effectively, the multiple advocacy system requires careful leadership and process management by chief executives and designated senior staff members. This can be achieved by designating different roles to different actors in the decisional group: magistrate (the chief executive who encourages debate among advisors and makes the ultimate choice), custodian (manager of the decision process, who has to make sure that the broadest possible range of advocates and viewpoints gets attention, brings in new advisors to argue for unpopular options, sets up alternative information channels, and provides for independent evaluation of options), and advocate.

It is obvious that multiple advocacy works only under certain conditions, that it entails a considerable potential for role conflicts among the officials (especially the custodian-manager), and that it is an expensive decision procedure in that it presupposes a considerable amount of high-level attention for any given decisional issue. These issues have been recognized by its proponents who are careful not to present it as a panacea for all the dilemmas of policymaking.

Groupthink and the quality of decision making

Locating the groupthink phenomenon within this trade-off context, it is apparent that groupthink raises the acceptability of decisions among the decision makers themselves and provides for quick decisions requiring relatively little resources. Yet it also produces decisions that may be highly controversial to implementing agencies and/or recipients. Most of all, it leads to ill-considered solutions to complex problems, i.e. it fails in terms of the substantive quality of decisional output. Now the challenge for any kind of prescription seeking to prevent groupthink is to enhance the substantive quality and the external acceptability, while at the same time preserving internal support among the decision makers and not posing irrealistic demands on the available decision-making resources.

The dilemma, in other words, is multi-faceted. It involves finding a balance between the need for group consensus about its decisional products and the self-corrective functions of in-group conflict in reaching adequate solutions. In terms of the relationship between the group and its organizational-administrative environment, mechanisms to prevent groupthink hang in the balance between the positive functions of external oversight and control, and the need for group autonomy to maintain flexibility and innovative capacity. In terms of the political context of decision, preventing groupthink may involve walking the tightrope between secrecy and openness, between constrained consultation and broad participation, and between maintaining decisiveness and democratic control of the executive.

Preventing groupthink (I): Janis' recommendations

Janis has offered nine recommendations for preventing groupthink. Most of these devices are designed to offset conformity pressures, to neutralize the steering role of the group leader, and to generate maximum diversity of opinions in deliberating about a policy problem. However, as Janis indicates, some of these recommendations may have drawbacks. Indeed, he reports experiencing 'considerable ambivalence' in formulating the prescriptions at all.[26] He regards them more as elementary precautions than as comprehensive solutions.

a) Each member must be critical evaluator of the group's course of action; an open climate of giving and accepting criticism should be encouraged by the leader.
b) Leaders should be impartial and refrain from stating their personal preferences at the outset of group discussion; they should limit themselves initially to fostering open inquiry.
c) Set up parallel groups working on the same policy question under different leaders.
d) When policy options are evaluated the group should split up in two or more subgroups, eventually coming together to compare and resolve their different assessments.
e) Each member of the group should privately discuss current issues and options with trusted associates outside the group and report back their reactions.
f) Different outside experts should be brought in from time to time to challenge the views of the core members.

g) There should be one or more devil's advocates during every group meeting.
h) In conflict situations, extra time should be devoted to interpreting warning signals from rivals and to constructing alternative scenarios of their intentions.
i) Second chance meetings should be held to reconsider the decision once it has been reached and before it is made public.

These prescriptions are no doubt useful in enhancing the quality of decision-making procedures. If implemented to the letter, most of them will be effective in forcing the members of decision groups to acknowledge the complexity of the issues, and mobilizing their critical facilities in the process of deliberation and choice.

Example 1: Cuban missile crisis. Janis' analysis of U.S. decision making during the Cuban missile crisis shows many of these principles in action: President Kennedy as cautious and unbiased leader, Robert Kennedy as devil's advocate with enough leverage to be really effective instead of a ritual voice of dissent, and parallel groups working on the same issue. To a certain extent, this decision process can also be viewed as an instance of successful multiple advocacy with the President as magistrate and his brother as custodian, with other senior and military advisors acting as advocates.[27]

Example 2: South-Moluccan hostage takings. In 1977, South-Moluccan terrorists captured a train and a primary school in the northern part of the Netherlands taking the train passengers hostage, as well as the schoolchildren and their teachers. The hostage crisis dragged on for more than three weeks with, apart from the release of the children, little hope for a negotiated solution without major concessions from the Dutch government. At this point, the Ministerial crisis center containing the Prime Minister and chaired by the minister of Justice had started to contemplate military intervention, plans and exercises for which had already been underway. There were a number of reasons for this: stress on the hostages and their captors was rising to intolerable levels with increased danger for dramatic outbursts and violence; there were public tensions between Dutch and Moluccan groups in the country; and political time pressures existed as there was a pressing need to free the political leaders from the crisis and to proceed with the formation of a new coalition government after the general elections that had taken place two days into the hostage takings.

To begin with, the situation seemed to be quite conducive to groupthink (stress, single group, isolation of the group, presence of clearly definable out-groups, perceived need for consensus on whatever decision that emerged from the crisis center), a combination of political dynamics and deliberate management counteracted potential groupthink tendencies.

To begin with, there existed serious personality and political differences and tensions between the two main authorities in the crisis center (prime minister and minister of Justice). These not only forestalled the development of amiability and esprit de corps, they also implied a constant if mostly latent struggle for de-facto leadership. As a consequence there was no single group leader dominating the discussion and manipulating the process. Secondly, the political sensitivities of this crisis during election and formation time led some of the group members to discreetly consult with confidants in their respective political and bureaucratic bases.

Equally, group isolation was broken by the fact that no single agency or coalition of experts was able to monopolize the flow of information and advice reaching the group: medics, psychiatrists, military personnel and political consultants were all involved, contributing different points of view and offering conflicting policy suggestions at different points in time (this in itself produced problems radically different from the dangers of quick consensus, namely the risk of paralysis). Fourthly, from the outset, the decision makers had advanced a two-pronged strategy whereby parallel negotiation and military scenarios were contemplated. Fifthly, next to the central-level crisis center there was a local policy center which monitored the daily course of events. During the crisis, marked differences of perspective between the policy center and the crisis center came to the fore. The policy center was much more sensitive to the pressures building up in and around the train and the school. It was, therefore, more prone to stress the urgency of the situation and the need for quick decisions. As such, it acted as one among several other advocates impacting on the ministerial crisis center where final responsibility located.

Ultimately, the decision was taken to end the crisis by force. This was not an easy process. In particular, the prime minister continued to object to the use of military force. The political and ethical implications of a surprise attack where discussed at length. When finally a consensus seemed to emerge, it was decided to postpone the meeting for some hours, giving each member of the center the opportunity for some private reflection.

The final decision was reached only at a second session, after which there was still long debate about the operational and safety ramifications of the proposed attack plan. The next morning, the train and the school were stormed. Six terrorists were killed as well as two train passengers. The other hostages came out unharmed.[28]

There are other examples of successful prevention of groupthink along the line of Janis' recommendations. Yet some caution is in order. As the Moluccan hostage case shows, personal and political factors other than deliberate management techniques may play a vital role in breaking through concurrence-seeking tendencies.

Personal experience, the personality mix in the decision group, the distribution of power and influence between group members, the timing of the issue vis-à-vis other ongoing concerns, the wider organizational and political configuration and its impact on the decision makers: all of these factors can work to overcome concurrence-seeking tendencies.

In this respect, one could also question the practical feasibility of some of Janis' recommendations (as well as those of other prescription-oriented analysts such as George). In particular, the underlying premise that decision makers will be motivated to comply with guidelines and rules of the game implied by the recommendations. For instance, there may be strong pressures upon a political leader faced with a major policy issue or crisis to display strong leadership. Under these conditions, it is unlikely that the chief executive will be patient enough to assume a neutral role encouraging free debate among his advisors, and wait for the results of the often complex and drawn-out advocacy process. Such an attitude, though conducive to high-quality decision making, may easily be interpreted as indecisiveness, and may cost the leader political credibility and support.

In advocating the use of multiple, implicitly competitive groups working on the same policy issue, Janis remarks that actors in a more adversarial decision process should be made aware of the fact that their primary loyalty should lie with the organization or government as a whole rather than with their sub-groups and bureaucratic factions.[29] This is not very realistic, given the balance of rewards and costs for the individuals concerned. Both formal (promotions, salaries) and informal (peer-group acceptance, leverage) steering mechanisms often lie with an actor's immediate work environment and superiors rather than with the broader organization and policy system. Hence, the incentives for continued hard-pitched bureaucratic politics cannot simply be offset with a call for a broader sense of duty. For such a call to be effective, the balance of rewards and costs should be altered. This is not easy to accomplish.

There is another set of practical difficulties. If one reconsiders the three basic criteria for high-quality policymaking, it appears that many of Janis' prescriptions would entail large costs, in that they mobilize many people, they entail built-in redundancies, and they take time (expert meetings, opponents-scanning meetings, second chance meetings). This goes for multiple advocacy as well (George mentions chief executives' participation and the availability of time as two of the preconditions of this model). The obvious risk of such costly procedures is that of input overload: decision makers are engulfed by problems that simply cannot all be handled in the rigorous manner. In the long run, the recommendations will backfire against the limited span of attention of key decision makers, staff members, and policy analysts. To circumvent this, a selection must be made: which problems are deemed so important as to warrant full-scale decision procedures advanced by Janis, George and others? How can such a selection be made sensibly before chief executives have themselves carefully assessed each of the issues at hand?

Can these critical considerations be neutralized in some way or another? Are there methods to preserve the strong points within these recommendations while altering the decisional costs associated with them? And is it possible to develop policy recommendations that do not contradict too bluntly the organizational and political imperatives that many policy decision makers are confronted with?

Are there heuristics for group decision making that are both effective in terms of improving decision quality, realistic, and cost-efficient? These questions cannot be answered in full yet. In part, the answer must be 'no': you cannot have it all in one magic formula. One may simply face up to the need to make real trade-offs: concentrating on a limited number of key issues and handling these properly, while taking risks by neglecting other policy problems that await decisions.

Preventing groupthink (II): supplementary provisions

Janis recommendations for preventing groupthink were derived from his theoretical and empirical analysis of groupthink, focusing largely on group cohesiveness and its ramifications (isolation, leadership practices enhancing real or apparent group unity). In the present study, a broader theoretical analysis has been developed. Taking the revised model of groupthink with its more fully elaborated scanning of the contextual preconditions of groupthink as a starting point, several additional recommendations can be formulated. In particular, they seek to prevent anticipatory compliance, and suggest specific political-administrative provisions counteracting groupthink tendencies. These recommendations are designed not to replace those discussed above, but can be used as alternative measures or in addition to the earlier provisions (at this point, there are no well-tested rules of application for the various recommendations, but it should become possible to devise a checklist of groupthink-inducing factors along with specific counteracting devices for practical use).

Break through group isolation: accountability and control

One obvious mechanism to improve group decision making is to impose external oversight and control. Holding decision makers accountable for their actions is one of the oldest ways in which organizations and political systems have sought to protect themselves against foolishness or questionable conduct on the part of elites. Hierarchical, external and political accountability (through periodic reviews, auditing, parliamentary scrutiny) constitute forms of 'backward policing.' They seek to improve the quality of decision making at time t by evaluating and, if possible, sanctioning decision makers' performance at time t-x. These forms of post-hoc control generally do not aspire to timely discover and readjust potential fiascoes, but are mainly directed to dissuade decision makers from initiating or participating in future mishaps. However, some accountability fora (such as permanent parliamentary committees) may even develop resources to engage in pro-active monitoring of ongoing policy ventures, that might enable them to engage in active steering of running projects.

In chapter 12, some potential unintended undesirable effects of accountability structures have been identified. Members of collective decision bodies can ignore or play down their personal responsibility for the outcomes of policy decisions, when there is no explicit and enforceable standard of individual accountability. This may cause them to be complacent when the group they take part in embarks on a questionable course of action. They lack incentives to intervene, as their personal fate with regard to the decision at hand is completely tied in with that of the other group members.

This changes when conditions are such that accountability and control by external fora may imply that decision makers are individually responsible.[30] Then, each group member is better motivated to challenge collective rationalizations and misperceptions underlying faulty group decisions. If he fails to do so, he will pay the price later.

The suggestion to upgrade structures of accountability on the basis of the principle of individual responsibility is not new. Nor is it free from practical problems that may limit its effectiveness. But it does suggest that the prevention of groupthink need not only be a matter of intragroup mechanisms of improvement. Manipulating the external context of group action and the premises of group members provides an alternative route.

Protect 'voice' within the policy arena: whistleblowing
The second prescription follows the same line of reasoning. As the compliance pathway to groupthink indicates, the balance of conflict and cohesion is not the only relevant dimension of the group process at work in groupthink. Groupthink may also occur because group members operating in an organizational and political hierarchy manifest in the in-group, that predisposes them to refrain from voicing any doubts and misgivings they might have. The suppression of doubts at work in groupthink is a clear manifestation of the harmful effects of compliance.

Where compliance is the problem, non-compliance may be a solution. To prevent compliance-based groupthink, group members should be encouraged to voice concerns rather than to voluntarily suppress them, to question assumptions rather than to accept them at face value, and to continue to disagree and debate when no satisfactory answers to their concerns are given by the rest of the group. If these countervailing mechanisms fail to alter the erroneous decision, deviant group members with serious concerns may contemplate another alternative: blowing the whistle. Whistleblowing refers to instances where individual organization members or civil servants disclose information about, or take a public stand against, failures or questionable practices they have become aware of through their membership of the organization or government; and this occurs without orders or permission from their superiors.

Whistleblowing is a form of bureaucratic disobedience that has stirred up considerable attention and controversy in the United States, Great Britain and elsewhere, triggered by famous (and notorious) cases such as Daniel Ellsberg's release of the Pentagon Papers, Frank Serpico's revelations about New York police corruption, Karen Silkwood's exposure of mismanagement in the nuclear power industry, and Clive Ponting's charges concerning the sinking of the Argentian warship Belgrano during the Falklands war.

The average whistleblower has a hard time. Before going public, most whistleblowers struggle with a serious role conflict: loyalty to the public interest on the one hand against loyalty to the team, to superiors, to the organization as a whole, and personal career and family consideration as on the other hand. Also, they may consider themselves to be so far down the road of complying with malicious or irrational practices that try think it better to remain about them (entrapment).

Furthermore, organizations do not like whistleblowing, and possess numerous power resources to put pressure on their members. Many whistleblowers fare badly after their revelations: they miss promotions, get fired, face harassment and threats, and find it hard to land in a new job (few organizations are eager to hire known 'trouble makers'). Finally, the whistleblower must face up to considerable political and legal consequences resulting from his actions. Whistleblowing in defense or foreign affairs may easily lead to charges of security breaches and treason, which may entail criminal prosecution.

Given all these constraints, whistleblowers are relatively rare. It is much easier to go along and conform. This might be changed if whistleblowers could count on legal or other forms of protection. Protecting whistleblowers may encourage potential dissenters in a policy group embarking on a disastrous course of action to escape the overt or implicit pressures for compliance in the group and its institutional environment.[31]

This is easier said than done, however. Whistleblowing provisions may not be sufficient to really safeguard public dissenters from the wide range of formal and informal sanctions that may be used against them. Also, it is hard to formulate appropriate criteria for whistleblowing, to prevent such provisions from being misused by the wrong people, such as sensation seekers and disgruntled employees. The genuine whistleblower acts out of motives related to the public interest. Yet on the basis of post-hoc argumentation only, the lines of distinction between genuine and improper users of whistleblowing provisions are hard to draw. Therefore, it is necessary to outline a more complex procedure. These are practical problems that may be overcome. In essence, whistleblowing constitutes another potentially useful instrument to prevent or mitigate groupthink.

Protect the right to say 'no' for motivated dissenters
A related problem of deviance from collective judgments concerns organizational actors that refuse to participate in the making or implementation of policies or decisions because this would violate their conscience: conscientious objection. This is a somewhat specific variant of deviance. First of all, the source of deviance is said to be explicitly moral. Secondly, the deviant does not necessarily want to prevent or alter the decision from being taken or implemented, he simply does not want to remain personally involved. This would force him to be involved in activities that he considers unjustifiable. In other words, whistleblowers pursue the 'voice' option while conscientious objectors claim a right to 'exit.'

At first sight, providing for such exit in the form of legal provisions concerning conscientious objection does not seem very helpful in improving the quality of decision making and protecting against policy fiascoes. From the perspective of the public interest, it does not matter much whether a disastrous policy is conceived of or implemented by officials A, B, and C, or by their colleagues C, D, and E. From this point of view, reasons other than overall quality of government must be probed in justifying conscientious objection. However, from the perspective of groupthink alone, this may be somewhat different. Groupthink leads group members to collectively neglect or play down the moral implications of their proposed course of action. When individual group members with private concerns about ethical issues overlooked or suppressed in the group as a whole know that they have a realistic exit option, they are likely to become less hesitant in voicing their concerns within the group before resorting to this final option. In doing so, they might be able to bring the ethical perspective back in. Needless to say, however, that institutionalizing this kind of exit option entails the same kind of demarcation and procedural problems encountered with whistleblowing. What types of objections are valid? Which steps should dissenters take before they can rightfully refuse to participate? And which safeguards against organizational retaliation should be offered?[32]

Manipulate decision rules and their acceptance: between consensus and majority vote
A very obvious way to prevent members of a decision group from maintaining an illusion of unanimity is to alter the rules governing group choice. To prevent groupthink, one may break through the common assumption that high-level decision groups should operate on the basis of consensus. Replacing this with one form of majority rule will relieve pressure on group members in minority positions. Under consensus rules they may refrain from voicing their concerns, either by self-discipline and a desire not to shatter group harmony (suppression of doubts) or following direct hints by the leader (compliance) or by fellow group members (mindguards; peer pressure). When consensus is no longer required, group discussion can be more open.

There are serious drawbacks associated with majority rule in high-level policymaking groups, however. First of all, installing majority rule may lead to a more adversarial group climate. Latent conflicts are easier brought out into the open. This can ultimately lead to the disintegration of the group. Secondly, especially in segmented groups (like coalition cabinets), adopting majority rule may make visible permanent majority-minority relations within the group. Ironically, then, it may effectively diminish the de-facto influence of minorities and dissenters in influencing the final outcome, despite a more open process of discussion.

In other words, majority rule may prevent the group from the dangers of concurrence-seeking at the group level, but at the same time it makes it easier for subgroups (i.e. majorities within the group) to force their opinions. This would simply mean that instead of the entire group embarking on a failing course of action, under majority rule one only needs a committed and uncritical subgroup of majority members to obtain the same result. If this would really be the case for any kind of very crucial group decision, the only option left to minority members that might eventually redress the balance would be to contemplate their voice and exit options

293

(see above).

A third major problem with majority rule can be derived from small group research indicating that under majority rule, group members are much less committed to the group decision than is the case with unanimous decisions.[33] In many major policy decisions, post-decisional commitment is crucially important in obtaining external support for policies (i.e. 'selling' the decision to various constituencies).

Finally, and perhaps most importantly, despite the fact that majority rule may be able to prevent pathologies of concurrence-seeking, research continually indicates that, *in general,* in comparison to cooperative unanimity groups, competitive majority rule groups simply produce inferior outcomes. They produce lower quality solutions, and member satisfaction is distinctly higher in consensus groups. Majority rule may easily boil down to either ritualized or highly fixed competitive interaction between group members. In both cases, they lack a willingness to critically examine and evaluate one another's arguments, which, ideally, does happen in consensus groups (provided they are able to maintain an 'open' climate).

A dilemma emerges: changed decision rules (i.e. majority rule) may be effective in preventing groupthink tendencies, yet at the same time, they have different but equally serious drawbacks. This dilemma between conflict and consensus might be reconciled, as suggested by George and by Gaenslen.[34] They both suggest a middle course: retaining consensus and cooperation as a basic requirement for group decision; but influencing the process of consensus seeking by introducing a more adversarial discussion process (i.e. multiple advocacy, as described above). As Gaenslen concludes: "In sum, I propose a project: the investigation in the laboratory of the possibility of combining advocacy with the desire for unanimity and with trust and friendship to create a decision process that is both relatively efficient and relatively democratic."[35]

Hence, the focus is back to where it was nineteen chapters ago: the idea of policy decision groups as genuine 'teams': consensual and collegial, but strongly task-oriented. After so many years of small group studies exploring the various ramifications of the problem, this seems a somewhat meager harvest. And indeed, in the more than seventeen years that have elapsed since George's elaborate presentation of the multiple advocacy framework, group analysts in Political Science and Public Administration have produced little to challenge the relevance of Gaenslen's call to further examine the possibilities of combining 'the best of both worlds' in a single meta-decisional framework for practical use by policymaking bodies. It is time to get to work.

Concluding remarks

This discussion of how to prevent groupthink may leave the reader somewhat sceptical about the chances of improving the quality of government action. The continued occurrence of decisional failures and policy fiascoes suggests that governments have difficulty improving their performance. Studies of government learning are generally pessimistic about the possibilities to upgrade the quality of government action and to induce policy makers to avoid repeating the mistakes of the past.[36] Not only is it difficult to implement proposed reforms and improvements. More fundamentally, each of the policy recommendations offered by prescription-oriented analysts has potential drawbacks which may offset the benefits. There are no golden formulas for solving permanently the dilemmas of government decision quality. There is no easy way to streamline the processes of organizational and interorganizational problem-sensing, information processing, and choice. There is no simple, if any, method to get individual officials to enact well-trained skills and professional and ethical norms, to escape the logic of collective action, and to manage bureaucratic complexity to make organizational behavior more morally responsible. The best one can do is to continue to try and understand the conditions of success and failure, to rethink standards of evaluating the quality of government, and to produce policy-relevant theories to stimulate improvements.

Notes

1. Crossman (1979), pp.76-77; describing February 25th, 1965.
2. Crossman (1979), pp.86-87; describing April 18th, 1965.
3. Crossman (1979), p.180; describing April 7th, 1966.
4. Crossman (1979), pp.540-541; describing April 29th, 1969; Barbara stands for Mrs. Barbara Castle, member of the Wilson cabinet.
5. See the full version of this argument as developed in Baylis (1989); this is not to imply that a single small group often emerges as the sole or dominant decisional actor - as explained in greater detail in chapters 9 and 10.
6. See Janis' cautious assessment of the advantages and potential drawbacks of 'a little knowledge of groupthink' among practitioners, Janis (1982a), pp. 275-276.
7. Janis (1968).
8. Sakurai (1976); Swap (1984); Hirokawa (1987); see also Buys (1978), for a more general, if not altogether serious, 'condemnation' of groups.
9. See: Raven and Rubin (1977); Latan (1982); Rabbie (1982).
10. In Janis' original model, the preconditions were mentioned but not operationalized further; also, he failed to analyze in any detail the intergroup dimensions of intragroup processes.
11. A crucial mediating factor here is the group members' belief that their group can actually prevail in the intergroup conflict. If this would not be the case, increased fragmentation and defection from the group would result.
12. Cf. Janis' analysis of conformity out of fear of recrimination, Janis (1982a), pp.299-300.
13. The cautiousness of this formulation is due to the fact that in the next few months and years, new material and facts concerning this case are likely to become available. It will be a challenge to see whether, in a few years from now, this interpretation of events will need to be modified.
14. Bachrach and Baratz (1970); Cobb and Elder (1972).
15. Goodin (1982); see also Allison (1971), model II.

16. Allison (1971), model III, Rosenthal (1988).
17. Jervis (1976), Lebow (1987).
18. Argyris and Schon (1978), model I learning versus model II learning (single-loop versus double-loop); see also Etheredge (1985), and Neustadt and May (1986).
19. Turner (1978); Perrow (1984), and Kouzmin and Jarman (1989).
20. For instance, Flowers (1977); for a more elaborate treatment of the problem, see Janis (1982b).
21. Note that this is not altogether self-evident. Longley and Pruitt (1980), for instance, have raised the question of whether groupthink is necessarily bad, and have concluded that his is not the case. For simple problem-solving tasks, concurrence-seeking may enhance group efficiency. Janis (1989), too, suggests that groupthink and other decision heuristics are dangerous only when it concerns complex policy problems requiring innovative solutions. The discussion about prevention, therefore, presumes this demarcation.
22. For a more elaborate treatment, see: George (1980), see also Schweiger, Sandberg and Regan (1986). In the small-group literature, member satisfaction with the group is often mentioned as a key requirement for evaluating group effectiveness, see Vroom and Yetton (1973), Gladstein (1984). The two diverse interpretations can easily be reconciled by subsuming member satisfaction under the broader category of support and acceptability, and by differentiating between internal acceptability (satisfaction of group members) and external acceptability (satisfaction of different groups of clients and implementing agencies). For the internal-external discussion with regard to group effectiveness, see Gladstein-Ancona (1987).
23. See Hall and Watson (1971); Nemiroff and King (1973); Vroom and Yetton (1973); Gaenslen (1980); Falk (1981); McGrath (1984); Schweiger et al. (1986).
24. See Gladstein-Ancona (1987).
25. See George (1972) and discussant I.M. Destler; George (1980); on the broader issue of managing a policymaking system, see Pika (1988).
26. Janis (1982a), p.262.
27. Note that the positive assessment of Kennedy's 1962 case is not wholly undisputed. For instance, Kennedy was not at all a neutral leader with respect to the basis question of whether the discovery of the missile building sites actually needed a forceful American response: McNamara's doubts ('a missile is a missile') in this respect were brusquely shoved aside. See Lebow (1981), McCauley (1989).
28. See for a more elaborate discussion of the case: Rosenthal and 't Hart (1989).
29. Janis (1982a), p.265.
30. Meeus and Raaijmakers (1984); 't Hart, Kroon, Van Kreveld (1989).
31. For a more elaborate treatment of whistleblowing provisions and the problems involved, see Bovens (1987b).
32. See Bovens (1987a), who distinguishes between orthodox and libertarian modes of conscience and formulates a number of operational criteria that may form the basis of a formal provision on this point.
33. See research on mock juries operating under different decision rules as conducted by, amongst others, Bower, Robinson, Nemeth and others, as reported by Gaenslen (1980), pp. 21 ff.
34. George (1972); Gaenslen (1980).
35. Gaenslen (1980), p.25.
36. Etheredge (1985); Neutstadt and May (1986).

Bibliography

Abcarian, G., and J.W. Soule (eds 1968), *Social Psychology and Political Behavior: Problems and Prospects*, Columbus: Charles E. Merrill.

Abelson, R.P., and A. Levi (1985), Decision making and decision theory. In: G.Lindzey, E. Aronson (eds), *The Handbook of Social Psychology*, vol. II, New York: Random House, pp. 231-309 (3rd ed.).

Aberbach, J.D., R.D. Putnam and B.A. Rockman (1981), *Bureaucrats and Politicians in Western Democracies*, Cambridge Mass.: Harvard University Press.

Abrahamsson, B. (1977), *Bureaucracy or Participation: The Logic of Organization*, London: Sage.

Allison, G.T. (1971), *Essence of Decision: Explaining the Cuban Missile Crisis*, Boston: Little, Brown and Company.

Ambrose, S. (1985), *Eisenhower, vol. II*, New York: Simon and Schuster.

Andeweg, R.B. (1985), The Netherlands: cabinet committees in a coalition cabinet. In: T.T. Mackie and B.J.W. Hogwood (eds), *Unlocking the Cabinet*, London: Sage Publications, pp. 138-154.

Andeweg, R.B. (1988), Centrifugal forces and collective decision making: the case of the Dutch cabinet. In: *European Journal of Political Research*, 10, pp. 125-151.

Argote, L. (1982), Input uncertainty and organizational coordination in hospital emergency units. In: *Administrative Science Quarterly*, 27, pp. 420-434.

Argyris, C., and D.A. Schon (1978), *Organizational Learning*, Reading Mass.: Addison-Wesley.

Arkes, H.R., and C. Hackett (1984), *The Psychology of Sunk Costs*. Unpublished manuscript, Ohio University.

Armstrong, S., M. Byrne, T. Blanton, et. al. (1987), *The Chronology: The documented day-by-day account of the secret military assistance to Iran and the Contras*, New York: Warner Books.

Aronson, E. (1984), *The Social Animal*, New York: Freeman.

Aronson, E., N. Blaney, C. Stephan, J. Sities and M. Snapp (1978), *The Jigsaw Classroom*, Beverly Hills: Sage.

Asch, S. (1951), Effects of group pressure upon the modification and distortion of judgments. In: H. Guetzkow (ed.), *Groups, Leadership and Men*, Pittsburgh: Carnegie Press, pp. 177-190.

Asch, S.E. (1952), *Social Psychology*, Englewood Cliffs: Prentice Hall.

Asch, S. (1956), *Social Psychology*, Englewood Cliffs: Prentice Hall, 2nd ed.

Austin, W.G., and S. Worchel (eds 1979), *The Social Psychology of Intergroup Relations*, Monterey CA: Brooks/Cole.

Axelrod, R. (1984), *The Evolution of Cooperation*, New York: Basic Books.

Bachrach, P., and M.J. Baratz (1970), *Power and Poverty: Theory and Practice*, New York: Oxford University Press.

Back, K.W. (1951), Influence through social communication. In: *Journal of Abnormal and Social Psychology*, 46, pp. 9-23.

Bandura, A. (1977), *Social Learning Theory*, Englewood Cliffs: Prentice Hall.

Barber, J.D. (1965), *Power in Committees: An Experiment in the Governmental Process*, Chicago: Rand McNally.

Barber, J.D. (1972), *The Presidential Character: Predicting Performance in the White House*, Englewood Cliffs: Prentice Hall.

Barber, J.D. (1989), *Politics by Humans: Research on American Leadership*, Durham: Duke University Press.

Barett, L. (1984), *Gambling with History: President Reagan in the White House*, New York: Penguin.

Barrett, D.M. (1988), Political and personal intimates as advisers: The mythology of Lyndon Johnson and the 1965 decision to enter the Vietnam War. Paper presented at the Midwest Political Science Association.

Barry, B. (1974), Review Article: "exit, voice and loyalty". In: *British Journal of Political Science*, 4, pp. 79-107.

Barton, A. (1969), *Communities in Disaster*, Garden City: Doubleday.

Baylis, T.A. (1989), *Governing by Committee: Collegial Leadership in Advanced Societies*, Albany: State University of New York Press.

Bazerman, M.H., T. Giuliano, and A. Appelman (1984), Escalation in individual and group decision making. In: *Organizational Behavior and Human Performance*, 33, pp. 141-152.

Beauchamp, T., and N. Bowie (eds 1983), *Ethical Theory and Business*, Englewood Cliffs: Prentice Hall.

Ben Zvi, A. (1977), Misperceiving the role of perception: a critique. In: *Jerusalem Journal of International Relations*, 2, pp. 74-93.

Berg, I.A., and B.M. Bass (eds 1961), *Conformity and Deviation*, New York: Harper.

Bergen, C.W. von, and R.J. Kirk (1984), Groupthink: when too many heads spoil the decision. In: *Management Review*, pp. 44-49.

Berkowitz, L. (1954), Group standards, cohesiveness, and productivity. In: *Human Relations*, 7, pp. 509-519.

Bettelheim, B. (1943), Individual and mass behavior in extreme situations. In: *Journal of Abnormal and Social Psychology*, 38, pp. 417-452.

Betts, R.K. (1977), *Soldiers, Statesmen and Cold-War Crises*, Cambridge: Harvard University Press.

Betts, R.K. (1981). Surprise despite warning: why sudden attacks succeed. In: *Political Science Quarterly*, 95, pp. 551-572.

Betts, R.K. (1982), Analysis, war and decision: why intelligence failures are inevitable. In: *World Politics*, 34, pp. 62-89.

Bill, J.A. (1988), *The Eagle and the Lion: The tragedy of American-Iranian Relations*, New Haven: Yale University Press.

Billig, M.G. (1976), *Social Psychology and Intergroup Relations*, London: Academic Press.

Billig, M.G. (1978), *Fascists: A Social Psychological View of the National Front*, London: Academic Press.

Bion, W.R. (1961), *Experiences in Groups and Other Papers*, New York: Basic Books.

Blake, R.R., and J.S. Mouton (1961), Conformity, resistance and conversion. In: *I.A. Berg and B.M. Bass (eds)*, op. cit. pp. 1-37.

Blake, R.R., and J.S. Mouton (1962), The intergroup dynamics of win-lose conflict, problem-solving and collaboration in union-management relations. In: M. Sherif (ed.), *Intergroup Relations and Leadership*, New York: John Wiley, pp. 94-140.

Blau, P.M., and W.R. Scott (1962), *Formal Organizations*, San Francisco: Chandler.

Blondel, J. (1982), *The Organization of Governments. A Comparative Analysis of Governmental Structures*, London: Sage.

Blondel, J. (1987), *Political Leadership: Towards a General Analysis*, London: Sage.

Boos, M., and R. Fisch (1987), Die Fallstudie in der Organisationsforschung. In: A. Windhoff-Héritier (hrsg.), *Verwaltung und ihre Umwelt*, Bonn: West-deutscher

Verlag, pp. 350-376.

Bovens, M.A.P. (1987a), Het geweten als bureaucratisch probleem. In: *Beleid en Maatschappij,* 14, pp. 87-98 (in Dutch).

Bovens, M.A.P. (1987b), Bescherming van "klokkeluiders". In: *Beleid en Maatschappij,* 14, pp. 160-171 (in Dutch).

Bovens, M.A.P. (1989), The Social Steering of Complex Organizations. In: *British Journal of Political Science,* 21, pp. 91-118.

Bozeman, B. (1987), *All Organizations are Public,* San Francisco: Jossey-Bass.

Brockner, J., J.Z. Rubin and M.C. Shaw (1979), Factors affecting with drawal from an escalating conflict: Quitting before it is too late. In: *Journal of Experimental Social Psychology,* 15, pp. 492-503.

Brockner, J., J.Z. Rubin and E. Lang (1981), Face-saving and entrapment. In: *Journal of Experimental Social Psychology,* 17, pp. 68-79.

Brockner, J., S. Nathanson, A. Friend, J. Harbeck, C. Samuelson, R. Houser, M. Bazerman, J.Z. Rubin (1984), The role of modelling processes in the 'knee deep in the big muddy' phenomenon. In: *Organizational Behavior and Human Performance,* 33, pp. 77-99.

Brockner, J., and J.Z. Rubin (1985), *Entrapment in Escalating Conflicts,* New York: Springer-Verlag.

Bronner, R. (1982), *Decision Making under Time Pressure,* Lexington: Heath.

Brown, R. (1986), *Social Psychology,* New York: Free Press, 2nd ed.

Brown, R. (1987), *Group Pressures: Dynamics Within and Between Groups,* Oxford: Basil Blackwell.

Brug, H. van der (1986), *Achtergronden van Voetbalvandalisme,* Haarlem: Vrieseborgh (in Dutch).

Brzezinski, Z. (1983), *Power and Principle: Memoirs of the National Security Advisor 1977-1981,* New York: Farrar, Straus and Giroux.

Burnstein, E., and A. Vinokur (1977), Persuasive argumentation and social comparison as determinants of attitude polarization. In: *Journal of Experimental Social Psychology,* 13, pp. 315-332.

Buys, C.J. (1978), Individuals would be better off without groups. In: *Personality and Social Psychology Bulletin,* 4, 1, pp. 123-125.

Caddick, B. (1982), Perceived illegitimacy and intergroup relations. In: H. Tajfel (ed.), *Social Identity and Intergroup Relations,* Cambridge: Cambridge University Press, pp. 137-153.

Caldwell, D.F., and C.A. O'Reilly (1982), Response to failure: the effects of choice and responsibility on impression management. In: *Academy of Management Journal,* 25, pp. 121-136.

Callaway, M.R., R.G. Marriot, and J.K. Esser (1985), Effects of dominance on group decision. In: *Journal of Personality and Social Psychology,* 49, pp. 949-952.

Campbell, C. (1983a), Political Leadership in Canada: Pierre Elliot Trudeau and the Ottawa model. In: R. Rose and E. Suleiman (eds), *Presidents and Prime Ministers,* Washington DC: American Enterprise Institute for Public Policy Research, pp. 50-93.

Campbell, C. (1983b), *Governments Under Stress: Political Executives and Key Bureaucrats in Washington, London and Ottawa,* Toronto: University of Toronto Press.

Campbell, C., and G. Szablowski (1979), *The Superbureaucrats: Structure and Behavior in Central Agencies,* Toronto: MacMillan of Canada.

Campbell, C., and B.G. Peters (eds 1988), *Organizing Governance: Governing Organizations,* Pittsburgh: University of Pittsburgh Press.

Campbell, D.T., and J.C. Stanley (1966), *Experimental and Quasi-Experimental Designs for Research,* Chicago: Rand McNally.

Cannavale, F.J., H.A. Scarr and A. Pepitone (1970), Deindividuation in the small group: further evidence. In: *Journal of Personality and Social Psychology*, 16, pp. 141-147.

Cartwright, D. (1968), The nature of group cohesiveness. In: D. Cartwright and A. Zander (eds), *Group Dynamics*, New York: Free Press, 3rd ed., pp. 91-109.

Cartwright, D. (1971), Risk taking by individuals and groups: an assessment of research employing choice dilemmas. In: *Journal of Personality and Social Psychology*, 20, pp. 361-378.

Cartwright, D. (1973), Determinants of scientific progress: the case of the risky shift. In: *American Psychologist*, 28, pp. 222-231.

Cartwright, D. and A. Zander (eds 1968), *Group Dynamics*, New York: Free Press, 3rd ed.

Cassese, S. (1983), Is there a government in Italy? Politics and administration at the top. In: R. Rose and E. Suleiman (eds), *Presidents and Prime Ministers*, Washington DC: American Enterprise Institute for Public Policy Research, pp. 171-202.

Charles, M.T. (1989), The Last Flight of Space Shuttle Challenger. In: U. Rosenthal, M.T. Charles and P. 't Hart (eds), *Coping with Crises: The Management of Disasters, Riots and Terrorism*, Springfield: Charles Thomas, pp. 141-168.

Chodoff, E. (1983), Ideology and primary groups. In: *Armed Forces and Society*, 9, pp. 569-593.

Chong-do-Hah, and R.M. Lundquist (1975), The 1952 steel seizure revisited: a systematic study in presidential decision making. In: *Administrative Science Quarterly*, 20, pp. 587-605.

Christopher, W. (ed. 1985), *American Hostages in Iran: The Conduct of a Crisis*, New Haven: Yale University Press.

Cobb, R.W., and C.D. Elder (1975), *Participation in American Politics: The Dynamics of Agenda-Building*, Baltimore: Johns Hopkins University Press.

Coch, L., and J. French (1948), Overcoming resistance to change. In: *Human Relations*, 1, pp. 512-532.

Cockburn, L. (1987), *Out of control: The Story of the Reagan Administration's Secret War in Nicaragua, the Illegal Arms Pipeline and the Contra Drug Connection*, New York: Atlantic Monthly Press.

Cohen, M.D., J.G. March and J.P. Olsen (1972), A garbage can model of organizational choice. In: *Administrative Science Quarterly*, 17, pp. 1-25.

Cohen, R. (1980), *Threat Perception in International Crisis*, Wisconsin: University of Wisconsin Press.

Colvin, I. (1971), *The Chamberlain Cabinet*, London: Gollancz.

Congressional Report (1988), *Report of the Congressional Committees Investigating the Iran-Contra Affair, with the Minority View*, New York: Random House (orig. publ. 1987).

Coser, L. (1956), *The Functions of Social Conflict*, New York: Free Press.

Courtright, J.A. (1976), *Groupthink and Communication Processes*. University of Iowa: PhD-thesis.

Courtright, J.A. (1978), A laboratory investigation of groupthink. In: *Communication Monographs*, 45, pp. 229-246.

Crossman, R. (1979), *The Crossman Diaries: Selections from the Diaries of a Cabinet Minister (ed. by A. Howard)*, London: Hamilton and Cape.

Crozier, M. (1964), *The Bureaucratic Phenomenon*, London: Tavistock.

Crutchfield, R.S. (1955), Conformity and character. In: *American Psychologist*, 10, pp. 191-198.

Cyert, R.M., and J.G. March (1963), *A Behavioral Theory of the Firm*, Englewood Cliffs: Prentice Hall.

300

Dean, J. (1982), *Blind Ambition*, New York: Simon and Schuster.

Dentler, R.A., and K.T. Erikson (1959), The functions of deviance in groups. In: *Social Problems*, 7, pp. 98-107.

Deutsch, K.W. (1963), *The Nerves of Government*, New York: Free Press.

Deutsch, M. (1949), The effects of cooperation and competition upon group process. In: *Human Relations*, 2, pp. 129-152.

Deutsch, M. (1965),Conflicts: productive and destructive. In: *Journal of Social Issues*, 25, pp. 7-41.

Deutsch, M. (1973), *The Resolution of Conflict*, New Haven: Yale University Press.

Diamant, A. (1981), Bureaucracy and public policy in neo-corporatist settings. In: *Comparative Politics*, 14.

Diamond, M., and S. Allcorn (1985a), Psychological responses to stress in complex organizations. In: *Administration and Society*, 17, pp. 217-239.

Diamond, M.A., and S. Allcorn (1985b), Psychological dimensions of role use in bureaucratic organizations. In: *Organizational Dynamics*, 14, pp. 35-59.

Dickenberger, D., and G. Gniech (1982), The Theory of Psychological Reactance. In: M. Irle (ed.), *Studies in Decision Making: Social Psychological and Economic Analysis*, Berlin: De Gruyter.

Diener, E. (1976), Effects of prior destructive behavior, anonymity and group presence on deindividuation and aggression. In: *Journal of Personality and Social Psychology*, 33, pp. 497-507.

Diener, E. (1977), Deindividuation: Causes and consequences. In: *Social Behavior and Personality*, 5, pp. 143-155.

Diener, E. (1980), Deindividuation: The absence of self-awareness and self-regulation in group members. In: P.B. Paulus (ed.), *Psychology of Group Influence*, Hillsdale: Erlbaum Associates, pp. 209-242.

Dion, K.L. (1979), Intergroup conflict and intra-group cohesiveness. In: *W.G. Austin and S. Worchel (eds)*,op. cit., pp. 211-224.

Dipboye, R.L. (1977), Alternative approaches to deindividuation. In: *Psychological Bulletin*, 84, pp. 1057-1075.

Dodd, L.L. (1962), Committee integration in the Senate. In: *Journal of Politics*, pp. 1135-1171.

Dogan, M. (ed. 1975), *The Mandarins of Western Europe: The Political Role of Top Civil Servants*, London: Sage.

Doise, W. (1969), Intergroup relations and polarization of individual and collective judgments. In: *Journal of Personality and Social Psychology*, 12, pp. 136-143.

Doise, W. (1978), *Groups and Individuals: Explanations in Social Psychology*, Cambridge Mass.: Cambridge University Press.

Douglas, M., and A.B. Wildavsky (1982), *Risk and Culture*, Berkeley: University of California Press.

Downs, A. (1967), *Inside Bureaucracy*, Boston: Little, Brown and Company.

Drabek, T. (1986), *Human Systems Responses to Disaster: An Inventory of Sociological Findings*, New York: Springer-Verlag.

Draper, T. (1987a), The rise of an American junta. In: *New York Review of Books*, October 8, 1987, pp. 47-58.

Draper, T. (1987b), The fall of an American junta. In: *New York Review of Books*, October 22, pp. 45-57.

Draper, T. (1987c), An Autopsy. In: *New York Review of Books*, December 17, pp. 67-77.

Dror, Y. (1968), *Public Policymaking Reexamined*, San Francisco: Chandler.

Dror, Y. (1986), *Policymaking under Adversity*, New Brunswick: Transaction Books.

DuBrin, A.J. (1984), *Foundations of Organizational Behavior: An Applied Perspective*, Englewood Cliffs: Prentice Hall.

Dunsire, A. (1978), *Control in a Bureaucracy*, London: Martin Robertson.

Easton, D. (1965), *A Systems Analysis of Political Life*, Chicago: Chicago University Press (2nd ed. 1979).

Edelman, M. (1964), *The Symbolic Uses of Politics*, Urbana: University of Illinois Press.

Edelman, M. (1977), *Political Language: Words That Succeed and Policies That Fail*, New York: Academic Press.

Edelman, M. (1988), *Constructing the Political Spectacle*, Chicago: Chicago University Press.

Eisman, B, (1959), Some operational measures of cohesiveness and their correlations. In: *Human Relations*, 12, pp. 183-189.

Ellemers, J. (1956), *De Februari Ramp*, Assen: Van Gorcum (in Dutch).

Elms, A.C. (1976), *Personality in Politics*, New York: Harcourt, Brace and Jovanovich.

Emery, F.E., and E.L. Trist (1965), The Causal Texture of Organizational Environments. In: *Human Relations*, 18, pp. 21-32.

Esser, J.K., and J.S. Lindoerfer (1989), Groupthink and the Space Shuttle Challenger Accident: Toward a quantative case analysis, in: *Journal of Behavioral Decision Making*, 2, pp. 167-177.

Etheredge, L.S. (1985), *Can Governments Learn?*, New York: Pergamon.

Etzioni, A. (1977), *A Comparative Analysis of Complex Organizations*, New York: Free Press.

Etzioni-Halévy, E. (1982), *Bureaucracy and Democracy: A Political Dilemma*, London: Routledge.

Falk, G. (1981), Unanimity versus majority rule in problem-solving groups: a challenge to the superiority of unanimity. In: *Small Group Behavior*, 12, pp. 379-399.

Feigenbaum, H.B. (1985), *The Politics of Public Enterprise: Oil and the French State*, Princeton: Princeton University Press.

Feldman, M.S., and J.G. March (1981), Information in organizations as signal and symbol. In: *Administrative Science Quarterly*, 26, pp. 171-186.

Fenno, R.F. (1959), *The President's Cabinet: An Analysis in the Period from Wilson to Eisenhower*, Cambridge, Mass.: Harvard University Press.

Fenno, R.F. (1962), The house appropriations committee as a political system: the problem of integration. In: *American Political Science Review*, 56, pp. 310-324.

Fesler, J.W. (1983), Politics, policy and bureaucracy at the top. In: *Annals of the Academy of Political and Social Science*, 466, pp. 24-37; 39-40.

Festinger, L. (1950), Informal social communication. In: *Psychological Review*, 57, pp. 271-292.

Festinger, L., S. Schachter and K. Back (1950), *Social Pressures in Informal Groups: A Study of Human Factors in Housing*, New York: Harper and Row.

Festinger, L., and J. Thibaut (1951), Interpersonal communication in small groups. In: *Journal of Abnormal and Social Psychology*, 46, pp. 92-99.

Festinger, L., A. Pepitone and T. Newcomb (1952), Some consequences of deindividuation in a group. In: *Journal of Abnormal and Social Psychology*, 47, pp. 382-389.

Fiedler, F.E. (1967), *A Theory of Leadership Effectiveness*, New York: McGraw-Hill.

Fiedler, F.E. et al. (1967), The effect of intergroup competition on group member adjustment. In: *Personnel Psychology*, 20, pp. 33-44.

Fischer, B.A. (1974), *Small Group Decision Making: Communication and the Group Process*, New York: McGraw-Hill (2nd ed. 1981).

Fischoff, B., S. Lichtenstein, P. Slovic, S.L. Derby and R.L. Kenney (1981), *Acceptable Risk*, New York: Cambridge University Press.

Fleming, R., A. Baum and J.E. Singer (1984), Toward an integrative approach to the study of stress. In: *Journal of Personality and Social Psychology*, 19, pp. 439-449.

Flowers, M. (1977), A laboratory test of some implications of Janis' groupthink hypothesis. In: *Journal of Personality and Social Psychology*, 42, pp. 178-185.

Fodor, E.M., and T. Smith (1982), The power motive as an influence on group decision making. In: *Journal of Personality and Social Psychology*, 42, pp. 178-185.

Ford, D. (1985), *Meltdown*, New York: Simon and Schuster.

Ford, D. (1986), *The Button*, London: Counterpoint.

Forsyth, D.R. (1983), *An Introduction to Group Dynamics*, Pacific Grove: Brooks/Cole.

Fox, F.V., and B.M. Staw (1979), The trapped administrator: Effects of job insecurity and policy resistance upon commitment to a course of action. In: *Administrative Science Quarterly*, 24, pp. 449-471.

Francis, W. (1962), Influence and interaction in a state legislative body. In: *American Political Science Review*, 56, pp. 953-960.

French, J.D. (1944), Experimental studies in personal pressure and resistance: II. Methods of overcoming resistance. In: *Journal of Gen. Psychology*, 30, pp. 43-56.

French, J.R.P., and B.H. Raven (1959), The bases of social power. In: D. Cartwright (ed.), *Studies in Social Power*, Ann Arbor: University of Michigan Press, pp. 150-167.

Freud, S. (1965), *Group Psychology and the Analysis of the Ego*, New York: Bantam (orig. publ. 1927).

Friedrich, C.J. (1963), *Man and his Government*, New York: McGraw-Hill.

Gabriel, R. (1985), Military Incompetence: *Why the American Military Doesn't Win*, New York: Hill and Wang.

Gaenslen, F. (1980), Democracy vs. efficiency: some arguments from the small group. In: *Political Psychology*, 2, pp. 15-30.

Gal, R. (1985), Commitment and obedience in the military: An Israeli Case Study. In: *Armed Forces and Society*, vol. 11, no. 4. pp. 553-564.

Galtung, J. (1968), Small group theory and the theory of international relations: a study in isomorphism. In: M.A. Kaplan (ed.), *New Approaches to International Relations*, New York: St. Martin's Press, pp. 270-302.

Gelb, L.H., and R.K. Betts (1979), *The Irony of Vietnam: The System Worked*, Washington: Brookings Institution.

George, A.L. (1968), Power as a compensatory value for political leaders. In: *Journal of Social Issues*, 24, pp. 29-49.

George, A.L. (1972), The case for multiple advocacy in making foreign policy. In: *American Political Science Review*, 66, pp. 751-785.

George, A.L. (1974), Adaption to stress in political decision making: the individual, small group, and organizational contexts. In: G.V. Coelho, D.A. Hamburg, J.E. Adams (eds), *Coping and Adaptation*, New York: Basic Books, pp. 176-248.

George, A.L. (1979), Case studies and theory development: the method of structured, focused comparison. In: P.G. Lauren (ed.), *Diplomacy: New Approaches in History, Theory and Policy*, New York: Free Press, pp. 43-68.

George, A.L. (1980), *Presidential Decision Making in Foreign Policy: The Effective Use of Information and Advice*, Boulder: Westview Press.

George, A.L. (1984), Criteria for evaluation of foreign policy decision making. In: *Global Perspectives*, pp. 58-69.

George, A.L. (1986), The impact of crisis-induced stress on decision making. In: *The Medical Implications of Nuclear War*, Institute of Medicine, Washington: National Academy of Sciences.

George, A.L., and J.L. George (1956), *Woodrow Wilson and Colonel House: A Personality Study*, New York: Dover.

George, A.L., and T.J. McKeown (1985), Case studies and theories of organizational decision making. In: *Advances in Information Processing in Organizations*, 2, pp. 21-58.

Gerard, H.B. (1953), The effect of different dimensions of disagreement on the communication process in small groups. In: *Human Relations*, 6, pp. 249-271.

Gero, A. (1985), Conflict avoidance in consensual decision processes. In: *Small Group Behavior*, 16, pp. 487-499.

Gilbert, M. (1966), *The Roots of Appeasement*, New York: New American Library.

Ginneken, J. van (1989), *Crowds, Psychology and Politics*, PhD-dissertation, University of Amsterdam.

Gladstein, D. (1984), Groups in context: a model of task group effectiveness. In: *Administrative Science Quarterly*, 29, pp. 499-517.

Gladstein-Ancona, D. (1987), Groups in organizations: extending laboratory models. In: C. Hendrick (ed.), *Group Processes and Intergroup Relations*, Beverly Hills: Sage, pp. 207-230.

Glazer, M. (1983), Ten whistleblowers and how they fared. In: *Hastings Center Report*, pp. 33-41.

Goleman, D. (1985), *Vital Lies; Simple Truths; The Psychology of Self-Deception*, New York: Simon and Schuster.

Golembiewski, R.T. (1962), *The Small Group*, Chicago: University of Chicago Press.

Golembiewski, R.T. (ed. 1978), *The Small Group in Political Science*, Athens: Georgia UP.

Golembiewski, R.T., W.A. Welsh and W.J. Cotty (1969), Empirical science at the micro level: Cohesiveness as concept and operation. In: R.T. Golembiewski, W.A. Welsh and W.J. Cotty (eds), *A Methodological Primer for Political Scientists*, Chicago: Rand McNally, pp. 67-89.

Gouran, D.S., and R.Y. Hirokawa (1986), Counteractive functions of communication in effective group decision making. In: R. Poole and R.Y. Hirokawa (eds), *Communication and Group Decision Making*, Beverly Hills: Sage.

Grandori, A. (1984), A prescriptive contingency view of organizational decision making. In: *Administrative Science Quarterly*, 29, pp. 192-209.

Green, D., and E.S. Connolley (1974), *"Groupthink" and Watergate*, Paper APSA, annual meeting.

Greenstein, F. (1982), *The Hidden-Hand Presidency: Eisenhower as a Leader*, New York: Basic Books.

Griffiths, R.F. (ed. 1981), *Dealing with Risk*, Manchester: Manchester University Press.

Grinker, R.R., and J.P. Spiegel (1945), *Men under Stress*, Philadelphia: Blakiston.

Gross, N., and W. Martin (1952), On group cohesiveness. In: *American Journal of Sociology*, 57, pp. 533-546.

Gross Stein, J. (1985), Calculation, miscalculation and conventional deterrence II: the view from Jerusalem. In: R. Jervis, R.N. Lebow and J. Gross Stein, *Psychology and Deterrence*, Baltimore: John Hopkins University Press, pp. 60-88.

Gross Stein, J. (1988), Building politics into psychology: the misperception of threat. In: *Political Psychology*, 9, pp. 245-271.

Gross Stein, J., and R. Tanter (1980), *Rational Decision Making: Israel's Security Choices*, Columbus: Ohio University Press.

Gruber, J.E. (1987), *Controlling Bureaucracies: Dilemmas in Democratic Governance*, Berkeley: California University Press.

Hackman, J., and C. Morris (1975), Group tasks, group interaction process and group performance effectiveness. In: L. Berkowitz (ed.), *Advances in Experimental Social Psychology*, 8, pp. 1-66.

Haldeman, H.R. (1978), *The Ends of Power*, London: Book Club Associates.

Hall, P. (1982), *Great Planning Disasters*, Harmondsworth: Penguin.

Hall, R.L. (1987), Participation and purpose in committee decision making. In:

American Political Science Review, 81, pp. 105-127.

Halperin, M.H. (1974), Bureaucratic Politics and Foreign Policy, Washington: Brookings.

Hamblin, R.L. (1958), Group integration during a crisis. In: Human Relations, 11, pp. 67-76.

Hamblin, R.L. (1960), Leadership and crises. In: Sociometry, 21, pp. 322-335.

Hambrick, D.E. (1981), Environment, strategy and power in top management teams. In: Administrative Science Quarterly, 26, pp. 253-276.

Hamilton, V.L. (1978), Obedience and responsibility: a jury simulation. In: Journal of Personality and Social Psychology, 36, pp. 126-146.

Handel, M.I. (1976), Perception, Deception and Surprise: The Case of the Yom Kippur War, Jerusalem Hebrew University, Davis Institute, Paper no. 6.

Hanf, K.I., and F. Scharpf (eds 1978), Interorganizational Policy Making, London: Sage.

Hanf, K.I., and Th.A.J. Toonen (eds 1985), Policy Implementation in Federal and Unitary Systems: Questions of Research and Design, Dordrecht: Martinus Nijhoff.

Hansen, S.B. (1985), On the making of unpopular decisions: a typology and some evidence. In: Policy Studies Journal, 12, pp. 14-42.

Hare, A.P. (ed. 1976), Handbook of Small Group Research, New York: Free Press, 3rd ed.

Hart, P. 't, and B. Pijnenburg (1989), The Heizel Stadium Tragedy. In: U. Rosenthal, M.T. Charles and P. 't Hart (eds), Coping with Crises: The Management of Disasters, Riots and Terrorism, Springfield: Charles Thomas.

Hart, P. 't, M. Kroon and D. van Kreveld (1989), Accountability, group decision making and conflict management in a prison experiment. Paper presented at the International Society for Political Psychology, Tel Aviv.

Hart, R.L.A. (1968), Punishment and Responsibility, New York: Oxford University Press.

Hayes, M.T. (1978), The semi-sovereign pressure groups: a critique of current theory and an alternative typology. In: Journal of Politics, 40, pp. 134-161.

Heclo, H. (1977), A Government of Strangers: Executive politics in Washington, Washington: Brookings Institution.

Hedberg, B.L.T., et. al., (1976), Camping on seesaws: prescriptions for a self-designing organization. In: Administrative Science Quarterly, 21, pp. 41-65.

Heller, F. , P. Drenth and V. Rus (1988), Decisions in Organizations, London: Sage.

Heller, J. (1983), The dangers of groupthink. In: The Guardian, January 31st.

Helm, C., and M. Morelli (1979), Stanley Milgram and the obedience experiment: authority, legitimacy and human action. In: Political Theory, 7, pp. 321-345.

Hensley, T.R., and G.W. Griffin (1986), Victims of groupthink: the Kent State University board trustees and the 1977 gymnasium controversy. In: Journal of Conflict Resolution, 30, pp. 497-531.

Herek, G.M., I.L. Janis and P. Huth (1987), Decision making during international crises: is quality of process related to outcome? In: Journal of Conflict Resolution, 31, pp. 203-226.

Hermann, C.F. (1969), Crises in Foreign Policy: A Simulation Analysis, Indianapolis: Bobbs-Merrill.

Hermann, C.F. (ed. 1972), International Crises: Insights from Behavioral Research, New York: Free Press.

Hermann, M.G., and C.F. Hermann (1975), Maintaining the quality of decision making in foreign policy crises, a proposal. In: A.L. George (ed.), Towards a More Soundly Based Foreign Policy: Making Better Use of Information, Report to the commission of government for the conduct of Foreign Policy, Washington DC: US Government Printing Office.

Hermann, M.G., and C.F. Hermann (1988), Hostage Takings, the Presidency and Stress. Paper presented at the International Society of Political Psychology, Meadowlands, New Jersey.

Hersch, S.M. (1986), *The Price of Power*, New York: Summit.

Heuer, R. (1981), Strategic Deception and Counter Deception: a cognitive process approach. In: *International Studies Quarterly*, 25, pp. 294-327.

Hewstone, M., and R.J. Brown (eds 1986), *Contact and Conflict in Intergroup Encounters*, Oxford: Blackwell.

Hickson, D., R. Butler, D. Cray, G. Mallory and D. Wilson (1986), *Top Decisions: Strategic Decision Making in Organizations*, Oxford: Blackwell.

Hilsman, R. (1959), The foreign-policy consensus: an interim report. In: *Journal of Conflict Resolution*, 3, pp. 361-382.

Hilsman, R. (1967), *To Move a Nation*, Garden City: Doubleday and Company.

Hinkle, S., and J. Schopler (1979), Ethnocentrism in the evaluation of group products. In: *Austin and Worchel, op. cit.*, pp. 160-173.

Hirokawa, R.Y. (1987), Why informed groups make faulty decisions. In: *Small Group Behavior*, 18, pp. 3-30.

Hirokawa, R.Y., and D.R. Scheerhorn (1986), Communication in faulty group decision making. In: R. Poole and R.Y. Hirokawa (eds), *Communication and Small Group Decision Making*, London: Sage.

Hirokawa, R.Y., D.S. Gouran and A.E. Martz (1988), Understanding the sources of faulty group decision making: a lesson from the Challenger disaster. In: *Small Group Behavior*, 19, pp. 411-433.

Hirsch, F. (1977), *Social Limits to Growth*, London: Routledge.

Hirschman, A.O. (1970), *Exit, Voice and Loyalty*, Massachusetts: Cambridge University Press.

Hoffman, L.R., and N.R.F. Maier (1964), Valence in the adoption of solutions by problem-solving groups: concept, method and results. In: *Journal of Abnormal and Social Psychology*, 64, pp. 264-271.

Hogg, M.A., and D. Abrams (1988), *Social Identifications: A Social Psychology of Intergroup Relations and Group Processes*, London: Routledge.

Hollander, E.P. (1978), *Leadership Dynamics*, New York; Free Press.

Holsti, O.R. (1977), Foreign policy decision making viewed psychologically: cognitive process approaches. In: G. Bonham and M. Shapiro (eds), *Thought and Action in Foreign Policy*, Basel: Birkhäuser, pp. 10-74.

Holsti, O.R. (1979), Theories of crisis decision making. In: P.G. Lauren (ed.), *Diplomacy: New Approaches in History, Theory and Policy*, New York: Free Press, pp. 99-136.

Homans, G.C. (1950), *The Human Group*, New York: Harcourt, Brace and World.

Horwitz, M., and J.M. Rabbie (1982), Individuality and membership in the intergroup system. In: H. Tajfel (ed.), *Social Identity and Intergroup Relations*, Cambridge: Cambridge University Press, pp. 241-274.

Huntington, S.P. (1961), *The Common Defense: Strategic Programs in National Politics*, New York: Columbia University Press.

Israel, I. (1956), *Self-Evaluation and Rejection in Groups*, Stockholm: Almquist and Wiksell.

Jackson, R.J. (1976), Crisis management and policy-making: an exploration of theory and research. In: R. Rose (ed.), *The Dynamics of Public Policy: A Comparative Analysis*, London: Sage, pp. 209-236.

Janis, I.L. (1945), *Morale attitudes and social behavior of American soldiers in post-war Berlin*, Unpublished memorandum for the European Theater of Operations, Information and Education Division, Research Branche.

Janis, I.L. (1949), Morale attitudes of combat flying personnel in the Air Corps. In: S. Stouffer (ed.), *The American Soldier II: Combat and its Aftermath*, Princeton: Princeton University Press.

Janis, I.L. (1958), *Psychological Stress*, New York: John Wiley.

Janis, I.L. (1968), Group identification under conditions of external danger. In: D. Cartwright and A. Zander (eds), *Group Dynamics*, New York: Free Press, pp. 80-90.

Janis, I.L. (1971), *Stress and Frustration*, New York: Harcourt, Brace and Jovanevich.

Janis, I.L. (1972), *Victims of Groupthink*, Boston: Houghton Mifflin.

Janis, I.L. (1980), In rescue planning, how did Carter handle stress? In: *New York Times*, May 18th.

Janis, I.L. (1982a), *Groupthink*, Boston: Houghton Mifflin, 2nd rev. ed.

Janis, I.L. (1982b), Counteracting the adverse effects of concurrence-seeking in policy-planning groups: theory and research perspectives. In: H. Brandstätter, J.H. Davis, G. Stocker-Kreichgauer (eds), *Group Decision Making*, London: Academic Press, pp. 477-501.

Janis, I.L. (1989), *Crucial Decisions: Leadership in Policymaking and Crisis Management*, New York: Free Press.

Janis, I.L., and L. Mann (1977), *Decision Making: A Psychological Analysis of Conflict, Choice and Commitment*, New York: Free Press.

Jenkins, B., and A. Gray (1985), Bureaucratic politics and power: developments in the study of bureaucracy. In: *Political Studies*, pp. 177-193.

Jervis, R. (1970), *The Logic of Images in International Relations*, Princeton: Princeton University Press.

Jervis, R. (1976), *Perceptions and Misperceptions in International Politics*, Princeton: Princeton University Press.

Jervis, R., R.N. Lebow and J. Gross Stein (1985), *Psychology and Deterrence*, Baltimore: Johns Hopkins University Press.

Jonas, H. (1984), *Das Prinzip Verantwortung*, Frankfurt: Opladen.

Jordan, H. (1982), *Crisis*, New York: Berkeley Books.

Kahn, A., and A.H. Reyn (1972), Factors influencing the bias towards one's own group. In: *International Journal of Group Tensions*, 2, pp. 33-50.

Kahneman, D., P. Slovic and A. Tversky (eds 1982), *Judgment Under Uncertainty: Heuristics and Biases*, Cambridge: Cambridge University Press.

Kaufman, H. (1981), *The Administrative Behavior of Federal Bureau Chiefs*, Washington: The Brookings Institution.

Katz, D., and R.L. Kahn (1978), *The Social Psychology of Organizations*, New York: John Wiley, 2nd rev. ed.

Keinan, G. (1987), Decision making under stress: scanning of alternatives under controllable and uncontrollable threats. In: *Journal of Personality and Social Psychology*, 52, pp. 639-644.

Kellerman, B. (ed. 1984), *Leadership: Multidisciplinary Perspectives*, Englewood Cliffs: Prentice Hall.

Kelley, H.H. (1979), *Personal Relationships: Their Structures and Processes*, New York: Lawrence Erlbaum.

Kelley, H.H., and M.M. Shapiro (1954), An experiment on conformity to group norms where conformity is detrimental to group achievement. In: *American Sociological Review*, 19, pp. 557-567.

Kelley, H.H., and J. Thibaut (1969), Group problem solving. In: G. Lindzey and E. Aronson (eds), *The Handbook of Social Psychology* (2nd ed.), Reading, Mass: Addison-Wesley, vol. 4.

Kelman, H., and V. Hamilton (1989), *Crimes of Obedience: Toward a Social Psychology of Authority and Responsibility*, New Haven: Yale University Press.

Kennedy, R. (1968), *Thirteen Days*, New York: Norton.

Khandwalla, P. (1972), Environment and its impact on the organization. In:

International Studies of Management and Organizations, 2, pp. 297-313.

Kiesler, C.A. (1969), Group pressure and conformity. In: J. Mills (ed.), *Experimental Social Psychology,* New York: MacMillan, pp. 235-306.

Kinder, D.R., and J.A. Weiss (1978), In lieu of rationality, psychological perspectives on foreign policy decision making. In: *Journal of Conflict Resolution,* 2, pp. 707-735.

Kingdon, J.W. (1985), *Agendas, Alternatives and Public Policies,* Boston: Little, Brown and Company.

Kissinger, H. (1979), *The White House Years,* Boston: Little, Brown and Company.

Klapp, O.E. (1969), *Collective Search for Identity,* New York: Holt, Reinhart and Winston.

Klapp, O.E. (1978), *Opening and Closing: Strategies of Information Adaptation in Society,* Cambridge: Cambridge University Press.

Kogan, N., and M.A. Wallach (1964), *Risk Taking: A Study of Cognition and Personality,* New York: Holt, Reinhart and Winston.

Kouzmin, A. (1979), Building a new Parliament House: An opera house revisited? In: *Human Futures,* 3, pp. 51-74.

Kouzmin, A., and A. Jarman (1989), Crisis decision making: towards a contingent decision path perspective. In: U. Rosenthal et. al. (eds), *Coping with Crises: The Management of Disasters, Riots and Terrorism,* pp. 397-435.

Kowitz, A.C., and T.J. Knutson (1980), *Decision Making in Small Groups: The Search for Alternatives,* Boston: Allyn and Bacon.

Kozielicki, J. (1981), *Psychological Decision Theory,* Dordrecht: Reidel.

Krantz, J. (1985), Group process under conditions of organizational decline. In: *Journal of Applied Behavioral Science,* 21, pp. 1-17.

Kreveld, D. van, and P. Sander (1986), *The effect of anticipated accounting on group task performance: A preliminary experiment.* Paper for the 21st International Congress of Applied Psychology, Jerusalem.

Kreveld, D. van, and B. van Houwelingen (1987), *Anticipated accounting and group processes.* Unpublished paper, Rijksuniversiteit Utrecht.

Krieger, M.H. (1986), Big decisions and a culture of decision making. In: *Journal of Policy Analysis and Management,* 5, pp. 779-797.

Kroon, M., and D. van Kreveld (1988), *Groupthink and accountability: a laboratory investigation.* Poster for the Conference of the Dutch Society for Psychology, Tilburg.

Kunreuther, H.C., and P.J. Schoemaker (1982), Decision analysis for complex systems: integrating descriptive and prescriptive components. In: G.R. Ungson, D.N. Braunstein (eds), *Decision Making: An Interdisciplinary Inquiry,* Boston: Kent Publishers, pp. 263-279.

Lacqueur, W. (1985), *World of Secrets: The Uses and Limits of Intelligence,* London: Weidenfeld and Nicolson.

Lagadec, P. (1982), *Major Technological Risk,* New York: Pergamon.

Lamm, H., and D.G. Myers (1978), Group-induced polarization of attitudes and behavior. In: L. Berkowitz (ed.), *Advances in Experimental Social Psychology,* vol. 11, New York: Academic Press, pp. 145-195.

Landau, M. (1969), Redundancy, rationality and the problem of duplication and overlap. In: *Public Administration Review,* 29, pp. 346-358.

Lanzetta, J.T. (1955), Group behavior under stress. In: *Human Relations,* 8, pp. 29-52.

La Porte, T.R. (ed. 1975), *Organized Social Complexity, Challenge to Politics and Policy,* Princeton: Princeton University Press.

Latané, B. (1981), The psychology of social impact. In: *American Psychologist,* 36, pp. 343-356.

Leana, C.R. (1985), A partial test of Janis' groupthink model: effects of group cohesiveness and leader behavior on defective decision making. In: *Journal of Management*, 1, pp. 5-17.

Lebow, R. (1981), *Between Peace and War: The Nature of International Crises*, Boston: Johns Hopkins University Press.

Lebow, R. (1987), *Nuclear Crisis Management: A Dangerous Illusion*, Ithaca: Cornell University Press.

Lentner, H.H. (1972), The concept of crisis as viewed by the US Department of State. In: C.F. Hermann (ed.), *International Crisis: Insights from Behavioral Research*, pp. 112-135.

Lerner, A.W. (1986), There is more than one way to be redundant: a comparison of alternatives for the design and use of redundancy in organizations. In: *Administration and Society*, 18, 3, pp. 334-359.

Levi, A. (1982), *Escalating Commitment and Risk Taking in Dynamic Decision Behavior*. Unpublished doctoral dissertation, Yale University.

Levine, J. (1980), Reaction to opinion deviance in small groups. In: P.B. Paulus (ed.), *Psychology of Group Influence*, Hillsdale: Erlbaum, pp. 375-429.

Lewin, K., R. Lippit and R. White (1939), Patterns of agressive behavior in experimentally created "social climates". In: *Journal of Social Psychology*, 10, pp. 271-299.

Lijphart, A. (1968), *Verzuiling, Pacificatie en Kentering in de Nederlandse Politiek*, Amsterdam: De Bussy (in Dutch).

Lijphart, A. (1977), *Democracy in Plural Societies: A Comparative Exploration*, New Haven: Yale University Press.

Lindblom, C.E. (1959), The science of muddling through. In: *Public Administration Review*, 19, pp. 78-88.

Lindblom, C.E. (1979), Still muddling, not yet through. In: *Public Administration Review*, 39, pp. 517-526.

Linz, J.J., and A. Stepan (eds 1978), *The Breakdown of Democratic Regimes*, Baltimore: Johns Hopkins University Press.

Lipsky, M. (1982), *Street-Level Bureaucracy*, New York: Russel Sage.

Lodewijkx, H. (1989), *Conflict en Agressie tussen Individuen en Groepen*, PhD-dissertation, University of Utrecht (in Dutch).

Longley, J., and D.G. Pruitt (1980), Groupthink: a critique of Janis' theory. In: *Review of Personality and Social Psychology*, 1, pp. 74-93.

Lott, A.J., and B.E. Lott (1961), Group cohesiveness, communication level and conformity. In: *Journal of Abnormal and Social Psychology*, 62, pp. 408-412.

Lott, A.J., and B.E. Lott (1965), Group cohesiveness as interpersonal attraction: A review of relationships with antecedent and consequent variables. In: *Psychological Bulletin*, 64, pp. 259-309.

Lucas, R. (1970), *Men in Crisis: A study of a coal-mine disaster*, New York: Basic Books.

Lutrin, C.E., and A.K. Settle (1985), *American Public Administration: Concepts and Cases*, Englewood Cliffs: Prentice Hall.

MacCrimmon, K.R., and R.N. Taylor (1976), Decision making and problem solving. In: M.D. Dunette (ed.), *Handbook of Industrial and Organizational Psychology*, Chicago: Rand McNally.

Mackie, T.T. and B.W. Hogwood (eds 1985). *Unlocking the Cabinet*, London: Sage.

Mackintosh, J.P. (1968), *The British Cabinet*, London: Stevens and Sons (3rd ed. 1977).

Maier, N.R.F. (1970), *Problem-solving and Creativity in Individuals and Groups*, Belmont: Brooks/Cole.

Maier, N.R.F., and A.R. Solem (1952), The contribution of a discussion leader to the quality of group thinking: the effective use of minority opinions. In: *Human Relations*, 5, pp. 277-288.

Mandel, R. (1984), The desirability of irrationality in foreign policy making: a preliminary theoretical analysis. In: *Political Psychology*, 5, pp. 643-660.

Maoz, Z. (1981), The decision to raid Entebbe: decision analysis applied to crisis behavior. In: *Journal of Conflict Resolution*, 25, pp. 677-707.

March, J.G. (1988), *Decisions and Organizations*, Oxford: Blackwell.

March, J.G., and H.A. Simon (1958), *Organizations*, New York: John Wiley.

March, J.G., R. Weissinger-Babylon (eds 1986), *Ambiguity and Command: Organizational perspectives on military decision making*, Marshfield: Pitman.

March, J.G., and J.P. Olsen (1986), Garbage can models of decision making in organizations. In: J.G. March and R. Weissinger-Babylon (eds), *op. cit.*, pp. 11-35.

Matthews, D. (1959), The folkways of the United States Senate: conformity to group norms and legislative effectiveness. In: *American Political Science Review*, 53, pp. 1064-1089.

May, E.R. (1973), *Lessons of the Past*, New York: Oxford University Press.

May, J.V., and A.B. Wildavsky (eds 1978), *The Policy Cycle*, London: Sage.

Mayer, J., and D. McManus (1988), *Landslide: the unmaking of President Reagan*, Glasgow: Collins/Fontana.

Mayntz, R. (1983), Executive leadership in Germany: dispersion of power or "Kantzlerdemokratie". In: R. Rose and E. Suleiman (eds), *Presidents and Prime Ministers*, Washington: American Enterprise Institute for Public Policy Research, pp. 139-170.

Mazlish, B. (1972), *In Search of Nixon: A Psychohistorical Inquiry*, New York: Basic.

McCauley, C. (1989), The nature of social influence in groupthink: compliance and internalization. In: *Journal of Personality and Social Psychology*, 38.

McDougall, W. (1927), *The Group Mind*, Cambridge: Cambridge University Press.

McGrath, J.E. (1976), Stress and behavior in organizations. In: M.D. Dunnette (ed.), *Handbook of Industrial and Organizational Psychology*, Chicago: Rand McNally, pp. 1351-1396.

McGrath, J.E. (1984), *Groups: Interaction and Performance*, Englewood Cliffs: Prentice Hall.

McLuckie, B.F. (1975), Centralization and natural disaster response: a preliminary hypothesis and interpretations. In: *Mass Emergencies*, 1, pp. 1-19.

Meertens, R.W. (1980), *Groepspolarisatie*, Deventer: Van Loghum Slaterus (in Dutch).

Meeus, W.H.J., and Q.A.W. Raaijmakers (1984), *Gewoon Gehoorzaam*, PhD dissertation: University of Utrecht (in Dutch).

Meeus, W.H.J., and Q.A.W. Raaijmakers (1986), Administrative obedience: carrying out orders to use psychological-administrative violence. In: *European Journal of Social Psychology*, 16, pp. 311-324.

Merton, R.K. (1957), *Social Theory and Social Structure*, New York: Free Press.

Meyers, A.E. (1962), Team competition, success and adjustment of group members. In: *Journal of Abnormal and Social Psychology*, 65, pp. 325-332.

Middlemass, K. (1972), *Diplomacy of Illusion: The British Government and Germany 1937-1939*, London: Weidenfeld and Nicholson.

Miesing, P., and J.F. Preble (1985), Group processes and performance in a complex business simulation. In: *Small Group Behavior*, 16, pp. 325-338.

Milburn, T. (1972), The management of crisis. In: C.F. Hermann (ed.), *International Crises*, pp. 259-280.

Milgram, S. (1961), Nationality and conformity. In: *Scientific American*, 205, pp. 45-51.

Milgram, S. (1964), Group pressure and action against a person. In: *Journal of Abnormal and Social Psychology*, 69, pp. 137-143.

Milgram, S. (1965), Liberating effects of group pressure. In: *Journal of Personality and*

Social Psychology, 1, pp. 127-134.

Milgram, S. (1974), *Obedience to Authority*, New York: Harper and Row.

Minix, D.G. (1982), *Small Groups and Foreign Policy*, Boulder: Westview.

Mintzberg, H. (1984), *Power in and around Organizations*, Englewood Cliffs: Prentice Hall.

Mintzberg, H., D. Raisinghani and A. Theoret (1976), The structure of "unstructured decision processes". In: *Administrative Science Quarterly*, 21, pp. 246-275.

Morgan, T. (1985), *FDR*, New York: Simon and Schuster.

Moorhead, G. (1982), Groupthink: hypothesis in need of testing. In: *Group and Organization Studies*, 7, pp. 429-444.

Moorhead, G., and J. Montanari (1986), An empirical investigation of the groupthink phenomenon. In: *Human Relations*, 39, pp. 399-410.

Moscovici, S. (1976), *Social Influence and Social Change*, London: Academic Press.

Moscovici, S. (1985), Social Influence and Conformity. In: G. Lindzey, E. Aronson (eds), *The Handbook of Social Psychology*, pp. 347-412.

Moscovici, S., and M. Zavalloni (1969), The group as a polarizer of attitudes. In: *Journal of Personality and Social Psychology*, 12, pp. 125-135.

Moscovici, S., and W. Doise (1974), Decision making in groups. In: C. Nemeth (ed.), *Social Psychology: Classic and Contemporary Integrations*, Chicago: Rand McNally.

Mulder, M., and A. Stemerding (1963), Threat, attraction to group and a need for strong leadership: A laboratory experiment in a natural setting. In: *Human Relations*, 16, pp. 317-334.

Mulder, M., J.R. Ritsema van Eck and R.D. de Jong (1971), An organization in crisis and non-crisis situations. In: *Human Relations*, 24, pp. 19-41.

Myers, D.G., and G.D. Bishop (1971), Enhancement of dominant attitudes in group discussion. In: *Journal of Personality and Social Psychology*, 20, pp. 386-391.

Myers, D.G., and H. Lamm (1976), The group polarization phenomenon. In: *Psychological Bulletin*, 83, pp. 602-627.

Nelkin, D. (ed. 1985), *The Language of Risk*, London: Sage.

Neustadt, R. (1960), *Presidential Power*, New York: Wiley (rev. ed. 1980).

Neustadt, R., and E. May (1986), *Thinking in Time: The Uses of History for Decision Makers*, New York: Free Press.

Ng, S.H. (1982), Power and intergroup discrimination. In: H. Tajfel (ed.), *Social Identity and Intergroup Relations*, Cambridge: Cambridge University Press.

Ng, S.H. (1984), Equity and social categorization effects on intergroup allocation of rewards. In: *British Journal of Social Psychology*, 23, pp. 165-172.

Niskanen, W.A. (1971), *Bureaucracy and Representative Government*, Chicago: Aldine Press.

Nixon, R.N. (1978), *RN: The Memoirs of Richard Nixon*, London: Book Club Associates.

Nordlinger, E. (1972), *Conflict Regulation in Divided Societies*, Cambridge: Harvard Center for International Affairs.

North, O.L. (1987), *Taking the Stand: The Testimony of Lieutenant Colonel Oliver L. North*, New York: Pocket Books.

Nossal, K.R. (1979), Allison through the (Ottawa) looking glass: bureaucratic politics and foreign policy in a parliamentary system. In: *Canadian Journal of Public Administration*, pp. 610-626.

Nutt, P.C. (1988), *Making Tough Decisions*, San Francisco: Jossey-Bass.

Olsen, J.P. (1983), Governing Norway: segmentation, anticipation and consensus formation. In: R. Rose, E.N. Suleiman (eds), *Presidents and Prime Ministers*, Washington: American Enterprise Institute for Public Policy Research, pp. 203-255.

Olson, M. (1965), *The Logic of Collective Action*, Cambridge: Harvard UP.

O'Reilly, C.A. (1983), The use of information in organizational decision making. In: *Research in Organizational Behavior*, 5, pp. 103-139.

Page, E.C. (1985), *Political Authority and Bureaucratic Power: A Comparative Analysis*, Brighton: Wheatsheaf Books.

Paige, G.D. (1968), *The Korean Decision, June 24-30*, New York: Free Press.

Parillo, V.N., J. Stimson and K. Stimson (1985), Rationalization and ritualism in committee decision making. In: *Small Group Behavior*, 16, pp. 355-371.

Payne, R. (1981), Stress in task-focused groups. In: *Small Group Behavior*, 12, pp. 253-268.

Perrow, C. (1979), *Complex Organizations: A Critical Essay*, Glenview Ill.: Scott/Foresman.

Perrow, C. (1984), *Normal Accidents: Living with High-Risk Technologies*, New York: Basic Books.

Pika, J.A. (1988), Management style and the organizational matrix. In: *Administration and Society*, 20, pp. 3-29.

Platt, J. (1973), Social traps. In: *American Psychologist*, 28, pp. 641-651.

Polsby, N.W. (1984), *Political Innovation in America*, New Haven: Yale University Press.

Preimack, J., and F. von Hippel (1974), *Advice and Dissent: Scientists in the Political Arena*, New York: Basic Books.

Prentice-Dunn, S., and R.W. Rogers (1983), Deindividuation in Aggression. In: *Aggression*, 2, pp. 155-171.

Pressman, J., and A.B. Wildavsky (1973), *Implementation*, Berkeley: California University Press (rev. ed. 1984).

Pruitt, D.G. (1971a), Choice shifts in group discussion: An introductory review. In: *Journal of Personality and Social Psychology*, 20, pp. 339-360.

Pruitt, D.G. (1971b), Conclusions: Toward an understanding of choice shifts in group discussion. In: *Journal of Personality and Social Psychology*, 20, pp. 495-510.

Quandt, W. (1977), *Decade of Decisions*, Berkeley: California University Press.

Quarantelli, E.L. (ed. 1978), *Disasters: Theory and Research*, London: Sage.

Rabbie, J.M. (1972), *Experimental Studies of Intergroup Relations*. Paper presented at the conference on the Experimental Study of Intergroup Relations, Bristol.

Rabbie, J.M. (1982), The effects of intergroup competition and cooperation on intra- and intergroup relations. In: V.I. Derlega, J. Grzelak (eds), *Cooperation and Helping Behavior*, New York: Academic Press.

Rabbie, J.M. (1986), Intragroepsprocessen in de politiek. In: J. van Ginneken en R. Kouijzer (red.), *Politieke Psychologie: Inleiding en Overzicht*, Alphen aan den Rijn: Samsom, pp. 75-80 (in Dutch).

Rabbie, J.M., and M. Horwitz (1969), Arousal of ingroup-outgroup bias by a chance win or loss. In: *Journal of Personality and Social Psychology*, 13, pp. 269-277.

Rabbie, J.M., and J.H.C. de Brey (1971), The anticipation of intergroup co-operation and competition under private and public conditions. In: *International Journal of Group Tensions*, 1, pp. 230-251.

Rabbie, J.M., and G. Wilkens (1971), Intergroup competition and its effects on intragroup and intergroup relations. In: *European Journal of Social Psychology*, 1, pp. 215-234.

Rabbie, J.M., and L. Visser (1974), Bargaining strength and group polarization in intergroup negotiations. In: *European Journal of Social Psychology*, 2, pp. 401-416.

Rabbie, J.M., F. Benoist, H. Oosterbaan, L. Visser (1974), Differential power and effects of expected competitive and cooperative intergroup interaction on intragroup and outgroup attitudes. In: *Journal of Personality and Social Psychology*, 30, pp. 46-56.

312

Rabbie, J.M., and L. Visser (1976), Gevolgen van interne en externe conflicten op de relaties tussen groepen. In: *Nederlands Tijdschrift voor de Psychologie*, 31, pp. 233-251 (in Dutch).

Rabbie, J.M., and J. van Oostrum (1977), *The effects of influence structures upon the intra- and intergroup relations in simulated organizations.* Paper presented to the International Conference on Socialization and Social Influence, Poland.

Rabbie, J.M., and F. Bekkers (1978), Threatened leadership and intergroup competition. In: *European Journal of Social Psychology*, vol. 8, pp. 9-20.

Rabbie, J.M., and H. Lodewijkx (1983), *Agression toward groups and individuals.* Paper presented to the East-West meeting of the European Association of Experimental Social Psychology, Varna, Bulgaria.

Rabbie, J.M., and L. Visser (1984), Deindividuatie en de ontwikkeling van normen in groepen toeschouwers, een veldexperiment. In: R. van der Vlist (red.), *Sociale Psychologie in Nederland, Deel IV: Samenleving en Individu,* Deventer: Van Loghum Slaterus, pp. 102-128 (in Dutch).

Rabbie, J.M., and H. Lodewijkx (1986), *Conflict and agression between individuals and groups.* Paper presented to the second International Kurt Lewin Conference, Philadelphia.

Rabbie, J.M., and H. Lodewijkx (1987), Een interactief gedragsmodel: een poging tot integratie. In: A. van Knippenberg, M. Poppe, J. Extra, J.J. Kok en E. Seydel (eds), *Fundamentele Sociale Psychologie,* deel 2, Tilburg: Tilburg University Press (in Dutch).

Rabbie, J.M., and M. Horwitz (1988), Categories versus groups as explanatory concepts in intergroup relations. In: *European Journal of Social Psychology*, 18, pp. 117-123.

Rabbie, J.M., J.C. Schot and L. Visser (1989), Social identity theory: a conceptual and empirical critique from the perspective of a behavioral interaction model. In: *European Journal of Social Psychology*, 19.

Radford, K.J. (1977), *Complex Decision Problems: An Integrated Strategy for Resolution,* Reston: Reston Publishers.

Radford, K.J. (1986), *Strategic and Tactical Decisions,* Reston, Reston Publishers.

Ramuz-Nienhuis, W., and A. van Bergen (1960), Relations between some components of attraction-to-group: a replication. In: *Human Relations*, 13, pp. 271-277.

Raven, B.H. (1974), The Nixon Group. In: *Journal of Social Issues*, 30, pp. 297-320.

Raven, B.H., and J.Z. Rubin (1977), *Social Psychology: People in Groups,* New York: John Wiley.

Regan, D.T. (1988), *For the Record: from Wall Street to Washington,* London: Arrow.

Richardson, J.J., and A.G. Jordan (1979), *Governing under Pressure,* Oxford: Robertson.

Rivera, J. de (1968), *The Psychological Dimension of Foreign Policy,* Columbus: Bobbs-Merril.

Rockman, B.A. (1981), America's departments of state: irregular and regular syndromes of policy making. In: *The American Political Science Review*, 75, pp. 911-927.

Rosati, J.A. (1981), Developing a systemic decision-making framework, bureaucratic politics in perspective. In: *World Politics*, 33, pp. 234-252.

Rose, R., and E. Suleiman (eds 1983), *Presidents and Prime Ministers: Giving Direction to Government,* Washington DC: American Enterprise Institute for Public Policy Research.

Rosenthal, U. (1984), The bureaupolitics of policing: the Dutch case. In: *Police Science Abstracts*, 12, pp. 1-14.

Rosenthal, U. (1986a), Crisis decision making in the Netherlands. In: *Netherlands Journal of Sociology*, 22, pp. 103-129.

313

Rosenthal, U. (1986b), *Governmental crisis decision-making: decisions at hectic moments.* Paper presented for the International Sociological Association, New Delhi.

Rosenthal, U. (1988), *Bureaupolitiek en Bureaupolitisme: Om het behoud van een Competitief Overheidsbestel,* Alphen aan den Rijn: Samsom (in Dutch).

Rosenthal, U., M.T. Charles and P. 't Hart (eds 1989), *Coping with Crises: The Management of Disasters, Riots and Terrorism,* Springfield: Charles Thomas.

Ross, L., G. Bierbrauer and S. Hoffman (1976), The role of attribution processes in conformity and dissent: revisiting the Asch situation. In: *American Psychologist,* 31, pp. 148-157.

Ross, R.S. (1989), *Small Groups in Organizational Settings,* Englewood Cliffs: Prentice Hall.

Rourke, F.E. (1969), *Bureaucracy, Politics and Public Policy,* Boston: Little, Brown and Company.

Rubin, I. (1977), Universities in stress: decision making under conditions of reduced resources. In: *Social Science Quarterly,* 58, pp. 242-254.

Rubin, J.Z., and J. Brockner (1975), Factors affecting entrapment in waiting situations: the Rosencrantz and Guildernstern effect. In: *Journal of Personality and Social Psychology,* 31, pp. 1054-1063.

Rubin, J.Z., J. Brockner, S. Small-Weil and S. Nathanson (1980), Factors affecting entry into psychological traps. In: *Journal of Conflict Resolution,* 24, pp. 405-426.

Rummel, R. (1963), Dimensions of conflict behavior within and between nations. In: *General Systems Yearbook,* 8, pp. 1-50.

Russel, D.E.H. (1982), *Rebellion, Revolution and Armed Force,* London: Allen and Unwin.

Ryan, P.B. (1985), *The Iranian Rescue Mission: Why it failed,* Annapolis: Naval Institute Press.

Sakurai, M.M. (1976), Small group cohesiveness and detrimental conformity. In: *Sociometry,* 38, pp. 340-357.

Salinger, P. (1981), *America Held Hostage: The Secret Negotiations,* New York: Doubleday.

Schachter, S. (1951), Deviation, rejection and communication. In: *Journal of Abnormal and Social Psychology,* 46, pp. 190-207.

Schachter, S. (1959), *The Psychology of Affiliation,* Stanford: Stanford University Press.

Schein, E. (1979), *Organizational Psychology,* Englewood Cliffs: Prentice Hall.

Schilling, W.R. (1962), The politics of national defense: Fiscal 1950. In: W.R. Schilling, P.T. Hammond and G.H. Snyder (eds), *Strategy, Politics and Defense Budgets,* New York: Columbia University Press.

Schlesinger, A. (1965), *A Thousand Days: John F. Kennedy in the White House,* Boston: Houghton Mifflin.

Schweiger, P.M., W.R. Sandberg and J.W. Ragan (1986), Group approaches for improving strategic decision making: a comparative analysis of dialectical inquiry, devil's advocacy and consensus. In: *Academy of Management Journal,* 29, pp. 51-71.

Segev, S. (1988), *The Iranian Triangle,* New York: Free Press.

Semmel, A., and D. Minix (1982), Small group dynamics and foreign policy making: an experimental approach. In: G.W. Hopple (ed.), *Biopolitics, Political Psychology and International Politics,* Boulder: Westview, pp. 94-113.

Shaw, M.E. (1981), *Group Dynamics: The Psychology of Small Group Behavior,* New York: McGraw-Hill, 3rd ed.

Shaw, M.E., and L.M. Shaw (1962), Some effects of sociometric grouping upon learning in a second grade classroom. In: *Journal of Social Psychology,* pp. 453-458.

Sherif, M. (1936), *The Psychology of Social Norms,* New York: Harper and Row.

Sherif, M., and C.W. Sherif (1953), *Groups in Harmony and Tension,* New York: Harper and Row.

Shils, E.A. (1951), The study of the primary group. In: D. Lerner, H.D. Lasswell (eds), *The Policy Sciences: Recent Developments in Scope and Method*, Stanford: Stanford University Press, pp. 44-69.

Shils, E.A., and M. Janowitz (1948), Cohesion and disintegration in the Wehrmacht in World War II. In: *Public Opinion Quarterly*, 12, pp. 280-316.

Shrivastava, P. (1987), *Bhopal: Anatomy of a Crisis*, Cambridge Mass.: Ballinger.

Shrivastava, P. (1989), *Managing the crisis at Bhopal* In: Rosenthal, Charles, 't Hart (eds.), pp. 92-117.

Sick, G.G. (1985), *All Fall Down: America's Tragic Encounter with Iran*, New York: Penguin.

Sick, G.G. (1988), *The domestication of hostage incidents*. Paper presented at the International Society for Political Psychology, Meadowlands, New Jersey.

Simon, H., D.W. Smithburg and V.A. Thompson, *Public Administration*, New York: Knopf.

Singer, J.E., C.A. Brush and S.C. Lublin (1965), Some aspects of deindividuation: identification and conformity. In: *Journal of Experimental Social Psychology*, 1, pp. 356-378.

Smart, C., and I. Vertinsky (1977), Designs for crisis decision units. In: *Administrative Science Quarterly*, 22, pp. 640-657.

Smith, P.B. (1972), *Groups Within Organizations*, New York: Harper and Row.

Smith, R.B. (1988), *Bureaucracy and Political Power*, Brighton: Wheatsheaf Books.

Smith, S. (1984), Groupthink and the hostage rescue mission. In: *British Journal of Political Science*, 14, pp. 117-123.

Snyder, E. (1958), The Supreme Court as a Small Group. In: *Social Forces*, 36, pp. 232-238.

Snyder, G.H., H.W. Bruck and B. Sapin (eds 1962), *Foreign Policy Decision-Making*, New York: Free Press.

Soelberg, P.O. (1967), Unprogrammed decision making. In: *Industrial Management Review*, 8, pp. 19-29.

Spiro, H. (1968), *Responsibility in Government: Theory and Practice*, New York: Free Press.

Sproull, L.S., S. Weiner and D.B. Wolf (1978), *Organizing an Anarchy*, Chicago: University of Chicago Press.

Stassen, G.H. (1972), Individual preference versus role-constraint in policy-making: senatorial response to secretaries Acheson and Dulles. In: *World Politics*, 25, pp. 96-119.

Staw, B.M. (1976), Knee-deep in the big muddy: a study of escalating commitment to a chosen course of action. In: *Organizational Behavior and Human Performance*, 16, pp. 27-44.

Staw, B.M. (1981), The escalation of commitment to a course of action. In: *Academy of Management Review*, 6, pp. 577-587.

Staw, B.M., and F. Fox (1977), Escalation: some determinants of commitment to a previously chosen course of action. In: *Human Relations*, 30, pp. 431-450.

Staw, B.M., and J. Ross (1978), Commitment to a policy decision: a multitheoretical perspective. In: *Administrative Science Quarterly*, 23, pp. 40-64.

Staw, B.M., and J. Ross (1980), Commitment in an experimenting society: an experiment on the attribution of leadership from administrative scenarios. In: *Journal of Applied Psychology*, 65, pp. 249-260.

Staw, B.M., and J. Ross (1987), Behavior in escalation situations: antecedents, prototypes and solutions. In: *Research in Organizational Behavior*, 9, pp. 39-78.

Stein, J.G. and R. Tanter (1960), *Rational Decision Moaking: Israel's Security Choices, 1967*, Columbus: Ohio State UP.

Steinbruner, J.D. (1974), *The Cybernetic Theory of Decision*, Princeton: Princeton University Press.

Steiner, I.D. (1974), Whatever happened to the group in social psychology? In: *Journal of Experimental Social Psychology*, 10, pp. 93-108.

Steiner, I.D. (1982), Heuristic models of groupthink. In: H. Brandstätter, J.H. Davis, G. Stocker-Kreichgauer (eds), *Group Decision Making*, London: Academic Press, pp. 503-524.

Stephenson, G.M., and C.J. Brotherton (1975), Social progression and polarization: a study of discussion and negotiation in groups of mining supervisors. In: *British Journal of Social and Clinical Psychology*, 14, pp. 241-252.

Stock, D., R.M. Whitman and M.A. Liebermand (1958), The deviant member in therapy groups. In: *Human Relations*, 11, pp. 341-372.

Stogdill, R.M. (1974), *Handbook of Leadership Research*, New York: Free Press.

Stoner, J.A.F. (1961), *A comparison of individual and group decisions involving risk*. Unpublished master's thesis, Massachusetts Institute of Technology, School of Industrial Management.

Stouffer, S. (ed. 1949), *The American Soldier, volumes I and II*, Princeton: Princeton University Press.

Suedfield, P., and P.E. Tetlock (1977), Integrative complexity of communications in international crises. In: *Journal of Conflict Resolution*, 21, pp. 169-184.

Suleiman, E. (1975), *Politics, Power and Bureaucracy*, Princeton: Princeton University Press.

Suleiman, E. (ed. 1984), *Bureaucrats and Policymaking*, London: Holmes and Meier.

Swap, W. (ed. 1984), *Group Decision Making*, Beverly Hills: Sage.

Swap, W. et al. (1984), *Destructive effects of groups on individuals*. In: W. Swap (ed.), op. cit., pp. 69-95.

Tajfel, H. (1982), *Human Groups and Social Categories*, New York: Cambridge University Press.

Tajfel, H. (ed. 1982), *Social Identity and Intergroup Relations*, Cambridge: Cambridge University Press.

Tajfel, H., and J.C. Turner (1979), An integrative theory of intergroup conflict. In: W.G. Austin and S. Worchel (eds), *The Social Psychology of Intergroup Relations*, pp. 33-48.

Tanter, R. (1966), Dimensions of conflict behavior within and between nations, 1958-1060. In: *Journal of Conflict Resolution*, 10, pp. 41-64.

Taylor, D.M., and F.M. Moghaddam (1987), *Theories of Intergroup Relations*, New York: Praeger.

Teger, A. (1980), *Too Much Invested to Quit*, New York: Pergamon Press.

Tetlock, P.E. (1979), Identifying victims of groupthink from public statements of decision makers. In: *Journal of Personality and Social Psychology*, 37, pp. 1314-1324.

Tetlock, P.E., and J.I. Kim (1987), Accountability and judgement processes in a personality prediction task. In: *Journal of Personality and Social Psychology*, 52, pp. 700-709.

Thibaut, J.W., and H.H. Kelley (1959), *The Social Psychology of Groups*, New York: John Wiley.

Thompson, D. (1980), Moral responsibility of public officials: the problem of many hands. In: *America Political Science Review*, 74, pp. 905-916.

Thompson, J.D., and A. Tuden (1959), Structures, strategies and processes of organizational decision. In: J.D. Thompson et. al. (eds), *Comparative Studies in Administration*, Pittsburgh: University of Pittsburgh Press.

Thompson, V. (1961), *Modern Organization*, New York: Alfred A. Knopf.

Tiger, L. (1969), *Men in Groups*, London: Nelson.

Tjosvold, D. (1984), Effects of crisis orientation on managers' approach to controversy in decision making. In: *Academy of Management Journal*, 27, pp. 130-138.

Tower Report (1987), *The Tower Commission Report*, New York: Bantam Books.

Tullock, G. (1965), *The Politics of Bureaucracy*, Washington: Public Affairs Press.

Turner, B.A. (1976), The organizational and interorganizational development of disasters. In: *Administrative Science Quarterly*, 21, pp. 378-397.

Turner, B.A. (1978), *Man-Made Disasters*, London: Wykeham.

Turner, J.C. (1981), The experimental social psychology of intergroup behavior. In: J.C. Turner and H. Giles (eds), *Intergroup Relations*, pp. 66-101.

Turner, J.C. (1987), *Rediscovering the Social Group: A Self-Categorization Theory*, Oxford: Basil Blackwell.

Turner, J.C., and H. Giles (eds 1981), *Intergroup Behavior*, Oxford: Basil Blackwell.

Turner, R., and L.M. Killian (1972), *Collective Behavior*, Englewood Cliffs: Prentice Hall (2nd ed.).

Turner, S. (1985), Secrecy and Democracy: *The CIA in Transition*, Boston: Houghton Mifflin.

Ulmer, S.S. (1965), Toward a theory of sub-group formation in the United States Supreme Court. In: *Journal of Politics*, 27, pp. 133-152.

Varca, P.E., and J.C. Levy (1984), Individual differences in response to unfavorable group feedback. In: *Organizational Behavior and Human Performance*, 33, pp. 100-111.

Verba, S. (1962), *Small Groups and Political Behavior: A Study of Leadership*, Princeton: Princeton University Press.

Verba, S. (1978), The small group and political behavior. In: R.T. Golembiewski (ed.), *The Small Group in Political Science*, Athens: Georgia University Press, pp. 82-100.

Verbeek, B.J. (1987), *Victims of Groupthink? The British Egypt Committee during the 1956 Suez Crisis*, Mimeo European University Institute, Florence.

Vinokur, A. (1971), A review and theoretical analysis of the effects of group processes upon individual and group decisions involving risk. In: *Psychological Bulletin*, 76, pp. 231-250.

Vlist, R. van der (1976), *De Risky Shift: Een Experimenteel Sociaal-Psychologisch Verschijnsel*, Leiden: Universitaire Pers (in Dutch).

Vroom, V.H., and P.W. Yetton (1973), *Leadership and Decision Making*, Pittsburgh: Pittsburgh University Press.

Wagenaar, W.A. (1987a), Wat dwaasheid heet, is wijsheid achteraf. In: *Psychologie*, 6 (in Dutch).

Wagenaar, W.A. (1987b), *De Oorzaken van Onmogelijke Ongelukken*, Deventer: Van Loghum Slaterus (in Dutch).

Wahrmann, R. (1977), Status, deviance, sanctions and group discussion. In: *Small Group Behavior*, 8, pp. 147-168.

Weick, K.E. (1979), *The Social Psychology of Organizing*, New York: Random House (1st ed. 1969).

Wetherell, M.S. (1987), Social identity and group polarization. In: J.C. Turner et. al. (eds), *Rediscovering the Social Group: Self-Categorization Theory*, Oxford: Basil Blackwell.

Wheeler, D. and I.L. Janis (1980), *A Practical Guide for Making Decisions*, New York: Free Press.

White, R.K. (1984), *Fearful Warriors: A Psychological Profile of US-Soviet Relations*, New York: Free Press.

White, R.K. (ed. 1986), *Psychology and the Prevention of Nuclear War*, New York: New York University Press.

Whyte, G. Groupthink Reconsidered. In: *Academy of Management Review*, 14, pp. 40-56.

Whyte, W.F. (1943), *Street Corner Society. The Social Structure of an Italian Slum*, Chicago:

Chicago University Press.

Wiegele, T.C. (1973), Decision-making in an international crisis. In: *International Studies Quarterly*, 17, pp. 295-335.

Wildavsky, A.B. (1979), *Speaking Truth to Power: The Art and Craft of Policy Analysis*, Boston: Little, Brown and Company.

Wilkenfeld, J. (1968), Domestic and foreign conflict behavior of nations. In: *Journal of Peace Research*, pp. 56-69.

Wilkenfeld, J. (ed. 1973), *Conflict Behavior and Linkage Politics*, New York: McKay.

Wilson, J.Q. (ed. 1980), *The Politics of Regulation*, New York: Free Press.

Wilson, W., and M. Kayatani (1968), Intergroup attitudes and strategies in games between opponents of the same or of a different race. In: *Journal of Personality and Social Psychology*, 9, pp. 24-30.

Wilson, W., and J. Wong (1968), Intergroup attitudes towards co-operative versus competitive opponents in a modified Prisoner's Dilemma Game. In: *Perceptual and Motor Skills*, 27, pp. 1051-1058.

Witte, E. (1972), Field research on complex decision making processes - The phase theory. In: *International Studies of Management and Organization*, 1, pp. 156-182.

Wohlstetter, R. (1962), *Pearl Harbor: Warning and Decision*, Stanford: Stanford University Press.

Wolf, G., and E.J. Conlon (1984), *The Ecology of Sunk Cost Problems*. Unpublished manuscript, University of Arizona.

Wolfenstein, V.E. (1967), Some psychological aspects of crisis leadership. In: L.J. Edinger (ed.), *Political Leadership in Industrialized Societies*, New York: Wiley, pp. 155-181.

Wong-McCarthy, W. (1976), *A Content Analysis of the Unedited White House Transcripts*. Unpublished Research Report (cited in Janis 1982a, p. 334).

Woodward, B. (1987), *Veil: The Secret Wars of the CIA, 1981-1987*, London: Headline.

Woolsey-Biggart, N., and G.G. Hamilton (1984), The power of obedience. In: *Administrative Science Quarterly*, 29, pp. 540-549.

Worchel, S., E.A. Lind and K. Kaufman (1975), Evaluations of group products as a function of expectations of group longevity, outcome of competition and publicity of evaluations. In: *Journal of Personality and Social Psychology*, 31, pp. 1089-1097.

Yin, R.K. (1984), *Case Study Research: Design and Methods*, Beverly Hills: Sage.

Ziller, R.C. (1964), Individuation and socialization: A theory of assimilation in large organizations. In: *Human Relations*, 17, pp. 341-360.

Zimbardo, P.G. (1970), The human choice: Individuation, reason and order versus deindividuation, impulse and chaos. In: W.J. Arnold and D. Levine (eds), *Nebraska Symposium on Motivation: 1969*, Lincoln: University of Nebraska Press, pp. 237-307.

Zimmerman, E. (1983), *Political Violence, Crises and Revolutions*, Cambridge Mass.: Schenkman.

Index

Accountability, 15, 17, 26, 181–92, 201, 202, 206, 245, 248, 250, 279, 290, 291

Advisors, 5, 6, 36, 172–81, 186, 200

Anticipation, 148, 149, 163, 165, 170, 198, 247, 248

Avoidance. *See* Collective avoidance

Bay of Pigs, 5, 10, 42, 52, 62, 155, 161, 188, 191, 279

Boland amendment, 217, 225, 239, 256, 260

Brockner, Joel D., 88, 89, 94–96, 119

Bureaucracy, 80, 133, 143, 145, 153, 161, 162, 173, 190, 199, 274, 280

Bureaucratic politics, 140, 143–55, 190, 198, 227, 235, 278, 281, 289

Cabinet committees, 132–36, 140–43, 148, 149, 152, 153, 178, 196, 273–75, 293

Carter, Jimmy, 13, 186–87, 215, 220, 222, 224, 231, 238

Case study method, 13, 14, 26, 209–12, 283, 284

Casey, William, 216–69, 280, 281

Cautious shift. *See* Choice shift

Choice shift, 73–78, 81, 82, 94, 118

Closed-mindedness, 8, 10, 11, 83, 251–55

Cohesiveness: desire for, 40, 41, 115; group, 6, 7, 8, 9, 14, 16, 21, 23, 25, 31–44, 48, 49, 53, 57, 59–63, 69–72, 96, 99, 105–108, 112, 115, 118, 120–24, 139–57, 178, 191, 197, 204, 206, 211, 236–40, 267, 268, 274–77, 280

Collective avoidance, 26, 182, 184–87, 192, 201, 202, 206, 245, 247, 279

Collective overoptimism, 26, 182, 187–92, 206, 245, 247, 279

Commitment, 53, 87–97, 154, 176, 177, 185, 229, 230, 246, 277, 281, 293

Compliance, 13, 14, 25, 39, 42, 47–63, 108, 115–17, 120, 161–78, 205, 211, 243–45, 280, 293; anticipatory, 59, 63, 105, 109, 161, 176–78, 197, 199, 200, 236, 245, 249, 256, 268, 274, 276, 278

Concurrence-seeking, 6, 7, 8, 11, 14, 15, 16, 17, 18, 22, 23, 24, 43, 47, 59–63, 70, 72, 97, 117, 121–25, 162, 201, 205, 275, 276, 282, 288, 293, 294

Conformity, pressures, 25, 37, 47–63, 71, 72, 115–17, 124

Crisis, decision making, 20, 25, 36, 62, 80, 84, 119, 147, 150, 151, 171, 187, 192, 196, 215, 220–26, 236, 246, 250, 269, 279, 287, 288

Crowds, 65, 68, 118

Cuban missile crisis, 58, 171, 173

Decision making: defective, 8, 10, 16, 18, 19, 22, 95; governmental, 129–57, 196, 201, 203, 278; political, 5, 6, 14, 41, 57, 80, 125, 129, 130, 134, 277, 278; quality of, 11, 17, 18, 20, 25, 38, 81, 131, 146, 181, 187, 284

Deindividuation, 25, 65–72, 83, 115, 117–19, 121, 122, 124, 139, 155–57, 197, 199, 204, 276, 283

Deniability, 244, 245, 262, 280

Deviants, rejection of, 54

De Rivera, Joseph, 38, 81, 171, 174–76, 200

Dunsire, Andrew, 165, 168–70, 176, 177

Eisenhower, Dwight D., 5, 171, 172

Entrapment, 87–97, 111, 115, 119,

321

Hart, Paul 't.
  Groupthink in government : a study of small groups and policy failure / by
Paul 't Hart.
      p.   cm.
Originally published: Amsterdam : Rockland, MA : Swets & Zeitlinger, c1990.
With new pref.
  Includes bibliographical references (p.   ) and index.
  ISBN 0-8018-4890-3 (pbk. : acid-free paper)
  1. Public administration—Decision making. 2. Decision-making, Group.
3. Policy sciences. 4. Iran-Contra Affair, 1985–1990. I. Title. II. Title: Group
think in government.
JF1525.D4H37 1994
351.007'25–dc20   93-46082
                                                                            CIP